PUNJAB (1920–1945)

Agrarian Problems and Role of Peasantry in Freedom Struggle

PUNJAB (1920–1945)

Agrarian Problems and Role of Peasantry in Freedom Struggle

S. D. Gajrani

Commonwealth

PUNJAB (1920–1945) : Agrarian Problems and Role of Peasantry in Freedom Struggle

First Published : 2009

ISBN 978-81-311-0252-7

Published by :
COMMONWEALTH PUBLISHERS PVT. LTD.
4831/24, Prahlad Street,
Ansari Road, Darya Ganj,
New Delhi - 110002
Ph. : 23272541, 23257835
Fax : 91- 011- 23257835
e-mail : campusbooks@hotmail.com
commonwealthbooks@gmail.com

Laser Typesetting by :
Stylish Laser Typesetter
Delhi - 110053

Printed at :
Roshan Offset Printers
Delhi

FOREWORD

I am glad to write this Foreword to a book which helps to fill a gap in the history of the peasant movements in Punjab. The author scarcely needs an introduction to the world of scholars in this area of study. He has already published two monographs on agrarian unrest in the East Punjab States in the years 1920-46 *(Peasants and Princes,* Patiala, 1986) and in Punjab *(Peasant Movement in Punjab,* Patiala, 1986). I am happy that a fuller account of the peasant movements in Punjab, based on his doctoral dissertation, is now being published.

This is an extended and modified version of the work Dr. Gajrani had done with professor J. S. Grewal and me in the early eighties. The subject of this dissertation has been touched upon tangetially, sometimes in a rather generalised fashion, by a number of competent scholars ; but it is the empirical richness of Dr. Gajrani's work which merits attentions. He deserves congratulations on his meticulous documentation and exhaustive research into almost all relevant primary sources. He has used not only the archival material at the Punjab State Archives at Patiala and the National Archives at New Delhi, but also a large number of the collections of private papers of the British administrators in crucial decision-making positions in the period 1925-1947. This enables us to get a much more complete account of the process and direction of policy making, both at the provincial and central levels, than was available to us earlier. His research into the contemporary newspapers and periodicals, as well as the tracts, pamphlets and memoirs written by leaders of the peasant movement, has unearthed much new data on the ideological and organisational dimensions of the peasant movement. Finally, a picture of the peasant movement in the round can be constructed now from the oral testimonies (made available by the Nehru Memorial Museum) and from the interviews conducted by Dr. Gajrani with some prominent personalities connected with that movement.

The value of a historian's personal acquaintance with the region and the people under study, and the empirical knowledge this enables him to bring to bear upon the theme of popular movements, needs to be emphasised. It is one of the ironies of post-independence Indian academia that mimicry of research in the West, imitation of what was modish there years ago, working out agenda of research set up in terms of problematics unrelated to countries such as ours, diminish academic appreciation of the work of scholars whose life experience is fundamentally related to their research interests, Over the last couple of decades a number of regional studies of popular movements of various kinds have been published ; some of them may be limited in scope, some of them may lack conceptual and methodological sophistication, but these works add a new dimension to the historians' outlook by engaging with problems in a manner that mere professional skill cannot be expected to attain.

Dr. Gajrani's aim has been to map the course of the peasant movement in a particular region he knows well, comprehending in his schema the structure of rural society, the economic and social existence conditions of the peasantry, and the localised movements in their complex inter-relationship with wider regional and national political forces. This is not an easy task. It is, however, part of a widely shared interest among researcher's including social activists, in different regions exploring facets of regional and historical specificities of popular movements in the colonial era and in more recent times. One hopes that their findings will eventually enable us to obtain an integrated picture. There remain, of course, many areas quite unexplored. One of these unmapped areas is the peasant mind, the peasants, categories of thought, their image of society, their idea of good life, their idea of 'exploitation' or 'justice', and their basic premises of social and political action. Another set of problems awaiting research is the quotidian struggle of the peasant against his exploiters—as distinct from the organised movements, under political leaders', which have a higher visibility in contemporary reports or later historical accounts.

In their attempt to re-assess the older historical paradigms, in the development of "history from below", historians of popular movements will, one hopes, address themselves to questions such as these. The terms in which these questions may be cast are diverse. But one seems to see a convergence of the concerns and interests of many historians such as Dr. Gajrani opening up a new field of enquiry. This trend of enquiry promises to offer a new perspective on the past of the Indian people.

S. Bhattacharya
Jawaharlal Nehru University

Preface

An attempt is made in this work to bring to light certain neglected aspects of the agrarian unrest and agrarian movement in the Punjab during the last quarter of a century of British rule in India. We are fully aware that at this stage of research our knowledge regarding agrarian conditions and class structure constitute only approximations towards infinitely complex phenomena which are not yet adequately explored. We are also aware that many myths have been built around the Punjab agrarian movement; the general aspects have yet to be explored and many essential sources yet to be adequately explored.

In the following pages, we shall try to focus our attention on the issues like the type of peasant organizations, the detailed history of the various peasant movements, their socio-economic base or the involvement of the different sections of the peasantry, the role of casteism and communalism, the ideological aspects and strategic perspective as well as the forms of struggle in the agrarian movements, the methods and nature of mass mobilization, and finally their achievements and failures.

In the first chapter an attempt has been made to sketch the economic background to the agrarian unrest characterizing the Punjab in the period 1920-45. A study of agrarian structure in the Punjab will help us to understand and bring out the socio-economic stratification of the Punjab Society, as also the nature of the major contradictions which gave birth to the peasant movement and peasant unrest. While one would bear numerous regional variations in mind the main feature of the basic economy of the Punjab was its conversion to colonialism at a rapid rate towards the close of the 19^{Th} century. We have outlined some of the fundamental changes in the agrarian scene in this context.

The growth and structure of landlordism as also technological changes in agricultural production have been described in the first Chapter of the present work. The heavy indebtedness of the Punjab peasantry is widely known, but its importance in relation to production is mainly discussed in the Second section of the first Chapter. Similarly, we also know that the Punjab did not make much progress in the field of modern industry which had been at one stage progressive in the Punjab. As a consequence after 1918, the pressure of the growing population on the land was felt in the Punjab. Its adverse after-effects have also been traced which have helped us in building up a true picture of the agrarian problems and agrarian movement as well.

In attempting to study the nature and character of this movement, we have to answer a basic question: Was the peasantry, more or less, a homogenous mass or was it comprised of various and perhaps, even, mutually hostile rural strata? The question is in turn linked to the process of internal differentiation within the peasantry under the varied impact of colonialism. Peasant activists and historians might not agree on the degree of internal differentiation and stratification which existed in the Punjab peasantry. But there is no doubt that a considerable degree of differentiation marked the agrarian structure of the Punjab, and that this affected the character of agrarian movements. We have investigated this question briefly in this work.

There is another important question. To what extent did this agrarian movement expose this contradiction or took cognizance of it? It is obvious that in order to understand its nature and character, we shall have to study the contradictions and also the relationship between various rural strata as well as relationships between these strata and other sections of the society, particularly urban social groups. It would be the task of the historian to investigate how in the consciousness of the participants in agrarian movements attempts were made to identify and determine the areas of potential or actual class conflict and class harmony, and to consciously accentuate or mute them in accordance with the broad view and the over-all strategy. An attempt has been made to answer these questions in the present work.

It is one of the objectives of this study to investigate the peasants' grievances and demands. These demands will help us to determine the social contents of the peasant movement. What was its social base in the Punjab? What was the involvement of the various sections of the peasants in this struggle? What more issues have been raised here. The failure that had to be faced by the radical leadership of different political groups related to this struggle has also been described. In the 6th Chapter, the approach and attitude of these groups towards this movement is cited.

Another significant set of questions relating to the structure and strategy of this movement has also been raised in the 4th and 5th Chapters. We shall see that the form that the Punjab peasants struggle adopted in the British Punjab as well as in the East Punjab States, was basically agitational and it was not different from the form adopted by the national movement. But there was inadequate relationship between the two. The Punjab Congress which favoured the urban groups and the moneylenders, failed to win over the peasantry in the anti-imperialist struggle. As a result, it remained weak. At the same time the British Indian Government was able to bring into operation some countervailing forces against the Congress: the Government followed two fold policy–repressive on the one hand and conciliatory towards some rural strata on the other. This continuation of repressive and reformist policies we have traced in the 7th Chapter.

Lahore, the provincial capital of the undivided Punjab, being out of reach, the scholars in India working on the history of the Punjab are placed under numerous constraints. In addition, there does not exist a single book on the Freedom Movement in the Punjab covering the period, 1920-45, which could be used for the necessary background of some of the issues discussed in this work. However, I have tried to build up an account of the agrarian unrest piece by piece, with the help of the available contemporary writings, newspapers, journals, the Government files and various other sources lying scattered in different libraries, archives and private collections.

I studied in original the proceedings of the Home Department (Political) : 1917-45; Proceedings of the Home Department: 1917-45; Proceedings of the Finance Department;

1913-30, 1931-38; Proceedings of the Department of Revenue and Agriculture: 1894-1910; Punjab State Agency Records (Patiala): 1920-39; Punjab State Agency Records (General): 1920-37; These proceedings are available at the NAI, New Delhi. I also consulted the Patiala State Records–Prime Minister Office Files at the PSA, Patiala. In these files I found many pamphlets in Punjabee language which helped me in building up my account of the peasant unrest and problems in the East Punjab States.

Punjab Legislative Council Debates: 1920-45; Punjab Legislative Assembly Debates Proceedings: 1937-40, Vol. I-XX; *Report of the Abiana Committee,* appointed by the Punjab Government in 1934, Lahore: 1934; *Enquiry Committee,* 1931, Vol. I; *Report of the Land Revenue Committee,* appointed by The Punjab Government in 1937-38; *Report of the Punjab Provincial Banking Inquiry Committee: 1929-30,* Vol. I, Calcutta: 1930; *Report of the Punjab Sources of Revenue Committee: 1931,* Lahore: 1931; *Reserve Bank of India Preliminary Report on Agricultural Credit: 1936: Review of the work of the Irrigation Department, Statistical and Statement: 1938-39;* etc., are other printed primary source material I have studied.

I have also consulted papers of Lord Willingdon, Joseph Austin, Chemberlain, Linlithgow, Viscount Morley, Montague, Birkenhead, Zetland, Malcolm Hailey, Erskine, etc., which are in microfilm at NMML, Teen Murti, New Delhi. I had to sit at the Punjab State Archives, Patiala for almost a year to study in original some of the valuable sources, such as Chamber of Princes' Records; Proceedings of the Punjab States' Council Meetings held at Lahore in 1940, Simla in 1942 and in Patiala in 1943; Faridkot State Records: Political Movement files; Kalsia State Records (Confidential) files; Kapurthala and Nabha States Records files, etc., I have also made use of Annual Administration Reports of Patiala, Nabha, Kapurthala, Kalsia, Faridkot and Jind states for the year 1911-1939, at Central State Library Patiala, Reference Section. Assessment reports of various districts and tehsels and the famine reports of various districts have also been consulted. Other important sources I have madc use of are the Meerut Conspiracy (1929-32) selected files and the *Kirti; The Kirti Lehar,* from February 1926 to November 1939, have been frequently used. This paper particularly tells us at length about the condition of the workers and peasants. It also exposes the exploitation of the poor peasants in the hands of the moneylenders and landlords; various articles published in its different issues in *Punjabee* language have been very useful. Some more *Punjabee* source for instance, 1 have studied *Ahlkari Sazahan* by Sahib Singh; *Dukhee Janta Ka Ubal* by Janga Singh; *Aap Biti* by Sahib Singh; *Praja Malerkotla Di Dard Kahani* by Giani Kahar Sing; *Ikk Jivan-Ikk Itihas* by Jagjit Singh Aulakh and *Bhagat Singh* by Tirlok Singh. I have also made use of the private papers of Prithvi Singh Azad, Dr. Chaman Lal, Sardar Sunder Singh Majithia, etc. as well as the Transcripts of approximately 50 freedom fighters' oral testimonies which are available at NMML, New Delhi.

In search of material, I had to contact persons who could give one the requisite information about the peasants' problems and their struggle. I collected information through interviews with Sardar Hira Singh Pathal, Sardar Sohan Singh Josh, Master Hari Singh, Sardar Jagir Singh Joga, Shri Brish Bhan, Shri Chhaju Mal, Pandit Kishori Lal, Sardar Isher Singh Majhail and some more freedom fighters who were closely related to the agrarian movement in the Punjab under British as well as in the East Punjab States. In the beginning was cold shouldered by some of them but my going to them time and again made them realize that I was a genuine seaker of information regarding their participation in the agrarian movement in the province.

The conclusions arrived at in this study are only such as primary or contemporary evidence has yieled. In case of oral information, I have tried to compare that with the contemporary documentary evidence. I have not allowed my judgement to be influenced by the reverence and the esteem in which the people of India in general and that of the Punjab in particular had held the leadership.

S. D. Gajrani

ACKNOWLEDGEMENT

My indebtedness to my supervisor Dr. Sabyaschi Bhattacharyya. Professor of History, Jawaharlal Nehru University, New Delhi, for his seasoned and generous help and keen interest in my work, is too deep for words. He watched my progress over the years and very kindly spared time for discussing my problems for weeks together and also going through all my drafts with his habitual thoroughness. He also graciously allowed me the use of his personal library. I am and would be for the rest of my life beholden to him for his very kindly and scholarly suggestions during the course of the writing of my dissertation. I am also grateful to Dr. J.S. Grewal, Vice-Chancellor (Formerly Professor and Head Department of History), Guru Nanak Dev University, Amritsar, who is my co-supervisor. It was entirely due to his encouragement that I finally undertook this study. He also has guided me with patience and kindness giving me freedom to persue my own ideas. That inspite of the constant and valuable criticism and suggestions given by my advisors many errors still have crept in is entirely due to my imperfections.

I shall always remember with deep gratitude the benign interest which Professor B.R. Grover, Director-ICHR, New Delhi (Formerly, Head Department of History, Jamia Millia Islamia, New Delhi) took in inducing me into research and placing me in the hands of two of the towering historians of the country. I am thankful to the large number of friends who helped me in my work. My friend Jagdish Jindal of Modi College, has gone through the complete manuscript and made valuable suggestions. I thankfully acknowledge the help he gave me. I am really indebted to my teacher Dr. Bhagat Singh for having acted as a sounding board for my ideas.

I take this apportunity of expressing my gratitude to the custodian of Archives of India, the Punjab State Archives,

Patiala, Archives of Contemporary History of India, Jawaharlal Nehru University, New Delhi and such libraries as I often visited in search of material. In particular, I would like to express my indebtedness to Dr. Y.P. Bajaj–Reader in History, Punjabi University, Patiala for giving me permission to use his personal collection of the *Jat Gazette*.

My thanks are also due to the UGC and the authorities of Universities Grants Commission for awarding me a Teacher Followship, without which I could not attain my life long dream of writing a Ph.D. dissertation.

In the end I must thank Kavita Gajrani, my wife for having given me invaluable help at every stage of this dissertation's preparation. She went through each page of the preliminary as well as the final draft, made valuable suggestions, gave me encouragement when 1 needed it and helped me check the type script. In fact, if any error of typing remains in this work, she shares the responsibility with me.

S. D. Gajrani

CONTENTS

Abbreviations

AICC	:	All India Congress Committee
AIKS	:	All India Kisan Sabha
CPI	:	Communist Party of India
Census	:	Census of India, Report
CSP	:	Congress Socialist Party
D.G.	:	District Gazetteer (Punjab)
GOI	:	Government of India
Ed.R.	:	Report on the progress of education in the Punjab (Annual)
NBS	:	Naujawan Bharat Sabha
NPR	:	Native papers (Journals and Periodicals) published in the Punjab, Report of the Government of India
PAR	:	Administration Report of the Punjab and its dependencies (Annual)
PCSP	:	Punjab Congress Socialist Party
PKC	:	Punjab Kisan Committee
PLCD	:	Punjab Legislative Council Debates
PLAD	:	Punjab Legislative Assembly Debates
PNQ	:	Punjab Notes and Queries
PPCC	:	Punjab Provincial Congress Committee
RCA	:	Royal Commission on Agriculture in India. Abridged Report, 1928
RCS	:	Report on the working of the Co-operative Societies in the Punjab (Annual)
SABI	:	Statistical Abstract of British India (Annual)
SGPC	:	Shiromani Gurdwara Parbandhak Committee
WPP	:	Workers' and Peasants' Party

Glossary

Abiana	:	Water Rate
Abwab	:	Cesses additional to land revenue
Ahlkar	:	An official; a functionary of the Government
Acre	:	A measure of land equal to 4840 Square Yards
Akali	:	Literally meening "immortal"; a member of the Akali Party
Anna	:	A Coin representing 1/16 of a Rupee
Barani	:	Unirrigated land depended on rain
Batai	:	Share Cropping; the system of cropping where revenue is a certain portion of the produce
Batawas	:	Those who made Batai
Banjar	:	Barren land; Culturable waste
Begar	:	Compulsory forced labour, Unpaid
Chahi	:	Land irrigated by well
Chak	:	A village or estate in Canal Colonies
Ghair Marusi	:	Non-hereditary
Hadbast	:	Joint boundary; demarcation of boundaries
Hissa Kashi	:	Provisional measure of land revenue base on the apportionment of farm produce
Kachhus	:	Those who made the apportionment
Kamin	:	A village menial
Kanungo	:	A revenue officer supervising the work of Patwaris

Kharif	:	Summer Crop
Khasra	:	Description of land
Kham	:	Cesses; Kacha
Likhari	:	Writer or accountant
Mahant	:	A head of a Gurdwara (Sikh Temple)
Malba	:	Fund out of which village expenses were defrayed
Malik Adna	:	Literally, inferior proprietor; secondary owner
Malik Ala	:	Literally a superior proprietor; he had a recognised over land, and claim to a certain share in the produce usually ranging 1.5 to 10 per cent; primary owner
Maurusi	:	hereditary
Muzara-Maurusi	:	Literally cultivator, used for tenant
Muafidar	:	Holder of revenue free grant
Nehri	:	Land irrigated by canal
Patti	:	A part or portion of a village, generally being the sub-division of a taraf; a share in a village
Pattidari	:	A definition of the land tenure given by the British administrator in which land was supposed to be divided and held in severlty by the different proprietors according to ancestral or customary shares which also determined the revenue payable.
Paimaish-i-arazi	:	Provisional measurement
Rabi	:	Winter Crop
Shamlat	:	The village common land
Tehsil	:	Sub-division of a district
Taqavi	:	Liberally, strengthening or assisting; the

		money advanced to cultivators for implements, seeds, digging wells etc.
Thikaripehra	:	A system under which villagers performed the duties of watchman
Zail	:	Sub-division of a tehsil, consisting of a number of villages
Zabti	:	Assessment of land revenue in Cash

1

The Socio-Economic Background and Origin of Agrarian Unrest

The main purpose of writing this chapter is not an exhaustive study of the agrarian structure but to focus the attention on those tendencies and areas within it which contained seeds of social tension and conflict. With this perspective in view, certain most important aspects have been highlighted. It is to be noted here that Primarily those aspects of social structure have been discussed which were, at a later stage, responsible for the rural unrest and peasants' movement as well.

One of the most favourite myths about Punjab was that it was predominantly a province of peasant proprietors.[1] But this notion had hardly any basis in reality. Punjab was as much a land of *Zamindars,* rich peasants, middle and small peasant proprietors, occupancy tenants[2], tenants-at-will and agricultural labourers and agriculture servants. Moreover, the rural society could be vividly seen as divided between the rural rich and the rural poor, with tenants-at-will and the agricultural labourers and servants constituting the most oppressed and exploited sections of rural Punjab. However,

1. Darling, M.L., *The Punjab Peasant in Prosperity and Debt,* Oxford, London—1925, xii, 4.
2. Only 8.75% area of the province was in the hands of occupancy-tenants : Home Department, File No. 196-197 (Land, Health and Education), 33-34; NAI : New Delhi; Douie, J.M., *Punjab Settlement Mannual,* Lahore : 1930, 62.

it may be noted at the very outset that in almost all the districts in the province, the land cultivated by owners was between 60 to 70 percent.[3] But it is a paradox that both agriculture and agriculturists[4] were in a depressed state from the very beginning of the period under review.

The pattern of landownership was highly differentiated.[5] In 1925, 58.3% of the owners owned less than 5 acres of land, had average holding of 2.6 acres, and cultivated 12% of the total land. 26.2% of the owners with holdings between 5 to 15 acres owned 26.6% of the land. Besides, 3.3% of the owners with holdings of over 50 acres owned 25.7% of the land, while

---

3. P.L.C.D., Vol. II, 1921; *Census 1911,* Vol. IV; *Census 1921*; Vol. XV; *Census 1931,* Vol. XVII; *Board of Economic Inquiry;* Punjab Agricultural Statistics, 1901-02 to 1935-36; Douie, J.M., *Punjab Settlement Manual,* Lahore 1930, 159; Linlithgow Collection (Microfilm, Acc.No. 2352, Vol. I, 1936-38), 'Speech by Marques of Linlithgow'.
4. Agriculturists were a very important class as on them depended the food supply of the people, nevertheless they were not treated well or helped by any one. Their very blood was squeezed out of them. The Government was contemplating the recovery from the agriculturists, alongwith the land revenue of 52 lacs of rupees which were spent on famine relief (alluding to the famine arrears of £342,500 due from the Punjab). Could there be a greater injustice then this. They must combine and work together. Otherwise Government would impoverish them completely. Agriculturists were comprised of the following categories : *(i)* Rent-receivers *i.e.,* noncultivating owners; *(ii)* Actual cultivating owners; *(iii)* Rent-payers as tenants; *(iv)* Agricultural labourers and *(v)* Those who depended on agriculturists. Vide, Weekly Reports of the Department of Criminal Intelligence. September 25, 1909—Home Department Political Proceedings, October, 1909, 110-17; P.L.C.D., Vol. XXIV, 1934, 149-51; Vol. VIII, Part-A, 1925, 225.
5. It is clear that landownership or cultivation on a provincial basis is not enough to characterise the class structure of the province. Other features such as regional variation, quality of land, available of water, capital intensity have also to be considered. We feel, however, that for our purposes the broader statistical categorisation is still quite serviceable.

7.5% of the owners with holdings of 20 to 50 acres owned 27.2% of the land[6]. The following table based on Calvert's study gives the distribution of land holdings of landowners and throws considerable light on the conditions prevailing in the Punjab countryside.[7]

Table 1.1. Distribution of owner holdings (1925)

Size of Holdings	*Percentages of the Total Owners*	*Percentage of the Total Cultivated Land*
Below 1 acre	17.9	1.0
Between 1-3 acres	25.5	4.4
Between 3-5 Acres	14.9	6.6
Between 5-10 Acres	18.0	15.1
Between 10-15 Acres	8.2	11.5
Between 15-20 Acres	4.3	8.4
Between 20-25 Acres	2.7	6.3
Between 25-30 Acres	4.8	20.4
And over 50 Acres	3.3	25.7
	Total : 99.9	99.9

It is really noteworthy to state that though 80% of the population was dependent on agriculture, only one person out of every eight owned any land at all.[8] A similar enquiry was conducted by the Board of Economic Inquiry, Punjab in 1939 to see if any change had taken place during the 15 years, duration *i.e.,* from 1925 to 1939. Its results are reproduced below.[9]

6. The Size and Distribution of Agricultural Holding in Punjab, Board of Economic Enquiry, Rural Publication, No. 4, 1925, 3.
7. *Ibid.,* Calvert, H., was the first who had studied this aspect of the agricultural problem in 1924 and the results of this enquiry were published in 1925.
8. Roberts, W. and Kartar Singh, *A Text Book of Punjab Agriculture : 1947,* 513.
9. *The Size and Distribution of Proprietory Holdings in the Punjab Agriculture : 1939,* 1.

Table 1.2. Distribution of Owner Holdings (1939)

Size of Holding		*Percentage of Owners*	*Percentage of Total Land*
Upto 1 Acre		20.2	0.8
From 1 to 3 Acres		28.6	5.2
" 3 to 5 Acres		14.9	6.2
" 5 to 10 Acres		16.6	13.1
" 10 to 15 Acres		7.3	9.1
" 15 to 20 Acres		3.6	7.2
" 20 to 25 Acres		2.2	5.6
" 25 to 30 Acres		3.9	14.8
50 Acres and above		2.4	38.0
	Total	100	100

This enquiry shows that the size of holdings in case of small landholders had further decreased while the holdings of big owners had increased. The study of the Board of Economic Enquiry also revealed a definite increase in the area owned by owners of over 50 acres at the expense of almost every other section of owners.[10] Its study again showed the congestion of owners in the lower group and the concentration of land in higher group. Peasant proprietors owing less than 5 acres can certainly be described as poor peasants. It has been calculated that in 1928-29, the monthly income of £ 5 acres holder was Rs. 11/- before payment in land revenue.[11] Most of these small owners were not very distanced from tenants or agricultural labourers in terms of their income condition. Merely, they were more heavily in debt. For example, in 1921, the debt's multiple of land revenue for small owners was 27 (Rs. 310/- per proprietor). While for large proprietors it was 10 (Rs. 570/- per proprietor).[12]

10. Roberts, W. and Kartar Singh, *A Text Book of Funjab Agriculture : 1947,* 514.
11. Brij Narain, "Agricultural Income", *The Tribune,* Lahore, December, 28, 1932.
12. Darling, M.L., *The Punjab Peasant in Prosperity and Debt,* 12-13.

Tenants formed the second but significant section of the rural society and played a significant role during the peasants (movement in the Punjab. In 1932, the tenants-at-will held, 48.2% of the area while occupancy tenants held 7.3% of it.[13] In 1935, the tenants constituted 31.8% of the rural working population.[14] The discrepancy between the two figures is well explained by the fact that many small owners rented out their small pieces of land and themselves worked as tenants at bigger holding.[15] This, of course, introduced a certain fuzziness in the class or stratum distinction between petty owners and tenants.

There did not exist any legal protection to the tenant-at will regarding security of tenure of fixity of rent. On the contrary, the increasing pressure of people on land forced the tenants to rent land on steadily worsening terms. Moreover, the terms of borrowing were much more unfavourable for the tenants-at-will for they could not offer land as security.[16] Besides, the occupancy-tenants were small in number and were becoming fewer.[17] They were, more often, assimilated to landowners for they paid only a very small quit rent in the form of *Malikana* or tribute.[18]

Agricultrual labourers constituted 14.4% of Punjab rural work force in 1920.[19] Even though wages relatively high—they ranged between Rs. 4.5 outside canal colonies and Rs.

13. Brij Narain, *India Before and Since the Crisis,* Allahabad, 1939, 605.
14. Brij Narain's article in *The Tribune,* March 16, 1935; According to the Census of 1931, this percentage was 29.3 : *Census of India,* Vol. VII, Part-II, Table-X, 160.
15. Calvert, H., *The Wealth and Welfare of the Punjab,* Lahore, 1936, 172.
16. *Report of the Punjab Provincial Banking Enquiry Committee :* 1929-30, Vol. I, 1930, 31.
17. Brij Narain, *India Before and Since The Crisis,* Allahabad, 1939, 605.
18. Calvert, H., *The Wealth and Welfare of the Punjab,* Lahore : 1936, 202.
19. Patel, S.J., *Agricultural Labourers in Modern India and Pakistan : 1952,* 29.

10/- in the canal colonies before the deperession[20]-unemployment was seasonal.[21] They were employed mostly at times of harvest and ploughing, for hardly any large scale cultivation with wage labour existed. However, their number was going up very rapidly. The rate of their increases was 58.7% between 1921-31 while population as a whole went up only by 13.5% [22] The agricultural labourers lived in extreme poverty. They had hardly any credit to enable them to borrow, for they were a 'poor risk'. They were the first to appear at the famine relief works in case of natural calamities.[23]

Almost all the landholders possessing over 50 acres of land of most of those owning between 20 to 50 acres were landlords. Between 50% to 50% of land was under their control. They constituted between 5.4 and 6.2 percent of the agricultural working population.[24] This in large parts of the province, it was the landlords who 'commanded the situation'.[25] However, there was considerable differentiation among the landlords with visible concentration of land at the top.

As mentioned earlier, another big section consisted of rick peasants or upper stratum of the peasantry. The benefits of commercialisation, irrigation and rise in prices were cornered by the landlords through the *batai* system and by the upper stratum of the peasantry who surpluses to sell whereas the rise in costs went against the tenents.[26] Rich peasants and

20. Darling, M.L., *The Punjab Peasant in Prosperity and Debt, 114.*
21. Calvert, H., *The Wealth and Welfare of the Punjab,* Lahore : 1936, 175. (There were very few permanently employed agricultural labourers).
22. Census, Vol. VII, Part-I, 1921, 220; also Part-II, Table-X; for detail, Spare, B.G., *Economics of Agricultural Progress : 1926.*
23. Calvert, H., *The Wealth and Welfare of the Punjab,* Lahore : 1936, 13.
24. *The Tribune,* 16 March, 1935; Census, Vol. VII, Part-II, Table-X, 160.
25. Calvert, H., *The Wealth and Welfare of the Punjab,* Lahore : 1936, 221.
26. *Ibid.*

Zamindars were also the beneficiaries of the Punjab farmers' debt legislation which enabled them to branch out or expand into rural money-lending in a big way, thus adding the surplus drawn through usury to land rent or profits of cultivations. On the contrary, the benefits of co-operative credit were also monopolised by the rural rich. The same strata were also acquiring control over land, transforming money of the small owners to the status of tenants-at-will.

In brief, prevalence of large holdings did not to capitalist farming or cultivating with wage labour either in the form of capitalist landlordism or capitalist farming. Invariably, the man who acquired more land than could be cultivated as family holding, took to renting out his land. This was because of the highly profitable *batai* system, itself the result of the overall colonial under-development.

The nature of the peasant unrest and struggle would be affected, or its objective determinants provided by the varying nature of contradictions or alignments between various agrarian classes and strata, between agrarian classes and urban social groups, and between the rural and urban people of the Punjab and imperialism and the colonial state. Besides, it would also be the task of the agrarian movement to identity area of potential or actual class conflict and class harmony and to accentuate or mute them in accordance with the broader view and larger political strategy.

The main contradiction of Indian society (including Punjab). Within whose frame work all other contradictions operated, was between the Indian people and colonialism which blocked their social progress and underdeveloped their economy. Any social and political movement would have to keep this in view. However, the *Zamindars,* peasant proprietors and tenants-at-will, who often paid half of the *abiana* and land revenue, had a more specific and directly apprehended contradiction with the British Government on the tissue of *abiana* land revenue. The demand of reduction in *abians* and land revenue could unite and mobilise the widest rural classes and strata against the British bureaucracy. Inelastic and high land revenue and *abiana* were a major mechanism for siphoning of agricultural surplus. Brij Narain calculated that these two payments constituted 40 to 50 percent of the peasants' costs of production.[27] Above all the Government was not ready to forgo them even during the calamitous depression years when as a result of the steep decline in agricultural products, the burden of Government taxes, which remained high, was increased manifold. The average remission of land revenue during the five years from 1929-30 to 1933-34 amounted to only 6%.[28] The combined burden of *abian* and land revenue amounted to Rs. 91.1 millions in 1938-39 while it was Rs. 86.6 millions in the predepression year of 1928-29 while prices were much higher.[29]

Other peasant demands would stem from the internal contradiction within rural society, *e.g.,* conflict between tenants-at-will and *Zamindars* and agricultural labour and peasant proprietors and landlords. These conflicts were confronted by the operation of rural credit.

The *Kisans* were forced into borrowing to pay land revenue and *abiana,* to maintain the necessary conditions of cultivation, and to meet his consumption needs, especially in times of crisis. The enormous size of the debt burden of the peasantry can be seen from the fact that it was in 1921 more than 19 times the amount of land revenue.[30] As early as in 1920's, 80% of the peasant proprietors were in debt.[31] According to Calvert, "the moneylenders" profits probably exceed those of all cultivators put together. Beside him, the professional class is considerable, the industrial class is insignificant, even trade and commerce take second place.[32] It was estimated in 1920's that at least 80% of the cultivators

27. Calvert, H., The Wealth and Welfare of the Punjab, 221-22.

28. Brij Narain, *Indian Socialism : 1937,* 64-65.

29. Brij Narain, *Indian Before and Since the Crisis,* Vol. II, 529; (Profits and Surplus of the Irrigation Department increased from Rs. 23.8 millions in 1928-29 to Rs. 29.3 millions in 1933-34), Vide, Brij Narain, *India in Crisis,* 21.

30. Darling, M.L., *The Punjab Peasant in Prosperity and Debt,* 13.

31. *Ibid.,* 5.

32. Calvert, H., *The Wealth and Welfare of the Punjab,* 256.

sold about 80% of their produce in the village to the village shopkeeper-cum-moneylenders.[33]

Before taking up the question of the varying nature of contradictions or alignments between different agrarian classes and strata, between agrarian classes and urban social groups, and between the rural and urban people of the Punjab and the colonial state, which affected the nature and course of the peasants' movement, let us have a look at the changes in the social and economic life of the province during the period of our study.

The most significant changes that occurred during this period, were the attenuation of the village and village community as an isolate the shift in the caste organisation brought about by the economic pressure and the impact of the new ideas and ideals which western thought and modes or living had brought with them and, lastly, the break up of the joint family system.[34] Thus, these changes shattered the off static society, transforming it slowly from a community pattern into an individualistic one. Before, we proceed further, let us compare the proportion of the urban and the rural population at the various Census years in the following table.[35]

Table 1.3. Rural/Urban Population in Census Years 1911-41

Year	*Urban*	*Rural*
1911	9.8	90.2
1921	10.3	89.7
1931	12.4	87.6
1941	14.7	85.3

33. *Report of the Punjab Provincial Banking Enquiry Committee,* Vol. I, 1930, 16, 48 & 196.

34. *Census 1911,* Vol. XIV, 29; *Census 1921,* Vol. XV, 94; Houseworth, F., *Purdah,* 248.

35. *Census 1931,* Vol. XVII (of Gurdaspur, Lahore, Sialkot, Gujranwala, Sheikhupura, Gujrat, Shahpur, Rawalpindi, Attock, Mianwali, Montgomery, Jhang, Lyallpur, Multan, Muzaffargarh and Dera Gazikhan); *Census 1941,* Vol. VI, 2-3; *Census of India Reports : 1921,* Vol. I, Part-I, 64; Agriculture-B-March, 1926, File No. Pros. No. 219-40, 1; Home Department-Land, Health and Education, NAI : New Delhi.

The figure of the above table clearly show the slow pace of urbanization. Urban-rural communication and transport was growing and the classic description of the self-sufficient village community hardly applies to early twentieth century Punjab. However, the traditional non-agricultural occupational groups, the *Teli,* the *Julaha,* the *Chimbs,* the *Tarkhan,* the *Mochi,* etc. still tried their trade.[36]

For the prosperity of the province and to tackle the problem of unemployment, both in rural and urban areas, and to improve the lot of the agriculturists, there was a strong need, especially of the agriculture based industrialisation as well as the development of cottage industries[37] in the Punjab. The industries in the Punjab could be divided into two classes *(i)* Cottage industries, and *(ii)* Organised and large scale Industries. In the case of the former the scale of operation was small, organisation limited and the supplies intended largely for meeting local need, while the latter were carried on in workshops or factories with power operated machinery, both for manufacture and trade.[38] Here, we shall discuss, in brief, the Cottage industries only.

---

36. P.L.C.D., Vol. XV, 1934, 150; Vol. XI, 1928, 312 (Among the cultivating class tenants-at-will, occupancy tenants, proprietors, *Zamindars,* absentee landlords, cultivating owner and any tenant including *Kamins*); also Vol. VIII, Part-A, 1925, 225 (These were *Teli, Julaha, Chimba, Tarkhan, Mochi,* who lived in the villages and played equally important role in village live); Hugles, H.H., Gen, Editor, *Punjab Village Survey : No. 1,* Chapter-V (For further details see Maine, H.S., *Village Communities in the East and West :* Six lectures delivered at Oxford with additional address, 3rd Edition : London, 1907, 125-56; Powell Baden, *The Origin and Growth of Village Communities in India : 1908,* 9-10; Morrison, *Th. Economic Transition in India* : 1911, 34; Mukherjee, R.K., *The Foundation of* Indian Economics : 1916, 3-5.

37. *Report of the Indian Industrial Commission,* 162; Anstey, V., *The Economic Development of India,* London : 1939, 228 (For further details also see P.L.C.D. Vol. VIII, 8.3.1925, 140; Darling, M.L., *Wisdom and Waste,* 370; Abbot, A and Wood, S.H., *Report on Vocational Education in India,* Delhi, Punjab and U.P. 1936-37, Delhi : 1937, 110.

38. *Reports on the Working of the Indian Factories Act in the Punjab,* Pars. 15-16.

Writers Darling, "Without this second string (rural cottage industries) to his bow the Punjab peasant proprietor must always be in debt".[39] The position of the cottage industry, however, was far from satisfactory during the period under review and was on the decline due to a number of causes. The cotton handloom industry was in bad shape. *The Paisa Akhbar,* a daily published in Lahore, of March 15, 1902 said that indiscriminate import and use of Europe made cloth had brought about the ruin of the weavers.[40] The influx or foreign piece-goods continued to affect adversely the fortune of the cottage industry workers throughout this period.[41]

The tariff policy of the Government of India exercised an adverse effect on the handloom industry. In 1930 Mr. Lionel Heath remarked, "The state of handloom industry is at a far lower ebb".[42] Further deterioration was reported in 1932 by the Indian Tariff Board, which wrote that the average earning of the weaver was "seriously reduced' due to "the increase in the cost of yarn on account of the protective duty".[43] The fact finding Committee (Handlooms and Mills), 1942, revealed that the yarn of above 20 counts used by the handlooms in 1939 was only 9.9% of the total yarns consumed by them, which indirectly exhibits that no less than 90.1% of the Cotton-goods produced by the weaver suffered from competition with the mills.[44]

In fact, the handloom industry could not stand against the organised industry. Thus, while the population of the Punjab increased between 1867 and 1911 by 13%, the handloom workers decreased by 69%.[45] They numbered 14, 797 in 1901,[46]

39. Darling, M.L., *Punjab Peasant in Prosperity and Debt,* 24.

40. *The Paisa Akhbar* (Lahore), March 15, 1902—Given in *Native Papers Report,* 1902, 203.

41. P.L.C.D., Speech of Abdul Haq on March 12, 1935.

42. Heath Lionel, *Review of the Condition of Hand-Weaving in the Punjab,* 1930, *(d).*

43. *Report of the Indian Tariff Board,* regarding the grant of protection to the Cotton Textile Industry, 1932, 170.

44. *Report of the Fact Finding Committee,* 16, 161.

45. Balkrishan, *Industrial Decline of India,* 1817, 188.

but only 2,68,254 in 1935.[47] In brief, nothing was done in this direction and the British wanted the Province to remain a mere producer of raw cotton for Lancashire Mills. The Punjab Administration Report for 1901-2 remarked that "the imported piece-goods were affecting adversely the fortunes of the cottage workers".[48] The decline of the cottage industry could also be inferred from the continuous call in the number of persons engaged in it. They numbered 42,048 in 1867; 32,361 in 1901; 17,023 in 1911[49] and only 13,394 in 1934.[50] Similarly, there was a rapid decline of the skills, tanning and weather industries.

One of the handicaps from which the cottage industries often suffered was the difficulty of obtaining cheap raw materials. Another was the poverty of the small artisan who lacked capital not only for the purchase of raw material and to meet the cost of production, but also to fill up the gap between production and final disposal of his goods. The middleman mostly financed the cottage workers. They also acted as the buyer of their products. When the financier happened to be money-lender, the small producer, who was unable to offer good security, obtained funds at high rates. The Punjab Banking Enquiry Committee revealed that the Punjab weaver had to pay interest at 12½% to 37%.[51] However, some times the middleman made advances without charging interest on the condition that all the products would be sold

46. *Administration Report of the Punjab and Its Dependencies* (Annual) 1901-02, 117.

47. *Indian Tariff Board* (Cotton Textile) II, (Evidence), 1934, 355; also see *Report of the Fact Finding Committee,* 201; Shah, K.T., *Industrialisation of the Punjab,* 1941, 63.

48. P.A.R., 1901-02, 117; see for details *Census Report-1911,* XIV, 500; *Indian Tariff Board,* II, 1935, 308; Badenoch, A.R., *Punjab Industries (1911-17),* 1917, 14, 140.

49. *Indian Tariff Board,* II, 1935, 347.

50. Lefroy, Maxwell H., *Report on an Inquiry into the Silk Industry-1,* 1917, 53; *Royal Commission on Agriculture in India* (Abridged Report : 1928), VIII, 211.

51. *Report of the Fact Finding Committee,* 1942, 86.

to him.[52] Another weakness of the Cottage industries was the absence of an organised system of marketing of the goods produced by them. In rural areas the production was largely for local consumption and only the surplus was sold to petty shopkeepers for disposal in adjoining areas. There were thus many gaps to be filled and strenuous efforts to be made in order to remove the numerous handicaps mentioned above. We shall consider the activities and policy of the Punjab Government to arrest the deterioration of Cottage industries and the methods it adopted to aid them in the sixth chapter of this work.

Another important features of the older socio-economic system was the communal pattern. It had its root in the social and political structural of the Punjab. Continual invasions and cultural confrontation had produced a society composed of three different but some times overlapping, segments—Hindus, Sikhs and Muslims,[53] each with its customs, boundaries and traditional elites. Virtually balanced population, with the western districts primarily Muslim and Eastern Hindu-Sikh, these communities shared a heritage of

52. *Report of the Fact Finding Committee,* 1942, 86.

53. The Muslim forming 5/9th of the population, Hindus were 3/9th of the population while the Sikh formed 1/9th of the population. Vide : Report of the Commissioner, appointed by the Punjab-sub-Committee of the INC, 4-5; Home Department, File No. 942/1922-Political, 36 NAI : New Delhi; *Census 1921,* Vol. XV, 95; P.L.C.D., Vol. XXVIII, 1935, 537-38 (The Rural and Urban population of each community between 1911-21 in the province as follows :

	Urban	Rural
General :	1,005,299	5,763,988
Sikhs :	178,150	2,885,994
Muslims :	1,424,931	11,878,060
Indian Christians :	392	144

Also see *The Punjabee* (Lahore), February 15, 1912 (For further details see Kassinger Tomi, Vilayatpur).

conflict involving war, rioting and struggle for converts.[54]

The break-up of the isolation of the village was especially striking in case of the villages within the easy reach of the biggest urban centres. This transition from the old to the new is a very remarkable event in the social life of the Punjab. Dr. Spare reported in 1926 : "The old days when each village was self sufficient unit replete with the industries, trades and professions necessary for its modest requirements are over".[55] The attraction of the rural life could not longer compete with that of the urban life, and the vitality of the village slowly declined. Moreover the ambition to rise in social scale became easier to fulfilled with the improvement of the means of communication.[56] A victim of the village community could now defy its undue harassment and shift to town bag and baggage.[57] By the turn of the 19th century, the position of the proprietary body as an authority over individual members and other inhabitants and considerably declined,[58] though it did not altogether succumb to the new powerful forces.[59]

---

54. Barrier, N.G., 'Mass Politics and the Punjab Congress in Pre-Gandhian Era', *The Punjab Past and Present,* Vol. IX-II, October, 1975 (Punjabi University, Patiala); The Punjabee (Lahore), February 15, 1912; Home Department, File No. 922/1922, 36 (For details see Mian Shah Din, 'Mohammedan Society in the Punjab', *The Indian Magazine;* Barrier N.G., The Punjab Government and communal Politics, The Punjab Past and present, 1970; Barrier, N.G., *The Sikhs and Literature,* Delhi : 1970; Kenneth Jones, *Communalism in the Punjab;* Dukhee Munsh Ram, *Jivan Bhai, Sahib Bhai, Mohan Singh Vaid* (Amritsar : n. d.).

55. Spare, B.G., *Economics of Agricultural Progress,* 1926, 19.

56. Memorandum prepared for the use of the Indian Statutory Commission by the Punjab Government, I, Part-I, 1928, 4-5; Saini, B.S., *The Social and Economic History of the Punjab* (including *Haryana and Himachal Pardesh*) 1901-39, Delhi : 1975, 42.

57. Spare, B.G., *Economics of Agricultural Progress,* 43; Mukherjee, R.K., *Economic Problems of India,* Vol. I, London : 1939, 265; Weld, E., *India's Demand for Transportation,* 1920, 81-82.

58. Powell Baden, *The Land System of British India,* Vol. I, 169.

59. *District Gazetter-Hoshiarpur : 1904,* 82; Saini, B.S., *The Social and Economic History of the Punjab* : 1901-39, 43.

Undoubtedly, the caste system,[60] influenced the social and economic life of the province, to a large extent. A source of rural tension was the existence of the depressed or untouchable classes who were subjected to humiliation and to many disabilities, not only social but economic as well.[61] While they constituted one-eight of the entire population of the province.[62] It will be equally interesting to know where they stood in terms of literacy. In this province in 1921-22, there were merely 7 per thousand who could read and write and only 2 per thousand in the native states and this too was the result of the philanthropic societies, such as the missionaries, the *Arya Samaj* and the Ahmadiyah people who had tried to find means for their education.[63]

Caste rule also regulated the actual methods of production, thus preventing experimentation and the exercise of initiative. For instance, in Darling's words, "proud of his faith more accustomed by common consent, the worst cultivator in the Punjab if he is a pure Rajput, is forbidden to touch the plough. On the other hand, the humble *Jat* is the very marrow and shoulder of the peasantry. Ploughing, weeding or reaping, he will bear the burden and the heart of the day, and at night take his turn at the well".[64] Another loss entailed by the caste system came from the rigid caste prejudices against the use of certain methods of improvement in agricultural and industrial productions.[65]

60. For details about caste system see Read Margaret, *The Land and Life of India* : 1934, 115; Mathew Arther, *Education of India* : 1926, 41-42.

61. Darling, M.L., *At Freedom Door,* London : 1949, 107; Wadia (PA) and Merchant (KT), *Our Economic Problem* : 1957, 72, 78.

62. P.L.C.D., Vol. III, January-March, 1922, 29.

63. P.L.C.D., Vol. III, January-March, 1922, 30.

64. Darling, M.D., *Punjab Peasant in Prosperity and Debt,* London : 1925, 35; This view is also supported by Sohan Singh Josh (Personal meeting with him : at Ajoy Bhawan, New Delhi).

65. The objection to the use of bone and night soil as manure for agricultural lands entertained by many castes was an instance in point. Vide. R.C.A., Par-84, Indian Government, *India in 1930-31,* 160.

Certain development in the late 19th century tended to impair the vitality of caste.[66] Now, the members of the higher castes under stress of economic circumstances were choosing careers, which 60 years ago would have been regarded with terror.[67] Thus, vocation ceased to be an index of caste and the question what a man was, was even more and more taking procedence over the question what his father was.[68] The gathering of men in cities and places of work like Government officers also weekend the caste restrictions and created an environment for a close social relationship, contacts and mutual understanding among them.[69] Again with the growth of nationalism, the larger recognition of the rights of the individual and the development of a spirit of criticism, the lower castes were becoming more self conscious and alive to the necessity of removing their old disabilities by concerned communal actions.[70] The Hindu-Muslim tension and the political rivalry and scramble for power during the period under review made even the conservative Hindu reconsider the question of the denial of the legitimate right of the untouchables to be classed as Hindus. This made the Hindus

66. Sarkar, J.N., Economics of British India : 1917, 47; Fuller, Bampylde, The Empire of India : 1913, 363; Weld, E., *India's Demand for Transport,* 1920, 89-90 (A high caste man may be well aware that his neighbour in a crowded railway carriage is an untouchable but is also more than aware that if he gives the situation a way by asking inconvenient questions, he will have to pay the difference in fare and change to a higher compartment. Discovering, that this silence has no outward results, he begins to wonder whether he could no ignore untouchability altogether) Vide. Blunt, Sir, E., *An Introduction to some Social Economic Problems of the Indian People :* 1938, 61; Saini, B.S., *The Social and Economic History of the Punjab,* 1901-39, 53.

67. Trevaskis, H.K., *Punjab of Today,* 1931, 206; Wadia and Merchant, *Our Economic Problems,* 1957, 27 and 78.

68. Trevaskis, H.K., *The Land of Five Rivers,* 1928, 59.

69. Read, Margret, *The Land and Life of India,* 1934, 119-20.

70. Ghurye, G.S., *Caste and Race in India,* 1932, 167-81.

more amenable to the influence of ideas of social reform and social equality.[71]

Another feature of the social super-structure was the joint family system. To some observers, this was the nearest approach to the ideal of social community.[72] Apart from kinship, the cohesion and solidarity of the joint family were based on social and religious traditions and the economic conditions of life and labour.[73] However, during the period under review, this system was fast disintegrating under the impact of various forces which the modern conditions brought to bear upon it. The consitition of a few families in the province was till based on some kind of joint living while others, especially in towns, had developed a definitely modern slant in their outlook on life.[74] With it the income of the family began to decrease.

We may briefly note the extent of literacy and education in rural Punjab for this was factor in the formation of consciousness and propagation of ideas among the masses. The first big step towards the instruction of the children of agriculturists was taken in 1918 when a give years programme for the extension of education in rural areas was launched.[75]

The progress of compulsory education was very slow as poverty of the rural population was perhaps the greatest

71. A sensation was caused by Dr. Ambedkar, Leader of the Hindu depressed class in 1936, when he announced his intention to leave the Hindu-fold alongwith his followers and embrace another faith promising equality of treatment. Vide. Jather Heri, *Indian Economics,* I, 1939, 106, For details see Farquhar, J.N., *Crown of Hinduism,* 1913, 175; Sitaramaya, P., *History of the Indian National Congress,* Vol. I, 1946, 52.

72. For details regarding the Joint Family System see Darling, M.L., *Wisdom and Waste in the Punjab Village,* 1934, 285; *Purdah,* 1932, 99-101; Wadia and Merchant, *Our Economic Problems,* 1957, 73.

73. Wadia and Merchant, *Our Economic Problems,* 1957, 81.

74. *Census: 1911,* Vol. XIV, 29; Hudson, T.C., *India Census Ethnography: 1901-31,* 63.

75. P.A.R., 1921-22, II, p. 13; also of 1924-25, 7; *Proceedings of the Department of Education, Punjab,* No. 18(A), dated July 16, 1948.

obstacle to complusion.[76] It was not easy to convince the illiterate parents, who needed the labour of their children to augment the family income, of the social and economic benefits of education.[77] The lack of strict enforcement of the final clauses of the Act and dilatory, intericate and expensive procedure for the conviction of defaulting parents were other important factors of its failure.[78]

In 1921, Sheikh Nur Illahi, the inspector of schools, Multan Division, started schools for illiterate adults in the rural areas on his own initiative. With this, a desire was aroused among other communities to start similar institutions suited to their own needs. But it harmed the interests of National solidarity.[79] Education of the depressed classes presented peculiar difficulties. The high-ups in the social scale were unmindful of the well-being of low castes, and objected to their admission to educational institutions because of the physical contamination supposed to be involved in touching them. This laid the foundation of great communal rivalry[80] and the socio-economic effects of communal strife can be easily imagined.[81]

It was during 1920-22, when the Non-co-operation movement had begun that Gandhi appealed to the masses to boycott the Government institutions and achieve complete success.[82] The Punjab Administration Report for 1921-22

76. *Punjab Government Report on the Compulsory Education Committee,* 1930, 4.

77. Punjab Government : *Land of the Five Rivers,* 2-6.

78. P.L.A.D., (Speech of Mian Abdul Haq on March 10, 1938), 10.3.1938.

79. Nurullah, S. and Naik, J.B., *A History of Education in India,* 1951, 585; For details also see P.A.R., 1909-10, 45; *Proceedings of the Department of Education :* Government of India, No. 1-2, A, October : 1917.

80. *Report of the Inquiry Committee on the University of the Punjab :* 1933, 150; P.L.C.D., (Speech of Abdul Hyat), July 24, 1937.

81. *Proceedings of the Ministry of Education :* Punjab Government, G.M. No. 210-G.S., dated 13.6.1923.

82. Rai, Lajpat, *His Life, Writings, Speeches,* Madras : 1918, 21-30, 63-70, 79-85, 208-09; Gandhi, M.K., *Autobiographical Writings,* ed., by V.C. Joshi, Delhi, 1965, 350-55, 848; Sitaramaya, Pattabhai, *History of the Indian National* Congress, Vol. I, 1946, 189-233.

described the situation in the province in these words :

> "For a time towards the end of 1920, and in the early months of 1921, the situation appeared serious. A few institutions cut all connections with the Government and University system.[83] By 1922 the tide had absolutely ebbed.[84] It is noteworthy that although discipline and work undoubtedly suffered,[85] this upheaval was not without its valuable lessons".

Now a demand for national education soon began to be put forward and gradually coincided with his Indian struggle for freedom. Almost all the political thinkers and leaders were of the view that the official system was unhelpful and even antogonistic to the national development.[86] Accordingly, Indians were to control national education. It was to create love and reverence for the motherland.

Before we take up the question of the burden of debt which was felt unequally by the larger and smaller owners, let us discuss some of the facts of agriculture and irrigation first. Infact, the condition of agriculture forced both the smaller and the larger peasants to borrow for making improvements.

Punjab was predominantly an agricultural province where agriculture was the chief industry. But it is a paradox that both agriculture and agriculturists,[87] were in a depressed state

83. P.A.R., 1921-22, II, 71.

84. Punjab Government : *Land of the Five Rivers,* 209; P.A.R., 1921, II, 71; Indian Government : *India in 1921-22,* 41.

85. Punjab Government, *Land of the Five Rivers,* 209.

86. Gandhi, M.K., *Young India,* 1919-22, 451; Lajpat Rai, *The Problem of National Education in India :* 1920, 28 (See also Mrs. Annie Beasant's writings).

87. Agriculturists were a very important class as on them depended the food supply of the people, nevertheless they were not treated well or helped by any one. On the contrary, their very blood was squeezed out of them. The Government was contemplating the recovery from them, along the land revenue of Rs. 52 lacks which were spent on famine relief. Could there be a greater injustice than this? They should

(Contd.)

from the very beginning of the period under review. The first thing that draws our attention in the study of the condition of agriculture in Punjab is the composition of the agricultural community. However, we have discussed this aspect earlier at length. But it will not be out of place to quote the following figures of the cultivators out of its total population of about 2358 crores, over 37 lacs possessed land,[88] while in U.P only about 12 lacs out of the population of nearly 4 crores owned land.[89] In Punjab those paid over Rs. 500/- as land revenue, numbered nearly 2135 *i.e.,* about 0.15% of the total population.[90] The agriculturist moneylenders were a main source of rural credit and according to some observers, they offered easy terms to poor farmers whenever they were in any need.[91] In the opinion of some observers, the agriculturist moneylenders were more sympathetic than the non-agriculturist moneylenders for the simple reason that unlike the latter, they were not shopkeepers, middlemen, and creditors, all in one; they neither used tricky weights, beams and measures, nor usurious practices. However, this view on the subject is challengeable. Agriculturist moneylender's avarice also approximated the insatiable greed of his non

combine and get-together, otherwise Government would impoverish them completely. Agriculturists comprised of 5 categories—see foot note No. 4 of this Chapter. Vide P.L.C.D., Vol. XXIV, 149; Vol. VIII, Part-A, 1925, 225; Weekly Report of the Director of Criminal Intelligence, September 25, 1909; Home Department, Political Proceeding, October, 1909, 110-17.

88. *Census of India,* 1931, Vol. XVII, Part-II, 2, 158-59; *Jat Gazette* (Muzaffargarh Report) 1.7.1931, 1; 15.1.1941, 3; 29.1.1941, 6; 5.2.1941, 1; P.L.C.D., Vol. XXV, 26.6.1934, 325; Vol. XXIII, 2.3.1933, 169.

89. P.L.A.D., Vol. XXIII, 24.4.1940, 327; P.L.C.D., Vol. XXIII, 2.3.1933, 646; Vol. XXIV, 1934, 325.

90. *Ibid.,* Calvert, H., *Wealth and Welfare of the Punjab,* 14-15; Bulletin of the Joint Development Board Punjab, 13 (Punjab Government : 1930) It further supports the point of view by reporting that big holdings were found in barran (unirrigated) tracts in the new settlement canal colonies which were sparsely populated.

91. P.L.C.D., Vol. XIX, 13.3.1942, 331; Vol. XXV, 28.6.1934, 328, 842-43; Vol. XXVIII, 2.11.1935, 1091; *Jat Gazette,* 1.6.1923, 8.

agriculturist counterpart, to remedy which the Government of the Unionist Party passed to Punjab Act of 1938, restricting the alienation of the land of an agriculturist debtor to a moneylender of his own section.[92]

But despite it, peasant proprietors dominated in the political organisation of the agriculturists. To cite an example, in 1935, the Unionist Party had 7 out of 8 members representing the Ambala Division in Punjab Assembly from among the peasant proprietors, and out of its eleven Sikh members eight belonged to the self-cultivators' class.[93] Besides, it is also noteworthy that *Zamindars* had adopted a very sympathetic attitude towards the tenants and cultivators. For instance, Jamal Khan, one of the big landholders, strongly supported the scrapping of the *Jinsi Batai* (sharing of Crops) system.[94] However, the condition of the peasants in general and the tenants in particular was very poor. They were at the bottom of their resources and got practically very little after meeting their rents.[95]

Some of the physical factors responsible for the backwardness of agriculture were : the uncertain character of rain-fall, floods, hailstorms, frosts and other vagaries of nature, which obviously had an injurious effect on the crop. Irrigation, undoubtedly, supplied a partial corrective to the deficiency of rainfall, but the effect of the other calamities mentioned above was altogether beyond human control.[96]

92. *Punjab Government Gazette* (Extra-ordinary), 16.6.1938, 80, 161; Saini, B.S., *The Social and Economic History of the Punjab* : 1901-39, 246.

93. P.L.C.D., Vol. XXVIII, 22.11.1935, 1091; P.L.A.D., Vol. XII, 4.3.1940, 50-51; P.L.C.D., Vol. VIII, 22.2.1928, 99.

94. P.L.A.D., Vol. XII, 4.3.1940, 50-51; Vol. XIV, 13.3.1942, 331; P.L.C.D., Vol. XXII, 29.3.1929, 1047-48.

95. *The Tribune* (Lahore), 11.4.1930, 11; *Report on the Administration of the Punjab And Its Dependencies for 1920-21,* Part-I, 7-8; P.L.C.D., Vol. XII, 1924, 629; Vol. XI, 1928, 321; Vol. XXIII, 21.3.1933, 668 (For more details see Part-II of the *Report on the Administration of the Punjab* and its Dependencies for 1920-21).

96. P.L.C.D., Vol. VII, 1924, 629; Vol. XXIV, 1934, 801-02, 1121 and 1138.

Besides the crop diseases, damage was also caused by wild animals.

It may be mentioned that 58% of the small holdings on an average measured 1.8 acre each and were thus not economical.[97] The agriculturist for the most part followed methods of extensive cultivation which were unsuitable in view of the smallness of the average holdings. The results was that the production was always low. Although the Department of Agriculture had introduced several types of improved implements, much remained to be done in this direction. The adoption of these implements was extremely slow due to several factors such as lack of capital, the smallness of holdings, ignorance, conservatism and inertia and the inability of the village blacksmith to repair them.[98] But gradually the value of improved agricultural implements had begun to be appreciated more and more, especially in the canal colonies.[99] One of the several factors responsible for the backwardness of agriculture and impoverishment of the cultivator was the unlimited sub-division and fragmentation of land. The *sub-division* of holding means the small size of the total area held or cultivated, while *fragmentation* implies the divisions of the holdings into a number of fragments 'or plots which are scattered through out the arable land of the village.

For the province as a whole, the average size of the owners' holding was between 7 to 8 acres.[100] An enquiry conducted

97. P.L.C.D., Vol. XXII, 2.3.1933, 169, 203; Vol. XXV, 23.6.1934, 338 (For further details see *Punjab Administration Reports :* 1911-12; *18 Months of Provincial Autonomy,* April 1, 1937 to September 30, 1938), Information Bureau, Punjab n.d.; Trevaskis, H.K., *The Punjab of Today,* 1931, 122.

98. P.L.C.D., Vol. I, 1921, 98-100 (Point No. 74—Question raised by Chaudhari Lal Chand).

99. P.A.R., 1923-24, 123-25; Darling, M.L., *The Punjab Peasant in Prosperity and Debt,* London : 1925, 180.

100. Calvert, H., *Wealth and Welfare,* 1936, 207-09.

by the Board of Economic Inquiry Punjab in 1939, revealed a further deterioration in the size of the holdings.[101] While according to Mr. Calvert, 58.3% of the owners cultivated less than 5 acres of land, according to the inquiry the percetage rose to 63.7, the land involved remaining the same.[102] 63.7% of owners in 1939 possessed uneconomic holdings as compared to 58.3% nearly 15 years ago. If the economic holding is to be regarded as equal to atleast 15 acres (as some observers *e.g.,*_M.L Darling thinks)[103] then in 1939, about 87.5% of the owners possessed land less than this and, therefore, they must have been living from hand to mouth. A large number of people took to agriculture for bare subsistence in the absence of any other mean of livelihood in the province, according to an inquiry made up by Mr. H. Calvert in 1927 on the extent of sub-division of the holdings of cultivators.[104] The results of the enquiry are shown in table 1.3. The category 'cultivator' as used by Calvert in his analysis did not discriminate between an owner and a tenant. The landless cultivators were much more numerous as compared to landowners.

---

101. *Board of Economic Enquiry, Prosperity Holdings in the Punjab* : Their Size and Distribution, Preliminary Report, 1.

102. It is not easy to define precisely the term "economic holding". Mr. Mann defines it as "One which will provide an average at the minimum standard of life considered satisfactory". Vide, *Land and Labour in Deccan Village*, II, 43 (According to *Keeling*, an economic holding should allow a man's chance of producing sufficient to support himself and his family in reasonable comfort after paying his necessary expenses.

103. Darling, M.L., *Punjab Peasant in Prosperity and Debt*, London : 1925, 33.

104. Calvert, H., *The Size and Distribution of Cultivators Holdings in the Punjab*: 1928 (Board of Economic Enquiry in Punjab), 14-15 (The average area cultivated by a cultivator was about 7.2 acres and the total number of cultivators was about 14% higher than that of owners). Vide. Robert, W. and Kartar Singh, *A Text Book of the Punjab Agriculture*, 1947, 47-48.

Table 1.3

Size	*Percentage of Cultivators*	*Percentage of Cultivated Areas*
1 Acre or less	22.5	1.5
Between 1 to 5 Acres	33.3	12.1
" 5 to 10 Acres	20.5	20.6
" 10 to 15 Acres	10.2	17.4
" 15 to 20 Acres	5.3	12.3
" 20 to 25 Acres	3.1	9.1
" 25 to 50 Acres	4.2	18.5
Above 50 Acres	0.9	7.9
Total	100	100

The fragmentation of cultivation was decidedly a more serious and more extensive evil than sub-division of holding and was carried to greater extreme. For example in a village in Jullundur district. Mr. Darling found that 1,28,000 acres were splintered into 63,000 fields and another 584 owners cultivated no less than 16,000 plots of which a large number were less than one-seventh of an acre. The size of an individual plot was sometimes as small as 0.006 of an acre, or 34.25 square yards.[105] Again in the village Bairampur in Hoshiarpur district, Mr. Ram Lal Bhalla found that 34.5% of the cultivators had over 25 fragments each.[106] This was typical of a widely prevalent situation. The sub-division and the fragmentation of land resulted in a host of evils. The multiplication of small fields involved a great waste of cultivable areas. It was also not possible to get full worth in terms of economic gains from

105. *Ibid.*, 47-48.

106. *Report on the Economic Survey of Bairampur : 1922*, 35 (The village lands were found to be divided into 1598 fields averaging about 1/5th of an acre each 38% of the holdings had over 30 fields and in three cases plots were so small—the smallest was only. 014 of an acre—that they had been lost sight of by their owners and had passed into the hands of others).

such poor equipment as the ordinary cultivator possessed, namely a pair of bullocks and a plough.

The plots were in some cases so small that it was hardly possible to turn the bullocks round while ploughing. The cost of maintaining the cattle and cultivator himself of course remained the same even if the holding was smaller than an economic one. Again, much time was wasted in shifting ploughs, cattle and manure from one field to another. Irrigation often had become impracticable, although sufficient water was available. Very often in order to save time, the cultivator tried to find a short cut through other peoples' fields. This, together with the disputes about boundaries, was the constant cause of litigation and endless quarrels among village fold.[107]

It is interesting to state that the peasant proprietor was a tenant as well as a receiver of rent. As started above 80.6% of the owners owned less than 10 acres while a size of holding considered cultivated by one yoke of oxen was about 14 acres.[108] In order to make it nearly an economic holding, this class of owners felt the necessity of taking some more land on rent if it was available or to rent their own land to a neighbour and themselves work merely as tenants on bigger holdings.[109] It is interesting to note that "as receivers of rent, more than six lakhs of the smallest landlord stand in the same position and have the same interests as some of the owners of the biggest estates"[110]

Tenancies were of two types :[111]

(i) Those which were held by tenants with rights of

107. Punjab Government : *Land of Five Rivers,* 122; R.C.A., 130; *Famine Enquiry Commission Report : 1945,* 261, 272, 457; *Agricultural Legislation-II.*

108. Calvert, H., *Wealth and Welfare,* 1936, 176.

109. Punjab Government : *18 Months of Provincial Autonomy* : April 1, 1937 to September 30, 1938, 2-3.

110. *Ibid.*

111. P.A.R., 1911, 52.

occupancy under the Punjab Tenancy Act XVI of 1881, and

(ii) Those which were held as tenancies-at-will.

It is worth mentioning that the tenancy in the Punjab was most prevalent in the backward areas, mainly in the districts of the South-east. In Hissar, about 60% of the cultivated land was leased out end in Gurgaon, about 52%.[112] Sustained and stable cycles of production could not be maintained due to the repeated crop failure and the insecurity of harvest. Direct investment for expansion of production did not appear to be an attractive proposition. In the central regions, with secure irrigation, comparatively more productive soil and developing markets, there was possibility of increasing production and returns per acre. Precisely because of this, population and capital tended to concentrate in this region. Here, in Jullundur and Ludhiana, almost 70-75 percent of the cultivated area was *Khudkashi.*[113] Thus, *Zamindari* was not dominant all over Punjab, even if we were to accept the formal and superficial argument that tenancy necessarily means feudal landlordism.

A large section of the occupancy tenants in the Punjab, consolidated their economic position successfully. The area cultivated by such tenants, was about 15 to 25 percent of the leased out land in Ludhiana and Jullundur, about 35% in Hissar and Ferozpur and as much as 60% in Hoshiarpur.[114]

The majority of the occupancy-tenants in contrast to the tenants-at-will, did not their rent in kind. Lump cash rents or revenue rates were more prevalent in the area held by occupancy tenants. This was significant since, landlords in general preferred rent in kind at a time of rising prices.[115] Even if the share of *Batai* did not change, the increased value

112. Percentages are calculated from *Land Revenue Administration Reports of Punjab of 1890, 1900 and 1910.*

113. *Land Revenue Administration Reports of Punjab for the years 1875-1925.*

114. *Ibid.*

115. *Ibid.*

of the product increased the income of the landholder. The sentiments of the landlords were expressed by Macleod and others who demanded a return to grain payment, "where they were urgently desired by the landowners,".[116] This desire was quite strong and widespread. "The proprietors", reported Gacroft, "cling to grain payment with a tenancity impossible to overcome".[117] However, it is clear fro m our evidence that the proprietors were not universally successful. In 80% of the area under occupancy tenants, cash rent was paid.[118] In Ferozpur, where there was a notable expansion of the area held by occupancy tenants, there was almost 90% increase in the area paying cash rents.[119] The general level of cash rents paid by the occupancy tenants was much lower than the rents paid by the tenants-at-will. Even when the occupancy tenants paid rent in kind, their dues were much lower than these of the tenants-at-will.[120] But it is to be noted that the limits of the difference varied from region to region.

The occupancy tenants, thus, had a great possibility of making profit through cultivation. They paid primarily cash rent at low rate. And the rents were supposed to be fixed.[121] of course, the rent increased, specially during the reassessments, but the rise was slower than the rate of price rise. The relative stability of rents at a time of rising prices meant that the proportion of surplus accruing to the landlords declined over time. And even if we assume productivity to be stagnant, the tenant could increase his income.

116. Foreign Department (Rev.) A-Pros.-January, 1870, Nos. 44-77, NAI, New Delhi.

117. *Settlement Report of Rawalpindi*, Para-303.

118. *Land Revenue Administration Reports of Punjab*, for the year 1924 & 1925.

119. *Ibid.*

120. *Ibid.*

121. Foreign Department (Rev.),-A-Pros.-January, 1870, Nos. 44-71 (See the Statement of Syad Jamal Ali, Extra Assistant Commissioner, Hissar District; Sohan Lal, Extra Assistant Commissioner, Jullundur District, and H.E. Parkins, Esquire, Deputy Commissioner Hoshiarpur District).

It is noteworthy to state that the landowners were positively hostile towards the section of occupancy tenants who managed to strengthen their economic position. When the former tried to maximise the rent, the latter struggled to retain a larger portion of the surplus. The relative position of the landlords and the tenants was determined in the process. It was reported in 1897-98 that in some districts. The tenants have so strong a position that the landlords can not afford to do any thing which would drive them away, no suits of enhancement are hence recorded.[122] The relative absence of such suits meant greater stability of the rent demand, which enabled the occupancy tenants of these regions to accumulate further. Landlords in such conditions, could profit more by cultivating their land through tenants-at-will. It is expects, therefore that the landlords would attempt to reject the occupancy tenants on some ground and to give the land to tenants-at-will.[123]

Since the occupancy tenants were difficult to dispossess, the landlords resorted to large scale ejection of tenants-at-will while only 20 to 40 occupancy tenants were ejected each year as 5 to 7 thousand tenants-at-will were dispossessed.[124] Here again, there were regional variations—the largest number being in the regions where there were reassessment operations. These large scale evictions, especially before the resettlements, were undertaken to prevent the growth of occupancy rights. In Hissar, for instance, it was reported "most of the notices in this district are not intended to turn out the tenants altogether from the village, but in some cases to raise the rent and in others to guard against the growth of occupancy rights by compelling the tenants to occupy an exchange of fields".[125]

The growing independence and strength of the occupancy tenants often implied that the landlords were squeezed out.

122. *Administration Report of Punjab* : 1990-1901.

123. *Ibid.*, (Consult Yearly Volumes).

124. *Ibid.*

125. *Ibid.* 1886-87.

While he had to pay an increasing revenue rate, he could not always successfully enhance the rent received from the tenant. Such tenants often expanded their cultivation by purchasing land from the owner. We are informed in many cases, "Occupancy tenants, who are not on good terms with their landlord, are prepared, at what appears to be absurdly high prices to buy up the remaining right of the landlord".[126] There was, of course, a section of occupancy tenants in some regions, who were dispossessed by the landlords and converted into tenants-at-will.

Compared to the occupancy tenants, those who leased in land as tenants-at-will had numerous disadvantages. Definitely they had a weaker position in relation to the landowner. From this, however, we can not deduce any general argument either about the real economic position of the tenants-at-will as a social group, or about the function and significance of this form of tenancy. They differed in different areas.

In districts like Jullundur, Ludhiana, in central Punjab, the tenants were not impoverished landless peasants. Over 60% of the cultivated area cultivated by tenants-at-will was held by either proprietors or occupancy tenants.[127] In 1911 this fact was again noted in Ludhiana, "the tenants are usually owners in the village".[128] According to the *Khasra Girdawari* records of village Tehong in Jullundur, 1923-24, there were 147 tenants-at-will. But of these only 25 (16.5%) were without land.[129] But the conditions were different in Gurgaon, Hissar and Rohtak. Around 1900, almost 40% of the cultivated area was leased

126. *Settlement Report of Hoshiarpur,* 1910-14; Foreign Department (Rev.)-A-Pros.-January, 1870, Nos. 44-71.

127. *Settlement Report of Ludhiana,* 1878-83 (As early as 1870's Gordon Walies made detailed investigations).

128. Land Revenue Agriculture, Revenue, A-Pros.-September, 1911.

129. *Punjab Village Survey,* No. 5; Calvert, H., *The Wealth and Welfare of Punjab,* 172,197, 202.

out to the tenants-at-will.[130] Partially this was due to the insecurity of the harvest. Moreover, a large proportion of the land was held by the moneylenders, who did not cultivate. Unlike in central Punjab, we find here, a large number of landless tenants.[131]

It is most appropriate to discuss the mode of tenancy prevalent among the tenants-at-will. The system of tenancy most widely prevalent among this class of the tenants in the Punjab was that of *batai* or share cropping. This involved payment of fixed share of the crop, usually half to the landlord. One of its features specific to Punjab, was that the peasant paid half the land revenue and half the water rate.[132] The system of *batai* led to intensive exploitation by the *Zamindar* who took a very high share of the net income. Calculations of the net income of a farm of about 28 acres in Lyallpur district given on *batai* showed that during 6 years from 1928-34, the *Zamindar's* share of net income came to Rs. 2,445 or 89.3% when the tenant's share came to Rs. 292 or 10.7%. This calculation, however, did not provide for the wages of the tenants and three other adult male workers of his family.[133] Brij Narain's estimate was that on an average, 80% of the income from land went to the landlords.[134] Most of the land under tenancy was under share rent. The area under cash rent was small and declining.[135]

---

130. *Land Revenue Administration Reports of Punjab,* 1900; Darling's Papers, 1/20, I.S. Notebook (C.SASA), (This is quoted by Mirdula Mukherjee in her Research-paper, "Aspects of Agrarian Structure in Punjab, 1925-27); Calvert, H., *The Wealth and Welfare of the Punjab,* 197; Douie, J.M.

131. *An Economic Survey of Bhadas—a village in Gurgaon district* of Punjab, (It reveals : "There is a steady demand of tenants in the village.........This demand for tenants has brought into the field people of the menial classes, though they are unable to secure land on favourable terms; neither are they very good cultivators).

132. Calverts, H., *The Wealth and Welfare of the Punjab,* 1936, 172.

133. *The Tribune,* Lahore, June 16, 1937 (Brij Narain's article).

134. Brij Narain, *India Before and Since the Crisis,* Vol. II, 561.

135. Calvert, H., *The Wealth and Welfare of the Punjab,* 196, 198, 204 & 238.

Calvert opined that unlike the English landlord, the Punjab landlord would invest practically nothing back on the land.[136] Naturally, therefore, under the conditions, tenants generally took little interest in improving the land and the method of cultivation, especially, the tenants-at-will who were aware of the possibility of ejection any time without adequate compensation. On the whole, the tenants kept poor live stock; grew less valuable crops, avoiding especially those requiring the sinking of capital in the land.[137] The proportion of land tilled by tenants, therefore, resulted in a heavy economic loss to the province.

The above discussion would remain incomplete if we do not discuss the condition of irrigation in the province. In the Punjab several regions did not get sufficient rain, and in others, it was ill distributed, and the only salvation lay in expanding irrigation.[138] The point is supported by the fact that out of the net area of 60.16 million tillable acres even in 1938-39, 30.94 million including 5.79 million fallow acres were brought under cultivation.[139] As regards irrigation cultivators grievances can be summed up under two heads, *(a)* need for lowering and rationalising irrigational dues; *(b)* streamlining the working of the irrigation department of the province.

The employees of the irrigational department were in the habit of drawing free labour in a high handed way from the villagers[140]. This department formed such rules from time to

136. Calvert, H., *The Wealth and Welfare of the Punjab, 1936,* 298.

137. Trevaskis, H.K., *The Punjab of Today,* Vol. II, 1931, 11; Mukherjee, R.C., *Land Problems of India,* 1933, 149-69; Indian Government : *India in 1917-18,* 141; Mukhtiar Singh, *Kisan,* 214.

138. Sohan Lal, *Development of Irrigation in the Punjab,* Lahore : 1925, 1.

139. *Agricultural Statistics,* Supplement No. 3 to publication No. 52, Board of Economic Enquiries, Punjab, Lahore : 1940, 8; Trevaski, H.K., *The Punjab of Today,* Vol. II, 1931, 329; Harris, D.G., *Irrigation in India,* London : 1923, 1-4; Wadia and Merchant, *Our Economic Problems,* 1951, 48.

140. *Jag Gazette,* 20.4.1927, 5; P.L.C.D., Vol. XXIII, 21.3.1933, 627.

time as allowed the closing of the canals for long periods, which also were very often ill timed causing damage to the Crops.[141] Canal officers exercised the powers vested in them under the *Aab-i-zai* rules in an unjudicious manner by imposing arbitrary fines,[142] while the persons declared guilty of making breaches in the canals were mostly those, who in fact suffered by the inundation of their fields by these breaches, which were quite often caused by the washing away of the banks by rains, or by the holes made by rats.[143] Again while imposing these fines, canal officers frequently flouted the rules by asking the so called guilty farmers to pay as fines, the highest water rates chargeable for cotton, sugarcane, crops etc., as against the sum permitted by the law which was equal to the watering charges for *Kahr* (first water after sowing of the crop) sown.[144] Moreover, the peasants, *Zaildars* and *Lambardars* were also severely punished if they failed to report these breaches at once to the canal officers or bring men to plug these holes.[145] Full water rates were charged even when it supplied only two waterings out of the four or five needed for a crop to mature.[146]

The *Kharaba* rules were very harsh. Under these rules, full remission in irrigation duty was granted, only if the crop of the canal irrigated field was less than 4 annas in a rupee,[147]

141. In the framing of their rules, the greatest defect still lay in the fact that the voice of the agriculturists were never taken into account. Vide P.L.C.D., Vol. XXIII, 21.3.1933, 655.

142. *Ibid.*, 657-58.

143. *Jat Gazette*, 20.4.1927, 3 (The point is well illustrated by the fact that in Rohtak District alone, *Aab-i-Zai* fine to the tune of Rs. 21, 692, Rs. 33, 186 and Rs. 33, 309 were realised respectively in 1924-25, 1925-26 and in the Kharif of 1926).

144. *Ibid.*, (Still the Collector or the Commissioner, with whom lay the appeals, more often than not upheld these unjust fines).

145. P.L.C.D., Vol. XXIII, 21.3.1933, 659-62.

146. To cite a few instances, in Rohtak district one *Zailar* was suspended, while another was warned. 3 *Numbardars* were dismissed and the Commission of 25 others was confiscated during 1924-26.

147. P.L.C.D., Vol. XXIII, 28.2.1933, 3; 656 and 627.

i.e. in case of 75% crop failure. The things were made still worse by the complicated procedure of claiming *Kharaba* benefits. Every owner of a field claiming *Kharaba,* had to file his application personally.[148] Besides this, every such field had to be inspected by the *lambardar* resulting in hardship to the applicants particularly when the number of the applications was large, because it took a long time to inspect all these fields.[149] But the cultivators could not afford to let the unmatured crops stand indefinitely in their fields. So they ploughed them for the next crop, and thus forfeited their claims to *Kharaba* remissions.[150]

The Chahi tax was realised even for the wells which, for one reason or the other, had become useless. For instance, in 1924-25, wells in *Khadar* area got filled in with sand and became inoperative but the *Chahi* tax was realised from the lands previously irrigated by these wells.[151] The working expenses of the irrigation departments were also exorbitant.[152]

As stated earlier, the water rate was the other major Government demand, almost equal in amount to the land

148. The example of the Shahpur assessment circle bore out the point in 1936, 4 *annas* wheat crop in the rupee harvested 2 mounds bring a total return of Rs. 4/- per acre, while the cost of production for the same excluding that of cattle maintenance, seeds, labour etc., stood at Rs. 13/-, *annas* 10 (water-rates Rs. 5/-; Land revenue Rs. 5.5; Local rate, 10 *annas, Malikana* (In the case of tenants), Rs. 2.5, Vide P.L.C.D., Vol. XXVIII, 17.3.1936, 627.

149. *Ibid.*

150. *Ibid.,* The Provincial Executive could enhance water-rates through an order even without consulting the provincial Legislature.

151. *Chahi* rate was levied in two ways : Firstly, it was fixed for a well, which was further distributed proportionately to the area irrigated by it. It was known as *Nal-Chahi* and secondly, to the land revenue of the areas irrigated by a well, some more amount was added. Vide *Jat Gazette,* 20.4.1927, 5; 27.5.1931, 7.

152. *Ibid.,* P.L.C.D., Vol. XVIII, 7.3.1931, 171, 405; P.L.C.D., Vol. XIX, 11.5.1931, 373; P.L.C.D., Vol. XX, 1.12.1931, 282-93; *Jat Gazette,* 4.3.1931, 1; 27.5.1931, 1; 6.1.1932, 2.

revenue demand[153]. It was even admitted by the Government that "Water rates have never had any scientific basis of assessment", and that canals were regarded as "the most important source of financing the requirements of the province irrespective of all theoretical considerations".[154] As a result, the water rate had no relation to the actual costs incurred in providing irrigation facilities. Profits or returns from canals, after allowing for expenses and interest on invested capital, varied between 12%, and were often closer to 15 to 16%.[155] Even in the years of acute depression, irrigation surplus stood at over Rs. 2 crores in 1930-31 and was equal to Rs. 3 crores in 1931-32,[156] *abiana* was even more inelastic than land revenue because the Government was under no obligation to reduce it, no matter how low the prices. This was one factor that cultivation costs were so inelastic, because *abiana* added up to a sizeable portion of total costs. In 1931, there were reports of peasants refusing to take canal water because they could not afford to pay the high water charges.[157] Besides, *abiana* could be enhanced at any time, there being no fixed period of settlement as in the case of land revenue. One such attempt at increase, in 1924, threatened to produce a major agitation which was averted by timely concessions and adept political manoeuvres involving the *'Zamindar Party'* on the part of Hailey, the Governor of the Punjab,[158] who remembered well

---

153. Darling, M.L., 1/21, Ts. Note Book (Quoted by Mirdula Mukherjee in her paper—"Aspects of Agrarian Structure in Punjab : 1925-47" read at J.N.U. on March 24, 1979).

154. Government Review of Report of Abiana Committee : 1934, Para 17 & 18.

155. Darling's, M.L., Papers, 1/21, Ts. Notebook, (Quoted by Murdula Mukherjee).

156. Brij Narain, *India Before and Since the Crisis,* Vol. II, 586.

157. *The Tribune* (Lahore) January 13, 1931.

158. Longley to Hailey, dated Simla—July 8, 1924, *(Hailey Papers,* M. S. S. Eur. E 220/6 *(a)* —& Hailey to G.D. Montmorency, P.S.U., dated Simla—July 8, 1924; Joint Secretary Department of Education, Health and Lands to Mr. Hailey dated August 16, 1924; *Hailey Papers,* M.S.S. Eur. E-220/6 *(b),* f 163 and f 277; Hailey to Hirtzel, dated November 13, 1924, *Hailey Papers,* M.S.S. Eur. E 220/6 *(c),* F 349 (and cited by Mrs. Mirdula Mukherjee in her research paper).

the lessons of 1907 agrarian disturbances and was not willing to let history repeat itself.

Many of the defects in the working of the irrigation system were due to the long standing anomalies in the Drainage Act of 1873. There was a need of removing these defects by overhauling this Act. Hence, the lack of irrigational means had further deteriorated the economic condition of the peasantry and this became one of the major factors which led to the rise of political consciousness among the peasants as well as the other rural masses.

Punjab seemed to have been marked out by nature as a prosperous agriculture region and yet its agriculture was in a backward condition. The living standard of the average tiller of the soil was pitifully low.[159] For instance, in Ferozpure and Lahore regions, in several villages, a considerable number of families were underfed.[160] Similarly, in Gurgaon and Hissar districts, living standard was perilously low; and shortage of food was generally the major cause of migration.[161] According to two Mohammedan Officials of Rawalpindi Division, the things were still worse. They say that the bulk of lower class of agriculturists was weak and unhealthy due to insufficient food.[162] Hence, the then prevailing complex economic structure of the province was responsible for the miserable economic condition of the peasants and this too led to unrest among the peasantry, between 1920-45.

Besides, the farmer had to feed wholly or partially all the

159. P.L.C.D., Vol. XXII, 1932, 637; Mukherjee, R.K., *Land Problems of India* : 1933, 3.

160. *Jat Gazette*, 24.3.1943, 1; Ganda Singh's Presidential remarks, Minutes of the Proceedings of the 30th meeting (December 4, 1970) of the Punjab History Society : Patiala).

161. P.L.C.D., Vol. XXII, 1932, 639-41.

162. P.L.C.D., Vol. I, 1937, 950 (Darling describes the pitiful and hard life of a *Jat* tiller which infact applies to the whole of agricultural community with rare exceptions, "as ploughing weeding or reaping, he will bear the burden and heat of the day and at night take his turn to the well".) Vide, Darling, M.L., *The Punjab Peasant in Prosperity and Debt*, London : 1925, 12.

Government officials, from *patwaris* upwards. Even the officials when on tours, were a source of misery and trouble to the poor *Zamindar.*[163] The real cause of the sad plight of the peasantry could be noticed in the anti-agriculturists and labour policy of the British rulers who were known as 'white traders'. The moneylenders enjoyed complete protection of the British Government and further enlarged their net of exploitation.[164] Hence, the white *baniyas* exploited the country through the black *baniyas.*[165] The British bureaucracy, being the Government of the capitalists, naturally gave concessions to the capitalists. The adverse economic effect of the political dominance of the white bureaucracy was that the Indians could not fix the prices of the commodities produced in their own country.[166]

Another evil of the British taxation policy was that it put 90% of the burden on the agriculturists including the self-cultivators, tenants and also on the agricultural labour and thus pushing them into the inextricable meshes of the moneylenders.[167] Moreover, inequality in distribution of land revenue and tax burden among different sections of

163. P.L.C.D., Vol. II, 1921, 181; Vol. VIII, Part I, 1925, 774; Vol. XVII, 1930, 217-18; *Bande Matram* (Lahore) Lajpat Rai editor, 10th July, 1920 & 15th March, 1921, Darling, M.L., *The Punjab Peasant in Prosperity and Debt,* London : 1925, 34; P.L.C.D., Vol. I, 2.7.1932, 950.

164. (Under the British rule, the moneylender was no longer at the mercy of the village community with his craftiness he fully exploited the complex legal system against the simple natured debtor.) Vide. Gopal Madan, Punjab Tenancy Act (N.d.), 12; Report of the Native News Papers : 1921, 379.

165. Shastri, R.S., *Samrik Jatti Sangh,* 335.

166. The Tribune (Lahore), 10.5.1930, 10.5.1930, 4; P.L.C.D., Vol. XVII, 1930, 217.

167. *The Tribune* (Lahore), 24.9.1936, 5; P.L.A.D., Vol. X-C, 24.1.1941, 270 (Unionist menifesto); *Jat Gazette,* 25.5.1921, 7; 13.1.1932, 5; 8.1.1941, 3 (Urban population was never asked to contribute its just share. It is also made clear by a letter written in 1909 by Sir L.W. Dane, Lt. Governor of the Punjab to the Central Government wherein urban committees contributed little to the exchequer) Vide Papers regarding the question of the abolition of fees in Primary School, 1910, 241.

agriculturists *viz.* big landlords and self cultivators, tenants, agriculture labourers, was noticed during the period under review. For instance, in 1934, agriculturists (having 30 to 50 acres of land) paid Rs. 0.01 crore out of the real total provincial revenues of Rs. 10.61 crores.[168] The budget of all the year (1920-21 to 1944-45) evinces, more or less, a similar position.[169]

The reason for such a continuous inbalance or why the Unionists who wielded influence in the Government, some times more and at others less, during 1923 and 1946, could not interfere with the inequitous incidence of taxation, was that they themselves represented the rich agriculturists class and not the poor peasantry. The gross injustice in this respect is illustrated by the fact that a section of the urban population in the Punjab paid Rs. 3.1 per head as taxes. As late as in 1940, when some new taxes had already been levied on the urban people in 1934; the condition grew still worse.[170]

Under the Government of India Acts of 1919 and 1935, the local Governments were assigned such sources of revenue as related to the taxation of agriculturists.[171] A still grievous incongruity was that the rural people had no say in spending the revenue,[172] and most of the benefits were enjoyed by the non-agriculturists.[173] Besides, there were the backward

168. P.L.C.D., Vol. XXIV, 20.3.1934, 1052.

169. The conclusion has been drawn from the statistics given in the Punjab Budgets with detailed estimate for the year 1920-21 to 1944-45.

170. Misra, B.B., *Administrative History of India,* 123; *Jat Gazette,* 8.1.1941, 8; P.L.C.D., Vol. XX, 1931, 262.

171. Statistical abstract for British India, 1920-21 to 1938-39, 298; Report of the joint select committee of Indian Constitutional Reforms : 1933-34, Vol. I, Part-II, 146; Government of India Act of 1919, Section 45-A; P.L.C.D. Vol. XV, 25.2.1930, 46-47; *Jat Gazette,* 8.1.1941, 3.

172. Hussain, A., *Fazl-i-Hussain : A Political Biography,* Bombay : 1946, 162, 273-78; *Jat Gazette,* 25.5.1927, 7 (It may be noted here that during 1927-35, The Governor directed hostility towards the Unionist Party and Sir Sikander's selfishness had made the voice of the rural people in this respect further feeble).

173. *Ibid.,* Report of the Punjab Sources of Revenue Committee, Lahore, 1931, 37.

districts of Dera Gazi Khan, Mianwali, Hissar, Rohtak, Gurgaon, Kangra and Hoshiarpur, where even drinking water was not available.[174] In view of the above stated financial inequalities, it is clear that urban and rural interests clashed and the urban classes stood in the way of rural improvement.

The distressing effect of the great economic depression on the Punjab economy can well be seen in the forecast of the provincial revenue receipts and expenditure prepared in 1932, by the Finance Department for the subsequent five years *i.e.* 1933-34 to 1937-38.[175] In order to have a better idea of the degree of economic distress in the Punjab, it would be proper to add that even the above quoted estimate by the finance member was an under statement of the bad finances of the province.[176] Hence, the class of agriculturists which until then, was considerably backward was being harassed and victimised by the urban population on one hand and the exploiters—the moneylenders and the Government on the other. The shortcomings which contemporary observers pointed out were as follows :

(a) In certain regions, settlements were made, for political reasons, so high that at later settlement even the settlement officers did not countenance them. For instance, revenue had been assessed quite high because their ancestors had risen against the Government in 1857;[177]

---

174. P.L.A.D., Vol. XIV, 6.12.1941, 855; Vol. XV, 24.1.1941, 270.

175. P.L.C.D., Vol. XXIII, 2.3.1933, 181 (It envisaged even without allowing for any further nation building activities, it will take up 5 years of slow recovery to wipe out the accumulated revenue deficit of Rs. 152 lakhs.

176. *Ibid.*, also Vol. XX, 3.12.1931, 240 (Prices of agricultural produce and other expenses began to rise after 1933-34, the period of distress could, during which the farmers sold gold under acute distress lasted to 1936-37) Vide. *Jat Gazette,* 9.12.1931, 3; For details also see Desai, T.B., *Economic History under British,* Bombay : 1968.

177. On average land revenue in the Punjab was Rs. 2/- per acre. Vide. P.L.C.D., Vol. X, 24.11.1927, 14; Darling, M.L., *The Punjab Peasant in Prosperity and Debt,* London : 1925, 231.

(b) The method of realising land revenue was archaic, inelastic, and unsympathetic and spared none. It left little beyond the wages of their labour with the cultivators. It would have been a sound principle to ask the poor peasants to pay taxes out of their holdings, the area sown and crop harvested. In fact, they paid their liabilities out of their minimum income while others (non-agriculturists) gave only what they could save out of their own income. To substantiate the point, this happened very often with the agriculturists of Gurgaon, Hissar, Muzaffargarh and Chambelipur, the most backward and famine hit districts of the Punjab, which got good rains only once in 5 or 6 years.[178] The system appears to be worse than the out dated *batai* system, since the Government did not share prosperity and adversity with the farmers. Hence, whether in a period of adversity or prosperity, they were always in a state of indebtedness. These conditions pressed the average cultivators, whose annual income was approximately Rs. 31.5 and who out of it paid Rs. 17/

---

178. Darling calculated for the whole Punjab that an agricultural cycle of 5 years gave one good order, one bad and three those which were neither good nor bad, since the quinquinnial cycle represents the average of both, areas having abundant rains like Kangara, Rawalpindi, Lyallpur with annual average rainfalls (For 1923-24 to 1936-39 in inches) of 113.12, 36.83, 23.12 respectively as against the provincial annual average of 20.39 inches for the same period, and those like Multan with scant rain (Multan's annual average rainfall for the year 1923-24 to 1938-39 was 6.6 inches), so it can be concluded that in the latter areas the rate of prosperous and average years must have been almost doubly spare than that stated in Darling's above cited remarks. Vide. Statistics given above have been calculated from the figures given in agricultural statistics of the Punjab : 1901-02 to 1935-36, Publication No. 52, Table No. 3 : Supplement Nos. 1, 2 & 3 to Publication No. 52, *Board of Economic Enquiry,* Punjab; *The Tribune,* Lahore, 6.2.1933, 7; P.L.C.D., Vol. X, 7.3.1927 & 24.11.1927, 139, 1940-42; Vol. XI, 22.2.1928 and 8.5.1928, 82 and 1011, 1025; Vol. XXIII, 24.3.1933, 178, 454-55; Vol. XXIV, 19.2.1934 and 6.3.1934, 576-77; Saini, B.S., The Social & Economic History of the Punjab, 1901-39, 415.

- (According to some about Rs. 26.25) as Government dues, to borrow most often from moneylenders[179] and thus be a victim of permanent embarrassment with no hope of being extricated in their life times from their meshes.[180] In 1925-26, the peasants paid Rs. 13.5 crores as interests while the land revenue demand for that year totalled only 4.5 crores.[181]

(c) No remission was granted, the reason thereof being :[182] Firstly, remission could only be given if the land revenue of that area had been suspended thrice successively; Secondly, if the produce from the area was not more than 4 *annas* in the rupee and thirdly, the ultra loyal servants of the Government would never let the crop estimates come as low as 4 *annas.* The net result was that very often the suspended land revenue was added on to the land revenue demand of the subsequent crop, many times to an indifferent crop. The situation becomes still gloomy if the corruption of the *patwaris* and other revenue officers is also taken into consideration. They forcibly extracted bribe. The example of Kharif 1934, substantiates the point. Of course, the Governor had declared 50% remission in land revenue in the flood hit areas of districts, Rohtak, Karnal, Gurgaon and Hissar. But the

179. Since the Punjab Government had not collected statistics during 1920's and 1930's that might have helped in calculating the average income of an agriculturist. So various calculations differing widely from each other have been made. Darling using the indirect methods calculated Rs. 75/- per annum as the average income of an agriculturist. Vide. P.L.C.D. Vol. XI, 8.5.1928, 1025; Vol. XXIII, 2.3.1933, 1203; Vol. XXIV, 19.2.1934, 329; Darling, M.L., *The Punjab Peasant in Prosperity and Debt,* London : 1925, 16; File No. 98-Lands-B-December, 1931, NAI : New Delhi, 48.

180. Report of the Famine Commission of India, 1901, 110; Darling, M.L., *The Punjab Peasant in Prosperity and Debt :* London : 1925, 18-20.

181. File No. 98-Lands-B-December, 1931; Darling, M.L., *The Punjab Peasant in Prosperity and Debt,* London-1925, 19.

182. *The Tribune,* Lahore, 6.2.1933, 7; P.L.C.D., Vol. II, 22.2.1926 and 8.5.1926, 82 and 1925; Vol. XXIII, 2.3.1933, 133 and 454.

patwaris declared that the Governor, the Revenue Members, the Financial Commissioners and the Deputy Commissioners, were nothing. It was their pen that was every thing, and added, "Let us see whether it is our pen, which rules here or the announcement made by the Governors".[183] It resulted in the criticism of the leaders of the Unionist Party who had advised the agriculturists not to gratify the *patwaris,* since either they got no remission where they actually needed 50% or received 50% though entitled to 100%.[184] Even when the Government ordered the collection of land dues in installments, collection officers insisted on full payment and thereby harassed the cultivators. Similarly, another stage of hardship faced by the cultivators was at the time of depositing part payments. They had to gratify petty officials like officer-in-charge of collections and balances. Not only the cultivators, even the lambardars had to tip such officers while remitting land revenue and this burden again fell on the agriculturists.[185]

(d) In contrast to realisation of income tax arrears, where-under only movable property of the defaulter could be auctioned, after defaulting the agriculturists' whole land, howsoever large a tract, could be confiscated for even smallest arrears and the balance after deducting the arrears was not payable to him, though the Government might have auctioned it for any huge amount. The sale of the crop, the cattle and movable and immovable property clauses of the land revenue Act (1887) were frequently wielded by the Government officials against the land revenue defaulters;[186]

183. P.L.C.D., Vol. XXIV, 1.3.1934, 492.

184. *Ibid.*

185. To mitigate this wrong with regard to the *Lambardars* Chhotu Ram suggested that the Government should waive postal rates altogether. Vide. P.L.C.D., Vol. XXIII, 2.3.1933, 21.3.1933, 182; 657 and 1017.

186. The Tribune, Lahore, 6.2.1933, 7; P.L.C.D., Vol. XXI, 10.3.1932, 355.

(e) The Government thought that the clamour of the cultivators against heavy taxation deserved no serious consideration since it was camel's habit to cry while being loaded, but that was a fallacious test of the capacity of the *Zamindars* to pay;[187]

(f) Ver scant consideration was given for the high cost of production while determining net assets to assess land revenue.[188] Land revenue fixed in the preceding settlement was not lowered even during the great economic depression during 1929-33, while the prices of agricultural commodities had registered a big fall vis-a-vis their prices during 1910-12, when the land revenue settlement was made.[189]

(g) In settlements, unusually high yields were assumed as basis of calculation. Per acre yields of even men like Colonel Brues, a member of the water rates enquiry Committee, were rejected, though he maintained thorough accounts of his farm. The method adopted to calculate the average produce of a yield was a very crude one. Settlement Officers took two *Kanals* of wheat, two *marlas* of sugar cane, etc. and applied the rule of three and struck the average produce of the whole field without allowing any discount for the

187. P.L.C.D., Vol. XXI, 12.3.1932, 355; Vol. XXIII, 233. 1933, 183.

188. Brij Narain, *Agricultural Workers and the Punjab Land Revenue Committee,* 10; P.L.C.D., Vol. XXVI, 22.3.1935, 727-28.

189. Average rates (in rupees, annas, pies) of some important agricultural commodities (prevailing in the Punjab) lending support to the point are tabled below :

Year	Wheat	Cotton	Gur	Toria	Grams
1910-12	3.04.4	8.15.4	1.14.0	7.04.8	3.15.4
1921-22	3.12.0	8.06.0	6.04.0	5.10.0	3.04.0
1933-34	3.09.0	4.11.0	1.08.0	3.08.0	2.02.0

The above figures are calculated by us from the statistics given in Punjab Government Gazette, for the year ending 31st December, 1933, Part-I (Statistical), 610; P.L.C.D., Vol. XXII, 2.3.1933, 184; Vol. XXIV, 1.3.1934 and 6.3.1934, 386, 578-81.

uncultivated lands. Directors of land records and agriculture used their revisionary powers very often to enhance estimates, but very seldom the other way round.[190]

Other causes of complaints were : *(i)* while making settlement no educated cultivator possessing independent views was consulted. Settlement Officers associated *numberdars* and *Zaildars* who were only *ji hazuri* (Yesmen) because their careers could be made or marred by the former;[191] *(ii)* In *bhai-chara* villages, where an estate did not belong to any single person, revenue officers under the doctrine of joint and several responsibility harassed many for the fault of one.[192]

It will be most appropriate to state here that the absolute impact of the colonial economy and administration forced all the sections of the peasantry to take recourse to the moneylender who played a crucial role in the economy, being the most important, and near monopoly source of credit and finance. The peasant was forced into borrowing to pay land revenue, to maintain the necessary conditions of cultivation, and to meet his basic consumption needs, especially in times of crisis. The enormity of the debt burden of the peasantry can be seen from the fact that it was, in 1921, more than 19 times the amount of land revenue.[193]

Both the larger and smaller owners equally felt the burden of debt. In 1921, debt's multiple of land revenue was 10 for the larger proprietors and 27 for the smaller ones.[194] Moreover, while the poor peasants borrowed out of economic necessity,

190. *The Tribune* (Lahore), 6.2.1933, 7; P.L.C.D., Vol. XXVII, 11.11.1935, 645.

191. P.L.C.D., Vol. XXVII, 11.11.1935, 635-45.

192. *The Tribune,* (Lahore), 6.2.1933, 7; P.L.C.D., Vol. XXI, 10.3.1932, 354.

193. Darling, M.L., *The Punjab Peasant in Prosperity and Debt,* London, 1925, 13; For details see Report of Punjab Provincial Banking Enquiry Committee, Vol. I. 1930, 16.

194. Darling, M.L., *The Punjab Peasant in Prosperity and Debt,* London-1925, 13-14.

the richer peasants often borrowed for making improvements. And in any case they borrowed from a position of strength. The conditions under which the agricultural labour and the tenant-at-will borrowed were even more harsh because they could not offer much security. However, these were two different problems and these issues must be emphasised because the entire Punjab official tradition as well as the Unionist anti-lender rhetoric chose to represent them as a single, homogenous agriculturists versus moneylender issue. The classic statement of this view in Darling's famous book, *The Punjab Peasant in Prosperity and Debt* proceeds on two basic assumptions. One—that the Punjab is prosperous; Second—that the Punjab is land of peasant proprietors, but both assumptions are questionable.[195]

However, if we find that Punjab was not a country of peasant proprietors, but that it was a highly stratified society with wide variation in income levels, then it is possible that the prosperity might be the prosperity of the few, and that there might be many others who borrowed not because they could, but because they must. Once we have introduced this distinction between causes of debt of various sections of society, we can proceed to discuss the indebtedness problem.

The indebtedness of the better-off *Zamindars* need not detain us for long. Probably, they borrowed out of improvidence, as Darling suggests, merely because with the enhancement of their security, as land value soared, they could borrow more. It was also highly likely that the money was frittered away on wasteful purposes, on conspicuous consumption and in spring feudal standards of grandeur. It is certainly true that very little, if any, of the loans taken were used for productive purpose such as land improvement, sinking wells, investing in better plough, better varieties of seeds, etc.[196] This borrowing, when it reached high levels and brought threats of sale of land in execution of decrees sought

195. Darling, M.L., *The Punjab Peasant in Prosperity and Debt,* London, 1925, 282.

196. This point is discussed in the second part of this Section.

by moneylenders, became a serious political problem. The Punjab Land Alienation Act, which tackled this problem at the turn of the century, merely sought to protect from sale the land of members belonging to agriculturist tribes and did nothing at all for providing for the essential credit requirements of those that needed to borrow for survival.[197] The result was the growth of a new class of agriculturist moneylenders,[198] who filled the credit vacuum, and strengthened their position by investment in moneylending, and cornering that part of the small peasants' surplus that was extracted by the old moneylenders. Insulated from competition by means of Land Alienation Act, this new class of agriculturist moneylenders cornered 75% of the mortgage debt of the province by 1929[199] because being themselves members of agriculturist tribes there was no restriction on their alienating the lands of defaulting debtors.[200]

In fact, these agriculturist moneylenders were notorious for lending only on security of land, because their main aim was the land and not the produce as in the case of the old merchant moneylender.[201]

---

197. This Act had, for a while atleast, before the moneylenders adjusted themselves to the new situation and before the growth of agriculturist moneylenders, resulted in a contraction of credit and the rise of interest rates, which had an obvious adverse impact on the small cultivator whose only security, land was devalued by the Act.

198. *Report of the Punjab Provincial Banking Enquiry Committee* 1929-30, Vol. I, 1930, 20 & 138; Darling, M.L., *The Punjab Peasant in Prosperity & Debt,* London : 1925, 229 & 280.

199. *Report of the Punjab Provincial Banking Enquiry Committee,* 1929-30, Vol. I, 1930, 139; *Darling Papers,* 1/21, TS, Notebook (Quoted by Mirdula Mukherjee).

200. *Report of the Punjab Provincial Banking Enquiry Committee,* 1929-30, Vol. I, 1930, 20.

201. Darling, M.L., *The Punjab Peasant in Prosperity and Debt.* London-1925, 229; *Report of the Punjab Provincial Banking Enquiry Committee,* 1929-30, Vol. I, 1930, 140; Report from Assistant Registrar of Co-operative Societies, Ambala, quoted in Darling Papers, 1/21, TS. Notebook (taken from Mrs. Mirdula Mukherjee's research paper).

The self-cultivating small peasant and the landless tenants and agricultural labourers, however, had a different problem—their need for credit as their precarious position in the production process forced them to borrow for paying the land revenue and *abiana*.[202] They might borrow, in *barani* tracts, to sink a new well or repair an old one,[203] since wells were a necessary condition for cultivation. They also borrowed for buying cattle lost through drought or disease or to replace an old one that died.[204] They might also borrow for the marriage of a daughter or son. In short, since at least 58.5% of the peasant proprietors and most tenants had holdings below the minimum required for making both and meet,[205] they existed at a precarious level of subsistence which did not allow for any reserves to tide over unkind season, uncontrollable price slumps, the onslaughts of disease[206] and other more

202. *Census of India,* Vol. XVII, 1931, Punjab Part-I, 53; Brij Narain, Article on 'Land Revenue and Indebtedness', published in *the Tribune,* Lahore, June 7, 1934; *Report of the Punjab Land Revenue Committee,* 1937, 2; *Report of the Indian Famine Commission,* 1901, 110 (By the close of 19th century land revenue realised was much less than the maximum fixed, but it varied greatly from district to district. Still the money borrowed to pay of the land revenue until then, alongwith the high rate of interest had accumulated into an embarrassing sum).

203. *Darling Papers,* 1/21 TS. Note Book (Quoted by Mirdula Mukherjee).

204. Calvert, H., *The Wealth and Wealth and Welfare of the Punjab,* Lahore—1936, 259; Darling, M.L., *The Punjab Peasant in Prosperity and Debt,* London : 1925, 250.

205. Darling opines that though minimum estimate for central Punjab is given 7 acres, almost every body agrees that if a family is to live comfortably, 10-15 acres in the minimum Vide. Article on 'The Economic Holding or the family farm' published in the agriculture Journal of India, Vol. XIII, Part-I, January, 1928; (For details also see Reed, S., and Cadell, P.R., *India the New Phase,* London : 1928, 97-98, 230; Mukherjee, A.K., *Economic Problems of Modern India,* Vol. I, London : 1939, 72; Darling, M.L., *The Punjab Peasant in Prosperity and Debt,* London : 1925, 18; Thornburn, S.S., *Punjab in Peace and War,* 1904, 352-53; *District Gazetteer,* Lahore : 1893-94, 69.

206. Darling, M.L., *The Punjab Peasant in Prosperity and Debt,* London : 1925, 211. (He informs that in the draught of 1920-21, the moneylender proved as indispensable as ever).

personal disasters, they were constantly in need of credit and often hopelessly in debt.

Thus, the debt existence was acknowledged as the principal cause of the sad state of affairs. Mr. Wolf rightly observed that, in India. "It is the bonds of debt that shackle agriculture".[207] Its presence definitely checked improvement in all directions and constituted one of the most serious problems of agricultural economy in the Punjab.[208] An enquiry regarding this problem made in 1929-30, by the Punjab provincial Banking Enquiry Committee, which based its conclusions on a comparatively comprehensive survey, put the total agriculture debt of the Punjab at Rs. 1350 millions in 1929 when in 1921 it amounted to Rs. 900/- millions, thus showing an increase of 50% on the estimate for 1921.[209]

Thus, rapid increase in the debt and the tendency in the increase of population at high rate, as the census figures for 1931 shows, requires no proof to show that the combination of these two factors must have had the far reaching consequences.[210] 'I can count on my figures', wrote the Settlement Officer of Muzaffargarh in the seventies, 'the men who are free from debt'. Twenty years later he wrote that things had become worse and that probably not more than 5% were free. Of Mianwali, it is said in the eighties, 23% of the Mohammedan proprietors were either ruined or irretrievably involved in debt. The late settlement officer says that 90% of the owners of the Muzaffargarh Tehsil were in

207. Wolf, H.W., *Co-operation in India,* 1929, 3.

208. Darling, M.L., *The Punjab Peasant in Prosperity and Debt,* London : 1925, 16-20.

209. *Report of the Punjab Provincial Banking Enquiry Committee,* 1924-30, Vol. I, Par. 222 (Total agricultural indebtedness of the British Indian Provinces in 1929 was estimated in the neighbourhood of Rs. 900 millions) Vide. *Report of the Central Banking Enquiry Committee,* Vol. I, 1931, Part-II, 77 (See for further details, P.L.C.D., Vol. VI, 1926, 924-26; Vol. XIII, 1929, 410; Darling, M.L., *The Punjab Peasant in Prosperity and Debt,* London : 1925, 3-5.

210. Darling, M.L., *The Punjab Peasant in Prosperity and Debt,* Lahore, 1936, 17; P.L.C.D., Vol. X-B, 1927, 1342; Vol. X-A, 1926, 90-96.

debt,[211] and in three more *Tehsils,* Mianwali, Jampur and Sangher, debt was atleast thirty times the land revenue. The figures given below, which are based on the official enquiry into mortgage debt, show the position in the tract as a whole :[212]

Table 1.5. Total Debt Proprietors and Occupancy Tenants Only

District	*In Lacs*	*As a Multiple of the Land Revenue*	*Per Cultivated Acre. Rs.*	*Per Head of the Rural Population & Rs.*
Mianwali	130	28	22	46
Muzaffargarh	191	22	26	35
Dera Ghazi Khan	168	22	13	40
Multan	200	08	17	25
Average	—	15	25	34

A glance at these figures will show that the debt in the west was much heavier than in the north. In Multan, it is true, the land revenue multiple is exactly the same as in Rawalpindi, but, as we shall see in a moment, the district had certain advantages over its neighbours. In the other three districts debt was for heavier, and Attock, with a land revenue multiple of eighteen, was the only district in the north that could be compared with them. If the West was compared with South, the conclusion was confirmed. Omitting Multan from the one and Karnal from the other, neither district was radically insecure, we have two groups of three districts for which the figures are as follows :

211. It is to be remembered that 90% of the population of Punjab was in debt. The Government must give the preference to the interest of 90% of the Punjab population which meant over 2 crores—rather than to the interests of a handful of moneylenders numbering not more than 40,000 in the whole province. Vide. P.L.C.D., Vol. XXVI, 1935, 423; Vol. V-I, 1926, 228-29; Vol. XXIII, 1933, 256-58.

212. *Report of the Punjab Provincial Banking Enquiry Committee,* 1924-30, Vol. I, Paras 222-225.

As a Multiple of the Land Revenue		For Cultivated Acre Rs.	Per Head of the Rural Population Rs.
South	17	15	36
West	25	21	39

In both the areas debt was undoubtedly heavy, but it was decidedly heavier in the west than in the south. For this, one reason was the smallness of holdings.[213]

Improvement of irrigation and opening of the Canal Colonies ushered in the Punjab an era of abnormal prosperity leading to an abnormal rise in the price of land.[214] The rise in price tempted the small land holders to sell their land or borrow amongst them, since the moneylenders who once considered land as useless, were now eager to lend against its fruits due to "..........the creation of property in land and the freedom with which that property could be alienated".[215] Some prominent factors apart from those discussed earlier, compelling the agriculturists to borrow from the moneylenders may be summed up as follows :

The complicated legal system of the British forced them

213. P.L.C.D., Vol. VIII, Part-I, 1925, 774; *Bande Matram,* Lahore, Lajpat Rai (Editor), July 10, March 15, 1921 (For details also see Darling, M.L., *The Punjab Peasant in Prosperity and Debt.)*

214. Board of Economic Enquiry, Supplementary 3 to Publication No. 52, Lahore : 1940, 6. Price of land were in rupees for acre *i.e.* from 30 in 1880-81 to 59 in 1895-96; 71 in 1901-02; 129 in 1910-11; 275 in 1919-20; 405 in 1929-30 and 475 in 1933-34; *The Tribune,* Lahore, January 12, 1939, 3; Calvert, H, *The Wealth and Welfare of the Punjab,* Lahore : 1936, 219; Sohan Lal, *Development of Irrigation in the Punjab,* Lahore : 1956, 1; Khushwant Singh, *The History of the Sikhs,* Vol-II, 151 (By 1939 out of the total cultivated area of about 30 million acres in the Punjab, approximately 10 million acres and 5 million acres respectively were being irrigated by canals and wells).

215. Misra, B.B., *The Indian Middle Class,* London : 1961, 15; Barrier, N.G., 'The Freedom and Enactment of the Punjab Alienation of Land Bill (1900)', *The Indian Economic and* Social Review, Vol. II, No. 2, April, 1965, 160.

to engage lawyers on heavy fees;[216] *Munsifs* Courts created in 1874-75 were mostly urbanites and ignorant of rural conditions;[217] Family feuds, complicated revenue and tenancy laws and altercations over canal waters resulted into excessive litigation;[218] In regions without irrigation facilities, there was insecurity of harvest due to uncertain rainfall, excessive sub-divisions and fragmentation of agricultural land and heavy mortality of livestocks.[219] Quite a potent reason was constituted by the unscrupulous methods of the moneylenders such as the falsification of accounts, the high rate of interest that doubled money and grain debts in two or three years.[220]

The rate of interest was no less in twenties and early thirties of the present century. It was as high as 20, 30 and 40% and

216. Thornburn, S.S., *Report on the Peasant Indebtedness and Land Alienation to Moneylenders,* Lahore : 1896, 47; Calvert, H., The Wealth and Welfare of the Punjab, Lahore : 1936, 372 (About 49% of the adult population attended the courts).

217. It is noteworthy here that the sale of land execution of decrees was almost unknown until 1873-74. Vide. *Ibid.,* Misra, B.B., *Administration of India,* 450.

218. Darling, M.L., *The Punjab Peasant in Prosperity and Debt,* Landon : 1925, 27 (It was calculated that a agricultural cycle of 5 years gave one good year, one bad and three cycle that were neither good nor bad. It was therefore, in good years that the peasants could most probably keep himself out of debt).

219. Royal Commission of Agriculture noted that due to uncertainty of animal life, cultivator was forced to keep reserves of Cattle, which he failed to feed properly resulted into the increase of his debt. Vide *Abridged Report of the Royal Commission on Agriculture* : 1928, 236 (The heavy cattle mortality constituted an important cause of the economic embarrassment of the cultivator is evidenced by the large percentage of loans given by co-operative societies in the Punjab, for the purpose of purchasing of cattle); Professor Carvor points out, small holdings invariably meant small incomes and in the Punjab where expenditure was less determined by incomes than dictated by customs and necessity small income sooner or later meant debt. Vide. Carvor, J.N., *Principle of Rural Economy,* 1911, 253.

220. Accepted rate of interest was described as *'dam dearbe Jins doons'* per year. Vide. Thornburn, S.S., *Report on Peasant Indebtedness and Land Alienations to Moneylenders.* Lahore : 1896, 47-50.

some times even 75% whereby one rupee could swell to Rs. 1,67,750 in 181/2 years.[221] As a result of these factors, by 1901-02, 32,87,387 acres in the province stood mortgaged with the moneylenders.[222] The reaction was so strong that some of the peasant debtors ultimately resorted to the murders of the Hindu and Sikh moneylenders.[223] This disgruntled peasantry was obviously threatening the internal security. As the Government was drawing the larger number of army recruits from among the Punjab peasantry,[224] it got alarmed as is revealed by a note of Fitzpatric, the Lieutenant Governor of the Punjab, to the Secretary of state, 'if landowners were reduced to the condition of tenants or labourers, they would constitute political danger of formidable dimensions'.[225] Similarly, veteran officials in the Indian administration expressed their fears about the political dangers involved in moneylending having become the largest industry of the province.[226]

The facility with which the ignorant and unthrifty

---

221. P.L.C.D., Vol. XXIV, 1934, 190, 830-31; Vol. X-B, 23.11.1927, 1343.

222. Saini, B.S., *The Social and Economic History of the Punjab,* 1901-39, Appendix-VII; Nanavati, *Indian Rural Problems,* Bombay : 1951, 224.

223. In the West Punjab, during the Cow riots, Mohammedan debtors often used these occasions and killed the *banias i.e.* mostly Hindu moneylenders or destroyed their records. Vide, *Punjab Administration Report,* 1891-92, 71; *Government of India* Proceedings : 1893-January, 311, 414-B; Khushwant Singh, *The History of the Sikhs,* Vol. II, 153.

224. During the first World War, Punjab sent 4 million soldiers to the different theatres of war. In 1939, almost as much as 60% of the soldiers of Indian army were being drawn from among the Punjab peasants. Vide, Travaskis, H.K., *The Punjab of Today,* 1931, 25; O.Dwyer, M., *India As I Knew It : 1885-1925.* London : 1925, 230; *The Tribune,* Lahore, January 12, 1934.

225. Government of India Records, *Agricultural Indebtedness And Transfers* Vol. II, Punjab, Correspondence, 2; Khushwant Singh *The History of the Sikhs,* 154.

226. *Records of the Punjab Government* (New Series), Vol. 3, 1899; *Government of India Revenue Proceedings;* 1894, December 11, 234-300; *Four Parliamentary Debates* Vol. III, 2.3.1892, 63-68; *Legislative Council of India Proceedings,* 1899, 330.

peasantry borrowed recklessly on the strength of the improved security of land, in course of time, led to reduction in their status from proprietors to tenants. On the other hand, in the Punjab, the moneylenders did not cultivate land themselves, but let it out on rent to their farmer—debtors. He did not invest any capital in improving it but contented himself with obtaining the best rent he could.[227] It was only in 1900 that the Government, realising that the transfer of land to non-cultivating classes was socially, politically, and economically dangerous, passed the Land Alination Act.[228] Of course, this Act, achieved its principal object of checking the alienation of land to the non-agriculturist to a remarkable degree, the moneylender, however, was "not willing to lose his hold on the cultivator".[229] He invented a new method of evading the provisions of the Act by resorting to benami transactions,[230] by which transfers were nominally made in favour of an agriculturist while the real benefit was not reaped by him.

Again as a measure of relief to the indebted and oppressed peasantry, the Government passed another Act called the Punjab Restitution of Mortgaged Lands Act; yet it failed to satisfy the indebted peasantry. Similarly, the Punjab Relief of Indebtedness Act (VII of 1934) was to protect the debtors; yet the poor sections of the community needed further protection against the unscrupulous moneylenders.[231] Although a free use of the Acts was made in the province, there legal provisions were reinforced with economic measures to support the poor peasant against the moneylenders. But the co-operative

227. Calvert, H., *The Wealth and Welfare of the Punjab,* Lahore : 1936, 271.

228. *Ibid.,* 246-264; P.A.R., 1901-02, 37.

229. *Report on Famine Inquiry Commission* : 1945, 465.

230. P.A.R., 1918-19, 19; P.L.C.D., Vol. XXVIII, 1934, 1143-54; *Report on the Land Revenue Administration of the Punjab for the Agriculture,* year ending the 30th September, 1929, 28-29; also of 1930, 19.

231. Punjab Act VII of 1934, Sec. 34, The Indian Civil Procedure Code : 1908, had provided for the imprisonment of the Debtor for the non-payment of his debt (Sections, 55-59, Order 21-Rule 37-40); For more details see the *Findings of the Central Banking Enquiry Committee*: 1931; *Report of the Famine Inquiry Commission* : 1945, 292.

societies set up by the Government provided quite an inadequate amount of loan and thus, inevitably threw the cultivator into the arms of moneylenders. As such the provision of suitable and cheap system of credit for the agriculturists, for combating rural indebtedness remained a great desideratum.

Another problem faced by the cultivators was that they could not realise a fair price for their produce. Farming was carried on, in most cases, by small peasant proprietors who had to depend on the moneylenders, because of their lack of access to adequate finance for marketing the produce. A further difficulty was presented by an inadequate provision of roads to enable the agriculturists to reach the market.[232] There was little wonder, then that the cultivator was forced to dispose of his produce at a disadvantage just when everybody was selling and the market was glutted.[233] There was a plethora of middlemen especially in the case of export staples. Large firms often entered into contracts with the cultivators, to whom advances of money were made in anticipation of the delivery of the produce and the pre-arranged price was always lower than the market price.[234]

An attempt at providing an alternative source of credit through co-operative credit societies we made. The process started in 1904,[235] but by 1939, the proportion of members of co-operative credit societies to families in rural areas was only 14%.[236] The total working capital of these societies in 1929 was Rs. 7 crores, 23 lakhs[237] whereas those moneylenders who were addressed to income tax, and who constituted 6,000 out of the total 55,000 in the Punjab, had invested a total capital,

232. *Report of the Punjab Provincial Banking Enquiry Committee*, 1929-30, 219-20, 252-53.

233. Wadia and Merchant, *Our Economic Problems*, 1957, 308.

234. *Ibid.*

235. An enabling Act was passed in 1904.

236. Brij Narain, India Before And Since the Crisis, Vol. II, 508-09.

237. *Report of the Punjab Provincial Banking Inquiry Committee*, 1929-30, 13.

of Rs. 22 crores. Besides the limited nature of the attempt, there were other factors why these societies were a failure in solving the problem of cheap and easy credit. Firstly, the membership rules were quite stern, and only well-to-do peasants were encouraged to join, as the danger of collapse of the societies if any members defaulted was great. Secondly, their procedures were much more cumbersome than the moneylenders and loans could not be taken at short notice. Thirdly, in backward areas, where most of the transactions between moneylenders and debtors were in kind, these societies were not population because they dealt only in cash.[238] Fourthly, those already indebted to moneylenders had to continue to deal with him till their accounts were settled. Also the fear of alienating the moneylender and his refusing to lend when an occasion arose which co-operative societies would not lend was strong. This fear was justified and was demonstrated in the time of depression when co-operative societies actually lent less than they did in normal times and even their members had to seek refuge with the moneylender.[239] Fifthly, their rates were not particularly attractive, as people with good security could borrow at almost the same rates from the moneylenders.[240] Sixthly, these societies were very exactly at the time of recovery.[241]

Consequently, we find that debt continued to increase at

238. *Punjab Revenue Department Proceedings,* June, 1930, No. 47.

239. Brij Narain, *India Before and Since the Crisis,* Vol. II, 509 (Loans to members of the Co-operative Societies in absolute amount declined from Rs. 24 lakhs in 1928-29 to Rs. 79 lakhs in 1932-33, and stood at Rs. 97 lakhs in 1936-37. Loans for member decreased from Rs. 53 lakhs in 1928-29 to Rs. 16 lakhs in 1932-33, and stood at Rs. 19 lakhs in 1936-37.

240. *Punjab Revenue Department Proceedings,* January, 1935, 16-17.

241. *Ibid., Darling's Papers,* Box I, Item No. 25 (Quoted by Mrs. Mirdula Mukherjee) Darling warned against the danger of Co-operatives pressing too hard for recovery and gives the example of a man who sold his daughter because the society was insisting on repayment.

an alarming rate,[242] and mortgage debt particularly (for the agriculturist moneylender rarely lent except mortgage), interest rates continued to be high, and the peasant remained embedded under this heavy burden. Only the old type of professional moneylender, threatened by the new political forces and losing his old position in the village, began to look elsewhere for investment opportunities. Because not many alternatives existed, he continued to lend in the village,[244] but on worse terms than before. The only change that occurred was in the personnel of rural moneylender landlords and other members of agricultural tribes with surpluses to invest grew stronger with their new resources from moneylending, as the political balance tilted in their favour. Hence, there is no gain saying the fact that co-operation did not succeed in curing all the economic and social ills from which the Punjab had been suffering. As a result, indebtedness of the poor peasantry continued to be a source of rural tension.

The Government's stiff land policy discussed above was considerably responsible for the loss of land by the cultivators, especially in the tracts with scant rainfall.[245] Not only lands, they had to sell their cattle, ornaments, and not very often,

242. *Report of the Punjab Provincial Enquiry Committee*, 16 (the total debt was estimated at Rs. 135 crores in 1929 of which 45 crores had been added since 1921. Before 1921, it had taken 30 years for Rs. 50 crores to be added).

243. Mortgage debt was estimated at almost half the total debt. Vide. Darling, M.L., *The Punjab Peasant Prosperity and Debt.*, London : 1925, 7; *The Report of the Punjab Provincial Banking* Enquiry Committee, 139 (The area mortgaged by agriculturists had increased from 190,000 acres to 328,000 acres between 1902-06 and 1931-36 Vide. *Darling's Papers*, Box I, Item No. 59 (Quoted by Mrs. Mirdula Mukherjee).

244. *Darling's Papers*, (Quoted by Mrs. Mirdula Mukherjee).

245. While the following table shows loss of lands by the agriculturists in Rohtak district (1926-27) to (1931-32), the case of the remaining alike districts was almost similar :

(Contd.)

their daughters too, in order to pay off their land revenue.[246] It was also alleged that the state had no right to claim for itself larger share in the produce from the land than in the case of other taxes, since land belonged to the tiller and not to the state; land revenue was a tax, not a rent.[247] The view seems to be convincing and was also supported by the taxation enquiry committee.[248]

For the betterment of agriculture, stress should have been laid on protecting the producers against the frauds being jointly perpetrated by the commission agents, weightmen, sackmen and brokers etc. Some of the funds charged from the agriculturists solely were really fantastic. For example, *Gaushala, Dharamshala* and several other such taxes were besides the freight charged from the producers for carrying commodities to buyers' goodowns. Another notable fraud of the traders as also reported by the Banking Inquiry Committee was that 49% of the weights and 69% of the scales used by them were designed for deceiving the agriculturists.[249]

On the other hand, the world depression further accentuated the differentiation within the peasantry. All rural classes and starta were adversely affected by the drastic fall in prices, but in varying degrees,[250] for which the Government

Year	*No. of Sales*	*Total Sales*	*No. of Mortgages*	*Total Mortgages Price in Rs.*
1926-27	67,001	5,87,13,459	1,47,014	6,18,29,672
1927-28	72,405	5,12,48,487	1,54,969	6,22,51,659
1930-31	64,871	5,13,66,715	1,44,791	5,53,20,330
1931-32	66,316	4,70,39,331	1,55,760	5,21,09,860

Vide. Statistics have been taken from P.L.C.D., Vol. XXIII, 27.2.1933, 59.

246. P.L.C.D., Vol. XXIII, 21.3.1933, 671.
247. P.L.C.D., Vol. II, 8.5.1928, 1024; P.L.A.D. Vol. XV, 27.1.1941. 312-13.
248. *Ibid.*
249. *Punjab Provincial Banking Enquiry Committee Report,* 1929-30, Vol. I, 219-20, 52-53, P.L.A.D., Vol. XVII, 1938, 594; Vol. VI, 14.11.1938, 555; *The Tribune,* Lahore, 23.4.1941—(Chhotu Ram's views), 2.
250. Darling, M.L., *Wisdom and Waste in Punjab Village,* 1934, 350.

apathy was no less responsible. A significant example of this can be cited by quoting the rate of wheat and other commodities being sold in the Punjab between 1928-29 and 1930-31. For this purpose, a table of the harvest prices of the principal crops is prepared which shows a noticeable decrease over last years' figures[251]

Table 1.6. Harvest Prices of the Principal Crops

Crop.	*1928-29*	*1929-30*	*Decrease or increase*	*1929-30*	*1930-31*	*Decrease or increase*
	Rs. A.P	*Rs. A.P*	*Rs. A.P*	*Rs. A.P*	*Rs. A.P*	*Rs. A.P*
Rice	3.13.0	3.04.0	0.09.0	3.04.0	1.12.0	1.08.0
Wheat	4.06.0	3.02.0	1.04.0	3.02.0	1.09.0	1.09.0
Barley	3.07.0	2.05.0	1.02.0	2.05.0	1.05.0	1.00.0
Jawar	4.07.0	4.02.0	0.05.0	4.02.0	1.12.0	2.06.0
Bajra	5.03.0	4.01.0	1.02.0	4.01.0	1.12.0	2.05.0
Maize	4.09.0	3.06.0	1.03.0	3.06.0	1.07.0	1.15.0
Gram	4.12.0	3.12.0	1.00.0	3.12.0	1.14.0	1.14.0
Rapeseed	7.00.0	5.12.0	1.04.0	5.12.0	3.13.0	1.15.0
Cotton-Desi	10.00.0	5.15.0	3.01.0	6.15.0	4.07.0	2.08.0
Unginned (American)	13.02.0	8.12.0	4.03.0	8.15.0	5.09.0	3.06.0
Sugar	6.02.0	6.05.0	0.03.0	6.05.0	4.02.0	2.03.0
Tobacco	9.15.0	10.00.0	0.01.0	10.00.0	7.03.0	2.13.0

Similarly, the fall in prices increased the land revenue burden for all revenue payers from landlords to tenants-at-will, but the impact of the increase varied. Deprecession hit hard as agricultural prices fell more than did the industrial

251. *Report on the Land Revenue Administration of the Punjab* for the agriculture year ending September 30, 1929; also the year ending September 30, 1931; P.L.C.D., Vol. XXIV, 1933, 673-74; File No. L & D.225/33/1933—Department of Land, Health and Education, NAI : New Delhi.

prices and the cost of agricultural production.[252] Moreover, as we have seen earlier, the fall in the land revenue and abiana was much less. Small holders and tenants-at-will were virtually ruined and were often unable to pay even the land revenue.[253] They were now in a radical mood. Moreover, even substantial farmers and small land-holder felt discontented.[254] Ground was now ready for the rise and spread of agrarian agitation in the province.

The contradiction between the debtors and creditors was sharpened further. On one hand, the debtor could not met his interest payment, on the other, the moneylender was reluctant to give fresh loans and if he did, he charged higher interest rates. He also clamourd for recovery of old loans as his own economic condition started deteriorating, for many moneylenders, especially the small one's, were hit quite hard by the depression, they were often unable to affect any recovery of the old loans.[255] But despite this the Government had not changed its policy, rather it followed the policy of benefiting the non-agriculturists, particularly the black-*banias*.[256] Hence, this evil had practically topped all economic growth. So helpless was the debtor and so extortionally oppressive were the creditors that besides economic slavery moral degradation had set in.[257]

252. Darling, M.L., *Wisdom and Waste in the Punjab Village*: 1934, 2; Brij Narain, *India Before and Since The Crisis*, Vol. II, 302, 307-10 and 313.

253. *The Tribune*, Lahore, Brij Narain's article, December, 28, 1932.

254. Darling, M.L., *Wisdom and Waste in the Punjab Village*, 168-169, 316 and 350.

255. *Ibid.*, 53, 101, 148-149 and 175.

256. P.L.C.D., Vol. XVII, 17.1.1931, 263-86; Vol. XXVIII, 1931, 931; Jat Gazette, 25.5.1927, 7; 1.6.1927, 8; 8.6.1927, 7; 27.1.1931, 1; Darling, M.L., *The Punjab Peasant in Prosperity and Debt*, London, 1925, 3-5; P.L.C.D., Vol. X-A, Jan-March, 1926, 90-96; Vol. X-B, 1927, 1342.

257. File No. Lands-B, December, 1931, No. 98, 69; P.L.C.D., Vol. XX, 1931, 298; Vol. VI, 1926, 228. (Their are instances where a debtors had to give his daughter or sister for immoral use in lieu of a little

(Contd.)

In brief, tax implemented by Kitchen, a British Official, towards the close of 1906, the increase in other land taxation, in irrigation and other payments extracted from the peasants were bound to cause discontent. The new Act limiting the right of land-owners in areas of settlement colonies, particularly the Chak colony, caused still greater unrest in the rural areas of Punjab. In addition to it, there was rumours about a revision of the right to hold land property, which greatly disturbed both the peasants and the land owners. As written earlier, the suffringe of the people were further aggravated by 13 years of almost constant crop failure and an epidemic of plague which according to official data caused the death of 65 thousand weekly in the province.[258] The disorder in the rural area was also caused by the action of the colonial Government itself. The several Government measures, such as extension of Land Alienation Amendment Acts to Canal Colonies from 1925 onwards, increased canal rates of the *Bari Doab* Canal, increased land revenue at Rawalpindi etc. were all obviously the causes for a great deal of excitement and agrarian unrest.[259] However, many other factors working in the same direction are discussed in the next chapter.

(Contd.)

recess for the payment of interest or debt. All that he grew which was very little under the circumstances was taken away by the moneylender towards the interest and he was to go the very day to get rotten food for his maintenance); P.L.C.D., Vol. XX, 1931, 240.

258. Navinson, H.W., *New Spirit in India*, London; 1908, 301.

259. The difference of policy in prosecuting the *Punjabee* (A popular local paper) and not proceeding against the *Civil and Military Gazette* (An organ of British Civil Service in the Punjab), the security of the sentence on the *Punjabee*, also caused excitement and unrest among the people. Vide, *Times of India*, May 25, 1907, 6.

2

Agrarian Unrest and the Peasant's Movement in the British Punjab

This chapter will attempt to examine the extent to which the peasantry of the British Punjab was awakened and organised and how peasant unrest developed in the period 1920-45. The aim of Section-I is to akettoh the historical background and to focus on those tendencies and developments which contained seeds of social, political and economic tension and conflict. A history of the Kirti Kisan Party is attempted in Section-II of the chapter. A brief history of the peasants' movement in various areas of British Punjab is traced in the third Section of the chapter.

As stated earlier, Punjab was not an industrially developed province. So unlike Bengal and Bombay regions, here the peasants and small landholders, instead of working-class were the first to take initiative in agitating against the oppressive and ruthlessly exploiting system of foreign imperialism[1]. The land tax imposed by Kitchen, a British official, towards the close of 1906, and the increase in other taxes, like that of irrigation and other payment extorted from the peasants were bound to cause discount. The new Act limiting the rights of land owners in areas of settlement colonies, particularly the Chanab colony, caused still greater unrest in the Punjab rural areas. There were also rumours about a revision of rights to hold landed property, which disturbed greatly the peasants as well as the landowners. All this happened against the

1. For details see Blyn, G., *Agricultural Trends in India* : 1891-1947, Philadelphia : 1966.

background of dire poverty, aggravated by 13 years of constant crop failure. The sufferings of the masses were further aggravated by an epidemic of plague which according to official date, caused weekly deaths of 65,000 in the province.[2]

In the Punjab, the various Government measures, such as the Land Alienation Act, 1901 the Land colonisation Act, 1990, the Transfer of Property Act, 1904, and the Punjab Pre-emption Act, 1905, provoked complex reactions from the political leaders. To some, it seemed to be a severe blow to the national unity and solidarity and an attempt to win over the favour of the Muslim *Zamindars* at the cost of the *Hindu-Bania*[3]. The Land Alienation Act, 1901 forbade the transfer of land from agriculturists to non-agriculturists through sale or mortgage. This Act adversely affected quite a large section of the society, especially the Hindu and the Sikh peasantry.[4]

Despite its sonorous claim that it was aimed at helping the poor peasantry out of the abyss of indebtedness, it was, in fact, a political measure designed more to debar the business classes from acquiring landed proprietorship than to help the distressed peasantry. A statutory distinction was draw between agricultural and non-agricultural classes to drive a permanent wedge between them. In the new situation the landlord and the rich peasant replaced the moneylender and reaped rich dividends resorting to the same nefarious mal-practices as well previously resorted to by the money-lender. The new order of things was worse for the poor peasantry,

2. Novinson, H.W., *New Spirit in India,* London : 1908, 301; P.L.C.D., Vol. VII-A, 1925, 367; Vol. X-B, 1927, 850; Vol. III, 1922, 98, 170, 232; Home Department File No. 225/33/1933-Land and Overseas. (For details also see the Fortnightly Report of the Punjab of the period under review. It will be clear that this state of affairs continued through out this period), NAI : New Delhi.

3. Hussain, A., *Fazl-i-Hussain : A Biography,* Bombay : 1947, 73; *The Punjabee,* March 21, 1907.

4. *Ibid.*

but it served the Government purpose admirably[5]. In another way the Act of 1901 proved a watershed. Embittered by the new deal meted out to them, the trading and business classes and other people, declared statutory non-agriculturists, became even more anti-Government and participated in or lent support to the national agitation. The Government, on its part, henceforth was inclined more towards the big landlords and rich peasants[6].

However, there was no significant sign of political upsurge except the under-current of dissatisfaction and friction in the Punjab before 1905. If at all three was some commotion in the political atmosphere, it as after the Congress Session in 1905. The Punjab had not even sent a delegate to represent it in the Ahmedabad Session of the Congress in 1902[7]. Moreover, as Lala Lajpat Rai once, pointed out, "Punjabees had shown very little political awareness to expose official injustice, highhanddeness and oppression........."[8]. But in 1907 the Punjab itself was in the threes of turmoil and as Lajpat Rai put it in 1908, "the only two provincers in which revolutionary movement established itself to any appreciable extent were

---

5. Hussain, A., *Fazl-i-Hussain : A Biography,* Bombay, 1947, 73; Fauja Singh, Presidential Address, Section-III, Indian History Congress : 33rd Session, December, 1974, Calicut, 6-7; *Annual Report on the Land Revenue Administration of the Punjab* for the year ending the 30th September, 1920, 1922 and 1923, 4; File No. 196-197-Agri-B-Feb., 1926, 23-24; P.L.C.D., Vol. XVIII, 1931, 298-301; Vol. XXIII, 1936, 1143-54; *Bande Matram,* June 18, 1921; *Paisa Akhbar,* August 28, 1921; *The Tribune,* April 29, 1923 (Editorial by K.N. Ray entitled 'The Land Alienation Act); Sharma, S.R., *Punjab in Ferment in the Beginning of the 20th Century,* Patiala : 1966, 11-12; (The Punjab Unionist Party tended to view the Alienation Act as a touch stone of their programme. But it was not acceptable to the small landlords. Thus, this Act was favouring the *Zamindars* whom this party represented).
6. Regarding the Land Alienation Act, see Appendix No. II.
7. Beasant Annie, *How India Wrough for Freedom,* Madras 1915, 352.
8. Rai Lajpat, *Political Future And India,* London : 1908, 301.

Bengal and the Punjab"[9]. Political awareness—which till 1907 was limited only to the urban areas of Amritsar, Ferozpure, Lahore, Sialkot, Rawalpindi and Lyallpur, now, became wide spread and its message could be carried to the villages on the issue of Colonization Bill. This Bill proposed to modify the canal colonizes tenures and increased the *abiana* in the *Bari Doab*. The Punjab Government's zeal to protect canal colonists created the very situation it most feared, and aroused countryside susceptible to anti-British propaganda[10]. The canal Legislation which out across the existing rights, and increased the rates along the *Bari-Doab* canal precipitated a unique population agitation. The campaign to alter the British policy, had a rural leadership and programme.

The colonies participating in the movement developed their own strategies without prior planning or co-ordination with urban organisations. Although mass demonstration brought out as many as 10 thousand protestors, the leaders did not stop at merely submitting petitions but escalated towards non-payment of land revenue and pressure through Indian Army Units. Propaganda such as cartoons, circulars and songs inculcating self respect and war like traditions of the Punjabees was designed to appeal generally to the illiterate

9. *Minute* by Sir Denzil Ibbetson, see *Autobiographical Writings of Lajpat Rai,* Jullundur : 1965, Appendix II, 228; File No. 5-AICC, Private Papers Section, NMML; New Delhi, 3.

10. Barrier, N.B. 'The Punjab Disturbances of 1907', *Modern Asian* Studies, 1967, 357-83 (This Bill was introduced in the Legislative Council on October 25, 1906, and was passed in February, 1907. It was contrary to the then nations of peasants' Proprietorship. It restricted the rights of colonisers to make will and denied them the right to cut trees in their lands. At the same time, the colonisation Bill was introduced in order to enhance the rate of water supplied from the Bari Doab canals) Vide. Sharma, S.R., *Punjab in Ferment in the Beginning of the 20th Century,* Patiala : 1966, 14-15; *Sedition Committee Report,* Calcutta, Supdtt. Government Printing : 1919, 142; *The Punjabee,* March 21, 1907; Daniel Argov's. *The Moderates and the Extremists in the Indian National Movement : 1923-24,* Bombay : 1967; Khushwant Singh, *The Sikhs,* Frinceton University Press : 1966, 157.

agriculturists. The Colonization Bill affected the Hindu as well as the Muslims in such a way that it provided a bond of unity.[11]

In fact, this bill sought to change the very basis of the land relationship in the Punjab. It attempted to deny the fruits of labour to the farmer who had been uprooted from the central Punjab districts to dog canals and irrigates the barren crown waste land in the western Punjab.[12] As a result of their labour, that area now became one of the most fertile regions in the country. The Punjab Government, then, made an attempt to modify the tenure system on the poles of introducing uniformity. The peasant believed that the Government planned to convert those lands into plantations on the lines of Assam, thus reducing the status of farmers from 1 and owners to cultivators.[13] In Rawalpindi, according to a new land revenue settlement, *abiana* taken from the *Bari Doab* was increased which further agitated the peasants.[14] A number of meetings were held to protest against this scheme.

Furzon's administration generated great political discontent in the country. The Punjab could not remain unaffected. The agitation that followed the partition of Bengal

11. Reginald Craddock, *The Dilmma in India,* London : 1929, 145; Barrier, N.G., "Mass Politics and the Punjab Congress in the Pre-Gandhian Era", *Punjab Past and Present,* Vol. XX-XX, October, 1975, (Punjabi University : Patiala), 350-51; *Sedition Committee Report,* Calcutta, Supdtt, Government Printing : 1919, 142.

12. The land was given to cultivators either free or very nominal rate. They were advanced cattle, implements, house building material and the like at a very low interest. Water was also supplied to them at moderate rates. According to the new Bill, it was proposed that the peasant was a mere tenant and the land belonged to the Government. This is corroborated by Wasti's findings : "The Punjab Government wanted to run the colony as a model form". Vide. Syed Wasti, *Lord Minto and The Indian Nationalists Movement : 1905-10,* Oxford : 1964, and G.T. Revenue, 1908, 15-B.

13. *Proceedings of the Punjab Council : 1907-08,* 100; Syed Wasti, *Lord Minto and The Indian Nationalists Movement : 1905-10,* 95; *Report on the Native News Papers,* 228-29; *Bari Doab Committee Report* in P.G. to G.I., 20 RI, January, 1908, G.T. Revenue, June 1908-15B.

14. *Ibid.*

also stirred the people of Punjab who sympathised with their brother in Bengal.[15] The biographer of Fazl-i-Hussain, writes that reaction to the unpopular administration of Curzon "roused the people from the state of lethargy" and that partition of Bengal and the Colonies Bill in the Punjab contributed to this.[16]

Ajit Singh, Sufi Amba Prasad and Agha Haider, who had organised the Anjumen-i-Muhabbat-i-Watan, and were to bring out a journal *Bharat Mata,* felt that this was an appropriate time to rouse the massen in the Punjab and they began to plan a massive agitation against the British.[17] A number of meetings were held (particularly in rural areas). The agitation, from the they beginning had the support of a large section of landowners as well as of the leading lawyers like Muhammad Shafi and Mian Shahabuddin as the measure was going to affect all the landlords in the west Punjab. In the mean time, the Punjab Government tried to rush through the Bill in the legislative Council despite requests made by the Indian members like Malik Umar Hyat Khan, Thakur Mohan Chand and Pratap Singh for sending the Bill book to the Select Committee for reconsideration.[18]

Meanwhile, violent disturbances took place at Rawalpindi

15. Rai Lajpat, *Writings and Speeches,* edited by Joshi, V.C., Delhi : 1966, 352; Sharma, S.R., *Punjab in Ferment in the Beginning of the 20th Century,* Patiala, 1966, 10.

16. Hussain, A., *Fazl-i-Hussain : A Political Biography,* Bombay : 1947, 78; *Report of the 34th Session of Congress,* Amritsar : 1922. A similar observation was made by Pt. Moti Lal Nahru in his Presidential address at the Amritsar session of the Congress in 1919; Barrier, N.G. 'Mass Politics and the Punjab Congress in the Pre-Gandhian Era', *Punjab Past and* Present, Vol. IX-II, October, 1975, 355.

17. *Liberal,* Lahore, 22.2.1920 (Editorial-Jai Gopal Tandon-Editor; Bal, S.S., *A Brief History of the Modern Punjab,* Lyall Book Depot, Ludhiana : 1974, 20; Back ground of members in Barrier, N.G., 'The Punjab Disturbances, in 1907', *Modern Asian Studies,* 1967, 201-05 (Swaran Singh, Pindi Dass, Kishan Singh, Sufi Amba Prasad, Kartar Singh, Ram Chand, Dina Nath and some others were the important members of the *Anjuman-i-Muhabbat-i-Wattan).*

18. *Proceeding of the Punjab Council, 1907-08;* 100.

on April 21, 1907, in a meeting which commenced with the soul stirring poems *'Pagri Sambhal O Jatta'* (O Peasant, guard your turban *i.e.* honour). Ajit Singh made a violent attack upon the increase in land assessment. He said that the peasants were the real rulers of the country. The *Rajas* were their *Kamins.* The Government and the chief officials were their servants.[19] He exhorted the peasants to stop cultivation until the amount was reduced and said, "The Punjab has also shaken off sleep after Bengal".[20] He appealed to the people not to lose courage but to march forward fearlessly. He asked them to boycott the honorary offices, and exhorted the Hindus and Muslims to unite. The then Deputy Commissioner served notice on Ajit Singh for his seditious speech, along with other organisers such as Gurdas Ram, Hans Raj and Amolak Ram. He asked them to face a public enquiry on Hay 2, at 11.00 a.m. A large crowd assembled outside the court. Fearing trouble, the hearing was postponed. The people were excited and they started damaging the Deputy Commissioner's lodge and other Government property. Consequently, several leaders connected with the agitation were arrested.[21]

The revolutionary group under the leadership of Ajit Singh and Sufi Amba Prasad, aiming to promote the political education of the masses, started distributing revolutionary literature written by them and published by the well known book agency, *Bharat Mata.*[22] The Punjab newspapers like *The*

---

19. Home Political (Deposit) July, 1907-08; *Report on the Administration of the Punjab and its Dependencies, 1921-22,* 1; Sharma, S.R., *Punjab in Ferment in the Beginning of the 20th Century,* Patiala : 1966, 10.
20. *The Hindustan,* May 3, 1907.
21. Barrier, N.G., 'The Punjab Disturbances in 1907', *Modern Asian Studies :* 1967, 455-56; Ibbetson to Minto, March 23, 1907; Barrier, N.G., The Punjab Disturbances of 1907; 'The Response of the British Government in India to Agrarian Unrest', *Punjab Past and Present,* October, 1975.
22. *The Hindustan,* May 17, 1907; *The Punjabee,* Lahore, May 22, 1907; Home Political-B-Nos. 25-26, January : 1910; Bal, S.S., *A Brief History of the Modern Punjab,* Ludhiana : 1974, 20; *The Tribune,* Lahore, December 20, 1910 (Editorial).

Hindustan and *The Punjabee* criticised the Government action regarding deportation of Lajpat Rai as "an act of blind vengeance".[23] It was expressed that an innocent, respectable and law abiding British subject was taken away from his family and friends for no reasons. Before his deportation, Lajpat Rai addressed largely attended public meetings. Being a supporter of the mass movement, he gave moral and material help to the organisers. On account of his anti British activities and his association with the *Arya Samaj,* he was considered by the British bureaucracy as the soul force behind the movement. Commenting on his association with the extremist agitators, V.C. Joshi writes, "Though some extremist agitators, among them the fire bend Ajit Singh, took advantage of the resentment among the peasantry to arouse their feelings against the Government, Lajpat Rai's aims and methods had been strictly constitutional".[24]

Because of the mounting political unrest in the province, colonisation Bill was vetoed by Lord Minto. The land tax and water-rates were reduced. In the mean while, in consequence of the repressive policy, the movement had gone under ground. However, secret meetings continued to be held almost daily. Sedition was spreading through theatrical performance, a powerful agency which had been fully used in Bengal as well. There was only tactical postponement of the agrarian agitation in order not to delay the release of Lajpat Rai and Ajit Singh.[25] After the release, Ajit Singh alongwith other

---

23. *The Hindustan,* Lahore, May 17, 1907; *The Punjabee,* Lahore, May 22, 1907; P.L.C.D., Vol. XII, 1929; 131; Duni Chand *The Ulster of India or An Analysis of the Punjab Problems.* Lahore : 1946, 2; Deniel Argov, *The Moderates and the Extremists in Indian National Movement : 1923-24,* Bombay : 1967.

24. Joshi, V.C. (ed.), *Lala Lajpat Rai's Writings and Speeches,* Delhi : 1966, 33; Sharma, S.R. *Punjab in Ferment in the Beginning of the 20th Century,* Patiala : 1966, 13; Home Deptt., File No. 203-204-Political : 1921, 13, NAI : New Delhi.

25. Syed Wasti, *Lord Minto and The Indian Nationalists 'Movement : 1905-10,* Oxford, 1964, 19 and 105; Barrier, N.G., 'Mass Politics and

(Contd.)

revolutionaries carried on his activities, the distribution of revolutionary literature in particular. The Punjab Government which had reluctantly released Ajit Singh now took all conceivable measures of suppression once again to meet the situation.[26] Hence, the agrarian unrest as well as the agitation in 1907 vividly displays that Ajit Singh and his young companions played a leading role in arousing anti-British feelings among the peasants, particularly in the western Punjab. The repressive policy of the Government that followed the agitation in the Punjab in 1907, gave rise to the revolutionary activities in the whole province.

We have to bear in mind the fact that the process of socio-religious transformation released by reform movements of the last quarter of the 19th century in the Punjab had prepared the masses for nationalist activity. At the same time the socio-religious movements had their limitations. Communal and religious affiliation tended to take predominance on other identities. Communal identity found expression in the British system which set the rules, goals and structures for formal political activities.[27] The British encouraged the belief that the Punjabees wishes could affect the policy, and introduced arenas of competition such as Municipal elections.[28] The Punjab

the Punjab Congress', *Punjab Past and Present,* Vol. XII, October 1975, 355-56; *The Tribune,* Lahore, February 15, 1907, 4; Notes by Charles Rivaz, February 12, 1907; Keep with to PRF 108-A, Punjab Revenue File, Board of Revenue, Lahore.

26. Syed Wasti, *Lord Minto And The Indian Nationalists' Movement : 1905-10,* Oxford, 1964, 105; *The Punjabee,* February 15, 1907 (Editorial by Lajpat Rai); *The Zamindar,* March 24, 1907; *The Punjabee,* April 20, 1907; *Civil and Military Gazette,* March 19, 1907.

27. Barrier, N.G., 'Muslim Politics in the Punjab', *The Punjab Past and Present : 1970;* Barrier, N.G., 'The Punjab Government and Communal Politics', *Journal of Asiatic Studies,* 1968, 363-79; Kenneth Jones, 'Communalism in the Punjab : *The Arya Samaj* contribution', *Journal of Asiatic Society, 1968,* 39-54; Munshi Singh Dukhi, *Jivan Bhai Sahib Bhai Mohan Singh Vaid* (Amritsar n.d.); Home Department File No. 1/60/1931-Public, NAI : New Delhi, 10; Karunakaran, K.P., *Religion And Political Awaking in India,* 22.

28. The Punjab case settlement illustrated in Barrier, *The Punjab Government.*

religious committees responded with efforts to influence the British as well as to control the new institutions. The associations such as *Arya Samaj* provided leaders and funds for political manoeurving and marshalled resources to determine the allocation of values, power and prestige within and without their community.[29] Religious application, often over-rode other considerations. It was alleged by a Sikh that almost every attempt to perpetuate Hindu-Muslim unity disappeared as election approached.[30]

By 1909, the Sikhs, the Hindus and the Muslims had evolved All-Punjab organisations; the Chief *Khalsa Divan,* the Punjab Muslim League, and the Punjab Hindu Sabha. Believing that survival depended on its size and over-all condition, each community tried to widen its membership, sphere of activities and strengthen its position through education, improved health, and boundary maintenance (*i.e.* new stress on symbols, purification and self identity as contrasted with other *Punjabees*). The *Arya Samaj,* for instance, sponsored *Shudhi* (cleansing, conversion ceremonies) among low caste agriculturists. The *Arya Samaj* propaganda tended to be in a *Sanakritized* language, intelligible only to the most educated. The *Samaj* despatched preachers or preaching team to instruct Hindus, and prevent conversion to Islam and Sikhism. The Sikhs already had a limited involvement outside the cities. The village based *Singh Sabhas* reinforced the lines of authority

29. On the various agitations see "Special Branch on the agitation against cow-killing", in G.P.I. (G.I. Public), January : 1884, 308-414B, NAI : New Delhi; P.G.G. (P.G. Committees), May, 1886, 9-12A (West Pakistan Record Office-Quoted by Barrier, N.G.; Evidence and Resolution in Report of the Public Service Commissions, Punjab Evidence (Calcutta : 1887).

30. Dukhi, Musha Singh, *Jivan Bhai Sahib Bhat Mohan Singh Vaid,* Amritsar, n.d., 71-73.

31. Nagar Singh (ed.), *Development in Sikh Politics :* 1900-1901; Gurdwara Gazette, April 1969, English Section, 6-7; Muslim League, Muhammad Shafi Memorandum, July 25, 1908, G.I.P., August 1908, 45-B (quotes Barrier); *Hindu Sabha,* Noting and Memorial in GIPOL (Home Political) October 1909, 29-31A; Harbans Singh and Jagjit Singh, *Singh Sabha Lehir,* in Ganda Singh (ed.), Punjab : 1849-1960, Ludhiana 1962.

within the community. The *Sabha* produced scores of publications,[31] usually in simple *Punjabee,* and sent out preachers to work upon illiterate villagers. Delegates attended fairs and visited historic *Gurdwaras,* both being the assembling spots for the dispersed and primarily agrarian Sikhs.[32]

These movements had the long range potential of influencing agrarian alignments. They also created new channels of communication which could be tapped, if essential. In 1908-09, for example the *Singh Sabha* contacted a large portion of community on the *Anand* marriage Bill.[33] The penetration of communal not works coincided with the emergence of another link among the agriculturists. Organisations of the *Jats,* the Rajputs and eventually the *Zamindars* began to meet in conferences, discuses issues and prepare resolutions. The Government provided impetus to the development by encouraging associations as a means of dealing with debt and related problems. Pro-agriculturist sentiment within the bureaucracy exhibited by the Punjab Alienation of Land Act and later by reserved seats for agriculturists, also stimulated political awareness. *Jagirdars*

32. For example, the publications discussed in Barrier, *The Sikhs,* and articles by Kenneth Jones and Barrier which deal with Sikh and Hindu movements; Barrier, N.G., 'Mass Politics and the Punjab Congress in the Pre-Gandhian Era', *Punjab Past and Present,* Patiala : 1975, 352; Home Department, File No. Public-1/60/1931, 23; Sharma, S.R., *Punjab in Ferment in The Beginning* of 20th Century, Patiala : 1966, 10 (The weekly meeting held at *Arya Samaj* hall, were generally meant for religious and social problems but invariably political affairs were discussed there. With the launching of civil Dis-obedience movement the members of this *Samaj* played a great role and prominent members were arrested and imprisoned), *Jyoti,* Lahore; Vidyawati Seth (Editoral) *Pratap* and *Parkash* of February, 1923, S.No. 80; Pt. Nanak Chand-Individual Collection : 1931-65, NMML : New Delhi, 2-4; Report of the Commissioners appointed by the Punjab Sub-Committee of the Indian National Congress, 4-5.
33. Talwar, K.C., 'The Anand Marriage Act', *The Punjab Past and Present,* No. II, 1968, Patiala : Punjabi University, 400-410.

and other landed aristocrats led the associations with the assistance of the retired officers, military personnels and lawyers who often purchased farm land to canal colonies.[34]

The *Kuka* movement was also responsible for the awakening in rural areas. Of course, it was almost entirely religious in character and resembled in all essentials the pre-modern militant religious sects which tended to come into conflict with the state apparatuses.[35] But, as the secretary of the Punjab Government wrote, "There is no doubt that the *Kukas* are the members of an organisation whose aim is to overthrow the British Government and to establish *Khalsa Raj* in its place.[36]

It was the First Great War that changed the *Punjabies'* attitude to the Empire.[37] Hardinge, in his speech, in the House of Lords, admitted that India had been bled white in the larger interest of the empire. The Punjab, especially the Amritsar district, had big share in army recruitment. Hissar too did not lag behind.[38] It is estimated that at the out break of the

34. *The Civil and Military Gazette* and *the Tribune*, occasionally printed articles on the associations : 1880-1910. For the British attitude towards rural classes and resulting policies see Barrier, N.G., *The Punjab Alienation of Land Bill of 1900*, 1965.

35. Ahluwalia, M.L., *Kuka-The Freedom Fighters of the Punjab*, Chapter V, 1965, For details see Fauja Singh's *Kuka Movement.*

36. Chatterjee, M.P., *Indian Revolutionaries in Conferences*, Calcutta : 1960; Bal, S.S., *A Brief History of the Modern Punjab*, Ludhiana : 1974, 16-17.

37. Mrs. Gauba, A., 'The Amritsar Conspiracy Case', *Proceedings—Punjab History Conferences*, Session VIII, December 15-16, 1973, 157-58.

38. P.L.C.D., Vol. XXVIII, 1936, 670-71 (People of Hissar, whether agriculturists or non-agriculturists gave their money freely and this district topped the list in the war loans. Similarly, they gave recruits beyond their required quota and it was promised to the people of Hissar district, over and again that the benefits of the irrigation through the Bhakra Dam Scheme should be given to them) Vide. P.L.C.D., Vol. XIV, 1924, 474; Vol. VI, 1926, 156-57; For further details

(Contd.)

war there were 100,000 *Punjabees* including residents of the Indian states, serving in the army of whom 87,000 were combatants; 3,80,000 of whom 2,31,000 were combatants, were enlisted during the war, making a total of 4,80,000 who served. This total represents one third of the entire contribution of India towards the forces of the empire.[39] Naturally Punjab expected some reward. After the war, however, the Government's apathy towards the wall being and aspiration of the people generated great resentment in the Punjab, since it had suffered more during the years of war. At the end of the war the Rowlatt Act came as a shock to the Punjab and to the rest of India.[40]

Moreover, O'Dwyer's administration abused the powers given to him by the Defence of India Act in suppressing all opposition to its authority. The Press had been gagged as a result of which it became impossible for the people of Punjab to have free ventilation of their grievances.[41] The Governor

also see Panandikar, S.G., *Some Aspects of Economic Consequences of the War for India,* Bombay : 1921, The author points out that India occupied second place after England in the British Empire for its expenditure during the war; Shah, K.T., and Khambatta, *Wealth and Taxable Capacity of India,* Bombay : 1924, 263-65.

39. Punjab Administration Report : 1921-22 (According to O'Dwyer, the number of fighting men raised during the four years of war roughly three hundred and sixty thousand, more than half the total number raised in India), Dwyer, *As I knew It : 1885-1925,* London : 1925, 215; Nehru, Jawahar Lal, *The Discovery of India,* New York : 1946, 359; Khambatta, K.J. and Sha, K.T., *Wealth and Taxable Capacity of India,* Bombay : 1924, 234.

40. Mrs. Gauba, A., "The Amritsar Conspiracy Case', *Proceedings Punjab History Conference,* 157-58; *The Nusrat,* March 28, 1919 (Translation of Dr. Satyapal Speech delivered on March 23, 1919, 11-12, under the heading-New Criminal Law : Passive Resistance Movement; File No. R-III, 10/2 (Private Papers Section, NMML : New Delhi), 1-3; File No. R-III, 12/3 AICC-Papers (The Rowlatt Act disturbed the public mind in the Punjab more than elsewhere), 41-44; *The Partap,* Lahore, 10.4.1920 (Editorial by Krishna-Editor); *The Akhbar-i-Aam,* April 10, 1920; File No. 847-1922, Home Department (Political), NAI : New Delhi.

41. Report of the Commission, appointed by the Punjab-Sub-Committee of Congress, Lahore : 1920 (Thereafter Congress Punjab Enquiry Committee Report 124); *The Leader,* Lahore, April 10, 1920.

pooh-poohed all aspiration towards self Government.[42] O'Dwyer belonged to that class of hardened bureaucrats of his time who were great admirers of Curzonian policies especially relating the Indian nationalists. This became particularly evident after the change of viceroyalty in April, 1916, when Chelmsford succeeded Hardinge. By then O'Dwyer had begun to pose as the uncrowned king of the Punjab. Even Chelmsford had to confess in private that the Punjab was almost O'Dwyer's estate.[43]

The Punjab administration led by O'Dwyer, had manifested hostility towards the politically aware class in more than one way during the war. It put about ten thousand *Punjabees* either behind the bars or in concentration camps on mere suspicion. It banned the entry of the national leaders like Tilak, B.C. Pal and Annie Beasant in the Punjab,[44] and used the restrictive provisions of the Press Act and the Defence of India Act with a severity unknown in the rest of the country.[45]

When the war came to a close and the growing tide of National awakening could not be contained in the Punjab despite the repressive measures, O'Dwyer became more vindictive. Within a few months, after the war, Gandhi started his Passive Resistance Movement. He thought of meeting the challenge with full force at his command. But being a calculating man O'Dwyer wanted to make out a reasonable case against Gandhi's movement so that the use of force which he intended might look justified in the eyes of law of the land. With that

42. *Disorder Enquiry Committee Report* (Calcutta : Supdtt, Government Printing India), 152; *Chelmsford Papers* (Microfilm), Roll No. 18, Letter No. 76, NMML : New Delhi, Chelmsford to O'Dwyer, February 10, 1917; *The Tribune*, Lahore, April 16, 1920-Editorial; *The Liberal*, Lahore, January 24, 1920.

43. *Ibid.*

44. Home Department (Political, March-1917, Proceedings No. 32, 13; Chelmsford to Chamberlain, Letter No. 28, September 15, 1916 (Microfilm), Roll No. 2, NMML : New Delhi : Home Department, File No. 5-Deposit (Political)-1921, NAI : New Delhi.

45. *Imperial Legislative Council Debates*, September 10, 1918, 299-303.

end in view, he took his legal Remembrancer into confidence and sought his expert opinion and advice. The Legal Remembrancer, as was expected of hi, suggested a way out for O'Dwyer by equating Passive Resistance Movement with a criminal conspiracy of waging war against the king.[46] They knew that in the Punjab, at any rate *hartal* meant some thing very much more than an orderly combination. So O'Dwyer wanted to cripple the nationalist activities, at least in the Punjab, and that could be done, in his view, only by giving the Martial Law a longer lease.[47]

The Jallianwala Bagh tragedy added fuel to the fire and the prevailing discontent among the masses mounted further.[48]

Pt. Nehru, in a conversation with Field Marshall Montgomery, once remarked that the Jallianwala episode marked a turning point in the Anglo-Indian relations. In essence, it was the culmination of the conflict between the British policies and the mounting Indian opinion fostered by Mahatma Gandhi's *Satyagrah* movement and nation wide agitation. While United Provinces, Madras, Calcutta and even Bombay remained largely calm, Punjab became a scene of serious political disturbances. In fact Jallianwala Bagh episode and the martial law in the Punjab had produced a tumultuous reaction. To Winston Churchill, the secretary of state for war, it was an "episode which appeared to be without parallel in the modern history of the British Empire, and it was totally an un-English and monstrous event". The Secretary of State for India Mr. Montague recorded that "Dwyer Committed a

46. *Evidence Before Disorder Committee,* Vol. VI, NAI : New Delhi, 191.

47. *Ibid.,* 196; *Chemsford Papers,* Roll No. 341; O'Dwyer to Chemsford, August 21, 1919 (Microfilm); File No. R-III, 10/2-AICC-Papers, NMML : New Delhi, 3.

48. Transcript, Gurdit Singh, (Note on Jallianwala Bagh episode in Hindi), NMML : New Delhi, 123-27. *The Punjabee* (Amristar), December 25, 1920; *The Liberal,* Lahore, 15th June, 1921; *The Punjab Administration Report of 1921;* Phillips, *Evolution of India and Pakistan,* 211. (For details see Dutta, V.N., *Jallianwala Bagh* in *Punjabi* and English also).

grave error of judgement". Mr. Asquith called it, "One of the worst outrages in the whole of our history".[49] In brief, it produced a feeling of horror, indignation and racial hatred. And, it had a far reaching impact on the political developments in the Punjab. It awakened the masses in the province and taught them to fight the British imperialism.[50] The acts of crime and terrible indignities committed in this period stirred a revolutionary feeling throughout the province the resulted in terrorism. The next decade in Punjab witnessed the formation of the *Babbar Akali* agitation in 1921, *Hindustan* Republic Association in 1925, the *Naujawan Sabha* in 1926, the *Kirti Kisan* Party in 1925-26 and other radical youth organisations.[51]

The same year, the District Committees were set up to stimulate political activities in the rural areas of the province. A conference in October was also convened which gave an out-let to the pent up feelings of the people against the Government. They started talking actively as the conference removed from their minds the fear of bureaucracy. Encouraged by the success, the leaders of the Punjab decided to invite the I.N.C. to hold its session in Amritsar.[52] Such a political stir in the province, as we shall see later, did not pass un-noticed in the rural areas.

It was in this atmosphere that the Rowlatt Bill was passed which invested the Government with extra-ordinary power

49. *Report of the Commissioner* appointed by the Punjab Sub-Committee of the INC, 158; Tara Chand, *History of the Freedom Movement in India,* Vol. III, Delhi-1972, 484; *Parliamentary Debates-House of Commons,* July 6, 1920, Fifth Series, Vol. 131, Col. 1715; File No. R-III, 12/2-AICC-Papers, 41-64; File No. 1-AICC, Papers, 15.

50. This account is based largely on : *(i) Report of the Commission* set up by the Punjab Provincial Congress Committee; *(ii) Disorder Enquiry Committee Report* (Hunter) in 6 Vols; *(iii)* Dutta, V.N., *Jallianwala Bagh,* Patiala : 1972; Mittal, D.C., "Jallianwala Bagh : Impact & Freedom Movement", *The Tribune,* April 12, 1976.

51. Hussain, A., *Fazl-i-Hussain : A Political Biography,* Lahore : 1946, 69.

52. *Ibid.,* 89; *The Punjabee,* Amritsar, October 25, 1920.

to suppress any kind of political agitation.[53] The agitation against the repressive Act began in Lahore under the leadership of Ram Bhuj Dutt, Duni Chand, Harkrishan Lal and Dr. Gokul Chand Narang.[54] In the Punjab, the outrages were largely due to the emigrants who returned from their homes with bitter feelings against the Government, which used the provisions of the Ingress Ordinance to prosecute them.[55] Almost all the emigrants were associated with the *Ghadr* Group. This group was founded not by the middle class youth, but by the *Punjabees* peasants who had migrated to the U.S.A. and Canada to earn livelihood.[56] Its chief, Hardial, categorically put forth the objective of their mission in his address to them :

> "Your duty is clear. Go to India. Stir up rebellion in every corner of the country. Rob the wealthy and show mercy to the poor........Arms will be provided to you on arrival in India. Falling this, you must ran-sack the police stations for rifles. Obey without hesitation the command of your leaders."[57]

---

53. *Congress Punjab Enquiry Committee Report,* Vol. II; File No. R-III, 12/2, AICC-Papers, 41-44; *The Akhbar-i-Aam,* Lahore, April 10, 1920 (Editorial-Gopi Nath); Distribution No. 160, Lahore, April 17, 1920; *The Pratap,* Lahore, April 10, 1920 (Editorial-Krishan), *The Leader,* Lahore, April 10, 1920 (Editorial-Shyam Lal); *The Tribune,* Lahore, April 16, 1920 (Editorial-K.N. Ray).
54. Sunderland, T.T., *Indian in Bondage,* Calcutta : 1929, 394; *The Tribune,* Lahore, April 16, 1920.
55. *Congress Punjab Enquiry Committee Report,* Vol. II-evidence, 203; *Disorder Committee Report,* 53; Hussain, A., *Fazli-Hussain : A Political Biography,* Lahore : 1946, 114-15.
56. Home Department, Political, A Proceeding No. 358 of December, 1916; Governor General to the Secretary of the State for India, November 24, 1916; *Sedition Committee Report : 1918,* 180; Mitra, *Indian Annual Register : 1922,* 53.
57. Tara Chand, *History of the Freedom Movement in India,* Vol. III, Delhi : 1972, 20-21.

The first issue of the Ghadr, spelled out unequivocally its aims and objects in the following words :[58]

> "Today, there begins in a foreign land but in our country's language a war against the British Raj.........what is our name? *Ghadr.* What is our work? *Ghadr.* Where will *Ghadr* break-out? In India".

In fact, the *Ghadrites* played an important role in rousing the rural masses and made them realise their duty to fight the British imperialism. The activities of the *Ghadrites* have been discussed in the second and third section of this chapter. At the same time, the non-co-operation under Ghandhi had spread among the masses. It stimulated numerous sections of the people to ventilate their grievances publicly and launch collective action for their removal. For instance, the Sikh League having passed a resolution on non-co-operation, urged the rural population of the Punjab to act upon it. The press in the Punjab in 1920-21 is out spoken about grievances accentuated by the war : the heavy influence of the rent caused unrest among the peasantry; the rise in prices without a corresponding rise in wages weighed heavily upon the factory workers; the sanitary conditions which caused epidemics like influenza in 1918 added to the misery and discontent.[59]

Of course, the non-co-operation movement failed but there is no denying the fact that it inculcated a new sense of self respect and fearlessness among the people especially in rural areas.[60] The activities of the *Akalis, Babbar Akalis,* the

58. Singh Khushwant, India's First Armed Revolution : The *Ghadr* Rebellion of 1915-A research paper read at *Asian History Conference,* 1961-62, New Delhi, 17; Juergenemeyer, Mark, Ghadr Source : Research on Punjabee Revolutionary in America, An Essay : *Punjab Past and Present—Essays in Honour of Dr. Ganda Singh,* 302-321.

59. *The Zamindara,* Lahore, October 28, 1920 (Editorial-Abdul Mazid Khan); *The Pratap,* Lahore, October 28, 1920 (Krishan-Editor); *The Desh,* March 5, 1921; *The Kesari,* March 5, 1921; *The Vakil,* March 6, 1921; *The Paisa Akhbar,* March 6, 1921; *The Zamindara,* March 9, 1921; *The Tribune,* March 6, 1921; *The Khalsa Advocate,* March 4, 1921; *The Akali,* March 14, 1921.

60. Tara Chand, *History of the Freedom Movement in India,* Vol. III, 507; Home Department, File No. 30-Deposit-1921, 1 (Letter from the Chief Secretary of the Punjab); *The Akali,* March 14, 1921; Coupland, *India : A Restatement,* 119.

Gurdwara Reform movement, the *Naujawan Sabha,* and the Lahore Conspiracy Case were some other internal factors of man consciousness in the Punjab. The British Government's repressive policy stimulated instead of making out revolutionary in revolutionaries such as Bhagat Singh and B.K. Dutt. The hunger strike by Bhagat Singh and others in the jail,[61] created tremendous stir and excitement through out the country.[62]

Let us now turn to the agrarian economic situation which brings us close to the cause of unrest among the peasantry. As pointed out in the first Chapter, the Government's policy of enhancing the land revenue after a certain number of years was more terrible for the poor *Zamindars* than even death.[63] In the 1920's and 1930's, the *abiana* question had begun to frighten the farmers. They feared that *abiana* already imposed might grow beyond the taxable capacity of the farmers and beyond any thing that had been imposed in other parts of the country.[64] It is interesting to note how much of his produce a *Zamindar* was required to sell to pay his *abiana.* In 1921, the rate of *abiana* was Rs. 3.12.0 and the rate of wheat was between Rs. 10 to Rs. 11 per *mound.* He had to sell 15 seers of wheat to pay his *abiana.* Then in 1930, the rate of wheat was Rs. 2.8.0, and the revenue was Rs. 5.12.0. The peasant had to sell to pay his *abiana,* 90 *seers.* Should not a *Zamindar* feel it?[65]

---

61. Home Department, File No. 255 KW of 1930 (Political, 59; *Imperial Legislative Council Assembly Debates,* Vol. IV. No. 9, September 14, 1929, 4.
62. Sandhu, V., *Yugdrashta Bhagat Singh* (Hindi), Varanasi : 1968, 106-07; Home Department, File No. 255 KW of 1930, 59-60; Home Department, File No. 13/11/1931-Political, 25 (Letter from the Government, the Punjab No. 117635B, dated Lahore the 10th February, 1930, it is stated that 16 out of 18 accused went on hunger strike on the 4th February and 15 were still on strike.
63. Home Department, File No. 45/V/1931-Political—*The Punch,* Lahore, May 19, 1921; *The Paisa Akhbar,* March 6, 1921; *The Zamindara,* Lahore, March 9, 1921; *The Tribune,* Lahore, March 6, 1921; File No. R-III, 3-X/3-AICC-Papers, NMML : New Delhi; Dutt, R.C., *Speeches : II,* 90; Bipan Chandra, *Economic Policies of Indian National Leadership :* 1880-1905, Delhi : 1966, 394.
64. P.L.C.D., Vol. VI, 1924, 404; Vol. XIV, 1934, 531-34.
65. P.L.C.D., Vol. X-B, 1927, 850; Vol. XVI, 1930, 45.

Similarly, the *Kharaba* rules were absolutely inadequate. The rule was that the *Kharaba* should be allowed if a *Zamindar* recovered nothing beyond the cost of seed and the cost of cultivation, which in the case of wheat came to Rs. 8/-. If unfortunately an acre of wheat yielded Rs. 9/- or Rs. 10/-, the *Zamindar* was falled upon to pay full abiana. That came to Rs. 12/- to Rs. 14/-. Where was he to find this money? But the Government did not intend to take any action to allay this dissatisfaction among the Zamindars.[66]

The normal clamities, such as famine, floods and draughts further added to the problems of the peasants.[67] Similarly, the lack of means of irrigation, the defective *batai* system, unpopular taxes, the repressive policy of the British of the time of the collection of the land revenue and high prices of various commodities were the root cause of all unrest and discontent among the peasantry in the Punjab.[68]

Among many other defects in the land system, the leaders of the agriculturists' class objected to the system of distribution of lease of the crown's lands on the following grounds :

83% of such land was sold or leased out to the landed capitalists;[69] and

The landlords capitalists[70] and lesses were very unfair because they passed on these lands to the poor tenants on harsh terms.[71]

---

66. P.L.C.D., Vol. XVI, 1930, 46.

67. P.L.C.D., Vol. III, 1928, 98, 170, 234; Vol. XIV, 1929, 258; *The Bande Matram,* Lahore, June 19, 1921; *The Paisa Akhbar,* Lahore, May 19, 1921; Land & Overseas—March-B, File No. 255-33/1933-Home Department, Political, NAI : New Delhi. *The Zamindar,* Lahore, July 14, 1921; *The Sansar,* August 13, 1921.

68. These defects have been narrated at length in Chapter-I of this work.

69. P.L.A.D., Vol. VIII, 20.3.1939. 438-39.

70. A landed capitalists, as the one who possessed wealth and invested it in agriculture only as a profitter and not that he loved it. Consequently, rather he bore malice against them. Vide. P.L.C.D., Vol. X, 17.3.1927, 521.

71. P.L.A.D. Vol. VIII, 20.3.1939, 438; P.L.C.D., Vol. X, 19.3.1931, 521; *The Tribune,* Lahore, January 4, 1927, 1.

During September 1924, and on January 4, 1927, the Punjab Government did some thing in this respect *i.e.* 2.5 lakh acres of land was reserved for sale to the small agriculturists only on higher purchase basis,[72] in the first instance. Again, out of the remaining 11.85 lakh acres too, major portion was set aside for sale to the agriculturists.[73] But it appears that in 1927, the Government reversed to its old policy of distributing these lands among the landed capitalists and it was repeatedly criticisd by the leaders of agriculturists' class and various political groups.[74] Capitalists were again benefited by this policy of selling the crown land through auction introduced by the British Government. The rising indebtedness was another powerful factor, as discussed earlier, which reduced the balance at the disposal of the peasants for the improvement of the agriculture was seriously reduced and this led directly to class discontent.[75]

Another significant factor to be noticed is that the Government in the early 1920's neglected the rural areas in providing some essential amenities. The statistics of that period, given below, oxhibits that whereas the Government

72. *Jat Gazette,* 20.4.1927, 3; P.L.C.D., Vol. X, 17.3.1927, 514-17 and 521.
73. P.L.C.D., Vol. X (Fazl-i-Hussain, Revenue Member), 17.3.1927, 514-17; *Jat Gazette,* 20.4.1927, 3.
74. While the first co-operative Bank was set up on February 16, 1924, with a view to facilitate the working of the co-operative Societies through the central Mortgage Banks etc; The Number of landed mortgage Bank rose from 3 in 1920 to 9 in 1926. The number of agricultural credit and non-credit Societies was enhanced from 3938 in 1918 to 8893 in 1923 and 19401 in 1939. Annual interest of rate of the mortgage Banks varied between 8-9% and those of the co-operative Societies ranged from interest free to 121/2% annually. Vide, *Punjab Administration Report :* 1920-21, 68; 1924-25, 137; *Annual Reports on the Working of Co-operative Societies : 1924,* 15; of 1925, 13; of 1926, 16-17; of 1935, 60; of 1939, 19; *Jat Gazette,* 25.5.1927, 7; 15.6.1928, 4; P.L.C.D., Vol. XVI, 7.5.1925, 1085-88; *Punjab Government Gazette* (Supplement), 11.2.1927, 25-26 (also see *Annual Reports of the Working of Co-operative Societies of 1918 and 1939*).
75. File No. Proceedings, 196-197, Agri.-B-1926 (Education Health and Land Department) NAI : New Delhi.

should have spent 90% of the funds allocated for this purpose, it only spent 10.3%.[76]

Table 2.1 Showing Expenditure Made by the Government on the Rural and Urban Health From 1919-20 to 1923-24

Area	*Expenditure on the Execution of Project (in Rs.)*	*Expenditure on Establishment (in Rs.)*	*Total Expenditure (in Rs.)*	*Total Expenditure in term of %age*
Urban :	18,64,726	1,12,680	19,77,406	89.7%
Rural :	1,98, 616	1,00,976	2,99,592	10.3%

The *Punjabee* in its issue dated April 4, 1906 brought to light the shocking sequel to the system of *Begar* as it then prvailed in the rural areas of the Punjab.[77] In brief, the condition of the agriculturists and agricultural labour was no better. In Gurgoan District, the standard of livng was perilously low. Similarly, in Rawalpindi division, in Lahore, it was alleged that 10% of the Hindu and 20% of the Mohammedan population were week and unhealthy due to insufficient food. Even the people of Hill tracts in Hazara, whether agricultural or grassier might generally be called a poor ill-grown, and underfed-looking race.[78] The Secretary of State, in a statement before the House of Commons on May 22, 1919, Confessed : "The position is not satisfactory. Rebellion and revolution have appeared internally".[79]

76. Statistics in preparing this table have been used from P.L.C.D., Vol. VI, 13.3.1926, 564-66.

77. *Begar,* which is another name for forced labour. Vide. *The Tribune,* Lahore, February 10, 1921; Home Department Political, File No. 105-Deposit-July, 1920; File No. 106/1920-Deposit; *The Bande Matram,* August 10, 1921; *The Pratap,* August 13, 1921. *The Tribune,* Lahore, June 6, 1921; 5; June 28, 1921, 7.

78. Dutt, Ramesh, *The Economic History of India : Vol. II, 1837-1900,* 446. For details also see Chapter I of this work.

79. For details see Bajaj, Y.P., *Sir Chhotu Ram and His Works,* Ph.D. Thesis, Kurukshetra University : 1972; Saini, B.S., *The Social and Economic History of the Punjab;* Tara Chand, *History of the Freedom Movement in India,* Vol. III, Delhi : 1972, 471.

As already discussed at length in the first part of this Chapter, the agitation that followed the partition of Bengal also stirred the masses of the Punjab. In the meeting held at Lahore in December 1905 to protest against the iniquitous act of the Government, Lajpat Rai appealed to the people of the Punjab to sympathise with their brethren in Bengal.[80] Consequently, one hundred and five delegates from the Punjab and the North-West Frontier province[81] attended the Congress Session held at Benaras in December, 1905 to demonstrate their readiness to suffer with the people of Bengal in their struggle against the vivisection of their province.[82]

The story of the achievements of the Russians had a tremendous impact on the thinking of the middle class nationalists as well as the lower classes. The influence of the Soviet experiment on the colonial patriots can best be judged by Nehru's book—*'Soviet Union'* based on a four-day visit to Russia and the septagenarian Tagore's letter to Russia. For the colonial countries of the world, the most significant lesson of the October Revolution was that the poor and the exploited could overthrow a tyrannical despotic rule if only they were properly aroused and organised.[83] The Punjab *Kirti Kisan Sabhas* and the Communist group up-held Soviet Russia as an ideal. The formation of the *Ghadr party* abroad and the abortive efforts made by their immigrating members to whip up insurrection in Punjab were considered portentous.

80. *Lala Lajpat Rai : Writings and Speeches,* Joshi, V.C. (ed.) Vol. X, 94, Delhi : 1966.

81. Annie Beasant, *How India Wrought for Freedom,* Madras : 1915, 416.

82. *Ibid.,* 427.

83. Tendulkar, D.G., *Mahatma,* Vol. I, 266; Nehru, Jawaharlal, *Discovery of India,* London : 1946, 312; Lord Chelmsford's speech reported in Times of India, September 9, 1928; also November 24, 1917; Mitra's *Indian Annual Register : 1921.* Calcutta : 1922, 271; Home Department, File No. 182 (1942) (1); File No. 28-R-III (Private Papers Section : NMML, New Delhi), 1-7; P.L.C.D., Vol. VIII, 1931; William Rushbrook, *India in 1919* (Foreward III); Home Department File No. 28/122-1935 (Political), Appendix to Notes, NAI : New Delhi.

Hijrat movement, an off-shoot of the *Khilafat* movement opened a new avenue for the Muslims, dissatisfied with the British Government, and for the intelligentsia of India, who had been unable to reconcile themselves with Gandhi's programme of non-violent non-co-operaton.[84] It swept away to Afghanistan more than 36,000 people.[85] (Later on they crossed into Russia). The Muhajir emigrants[86] brought inspiring accounts of the October Revolution. The Bolshevik revolution inspired vision of a new political, social and economic order in the minds of radical youth. Besides, penetration of the Marxist ideology into Indian life and thought was an epoch making event. Under the impact of Soviet Russia's example, Communist cells sprouted up in various parts of the country. For instance, Ghulam Hussain in lahore formed nucleus of a Communist Party.[87] He started an Urdu paper called *Inquilab* and propagated Marxist ideology in Lahore and the surrounding area. Russia had received Rs. 6,000 for this purpose in Kabul either from Roy's agents or from the Soviet Russia Embasay. He received an additional sum of Rs. 16,000 for this purpose in Kabul.[88] However, it is to be remembered that the Communist Group in the Punjab existed as an illegal body in the beginning. It was neither strong, nor influential.

84. Adhikari, G., *Documents of the History of the Communist Party of India : 1917-22,* Vol. I, P.P.H.New Delhi : 1971, 36-37.

85. Usmani Shaukat, *Peshawar to Mascow,* Delhi : 1927, Regarding the total number of Muhajirs Shaukat puts the figure at 36,000, while Baksh estimated it about one lakh and M.N. Roy specified it as 50,000; Vide, Adhikari, G., *Documents of the History of the Communist Party of India 1917-22,* Vol. I, P.P.H., New Delhi : 1971, 37.

86. Home Department, File No. 103, Part-K, Appendix B of 1923 (Political); Abdul Majid, Ferozuddin Mansoor, Fazal Illshi Quarban, Abdul Hamid, Aziz Ahmed hailed from the Punjab.

87. Gene, Overstreat and Marshall Windmiller, *Communism in India,* University of California Press : 1939, Chapter-II, 43.

88. Kaye, Cecil, *Communism in India : 1924-27,* Calcutta : 1927, Chapter-I, 13. It is Hussain's expenditures which figures in British not to the Soviet Government of May 1923, the text of which is given in *The Times,* May 9, 1923, II; *Documents of the History of the Communist Party in India,* (M.N. Roy's letter dated December 19, 1922), 595.

These groups were nothing more than organs of propaganda or ideological centes at this stage.

In brief, the *Ghadr* and the *Hijrat* movements, though not inspired by the Russian example, were the first of the Indian political organisations to establish contact with the Soviet Government. Undoubtedly, the *Ghadrites* made special efforts to stir-up a rebellion among the military forces in Punjab and that was why the British rulers were particularly anxious to save the Sikh soldiery from the impact of the Soviet Revolution and the Punjab disturbances. Many of these soldiers became active political workers after their release from the army and joined the Gurdwara Reform movement of the 20's and the Akali party and the Punjab *Ryasti Praja Mandal* on their formation in 1923 and 1928 respectively. At least a section of these ex-soldiers enrolled themselves in the Peasants and Workers' Party of Punjab which also came into being in 1927-28 and which later merged into the Communist Party.[90]

In 1922, Bhai Rattan Singh and Bhai Santokh Singh revived the *Ghadr* Party and the latter took initiative to establish contact with the Communist International. Santokh Singh and Sohan Singh Bhakna travelled through Moscow, attended the fourth Congress of the Communist International and from then on, the *Ghadr* Party, an a whole functioned more or less as a Communist Organisation.[91]

It is noteworthy that in so far as the politics in *Doab* region was left and radical oriented, it was due largely to the influence of the *Ghadrites.* The *Babbar* Akalis whose main field of operation too was the *Doab* area were also inspired by the

89. For more details see, *The Times,* March 20, 1920; *India in the Year 1919,* Government of India, 168; *India in 1922-23,* Government of India, 156; P.L.C.D., Vol. IV, 1365.

90. Reference quoted by Fyodorov, V., *"October Revolution : Its Impact on India's Struggle for Independence",* Soviet Land, New Delhi : 1967, Vol. XX, No. 13, 11.

91. Josh, Sohan Singh, *Baba Sohan Singh Bhakna* (Pbi. ed.), XVI of Forward; *Bande Matram,* November 13, 1921 (Lala Lajpat Rai's open letter to the Government of India).

Ghadr Group and the Gurdwara Reform Movement in 1921-23.[92] As already noted, the *Ghadr* party had also set up contacts with Soviet Communists and sent some of their members for training. Some sikh peasants were sent from Punjab too.[93] Among those who remained in Moscow were Teja Singh Swatanter, Achhar Singh Chhina, Bhai Santokh Singh, Baba Dula Singh, and Baba Karam Singh Dhut. So the Muslim *Muhajirs* (who had visited Soviet Russia between 1922-25) and the Sikh *Ghadrites* became the pioneers of radical thought in the Punjab and they were clearly inspired by the October Socialist Revolution.[94] During 1920-30, young revolutionaries both in the Punjab and U.P. were taking keen interest in socialism.[95] Many were in touch with the Communist Group.[96] Moreover, socialism had made a deep impact on the people of the Punjab as it represented a new state structure in which power now rested in the hands of workers and peasants.[97] In short, it were the revolutionary terrorists who put the people in the Punjab against their exploiters whether the British or native. Their role in also discussed at length in chapter—of this work.

Above all the change in the policy of the Labour Party, in

92. Makhsuspuri, Sunder Singh, *Babbar Akali Leher* (Introduction by Dr. Bhag Singh), 39; Walia, Romesh, 'Freedom Movement in the Punjab and Soviet Revolution' : A Research Paper—Published in the *Proceedings of the Punjab History Conference,* Session-VII, September 29-30, 1972, 259.

93. *Ibid.,* 260; *The Tribune,* November 19, 1921.

94. Home Department, File No. 6/9/1936 (Political), 34; *Documents of the History of the Communist Party in India* (M.N. Roy's letter dated 19th November, 1922), 595.

95. Roy, M.N., *India in Transition,* 131-35.

96. Many of them including Bhagat Singh might have been influenced by the Kanpur Balshevock conspiracy case since they were present in Kanpur at that time.

97. The Philosophy of the Bomb; also see Bipen Chandra's, A Research Paper, "The Ideological Development of the Revolutionary Terrorists in Northern India in the 1920's", *Socialism in India-1919-39,* NMML : New Delhi.

England, towards the Indian affairs during 1918-19 left deep impact on the minds of the *Punjabees.* A brief survey of this change is as follows :

The labour party adopted two resolutions on Indian affairs during 1918-19, which indicated the dual nature of its approach. The Nottingham Conference, apropos of the Montague Chelmsford Report, supported the demand for Home Rule for India, and urged all labour members to press for legislation without undue delay, in order that these people (Indian) shall be given their just rights which had been denied to them throughout all times, including the rights of self Government.[98] The resolution adopted by the Second International at Berne in February 1919, went further and showed that some Labour leaders thought it their duty to help the reconstruction of Indian society. It urged for the repeal of the Rowllat Act.[99] It also demanded that the land and soil, railways and mines of India should be socialised.[100]

The emergence of the Comintern in March 1919, the call for a world revolution and its insistence that all the parties wishing for affiliation have the adhere to the disciplines of the 21 points enunciated in 1920,[101] created dilemmas for the internationally minded socialists of the Labour Party. Upto 1923, these international tensions did not affect the relations between the Indian and the British left wings. In this period, the British Labour Party, while sharply critical of the Rowlatt Act and the Amritsar Massacre, expected the Indian politicians to abandon non-co-operation and try to work the Government of India Act of 1919.[102] A resolution passed by the National

98. *Labour Party Annual Report,* 1919, 205.

99. *Ibid.,* 206.

100. Douse, L.E., *Left in the Centre : The Independent Labour Party : 1893-1940,* London, 24-27.

101. Cab, G.D.H., *Communism And Social Democracy : 1914-31,* Part-I, London, 334; Kermit, E. Machanzie, *Comintern And World Revolution : 1928-43,* New York : 1964, 132-35; Dass, R.K., *The Labour Movement in India,* New York : 1927, 86.

102. *Labour Party : Annual Report,* 1920, 37.

Joint Council of labour, a fairly representative cross-section of the trade union and Labour Party leadership in February, 1922, criticised, "Political arrests" deplored non-co-operation, re-affirmed Dominion status as the goal of the Indian Government.

On the eve of the Simon Commission's arrival, the 5 years of association between the Indian labour leaders and the left-of-centre members of the British Labour Party (Whether trade unionists or the I.L.P.) had led to a sympathetic understanding on many issues, if not on all. It was symbolised seven months after the Brussels Conference, at the Labour Party's Annual Conference at Blackpool in October, 1927, when George Lansbury carried a unanimous resolution to grant Dominion Home Rule in India.

It was just in the beginning of 1928 that the Punjab *Kisan* Party was formed. This party, representative of a distinct and novel dimension of the militant movement, seemed to be a revival of the *Ghadr* Group in the United States. The *Ghadr* Group was a source of inspiration and by far the most important formative factor in the rejuvenation and the growth of the militant natonalism in Punjab . Futility of its experiment with violent means led to a search for new and effective forms of struggle against imperialism and capitalism, which later emerged as an agrarian movement in this province. However, it is absolutely wrong to assume that the Punjab *Kirti Kisan* Party was merely a foster child of the *Ghadar* Group[103] and that its organisation and ideology remained more or less subservient to its mentor.

Before we analyse its growth, formation and programme, let us have a look at the history of its weekly paper—the Kirti[104] which was the basis of the *Kirti Kisan* Party.

---

103. Williamson, H., *Communism in India, 1935* (Compiled in the Intelligence Bureau, Home Department, Government of India : 1933, revised upto 1935), 271.

104. *The Kirti,* May, 1927; November, 1928 (*The Kirti* was a monthly under the Communist influence. As is clear from its first issue that Santokh Singh went to Kanpur and attended the Communist and Trade Union Conference in December, 1925), Vide. *The Kirti,* February, 1926.

The need of having an independent ideological paper in *Punjabi* had, at first, been discussed by the *Ghadr* Group leadership.

Rattan Singh, in one of his letters from America, had impressed upon Ishar Singh of Kabul centre the need of Having a newspaper of their own.[105] In a party meeting held towards the end of 1922, it was decided to send *Bhai* Santokh Singh[106] and *Bhai* Rattan Singh[107] to India for starting such a paper and organising peasants and workers. It was also stipulated such a paper and organising peasants and workers. It was also stipulated to establish a connecting link with the Workers' and Peasants' Party in San Fransisco. In accordance with the party directive, both the leaders made a surreptitious entry into India in May, 1923.[108] But they were arrested in the independent trible territory of N.W.F.P. and realsed on security towards the end of the year. Soon, the following notification was published in different Newspapers in January, 1926.

"A monthly journal called the Kirti will soon start

105. Home Department, File No. 235/1926-Political (The efforts were being made to send money soon for this paper. It was in early 1926 that Santokh Singh received Rs. 10,000/- from Kabul and receipt of sums of Rs. 2700/- and Rs. 5000/- were also reported from America) Vide. *The Kirti,* November, 1928.

106. Home Department, File No. 233/II, 1926-Political, NAI : New Delhi, 26, (One time Santokh Singh was Assistant Secretary of the *Ghadr* Group in America. During the first world war, he was engaged in anti-British conspiracy in Seam and he was eventually convinted in the San-Fransisco Conspiracy Case).

107. *Ibid.;* File No. 235/II-1926, NAI : New Delhi.

108. Williamson, H., *Communism in India-1935,* 261 (Writing about their first entry in May, 1923, the British Intelligence Report said, "In May, 1923, They left for India, financed to a moderate extent by the Communist international". Their aim was to work at the Indian and the scheme formulated in Kabul, which included the formation of secret revolutionary societies clocked at communal organisations, the fomenting of trouble among the independent frontier tribes, the assassination of British Officers, and the selection of young Sikhs for training in foreign military school.

publication from Amritsar. It will be the voice of Indian workers living in America and Canada and will be dedicated to the secred memory of those martyrs who had awakened the sleeping Indian at the time when the service was far higher then it is now, and whose ideals were regarded by our own people as well as by outsiders as an absolutely vague dream. It will sympathise with all the workers throughout the world, the entire female sex, the subjugated, the wake and oppressed nations and the subjugated Indian."[109]

Its first issue was published in February, 1926. The *Kirti,* besides emphasising the value of organised labour, was explicit in the advocacy of its revolutionary aims.[110] It consistently praised the cause and ideals of the *Ghadrites* of 1914-15 and glorified the *Babbar* Akalis as heroes and martyrs. It also recalled such events as the *Budge—Budge* riots, the *Guru-Kae-Bagh* episode, the *Jallianwala Bagh* tragedy and the *Jaito Morchas.* Hence, this paper not only prepared the base for the formation of the *Kirti Kisan* Party but also appealed to the revolutionary ardour of the peasants and workers and tried to bring them in the fold of freedom struggle for the country.[111]

While outlining the policy of the *Kirti,* Santosh Singh in one of his articles criticised Gandhi's programme of attaining *Swaraj* within one year and that too by non-violent methods. He also attacked the right wing of the Congress Party for not

109. *The Kirti,* February, 1926 (Bhai Mohan Singh Vaid, Section-Punjabi University Library, Patiala); Home Department, File No. 235/1926, NAI : New Delhi.

110. (Babbar Akali Movement was a terrorist movement. Its rise is ascribed to Kishan Singh Gargaj. It was the Party of the Sikhs of *Doab* who wanted to oppose the Government on violent lines. As a result of their propaganda, the feelings of the Sikhs were inflamed to a dangerous pitch and the prestige of the Government sent to a very low level) Vide. Home Department, File No. 200/1926-Political, NAI : New Delhi.

111. Home Department, File No. 235/II of 1926, NAI : New Delhi; *The Kirti,* February-March, 1926.

allowing the passage of the resolution seeking to organise workers and peasants.[112] In the next 5 issues *i.e.* from March to September, there appeared a serialised essay on the agrarian questions under the title "Our Hardworking Peasants". It was written by Santokh Singh as a Comment on the views of the *'Sunday Times'* correspondent who according to the article, had expressed the idea that all the land should be converted into big plots, each not less than 50 acres and that the owners of the land should become peasants and the peasant tenants should become wage workers with land. The ultimate advantage will go to the present day farmers and tenants who will work as the wage labourers. Of course, there was no easy solution to the problem of poverty of the peasantry and the development of agriculture. These two issues were closely interconnected. And, solution to the problem was impossible without a change in the existing distribution of land. Such a change was a evolutionary step which would usher in a completely new era.[113] Another issue of this paper suggested the following solution to the agrarian problems :

> "The nation should be the owner of the land. Keeping in view the different needs, big fields of land should be given to the tenants' companies but the occupancy should not be given the right to sell or rent land, to give it on share cropping or to get profit by exploiting other workers. It should have the right to use land in order to carry on production. There should be no revenue or it should be very small. However, it should not be so low, as to transfer the main burden of taxation from the agricultural industry to other industries. To run the company work, the capital should be arranged by the state apparatus. Instead of bringing all land under *bandobast* at one stroke, small

112. *The Kirti,* February, 1926 (He recalled Hazrat Machani's words from speech delivered at the communist conference held in Kanpur, on December 26, 1926. "To win Swaraj we must fight for the betterment of the life conditions of the working people". For details see Adhikari, G., *The First Indian Communists Conference (Marxist Miscellaneous).*

113. *The Kirti,* March, 1926.

portions of land should be brought under piece meal. Arrangements should be made to use the latest equipments and knowledge or agronomy in agriculture, otherwise the whole attempt would be futile".

It is to be noted that the agarian question was posed and solved in a purely economic way. He put the fundamental questions : What sort of economic system in agriculture could and the miseries of the masses? He also replied : The socialisation of agriculture. However, he did not pose the further question : Under what sort of political state apparatus and under the leadership of what social class or classes was the achievement of such an agrarian system possible? The agrarian problem discussed above vividly displays that the *Kirti* was the voice of the peasants and workers. It in fact, prepared the base of the *Kirti Kisan* party and the *Kisan* agitation in the thirties, not only in the Punjab but in various other parts of the country also.[114]

It will not be out of place if the word *Kirti* is defined here. The *Kirti* is any one who does his work with his own hands and does not exploit others.[115] According to this definition, is difficult to include the peasants among workers. But when compared to the capitalists, farmers were also included in the camp of working class because they were also oppressed by the capitalist. Now it was strongly felt that the organisation of the labour class including the peasants was desperately needed which alone would break the shackles of India and

---

114. *The Kirti* was banned in the Punjab, so it was shifted to Meerut, U.P., and now it appeared in the name of *Kirti Lehr*. However, it reached in the different *Illaqas* of the Punjab. It too reached Bengal, Calcutta etc. (This information is based on the fortnightly reports—Home Deptt. Political, NAI : New Delhi, and *The Kirti* of this period); Personal meeting with Sardar Sohan Singh Josh, Ajay Bhawan, New Delhi.

115. According to S. Santokh Singh, the word *Kirti* is the exact translation of the word labourer. He is that person who has no capital and means of production and earns his living by working for others. Similarly the *Kirti Shareni* is that class of people who have no capital or means of production. Vide. *The Kirt,* March, 1926.

could lead to liberation. However, it was not clear, what sort of organisation? What would be its politices? What sort of strategy and tactics would be followed to pursue this politics? Hence, this paper was mainly and basically devoted to the problems of the working class movements. But not a single article was contributed to the practical problems of the Punjab peasantry during the period between May 1926 and August 1926.[116] However, after the death of Santokh Singh on 19th May, 1927[117], the Kirti entered the second phase and three was a clear emphasis on the problems of the peasantry.

Questions were varied as to the means to achieve the objective of the *Kirti*. The *Kirti* constantly expressed its concern towards extrication of the working class from the influence of 'bourgeois ideology' by forming a strong organisation of the labourers and peasants.[118] In its April 1927 issue, the *Kirti* expressed the view that there was a need for the formation of a *Kirti Kisan* Party.[119] As a result of this announcement, it now started using the term Kirti Kisan instead of Kirti only, which now included carpenters, black-smith, peasants and other workers engaged in different professions.[120]

The *Ghadr* Group[121] had increased its influence among the peasants of the Punjab, who actively participated in 1919-22 agitation, to evolve towards a clear ideology as a party of working classes. In the *Kirti* which was the only journal of its kind in the country, we find a conscious and sustained approach towards international class orientation. At a political Conference held in 1927, in Amritsar, the majority opinion

116. *The Kirti,* April, 1926; Supported by S. Sohan Singh Josh—Personal meeting—Ajay-Bhawan, New Delhi.

117. *The Kirti,* May, 1927; *The Kirti,* December, 1927; also *The Kirti* No. 3, 1926.

118. *The Kirti,* February, 1927; September, 1927.

119. *Ibid.,* June, 1927.

120. *Ibid.,* May, 1927 (For details also see Bhagwan Singh Josh's M. Phil thesis entitled 'Communism in the Punjab' (unpublished work—JNU, Library, New Delhi).

121. It was a political Faction of the Punjab Peasants.

expressed itself against the reformist leadership of the INC.[122] Hence, the left wing in the Punjab was constituted by individuals drawn from *Muhajirs*, nationalist youth, Akali militants and the members and sympathisers[123] of the *Ghadr* Group. What brought them together was their desire to organise the oppressed sections of the society in an uncomprising struggle against imperialism, feudalism and exploitation.[124]

The return of the emigrants provided the human channels through which the ideas of the outside world were injected into the life of certain starta of rural Punjab. The emigrants were mostly *Jat* Sikhs and thus the ideas they brought to Punjab were confined mainly to the Sikh peasantry. The impact of the infusion of the new ideas was very weak on the small land holders with their conservative self-sufficiency and indifference to the greater issues of the age. This was the social basis on which the *Kirti* operated. It is interesting to note that at the very beginning, the militant Akali and the *Kirti* were embodied within the same person. But after some time, when the Akali leadership compromised with the colonial authorities, the process of differentiation of ideologies began.[125]

We have already described how the *Ghadr* sent emissaries to India in 1923. Among these emissaries, the founder of the journal *Kirti*, Santokh Singh was one who managed to stay behind in India while his companions were deported or arrested. He got in touch with the radical-minded workers of

122. The Communist International between the 5th & 6th world Congress : 1924-28. (A Report on the position of in all section of the world communist party), ACHI, J.N.U., New Delhi.

123. Members and Sympathisers of the *Ghadr* Group abroad were mostly Sikh agriculturists, having a theological cost of mind. They read Marx's Capital and recited the hymns of *Gurus* at the same time.

124. *The Kirti*, February, 1929 ('Bolshevik Propaganda in India'-An article published in this issue).

125. *Ibid.*, (In the beginning important Akali leaders were Jathedar Udham Singh Nagoke, Darshan Singh Pheruman and Gurmukh Singh Musafir. They had close relations with the *Kirti* during this period).

Lahore, Dhariwal and Amritsar. Keeping in view the object of organising peasants and workers, he explored the possibilities of launching his project and a peasants' party in the Punjab. The presence and active participation of Bagh Singh 'Candian' a *Ghadrite* emissary, at the inaugural meeting of the Punjab workers' and peasants' party on April 12, 1927,[126] indicated the earnest desire of the *Ghadr* Group to set up rapport with the radical minded workers in the Punjab. It was in September, 1927 that the Kirti informed its leaders that a Workers' and Peasants Conference would be held in Hoshiarpur on October 6th-7th, 1927, in which their problems would be discussed. It was also said that a similar Conference would be held in Lyallpur in the last days of September. All those who were opposed to imperialisms, enter hearty greetings to the former Conference,[127] presided over by Sardar Sohan Singh Josh.[128] In these Conferences, the conditions of the peasantry was discussed at length.[129] Some Akali leaders offered their co-operation, should the *Kirti* Group leader succeed in building a *Kirti* organisation under their leadership.[130]

Mr. Abdul Majid, Sohan Singh Josh, Kedar Nath Sehgal and Philip Spratt, a Communist emissary attended the *Kirti Kisan* meeting, held at Amritsar, on September 12, 1927. The Amritsar group had 60 members to begin with. It was to establish close links with the Congress and thus become a party of the anti-imperialist movement. It was resolved at the Conference that after creating their permanent organisation with a political programme, they would co-operate with the

---

126. *Meerut Conspiracy Case,* Sessions Judgement, 1930, Vol. I, Part XXXIX, NAI : New Delhi, 594.

127. *The Kirti,* October, 1927; Home Department, File No. 1819/1927-Political, NAI : New Delhi.

128. Personal Meeting with Sardar Sohan Singh Josh.

129. S. Darshan Singh Pheruman, Gurmukh Singh Musafir and Jathodar Udham Singh etc. were the most prominent Akali leaders. Vide. *The Kirti,* October, 1927.

130. *Ibid.,* Fortnightly Report of October, 1927, NAI : New Delhi.

I.N.C. in every possible way and would always support the left group in the Congress.[131] Some held the opinion that the biggest task before them was the organisation of the workers. Among the workers in the Punjab 90% were peasants. In other words, the workers' organisation in Punjab primarily meant the organisation of the peasants.[132] The Punjab *Kirti Kisan* Party had framed a statement of its aims and objects and rules and regulations. The following resolutions were passed at the Conference, held at Amritsar :

(i) For the liberation of the country a strong party of *Kirtis* (workers and peasants) should be formed. Its aim should be a complete independence from British imperialisms;

(ii) To liberate workers and peasants from every sort of political economic and social slavery and to set up their United Republic;[133]

(iii) It was also resolved to declare support to the Chinese freedom struggle and the Russian Revolution; and establishment of a *Kirti* or *Bolshevik* type state;

(iv) Small holdings should be exempted from revenue and the *Kirti* branches, therefore, should be set up, to oppose the Government revenue demand in such cases, in every district;

(v) The revenue should be reduced. It should be imposed on production and not on land;

(vi) All means of production should be nationalised;

(vii) Land should be taken away from the landlords without compensation and it should be divided among the cultivators;

---

131. *The Kirti,* October, 1927.

132. *Ibid.*

133. *Meerut Conspiracy Case Papers,* Sr. No. 167, Exhibits No. 334 (T), 771-Aims and Objects and Rules and Regulations of the Punjab *Kirti Kisan* Party, NAI : New Delhi.

(viii) Village *Panchayats* should be reorganised and they should include the elected representatives of cultivators, and other rural workers. They should be entrusted with the authority to impose revenue on the peasants;

(ix) Government should give loans to the cultivators. It should provide the peasants with machines, seed and scientific assistance;

(x) The wages of the industrial workers should be increased and working hours should not be more than 8 hours;

(xi) The immediate aim of the party was to accomplish a thorough democratisation of India,[134] leading to political, economic and social emancipation of the masses.[135] Obviously, it was formed with the primary object of organising workers and peasants. Their active involvement and support were regarded as the decisive factor in the war against imperialisms in general and British imperialism in particular.

Another Conference was held in Lyallpur on 17th October in *Chak* No. 50. It was presided over by Tara Singh, a local peasant activist *Desh Sewak Kirti Sabha* was formed and its office bearers were elected.[136] As stated a above, at the beginning of 1928, it had been announced that the Kirti would start the work of organising its poor brethren.[137] In line with this aim, another Conference was called at Amritsar.

134. *Ibid.*, also Sr. No. 161, Exhibit No. P. 548 (15), 922-26, Constitution of All India Workers' and Peasants' Party. A Comparison of these two documents show that the Punjab *Kirti Kisan* Party and All India Workers' and Peasants' Party shared their aims and objects. Rasul, M.A., *History of the All India Kisan Sabha,* Calcutta : 1974, 57-59.

135. *Ibid.*, Sr. No. 19, Vol. 14, Joint Statement of Nimbkar, R.S., and others, NAI : New Delhi, 4892.

136. *The Kirti,* November, 1927; Fortnightly Reports of the year 1927, Home Department Political, NAI : New Delhi.

137. *The Kirti,* February, 1928; supported by Sardar Sohan Singh Josh, Personal meeting on November 19th, 1976, Ajay Bhavan, New Delhi.

On the invitation of Sohan Singh Josh and Bhag Singh 'Canadian', this Conference met on April 12, 1928 at 6.00 P.M. in Jallianwala Bagh, at Amrritsar. From different districts, more then 60 persons including Dr. Satyapal, Gopal Singh Qaumi, Hans Raj, K.N. Sehal, Master Kabul Singh, Ram Chand, M.A. Majid and Ferozedass Mansoor participated. It was unamiously resolved that a party named *Kirti Kisan* Party might be formed in order to organise the workers and peasents, and those who were attending should be considered its members. Sohan Singh Josh and M.A. Majid were elected Secretary and joint-Secretary respectively. A five member committee[138] was appointed to prepare the party's constitution. The rules would be formulated soon and a real programme of organising the workers and peasants would be started.[139] The second *Kirti Kisan* Conference was held in Lyallpur from the 28th to 30th September, 1928 alongwith the Punjab Provincial Political Conference.[140] Representatives of the *Kirti Kisan* organisation including the *Kirti Dal* of Bengal, participated.[141] It directed the workers and peasants to get

138. *Ibid.*, also of May, 1928 (Sohan Singh Josh, Gopal Singh Qaumi, Hira Singh, M.A., Majid and K.N. Sehgal were the members of this Committee), supported by Lala Ram Chand-Personal meeting : Delhi.

139. *Meerut Conspiracy Case*, Sr. No. 211, Vol. III (1), NAI : New Delhi; *The Kirti*, May, 1928 (See Sohan Singh Josh defence statement).

140. Philip Spratt played a key role in bringing together the labour group of Abdul Majid and the *Kirti* group, by impressing upon them the need to form a workers' and peasants' party in the Punjab. He stayed at Lahore for 3 months *i.e.* from June to August, 1927. He held discussions with the leaders of all the leftist groups including Bhagat Singh. According to a CID Report : On the night of 28th November, 1927, a secret meeting of the Communist Party was held in the house of Shaukat Usmani at which both Spratt and Broadly were present, and representatives from Bombay, Bengal and Punjab also attended it. Obviously, the *Kirti Kisan* Party worked under the impact of the leftist ideology. It would be more appropriate to call this party as the leftist group.

141. Ray, Subhodh (ed.), *Communism in India :* Unpublished documents, 1924-25, 1972, 57 (There was a *Kirti Dal* Bengal : A Group of Sikhs in Calcutta who were under the impact of Punjab *Kirti Kisan* Party. Later on it merged with Workers' and Peasants' Party of Bengal.

organised in order to solve their problems such as *begar* (forced labour), lack of irrigation water, reduction in taxes, land revenue and abolition of *abiana, Malba, Chowkidara* etc.[142]

In the newly colonised areas of the Sargodha district, the *Kirti Kisan* Party advised a boycott of the *Zamindara* League initiated by Sir Chhotu Ram and exhorted the peasants to organise committees of the farmers.[143] Formation of such committees linked with the *Kirti* Kisan Party also suggested to the peasant of Amritsar district.[144] The third Punjab Provincial workers' and Peasants' Party Conference was held in Rohtak on March 10, 1928. The change in name from the *Kirti Kisan* Party to the workers' and Peasants' Party pointed towards the close linkage which this group had developed with the Communist groups in the country. According to Sohan Singh Josh, the workers' and Peasants' Party had its branches at Ludhiana, Rohtak and the Bengal *Kirti Dal* in Calcutta. It also organised various unions in Amritsar.[145]

These Units were advised that they must fight not only imperialisms and feudalism but the bourgeoisie as well.[146] Moreover, being fully aware of the British strategy of divide and rule, the *Kirti Kisan* laid special emphasis on the fraternity of common economic and class-interest. It was the *Kirti Kisan* leadership which defined the nature and scope of the revolution and its tactics with considerable clarity.[147] As stated earlier, the *Kirti Kisan* Party had lost faith in total reliance on

142. *The Kirti,* November, 1927.
143. *Ibid.,* April, 1929.
144. *Ibid.,* June, 1929.
145. *Meerut Conspiracy Case,* Sr. No. 211, Vol. No. III (1), NAI : New Delhi, 295; Ray, Subhodh, *Communism in India : Unpublished Documents-1924-25,* 57.
146. *Ibid.*
147. Meerut Conspiracy Case, Sr. No. 212, Vol. 3(2), 516, NAI : New Delhi; (For a list of the immediate demands of the Punjab *Kirti Kisan* Party); Home Department, File No. 12/3/1936-Political; AISPC-Papers, File No. 139 (Part-I), 1937-42, NMML, Teen Murti, New Delhi.

violence as well as in means violence in bringing about radical change in social and economic set-up, still it too did not rule out resort to force. But individual terrorism was strongly condemned by the *Kirti Kisan* leaders.[148] Thus, this party contemplated and practised the use of force for bringing about national revolution and disbanding terrorist elements.[149] As opposed to the *Ghadr* methods, the workers' and peasants' organisation was the watchword of the policy of the Punjab *Kirti Kisan* Party, which worked on two level—mass movement and real terrorism. It displayed the difference between the attitude of both these parties towards the tactics of revolution. It also indicated the ideological maturity of its leadership in the province. Realising the importance of propaganda in organising the workers and peasants on the basis of economic principles.[150] *Bhai* Santokh Singh publicised the principle of socialism and created class-consciousness among its readers,[151] who were generally peasants and workers.

Throughout its career, the *Kirti* continued to disseminate the ideas and ideals espoused by its founder. Views of Karl Marx of private property, nature of class struggle and ultimate establishment of the dictatorship of the proletariate were explained in the idiom of the masses.[152] It was also to educate

148. Joint Statement of R.S. Nimbkar and Others, 5170 (Use of need-terrorism was sanctioned by the Punjab *Kirti Kisan* Party. Defining its scope, Sohan Singh Josh observed, "individual terrorism and need terrorism should not be mixed up together. The latter should be employed only when the state machine is captured by the proletariat and before". Vide *Meerut Conspiracy Case Papers,* Sr. No. 218, 324—Statement of Sohan Singh Josh in the court of R.L. Yanke, Additional Session Judge, Meerut.

149. Joint Statement of R.S. Nimbkar and others.

150. *The Kirti (Jivan Bhai* Santokh Singh in Punjabee), Amritsar, July, 1927, 13-15; also see its last instalment in the issue of June, 1929, 17-19.

151. *The Kirti,* Amritsar (Comrade Karl Marx), May, 1929, 56-59; *The Kirti,* April, 1929 (Mahatma Karl Marx), 7.

152. The title page of all the issues of the *Kirti* is based on the following lines : "Workers of the World Unite", "You have nothing to lose but your Chains of slavery".

the workers and peasants, in the Punjab, in the application of the Marxian principles to their political, social and economic problems.[153] It is also to be noted that in spite of the threats of searches into its offices, confiscation and arrest of its editors,[154] the *Kirti* fulfilled its role of moulding public opinion by promoting its sale which would continue the campaign of revolution.[155] The peasants, workers and petty bourgeoisie, especially the youth of the lower middle-class formed the bulk of its readers. They were the most suitable recipients of the *Kirti* message of Socialism, class-struggle, freedom of Press and complete independence.[156]

It is to be noted that the contact between the leadership of the *Kirti Kisan* Party and the *Ghadar* Group in the United States continued. It served as an effective channel of communication between the two factions.[157] The articles notably "Union and *Kisan*",[158] "Hindustan *Naujawan* and Terrorism",[159] and "Arrest of Santa Singh at Madras", in the *Kirti* highlighted its ideological stand on various issues such as the official policy of arresting the *Ghadr* emissaries in India and the various faces of the *Kirti Kisan* movement in the Punjab.

After noting this programme, aims and objects, one can not deny the fact that the *Kirti Kisan* Party had Marxist learnings. In fact, it was a mixture of left nationalism and democratic revolutionary tendencies.[160] It upheld Russia as

153. *Ibid.*

154. *Meerut Conspiracy Case Papers* (The Government of India confiscated many of its issues. For instance, notable ones were dated June, August, December, 1929. Its editors Daljit Singh and Arjan Singh Gargaj were also arrested).

155. *The Kirti,* December, 1929 *(Farangh Shahi Da Takhta Hal Giya),* 1-3.

156. *Ibid., The Kirti,* August, 1930 *(Kirti Lehr Nahin Dabegi),* 50.

157. *The Kirti,* February-1928, 77-78; Brij Narain's article—*Zamindar-te-Kisan,* in *The Kirti,* March, 1930, 16-19.

158. *The Kirti,* February, 1930, 3-8.

159. *Ibid.,* (For its text), 9-13.

160. Personal meeting with S. Sohan Singh Josh; also supported by Master Hari Singh—Personal interview : The Communist Office, Chandigarh.

an ideal.[161] However, it did not put forward a systematic and coherent programmes to follow. The question which is yet to be replied was how to realise the above mentioned programme and who would assume the leadership in this fight against capitalism, imperialisms and feudalism was a vital aspect of the *Kirti Kisan* ideology? The working class and the peasantry allied with each other in bringing about political, social and economic revolution. But the more articulate of them felt that workers and peasants should be separately organised on a common programme according to their needs, and in order to win freedom, the path of revolutionary mass action should be followed. To achieve complete freedom from the British rule by allying themselves with the middle class would be the first step towards their victory but the aim should be to establish an absolute democratic republic of workers and peasants,[162] where the latter would engage themselves in agriculture on small holdings while the state apparatus would be managed by the working class.[163]

It will not be out of place to state that there was no direct link between the leaders of the ex-soldiers and the *Kirti Kisan* Party. However, the C.I.D. authorities reported that at the third Conference of the *Kirti Kisan* Party, an insidiuous attempt

161. For details see K.N. Sehgal's Presidential address, delivered by him at workers' and Peasants' party Conference held in Meerut on October 13th to 15th-1923) Vide. *Meerut Conspiracy Case Papers,* Sr. No. 161, Exhibit No. P 172 (T), 683; also see the views of M.A. Majid delivered on 18.8.1928 at Jallianwala Bagh, Vide. *Meerut Conspiracy Case Papers,* Sr. No. 205 (1), Exhibit No. P. 1884 (2) (T), 40; Cross examination of Sohan Singh Josh before R.L. Yorke, May 18, 1931, Vide. *Meerut Conspiracy Case Papers,* Sr. No. 218, 231-32 and 348; *The Kirti* March, 1929; Lenin, V.I., *Alliance of the Working Class and* Peasantry, 340-46; Carr. B.H. *Socialism in one Country,* Vol. I.

162. For details study, see *Meerut Conspiracy Case Papers,* Exhibit No. 621 (T), 846; Exhibit No. p. 1882 (T), Sr. No. 161, 845-46; Exhibit No. 238, Sr. No. 218, 324; Sr. No. 545, 3, 9-10; *Janvani,* June 21, 1928.

163. For details see *The Kirti,* March-1929; Lenin, V.I., *Alliance of the Working Class and Peasantry,* 340-46, 351; Carr. E.H., *Socialism in One Country,* Vol. I.

was made to undermine the loyalty of the soldiers.[164] Because of the economic hardships, certain sections of the peasantry which formed the recruiting base of the army and contained large number of military men were becoming susceptible to the Congress propaganda in the villages. On January 7, 1929, ex-soldiers in order to seek an interview with the Governor to express their grievances.[165] They refused to leave the place when ordered to do so by the police. Many of them were arrested. Serious discontent prevailed among those ex-millitarymen of Sheikhupura district who were demobilised without a pension or a grant of land. They did not believe the declaration of the Government that it had no further land available for distribution. The centre of agitation was Lahore villages. The villages of Sahad, Natheka, Toria, Mirpur and Doneka were seriously affected.[166]

Moreover, the emphasis shifted to *Kisan* agitation between 1930-39. The district *Kisan* Committees which were actively organising agitation for the fulfilment of their demands, already mentioned above, threw up new leaders known as *'babas'*. In brief the Punjab *Kirti Kisan* Party survived inspite of repression and reprisals, for it assumed new form in response to the changing political situation. However, much has been written in connection with its activities, in the third section of this chapter.

The Punjab peasants, of course, waged heroic struggle for the demands of their community, but their role in the country's war of liberation was very significant. In brief, their struggle, as discussed in the section here to before of this chapter, was against imperialism, feudalism and exploitation. During the

164. Home Department File No. 233 of 1930-Political; File No. 130 and K.W. 1930-Political, NAI, Supported by S. Sohan Singh Josh (For details also see the Fortnightly Report of this period).

165. Anup Singh belonged to a military family. In 1921, he established an ex-soldiers Association. In his patition to the Viceroy he narrated the long story of injustice done to him by the local authorities and assured his long standing loyalty to the Empire. This petition informs that the membership of this Association was 30,000, Vide. *Ibid.*

166. Home Department, File No. 233 of 1930, NAI : New Delhi.

first imperialist war, the English Government had burdened the people, particularly the farmers, with the heavy taxes of war.[167] From the middle 1920's depression and from 1929 a world depression caused a crisis in agriculture. The various hardships which were faced by the peasants just before the start of their movement in the province, have already been stated in the first chapter as well as in the first section of this chapter.

At the very outset it is to be noted that there was no organised peasant movement in Punjab, till late 1920's. However, it does not mean that there was no agrarian unrest and agrarian agitation at all. The political work and propaganda among the peasantry by various political factions and the agrarian agitation of 1903, though a very partial one, had been preparing the ground for a strong peasant movement. Undoubtedly, Punjab became one of the provinces where the building up of regular peasant organisations and movements on various urgent issues of *Kisan* interest on a local or provincial scale began in right earnest.[168] We have already discussed the peasant agitation of 1907 in the first section of this Chapter. Let it be noticed that the *Ghadr* Party, organised in the U.S.A. in 1913, was mostly based on the peasant immigrants from Punjab. During the war, 8 thousand returned to India and the *Ghadrites* set up a radical, revolutionary political tradition in Punjab. The spirit of rebellion they generated was vividly seen in the later movements of the *Akalis, Babbar Akalis, Kirtis* and Communists. It is appropriate to state here that the rank and file of the Akali volunteers came from the Sikh peasantry. The Sikh peasantry formed the

167. *Khalsa Advocate,* August 17, 1918 (India contributed 10 lakhs of men but many of them were *Punjabies.* Punjab in fact bore the heaviest share of the burden of war and the Empire), Hari Singh, *Punjab Wich Kersani Laher* (The Peasants' movement in Punjab—Before and After Independence) in *Punjabi, Souvenir,* January : 1976 issued by C.P.I., supported by Ishar Singh Majhail (Personal Meeting on 10.12.1976, Gali No. 2, Arjun Nagar, Patiala-1.)

168. Rasul, M.A., *A History of the All India Kisan Sabha,* Calcutta : 1974, 2.

backbone of the Akali movement,[169] which stirred up the rural Punjab. Similarly, the *Babbar Akali* movement was based socially and politically on the *Sikh Jat* peasantry of Central Punjab. Though these movements can not be described as part of the peasant movement, one can not deny the fact that these movements generated a new spirit among the peasantry. More details, we can find in the first section of the fifth Chapter, the involvement of the peasantry in the war of independence before 1920.

It will not be out of the place to cite a few instances of agrarian unrest in the early part of the 1920's. A few villages in the Lahore and Jullundur districts which wished to take the lead in 'non-payment' and which had been dissuaded by some of the leading non-co-operators, were approached on the subject.[170] There had also been some village meetings in Hoshiarpur region in connection with non-co-operation. Some agitation had been worked up in Shujabad *Tehsil* of the Multan district against the new rates of assessment.[171] The common and the most consistent demand of the peasants' agitation was for the reduction of *abiana* and land revenue. The *Kirtis* had raised it repeatedly during 1926-29. It was put forward by the second *Kirti Kisan* Conference held at Lyallpur from 28th to 30th September, 1928.[172] This Conference also raised the issue of begar (forced labour) in 1928.[173] An allied demand often raised in Conferences and meetings, exemption of small uneconomic holdings from land revenue. It was also raised by the *Kirtis* during 1926-29. A resolution to this effect was

169. For details see Mohinder Singh, *The Akali Movement,* Delhi : 1978, (Particularly Chapter V and VIII), 143, Buddha Prakash, 'Reflexians on the Agrarian uprisings of the Ninteen-Twenties' : Seminar on Socialism in India : 1919-39, November 28-30, 1968, NMML : New Delhi.

170. Home Department, File No. Pros. July, 1921-1 Deposit, Political; File No. 66-Pros. Dec. 1920, Deposit, Political, NAI : New Delhi.

171. Home Department, File No. Pros. 45-June, 1921-Political, Deposit, NAI : New Delhi; P.L.C.D., Vol. XIV-1929, 612.

172. *The Kirti,* November, 1928.

173. *The Kirti,* November, 1928.

passed in the first *Kirti Kisan* Conference held in Hoshiarpur in October, 1928.[174] In brief, the *Kirtis,* during 1926-29, did raise the demand for taking away land from the landlords without compensation and its division among the cultivators. But the demand was put forward in too general and abstract a manner.

A mass meeting of *Kisans* was held at Garhi in the Hissar district on 10th November, 1929. They resolved not to pay *abiana* to their landlords till their legitimate grievances were redressed.[175] Even in 1924, a meeting was held at Lyallpur on youth June to protest against the enhancement of the water rates.[176] Thus, the agrarian agitation had started since the early part of 1920 and it continued to be fostered by the Punjab *Kisan* Committee at Amritsar, Lahore, Jullundur, Hoshiarpur, Ludhiana, Ferozepure, Multan, Montgomery, Lyallpur etc.

The peasant organisations, systematically, cropped up throughout the Central Punjab at the end of the 20's and the beginning of the 30's. *Zamindara Sabha* was active in Amritsar. It was holding series of Conferences to protest against the proposed reassessment of the district. The peasant movement was also backed by the *Kirti Kisan* Party, the Congress workers and the Communist organisation. It was in April 1930 that the Hissar *Kisan Sabha* headed a campaign against the payment of rents in kind to the landlords.[177] Congress gave special attention to the intensification of rural propaganda in the region of Lahore, Amritsar and Lyallpur. In the Bastern districts which were the home of Hindu *Jats,* both the Congress and the *Zamindara* League led agitation had spread to a serious extent to all the minor towns and many of the villages.[178] In

174. *The Kirti,* October, 1927.
175. P.L.C.D., Vol. XIV, 1929, 708.
176. File No. 25/1924-June, Home Deptt., Political, NAI : New Delhi.
177. Home Department, File No. 18/11/1930-Political, NAI : New Delhi.
178. *Ibid.,* (The nature of the conflict is not given in the fortnightly report in this file).

Sheikhupura also the peasant agitation was launched against the payment of land revenue.[179]

The Lyallpur *Zamindara Sabha* held a series of meetings in the countryside. There, resolutions were passed demanding that the land revenue be paid in kind and not in cash, since the fall in prices had raised the revenue burned manifold. Another important *Zamindara* meeting was held at Lyallpur on June 20, 1930 under S. Mangal Singh's presidentship. In his Presidential address, he observed that "even the most well-to-do among us are finding it impossible to make both ends meet".[180] The Congress too urged the Government to take steps towards affording substantial relief to the agriculturists by giving effects to the demands as follows :

(i) 58% of the agriculturists of the Punjab own less than 5 acres of land and to tax these uneconomic holdings was against equality, justice and all fair canons, of taxation;

(ii) At least 50% general remission in the land revenue and *abiana* and in special cases, more remission be given to meet particular requirements;

(iii) Reduction in *abiana* be made and *Chahi* rate should be abolished. The total receipt of *abiana* should be equal to the cost of administration plus the interest charged on the Capital spent in the construction of the canals;

(iv) *Bagar, Thikripehra* and *Chaukidara* tax should be abolished;

(v) The Punjab *Zamindars* should be consulted at every stage of the process of constitution making;

(vi) The Government should declare the formation of a Cotton Corporation and should actively begin the purchase of Cotton at fixed rates;

(vii) Land Revenue should be on the basis of Income-Tax and small holdings should be exempted;

179. *Ibid.*

180. *The Tribune,* Lahore, June 23, 1931.

(viii) The reduction of the exchange ratio of 1s.6d. to 1s.4d.;

(ix) The imposition of prohibitive duty on foreign wheat and cotton goods;

(x) Substantial reduction in Railway freight and agricultural products to Karachi, Bombay, Calcutta and other places;

(xi) Responsible Government, with complete control over the finances and the army, be immediately established in the country.

The Conference made it clear that the peasants were not satisfied with the scale of remission of land revenue granted to them so far.[181] In the south-east of the province, the farmers were finding it very difficult to pay *abiana*. The *Nili Bar Zamindars'* committee of Montgomery and Multan districts in its meeting on July 18, 1931, could not come to a definite decision as far as the non-payment of revenue was concerned. It told the peasants of the area that those who had the means to pay should do so.[182]

The *Kirti Kisan* Party held the annual Conferences in 1930 and 1931, in Lahore and Karachi respectively. The speeches at the *Kisan* Conferences showed that the Punjab Communists were also following the political line of the Communist Party in India.[183] At this time, the *Kirti Kisan* Party had acquired a slight foothold in parts of Amritsar district.[184] In Jullundur also, the *Kirt Kisan Sabha,* with the help of *Akali Dal* held meetings in which the small agriculturists were advised to agitate for the immediate reduction of land taxations.[185] The

181. On May 21, 1931, Government announced remission of land revenue and *abiana,* which amounted to Rs. 1084 lacs. It meant 5 *annas* in the rupee in case of land revenue.

182. Home Department, File No. 18/3/1931-Political, NAI : New Delhi.

183. *The Kirti,* January, 1930.

184. Home Department, File No. 18/4/1931-Political, NAI : New Delhi.

185. Home Department, File No. 18/5/1931-Political, NAI : New Delhi.

Congress and moneylenders' methods were attacked[186] and the sympathisers of the *Kirti Kisan* Party from among the *Ghadrites'* tried to capture offices in the Congress Committees and to utilise the Congress organisation to spread its propaganda.[187] Inspite of carefully selected prosecutions of the *Kirti Kisan* Party workers, the agitation continued in Amritsar district and was beginning to obtain a front hold in the Sheikhpura and Gurdaspur districts.[188] Of course, the remission had the effect of taking a great deal of the sting out of the agitation but it was still continuing in the districts of Central Punjab while the peaceful districts of North-West received it with genuine appreciation.[189]

The situation of deep economic crisis was putting a severe strain on the economic structure of the province. Credit to the peasants was restricted and the efforts of the moneylenders to recover debt were causing a bitterness which, where the creditors were Hindus and debtors Mohammedans, was developing along communal lines.[190] In the districts of Jhang, Muzaffargarh and Multan, communal tension was rising and the Government was expecting a wide spread attack by the Muslim peasantry on the Hindu usurper such as had occurred in this region of the province in 1925.[191] Attempts of the *Kirti Kisan Sabha* workers to influence the various *Zamindara Sabhas* and unite them not a single body were considered by

186. Congress was identified with the moneylenders and the later supported the Congress occasions, whenever the Congress party in the Legislative Assembly, had to support or oppose any agrarian Bill put forth by the Unionist Party but with a motive to denouncing the Congress in the eyes of the small agriculturists. For details see also Chapter IV. For this see, P.L.C.D.; and the Fortnightly report of this period, particularly when the Agrarian Bills were put in the Assembly for debate; and also see P.L.C.D.

187. Home Department, File Nos. 18/5/1931-Political : 31/III/1931-Political, NAI : New Delhi.

188. *Ibid.*

189. Home Department, File No. 18/6/1931-Political, NAI : New Delhi.

190. *Ibid.*

191. Home Department, File No. 18/7/1931-Political, NAI : New Delhi.

the Government to be a very dangerous move. These *Sabhas* had hitherto occupied themselves in endeavouring to ameliarate the lot of the *Zamindars* by constitutonal methods. But now their link with a revolutionary party like the *Kirti Kisan* Party were considered to be a 'very serious matter'. To stamp out the *Kirti* influence, the familiar method of 'Carrot and the stick' was used. However, the *Kirti Kisan* Party continued to pursue its activities. A *Kirti Kisan* Conference was held at Nankana Sahib on November 12-13, 1932. It was attended by 2000 people.[192] In the later half of the year 1933, a few meetings were held in Amritsar and Hoshiarpur districts.[193] In these meetings, the peasants' demands were supported. But the Government put ban on some of the organisations such as the *Kirti Kisan* Party; The *Babbar Akali;* The Communist etc. : As a result of the policy followed by the British Government, individuals active in the above organisations, sought to group themselves under the Punjab *Kisan Qarza* Committee's banner. Its first meeting was held at Amritsar on March 3, 1935. It was decided to organise small committees in rural areas to assist the peasants to obtain as much benefits as possible from the relief provided by the indebtedness Act.[194] A number of meetings and Conferences were held and the Jullundur district *Qarza* Committee set up 60 branches at various places in the district.[195] It held small village meetings at which speakers combined agrarian agitation with Communist propaganda.[196] During the month of October 1935, the *Doab* rural uplift conference was organised by the Communists at Patara in Jullundur district. It demanded the cancellation of debts and assessment of land

192. Home Department, File No. 18/6/1932-Political, NAI : New Delhi, Williamson, H., India and Communism : 1935, 28-29.
193. Home Department, File No. 18/1/1933-Political; 18/3/1933-Political, NAI : New Delhi.
194. Home Department, File No. 18/3/1935-Political, NAI : New Delhi.
195. *The Kirti,* December 22, 1935.
196. The Home Department, File No. 18/II/1935-Political, NAI : New Delhi.

revenue on the basis of income tax and also urged the villagers to set up *Qarza* Committes.[197]

It is to be noted that the leftists, organised under the banner of the Punjab *Kirti Kisan Sabha,* were the only politically organised group which sought to mobilise the poor and small holding peasants both against the moneylenders as well as the landlords. It is in this context that we shall make an attempt to discuss the organisation and politicalisation of the peasantry and the countervailing influences of the Unionist Party in close collaboration with the British imperialism.

Undoubtedly, this coincided with the rising peasants' struggle under the banner of All India *Kisan Sabha* throughout the length and breadth of the country which pressed for agrarian legislation. After the achievement of considerable unity in the ranks of the Punjab Socialists under the CSP, the peasants' agitation made a headway in Punjab. The Punjab *Kisan* Committee (PKC hereafter) was formed in March 1937 and was affiliated to the All India *Kisan* Committee.[198] Baba Jawala Singh was its first President. The Working Committee represented all bodies with socialist leanings.[199] The first Conference of the *Kisan* Committee met at Lyallpur in October 1937. 450 Delegates attended this Session when the total number of delegates was 500.[200] The size of the audience varied between 15 to 20 thousand persons.

The Punjab Kisan Committee now decided to intensify the agitation for cancellation of debts, the assessment of land revenue on income tax basis and exemption of uneconomic holdings from taxation. There it is to be noted that debts of the agriculturists moneylenders were also included in this demand. The PKC demanded that actually tillers of the land and not the big landlords should be the owners of the land.

197. *Ibid.*

198. It is alleged by others that Punjab *Kisan* Committee was set up in 1936, and was known then as Punjab *Kisan Sabha,* Vide. *Satyug,* (*Punjabi* weekly), December, 1975, 42.

199. *National Front,* October 31, 1938.

200. *The Kirti Lehr* (Meerut), October 23, 1938.

The Conference passed in all 26 resolutions. It condemned the functioning of the bandobast committees and deemed them to be harmful to the interests of the *Kisan* Committee. It, therefore, appealed to the organisers of these Committees to merge them into the *Kisan* Committee.[202] According to one source; the total membership of the PKC in February, 1938 was sixty thousand while in April it was reported to be 73 thousand, 4 hundred and 69.[203] In July, there were 1800 *Kisan* Committees in the Punjab.[204] In the Jullundur district, the *Kisan* Committees of Cheema Kalan, Atta, Majeian, Karnana and Bahadurgarh were quite active in their respective circles. Hence, in 1938, Punjab occupied the second position in the All India *Kisan Sabha* membership figures.[205]

It is worthwhile to state that the four districts of the Central Punjab—Lahore, Amritsar, Jullundur and Ferozepur dominated so far as the membership in the PKC was concerned. Again these districts—where the small holding peasantry predominated—was precisely the area which had a tradition of militant anti British struggle from the days of the Akali agitation which had consisted of Sikh peasants. Even the leadership of the PKC was drawn from this area and most of it had matured through the *Ghadr* and *Akali* struggles. However, in the region of Western Punjab such as Multan and Montgomery where the percentage of the rent paying tenant cultivators was very high, the PKC was almost a negligible force.[206] The question which needs to be answered

201. *Ibid.*, Home Department, File No. 18/10/1937-Poll., NAI : New Delhi.

202. *The Kirti*, June 12, 1938, (Representatives number from each district are also given. Details of delegates from various Police Stations (Area-wise) are also available, Vide the *Kirti Lehr*, Meerut, July 24, 1938.

203. *The Kirti Lehr*, February 27, 1938.

204. *Ibid.*, July 31, 1938.

205. *Ibid.*, July 28, 1938; *National Front*, June 5, 1938.

206. The number of PKC members belonging to Multan and Montgomery (where rent paying cultivators were roughly 75% to 80%) districts

(Contd.)

is, why did the PKC failed to acquire a mass base among the tenants of North-West Punjab?

It was in the forties that the leaders and the members of the PKC toured North-Western Punjab, and made efforts to organise the *Nili Bar* tenants. However, the tours were limited to a few villages and these too were occasional. As a result, they failed to concentrate their energies on this region. The reason for their failure to acquire a mass base becomes additionally clear when we examine their method of propaganda for the politicalisation of the peasantry. The most popular method of approaching the peasantry was to organise a tour of prominent leaders of the PKC belonging to a particular area and to hold meetings. But the fact is that in many villages, the loyalists *i.e.*, the *Lambardars* of various *Pattis,* the landlords and the ex-servicemen were under pressure of the local police in their villages; it was obligatory for them to prevent such political activity as an essential qualification for holding the status of *Zaildar* etc. in the village.[207]

This village level leadership was lacking in areas cultivated predominantly by tenants, the bulk of whom were Muslims. The reasons for the existence of such local village leadership in the Central Punjab and its non-existence in the North-Western Punjab can be traced back to the definite pattern of politicalization in the Punjab in the first quarter of the 20th century, which we shall discuss in the sixth chapter and to the differing class-structure in the countryside discussed in the first chapter respectively.

The peasant movement in the Punjab emerged as an organised force for the first time during the period when the Unionist Party formed its ministry in the Punjab in 1937. A number of Conferences were held by the PKC at various places

---

where on 1865 as compared to the Central Punjab region (Only Amritsar, Lahore and Jullundur districts) where the membership was 26, 199, 14, 817 and 7, 429 respectively). Vide *The Kirti Lehr.* February to July, 1938, also see Fortnightly Report of 1938-Home Deptt., Political, NAI : New Delhi.

207. *The Tribune,* Lahore, April 28, 1938.

such as Bhakna (Bhatinda), Chhjewal (Ludhiana), Daudhar (Ferozepur), Gobindpur (Gurdaspur), Anandpur (Hoshiarpur), etc. Swami Sahajanand, the Secretary of the All India *Kisan Sabha,* presided over a *Mazdoor Kisan* Conference at Barapind (Jullundur) which was held from September 21st to 24th, 1937.[208] Another Conference was organised by the Amritsar district *Kisan Bandobast* Committee at Naushera Punam on 29th and 30th September. Ten thousand people attended it. The various problems and demands of the farmers were discussed in these Conferences.[209]

In Amritsar district, the socialists and the Communists held almost daily meetings and *dewans* in some village or the other. Rural propaganda was almost continuously carried on in the Batala *Tehsil* of Gurdaspur.[210] The Deputy Commissioner of Gurdaspur had expressed the opinion that the activities of the *Kisan* agitators had reached a stage where action by the Government was required.[211] It will not be out of place to state that in the year 1937, a series of workers strikes took place in many small factories of Amritsar. All the strikes were launched under the leadership of the Labour Federation which was managed by a group of Communists who constituted the Punjab branch of the CPI and was known as the Sohan Singh Josh group.[212]

The year 1938 was the year of active agrarian movement. Like the peasant organisations in many other provinces, the Punjab *Kisan* Committee took an active part in organising and

---

208. Home Department, File No. 18/9/1937-Political, NAI : New Delhi; *The Kirti,* September-1937, Master Hari Singh, *(Punjab Wich Kirsani Laher'* (Punjabi), Souvenir, issued by the C.P.I. January, 1976.

209. Home Department, File No. 18/6/1937-Political, NAI : New Delhi.

210. Home Department, File No. 18/3/1937-Political, NAI : New Delhi.

211. *The Kirti Lehr,* Meerut, June 26, 1938; Master Hari Singh, *'Punjab Wich Kirsani Laher' (Punjabi), Souvenir,* issued by the CPI, January, 1976.

212. Master Hari Singh, *'Punjab Wich Kirsani Laher', (Punjabi), Souvenir,* issued by the CPI, January-1976; This view is also supported by Sardar Sohan Singh Josh in personal meeting at Ajoy Bhawan, New Delhi.

to a large extent, providing leadership to all the peasant agitations throughout the state, especially the agitations conducted by the peasants of Amritsar, Lahore, Hoshiarpur and the Canal colony districts. In the Punjab, the Communists, the workers and the revolutionary *babas* built up organisation in the peasants' movement.[213] It is worthwhile to mention here that almost all the peasants' Conferences were organised by the CBP and the PKC. Moreover, each of these was preceded by regular, smaller village meetings urging the peasants to attend the larger meetings and explaining to them their objectives etc.[214] The larger Conferences were most often attended by leaders of all India fame, for example, Pt. Nehru, Prof. N.G. Ranga, Jai Prakash Narain, Swami Sahajanand Saraswati, and many others.[215] Later, the local leaders made efforts to keep up the momentum imported by the distinguished visitors.[216] Through all these conferences socialist ideas were disseminated among the peasantry as also many other section of *Punjabee* society.

Due to the fall in the prices of foodgrains, it became difficult for the peasants to pay off *malia* and *abiana*. But in many districts, the Government made new settlement *(Bandobast)* and raised the land revenue *(malia)*. A general impression of the poor economic conditions of the large section of the peasantry can be gathered from the simple fact that

213. For details see *Kirti Lehr,* 10th July, 7th August, 8th September, 11th December, 1938; *National Front,* 29th November, 4th December, 1938; Home Deptt,-Political, File No. 18/3/1938, 18/6/1938; Rasul, M.A., *A History of the All India Kisan Sabha,* Calcutta ; 1974, 24.

214. *The Tribune,* Lahore, 9, 13, 14, 30 June; 15, 17, 18 September, 1936, Home Department-Political, File Nos. 18/12/1936, 18/3/1936, 18/2/1937, 18/4/1937, 18/6/1937, 18/8/1937, *Congress Socialist,* Vol. II (New Series), No. 35.

215. *The Tribune,* Lahore, 4th June, 1st August, 1936; 7th April, 12, 23 September, 1st October, 1937; Home Department-Political-File Nos. 18/11/1936; 18/3/1937; 18/5/1937; 18/6/1937; 18/7/1937; 18/8/1937; 18/9/1937; 18/10/1937; *Congress Socialist,* Vol. I (New Series), Nos. 25, 27, 34, Vol. II Nos. 33, 39, 41.

216. Home Department-Political, File Nos. 18/9/1936; 18/10/1937.

during 1938-39, many *Lambardars* and hundreds of peasants of Lahore district were arrested due to their inability to pay land revenue in time.[217] In 1939 at the time of the meeting of the Assembly, the peasants of Lahore declared to demonstrate in Lahore against the increased *malia*. The Government clamped section 144 in many parts of the city and prevented the procession from proceeding towards the Assembly. The farmers violated the section 144 and courted arrests. Soon this *morcha* became the *morcha* of the peasants of the whole Punjab.[218]

The *Jathas,* of course from various districts,[219] started marching towards Lahore on foot. Three to four thousand farmers were sent to Jails. The *morcha* was still continuing when the second World War started. The *Akali* peasants of Lahore division also took part in this *morcha*. The initiators of the *morcha* were the farmer leaders of Lahore : Yog Raj and Tehal Singh. Then the Punjab *Kisan Sabha* also lent support to the morcha.[220] Inspite of old age, Baba Sohan Singh Bhakna and Bhag Singh Canadian etc. took part in the *morcha* and went to jail.

On July 20, 1938 the *Bandobast* Committee (Akali) and

217. *Kirti Lehr,* June 4, 1939, *Kirti-Jan.* 16, 1936, (In May 1939, The P.K.C. decided to make the agitation state-wide and presented the Government with a charter of demands) Vide. *National Front,* 28th May, 1939.

218. File No. 18/3/1939, 18/6/1939, Home Department-Political, NAI : New Delhi.

219. (District Committees of the PKC were asked to send *Jathas* of volunteers to court arrests at Lahore. Such *Jathas* were sent from Ferozpur, Ambala, Jullundur, Amritsar, Gurdaspur and Lyallpur districts. These *Jathas* carried an active agitation in the villages through which they passed on their way to Lahore) Vide *Kirti Lehr,* 31 July, 1939; *National Front,* 27 August, 1939.

220. *Kirti,* October, 1939; File No. 18/3/1939, Home Department-Political, NAI : New Delhi; Nurpuri, Chanan Singh, *'The Great Morcha of Lahore and Harsa Chhina',* (an article in *Punjabi*) published in Souvenir, issued by the CPI in 1976. Home Deptt. Political, File No. 18/7/1938, 18/8/1938; *Kirti Lehr,* 31st July, 1938, *National Front,* 9 October, 1938.

the PKC held a huge demonstration at Amritsar. Consequently the peasants of Amritsar violated section 144 and demonstrated against the increased *malia,* reduction of canal outlets in a number of villages, and the burden of *Malba, Chowkidara, Chahi* and other local taxes. They were severely *lathi* charged in which over 300 were injured and 145 *Kisan* activists were arrested.[221] In this demonstration also, the Congress took part.[222] As a result of the peasant movement, the Punjab Government declared its intention to implement sliding scale in *malia.* Accordingly it was decided to decrease the *malia* in view of the fall in the prices of crops beyond a certain level.[223]

In Jullundur district since long irrigation had been done with the help of wells. After 1930, there set in a long dry period and the level of the water in wells went down. The peasants of the district demanded that a canal be dug in the *Doaba* and in this connection, in 1937, 50,000 peasants demonstrated in which included all types of peasants participated.[224]

During the British rule, *Malba* was also charged in addition to *malia.* The real purpose of *malba* was to help the poor helpless persons but this amount was spent on the entertainment of the Government officials. The peasants started a movement against it. At several places, as in the

221. Home Department-Political, File Nos. 18/3/1939, 18/4/1939, *Kirti Lehr,* April 2, 1939.

222. *Akali Ten Pardesi :* P/6, August 3, 1939; File No. 84 (Collection of Private Papers-Sunder Singh Majithia), Nehru Memorial Museum and Library (N.M.M.L), Wadhawa Ram, Some Memoirs of *Nili Bar—Bane Utte Udho-Adh* (An article in *Punjabi*) published in a *Souvenir* issued by CPI in 1976; Home Department-Political, File Nos. 18/8/1938; *National Front,* 9 October, 1938; *Kirti Lehr,* 31 July, 1938.

223. *Kirti,* May 1, 1936; *Kirti Lehr,* Meerut, July 3, 1939, Master Hari Singh, *'Punjab Wich Kirsani Lehr' (Punjabi), Souvenir,* issued by the CPI, January, 1976; also see Home Deptt.-Political File Nos. 18/4/1931, 18/5/1931, 18/7/1938, 18/8/1939; NAI : New Delhi. (After independence, this demand was conceded).

224. Home Department-Political File No. 18/3/1939; NAI : New Delhi.

village Mahilpur of Hoshiarpur district, the collection of *Malba* was discontinued. The state Government announced in the Assembly that the Government had nothing to do with *malba*. It was the choice of the villagers whether to collect it or not. The announcement marked the success of the farmers' movement. After this the collection of *malba* was generally stopped.

In the second half of March 1939, the Lahore district *Kisan* Committee declared a plan to mobilize 50,000 tenants to stage a protest demonstration; but according to the police, only 300 men turned up.[225] According to another source, the number of demonstrators was 8,000.[226] A contemporary Government report stated that the Premier offered to receive a deputation of the peasants but refused to allow certain professional agitators who themselves were not peasants, and were not inhabitants of Lahore district, to act as spokesman of the deputation.[227] When the demonstrators defied Section 144 Cr.P.C., 103 persons were arrested on the spot. The demonstration was staged on 23rd March and till the end of the month, 374 persons had been arrested.[228] Small batches of peasants gathered daily to defy section 144 and demonstrated before the Assembly Chamber. The Congress members of the Assembly and the city 'rif-raff' (as the British officials put it) openly supported the demonstrations.[229] The *Kisans* were determined to continue their civil disobedience until their demands were met. They demanded that action on the new settlement should be postponed for three years. The Akalis actively participated in this agitation and till the end of April, 100 men were arrested, including 24 Akalis.[230] *Kisan* Committees in the Kasur Sub-Division of Lahore and Dipalpur *Tahsil* of Montegomery refused to use canal water as a protest

225. Home Department-Political, File No. 18/3/1939; NAI : New Delhi.

226. *Kirti Lehr,* April 2, 1939.

227. Home Department-Political, File No. 18/3/1939; NAI : New Delhi.

228. *Ibid.*

229. *Ibid.*

230. File No. 18/4/1939, Home Department-Political, NAI : New Delhi.

against the enhancement of revenue under the new settlement in Lahore.[231]

In the middle of May, 1939, the Control of the agitation was taken over by the PKC in order to give a state-wide dimension to the agitation.[232] A charter of demands which enlisted, apart from general demands, the specific demands of the peasants of the various areas, was presented to the Government.[233] District level Committees were directed to send volunteer *Jathas* to court arrest at Lahore. *Kisans Jathas* from various districts such as Ambala, Jullundur, Gurdaspur, Amritsar, Ferozepur and Lyallpur proceeded towards Lahore and on their way passed through villages denouncing the high-handedness of the ministry in the Punjab. Almost all the *Jathas* were intercepted by the police and later on arrests of prominent agitators started in the villages. Was approaching and the Government decided to take firm action against the *Kisan* in order to stop further misleading.[234] All India *Kisan Sabha* decided to observe 4th June as the 'All India Punjab *Kisan* Day' in order to express their solidarity with the Punjab peasants.[235] On June 17, the Government issued a communique warning that firm action, including the use of the ordinary criminal law and the Criminal Law Amendment Act, would be taken against the organisers of *Kisan Satyagraha* in Lahore.[236] The struggle continued for three more months. About four thousand persons were thrown behind bars.[237] Though internal dissensions weakened the agitation, it was mainly the iron heel of the imperialist repression that crushed the agitation.

The second Provincial *Kisan* Conference met at Sargodha

---

231. *Ibid.*

232. *National Front,* May 28, 1939.

233. *Ibid.*

234. File No. 18/6/1939, Home Department-Political, NAI : New Delhi; *Kirti,* 31 July, 1939; *National Front;* August 27, 1939.

235. *National Front,* June 11, 1939.

236. *Ibid.,* June 25, 1939.

on 5, 6 and 7th September, 1939. Baba Rur Singh presided over it.[238] It expressed its determination to carry forward the banner of struggle by organising more peasants into ranks of the PKC.

At the end of the August 1939, Sikander Hyat declared that he guaranteed that the manpower and resources of the Punjab would be unhesitatingly placed at the disposal of Great Britain.[239] The repressive machinery of the state was brought into full swing against the opponents of war.[240]

The *Kisan Sabha* also launched a movement to relieve the peasants of the heavy burden of debts. However, it is to be noted that the peasant movement did not take up the problem of indebtedness till 1935 and not very rigorously even after that. It was with the formation of the Punjab *Kisan Qarza* Committee in March 1935 by the leftist leaders of the various banned organisations that the problem was taken up.[241] The *Kisan Sabha* started supporting the public war. The open activities of the *Kisan Sabha* were recommended. It launched a campaign to increase agricultural production and supplementing it with some demands, it started a struggle. In 1943, there was a severe famine in Bengal which claimed many lives. The Punjab *Kisan Sabha* started a campaign to help the famine victims of Bengal and collected fairly large funds, food and clothes for them.[242]

After the war, in 1946, the peasant movement again gained momentum. The tenants' agitations have already been referred to. In 1946, under the leadership of the Communist Party and

237. *Kirti Lehr,* July 9, 1939.

238. *National Front,* September 10, 1939.

239. *Ibid.,* August 27, 1939.

240. Home Department-Political, File No. 18/6/1942, NAI : New Delhi.

241. *Ibid.,* 18/3/1935 (The Committee organised smaller committees in the rural areas to help the peasants derive full benefits from the existing Deptt. Relief Legislation).

242. Hari Singh, *'Punjab Wich Kirsani Laher' (Panjabi),* issued by the CPI a *Souvenir* in January, 1976.

the Punjab *Kisan Sabha,* the *'Moghas' Morcha* of Harsa Chhina was fought. In six villages of the Chhina area of District Amritsar, the Government narrowed the *'Moghas'* (outlets) of the canals under the pretext of the remodelling of the *Moghas* and canals, and thus decreased the quantity of water but retained the old rates of abiana. It affected actually the farmers and the farmers of the area started a *morcha* against it. The peasants all over the Punjab supported the *morcha.* A large number of peasants were sent to jails.[243] Those who went to jail included Sohan Singh Josh, Achhar Singh Chhina and Gurdial Singh Dhillon. The Akali leaders of the district also took part in it but in the end they tried to sabotage the *morcha.*[244]

The whole District Committee (it consisted of only 5 members then) comprised the Action Committee. Being the state organiser of the District Party, Comrade Teja Singh Swatantar was the adviser of the *Morcha.* A big Conference was held at the bridge of the canal and the Congress and the Akali parties were also invited to participate. Isher Singh Majhail and Avtar Singh Siddhu represented the Congress. They announced that they would take active part in the *Morcha.*[245] But under the Sikander-Baldev Pact, Baldev Singh of the Akali Party had taken Sunder Singh Majithia's place in the Unionist Party ministry and many *jagirdars* and capitalists had joined the party. Thus neither the Akali nor the Congress leaders made any sincere contribution to the *morcha.* On the very first day, they started talking of striking a compromise.

243. Nurpuri, Chanan Singh, 'The Great *Morcha* of Lahore and Harsa Chhina', (An article in *Punjabi*), published in a *Souvenir* issued by the CPI in January, 1976; Master Hari Singh, *'Punjab Wich Kirsani Laher', (Punjabi), Souvenir* issued by CPI in January, 1976.

244. File No. 18/10/1932; File No. 18/12/1938; Home Deptt.-Political, NAI : New Delhi; Nurpuri, Chanan Singh, *'The Great Morcha of Lahore and Harsa Chhina', Souvenir,* issued by the CPI, January : 1976.

245. File No. 18/4/1939, Home Department-Political, NAI : New Delhi; Master Hari Singh, *'Punjab Wich Kirsani Laher' (Punjabi)—Souvenir* issued by the CPI, January : 1976.

A big conference was held in front of the bridge.[246] With a large iron *mogha* on his shoulder, Achhar Singh Chhina led a *Jatha* to replace the small *mogha*.[247] Following was a 10 to 15 thousand strong crowd. Chhina told Majhail that in case of a lathi charge, he (Majhail) would be held responsible as he was a party to the Baldev Singh ministry.[248] The latter, then, went to the S.S.P. under whose command a police party was guarding the bridge to persuade him not to take any action. However the members of the *Jatha* were arrested peacefully. Every day the *jathas* were arrested while trying to break the *mogha*.[249] S. Gurdial Singh Dhillon of the Akali Party also courted arrest alongwith a jatha of 222 persons.[250]

The continue strength of the *morcha* put the Congress and Akali leaders in an embarrassing position. At last, at a large gathering in the village Sahinsara, Majhail alongwith *Jathedar* Udam Singh announced S. Baldev Singh's message, "Call off the *morcha* and the *moghas* will be widend". But according to Dalip Singh Tapiala, it was but a move to sabotage the morcha".........[251] The *morcha* continued. A *jatha* was also sent to the office of the Amritsar Canal under the leadership of S. Mohan Singh Mahawa. There were a large number of encounters with the Police. This *morcha* yielded good results for the Communist party.

---

246. Nurpuri, Chanan Singh, *The Great Morchas of Lahore and Harsa Chhina;* Master Hari Singh, *'Punjab Wich Kirsani Laher, (Punjabi)—Souvenir* issued by the CPI, January : 1976; File No. 18/4/1943; Home Department-Political, NAI : New Delhi.

247. Nurpuri, Chanan Singh, *The Great Morchas of Lahore and Harsa Chhina, Souvenir* issued by the CPI, January : 1976.

248. Personal meetings with S. Laher Singh Majhail (Patiala), Master Hari Singh (Chandigarh); File No. 18/5/1943; Home Department-Political, NAI : New Delhi.

249. File Nos. 18/8/1938; 18/3/1939; *National Front,* May 28, 1939; *Kirti Lehr,* July 31, 1939; Home Deptt.-Political : NAI New Delhi.

250. File No. 18/6/1939; Home Deptt.-Political; *National Front,* June 11 and 25, 1939; Nurpuri Chanan Singh, *The Great Morchas of Lahore and Harsa Chhina, Souvenir,* issued by the CPI in January, 1976.

251. *Ibid., Kirti Lehr,* July 9, 1939; *National Front,* September 10, 1939.

After the formation of the state Kisan Sabha under the Presidentship of Baba Jawala Singh, attention was paid to the farmers of *Nili Bar.* During 1922, and 1928, the head *Submanki* and the *'Nahri'* (Canal) Sutlej Valley projects were completed. The vast barren areas of Montegomery and Multan districts which were totally depended on rain got reclaimed.[252] However, the old areas of *Nilibar* were here and there irrigated by six monthly canal and well facilities but these were very rare. Most of the uniirrigated areas were waiting for the waters of the Nili river. The soil was extremely hard. The normal yield per acre of cotton was 20 to 30 *maunds* and that of wheat 25 to 40 *maunds.* Apart from the local farmers a large number of poor farmers from other districts of the Punjab also got settled there. They did agriculture on *Batai* basis.[253] There were two types of land set-ups. On one side there were big *Poojes,* the *Gurus,* the *Pirs,* the *Bedis,* the *Daulatanas,* the *Nigriala,* the *Muzaffargarhis,* the *Pathans,* the *Shergarhis,* the *Gaddhi Nashine* of the *Pir Baba Faridi* etc., whose ownership was 12,000 to 40,000 acres.[254] The second was the company who took the Government land of the whole villages on *Patta* for 3 to 5 years. They sucked the blood of the farmers; so much so that even after yielding the crops of the year, the farmer found himself under debt to the tune of Rs. 2000/- to Rs. 3000/-.[255] In this region, these companies had their own leather coin in circulation. They had also opened their own shops for the supply of the articles of daily use in these

252. Wadhawa Ram, 'Some Memoirs of Nili Bar'—*Banne-Utte-Adho-Adh,* An Article in *Punjabi* published in a Souvenir, issued by the CPI on January 26, 1976.

253. File No. 18/10/1932; 18/14/1933; Home Department-Political, NAI : New Delhi.

254. File No. 18/7/1938; Home Department-Political, NAI : New Delhi; Wadhawa, Ram, 'Some Memoirs of Nili Bar'—*Banne-Utte-Adho-Adh,* An Article in *Punjabi,* published in a *Souvenir* issued by the CPI in January : 1976.

255. Wadhawa Ram, 'Some Memoirs of Nili Bar—*Banne-Utte-Adho-Adh',* *Souvenir,* issued by the CPI, January : 1976; Master Hari Singh *'Punjab Wich Kirsani Laher (Punjabi), Souvenir* issued by the CPI in January : 1976.

villages.[256] They would pay the leather eight-*anna* or four-*anna* coins for the picking up of cotton and then they would get back these coins by providing *Gur,* Rice etc. from their shops.[257]

None dared to complain if the *jagirdar* seized the belongings of a villager, beat him and turned him out of the village. The whole population was under the awe of the *jagirdar.* To charge various kinds of gifts and bribes and get work without making any payment were the traditional privileges of the *jagirdars.*[258] The companies too were in no way less taxing. They would deduct 16 *seers* of grains per *mound* without any reason. Out of the remaining 24 *seers,* 12 *seers* would fall to the share of the company and only 12 *seers* were credited to the *muzara i.e.* out of a *mound* the *muzara* go only 12 *seers* and the company 28 seers. But the *muzaras* were not given the crops. The food-grains were all stored in the godown of the Company.[259] The accounts of the Hari were cleared in the month of *Sawan* and those of the *Sawani* in *Chet;* but on each occasion, the farmer found himself under debt for Rs. 3 to 4 thousand instead of getting anything for the labour of the whole year.[260]

At the time of the issuing of new *Pattas,* after 3 to 4 years the owners of the Company would change. Therefore they did not have as much hold on the *muzaras* as had the *jagirdars.* That is why the struggle first was launched by the *Muzaras* in the Bar against the companies. It was the time when, at the begnning of 1937, Baba Jawala Singh reached the Nili Bar alongwith his companions.[261]

---

256. *Ibid.*

257. Personal meeting with S. Hari Singh; *Kirti Lehr,* May 1, 1938.

258. *Kirti Lehr,* May 1, 1936; June, 1938.

259. Wadhawa Ram, 'Some Memoirs of Nili Bar-*Banne Utte Adho-Adh',* *Souvenir* issued by the CPI, January : 1976.

260. Master Hari Singh, *Punjab Wich Kirsani Laher (Panjabi),* Souvenir, issued by the CPI, January : 1976.

261. Nurpuri, Chanan Singh, *'The Great Morchas of Lahore and Harsa Chhina', Souvenir,* issued by the CPI, January : 1976; *Kirti Lehr,* December, 1938.

In some of the areas of the districts of Multan and Montgomery, it was a practice with the Government to invite tenders in order to allot land to the highest bidder. These tender-holders further divided these lands among the rent paying cultivators. After the depression, tenders of the Government by lessees had so risen through competition that the lessees in order to make a profit, had been adding to the standard rents various other exactions. About 25,000 tenants of Nilibar, a colony in Montgomery district, went on strike against additional exactions to the standard rent and refused to pick cotton or sow wheat.[262] Similarly the tenants of more than twenty villages in Talamba Thana, Multan district struck work in September, 1938 and the strike lasted for about a month.[263] The PKC held a number of Conferences in the area of Bunewal, Sohuka, Aarafwala and Vehori. Kartar Singh, Jalwant Singh, Harbans Singh and Amir Haq were some of the *Kisan* Committee workers who carried on propaganda in these areas.[264] In both cases, the Government and the tender-holders were compelled to negotiate and concede many of the immediate demands.[265] The more important demands were :

(a) Bagar of all kinds be stopped at once; *(b)* no tender-holder shall have the right to expect illegal taxes from his *muzaras; (c)* no tender-holder shall eject any tenant for his participation in the strike; *(d)* the peasant shall pay the price of green fodder at Rs. 3/- per unit instead of Rs. 6/-; *(e)* Cotton and other crops shall be divided half and half in the field itself; *(f)* water for drinking purposes would be provided to the *muzaras* by the holders.[266]

In the month of March, 1938, the peasants of the different Chaks in the Montegomery district sent applications to the

262. *Kirti Lehr,* December 11, 1938.

263. *National Front;* December 4, 1938, & December 6, 1938.

264. *Kirti Lehr,* August 7 and September 8, 1938.

265. *National Front,* November 27, 1938, *Kirti Lehr,* July 10, 1938; Rasul, M.A., *A History of the All India Kisan Sabha,* Calcutta : 1974, 24.

266. *Ibid., Kirti Lehr,* July 10, 1938.

Commissioner threatening *Kisan Satyagrah* if their rents were not reduced.[267] A number of the PKC's suggested the farmers to get organised and form local committees.[268] Two months later, they ceased to work as a protest against the exactions of the temporary lease of the Government land and demanded that the same concessions be granted to them as the Government had recently accorded to the tenants in Nili Bar.[269] The *muzaras* of 15 *chaka* in the *Khanewal tehsil* went on strike under the leadership of the District *Kisan* Committee of Multan and Montegomery. They refused to pick cotton and sow the wheat crop.[270] Tenants struck work for about 30 days when ultimately an agreement was reached. According to the police, the agrarian unrest in this *tehsil* was instigated by the local Congress Committee, helped by the Communists and Socialists of the *Kisan* Committee.[271] The Cotton Growers Association was willing to discuss matters with the tenants and to meet their demands as far as possible but it refused to allow the Congress or any other outside body to act as an intermediary.[272] This gave rise to fresh problems. A great difficulty arose where tenant lessees succeeded in getting land which at that time was being cultivated by other tenants who had to be ejected because the lessees wanted to cultivate the land themselves.[273]

The process of finding a foothold among the peasants in

---

267. File No. 18/3/1938, Home Deptt.-Political, NAI : New Delhi.

268. *Ibid.*, Personal interview with Master Hari Singh (Chandigarh).

269. File Nos. 18/3/1938, 18/6/1938, Home Department-Political, NAI : New Delhi, Hari Singh, *'Punjab Wich Kirsani Laher' (Punjabi), Souvenir,* issued by the CPI, January : 1976.

270. Wadhawa Ram, 'Some Memoirs of Nili-Bar—*Banne-Utte-Adho-Adh',* (An article in *Punjabi*) published in a *Souvenir,* issued by the CPI, January : 1976. File No. 18/6/1938; Home Department-Political, NAI : New Delhi.

271. Home Department-Political, File No. 18/11/1938, NAI : New Delhi.

272. *Ibid.*

273. File No. 18/2/1939, 18/4/1939, Home Department-Political, NAI : New Delhi.

some of the villages of Multan and Montgomery began in January, 1938 and by the beginning of next year, the PKC was able to create some pockets of influence.[274] The peasants under the leadership of PKC leaders put up resistance when, number of times, armed attempts were made to eject them. A movement in Multan district started on April 12, 1939 when the colonisation officer sought the help of the police in ejecting the old peasants from certain plots. Sixteen tenants were arrested for obstruction. Despite all this, about a hundred *muzaras,* next day, entered the fields and began to plough them but they were dispersed with the help of police and 18 of them were also arrested. Congress leaders of some standing avoided any association with this agitation and they considered it an ill advised agitation.[275]

The agrarian movement of the peasants of the Lyallpur district which raised the demands for reduction of land revenue and water rates gained considerable momentum in July 1938, when the irrigation department remoulded the canal outlets. Six *jathas* varying in number from 60 to 550, aggregating in all to 15,000 marched from different places in the district to head-quarters, where a procession was taken out on June 10, 1938. It was alleged that the demonstrators numbered about forty thousand and that 90% of them were Sikhs.[276] The movement became more vigorous in the next month and many meetings were held in the villages.[277]

In the beginning of 1938, it was decided by 164 villages of Rajabaha area to start a boycott of canal waters in order to

274. File No. 18/3/1939, Home Department-Political, NAI : New Delhi. (For more detail see a Police Report given in thiis file).

275. File No. 18/4/1939, Home Department-Political, NAI : New Delhi; Wadhawa Ram 'Some Memoirs of Nili Bar—*Banne-Utte-Adho-Adh',* *Souvenir,* issued by the CPI, January : 1976, supported by Master Hari Singh-Personal meeting with the individual.

276. File No. 18/6/1939, Home Department-Political, NAI : New Delhi; Personal interview with Sardar Sohan Singh Josh.

277. File No. 18/7/1938, Home Department-Political, NAI : New Delhi; *Kirti Lehr,* July 3, 10, 1938.

compel the Government to increase the water supply.[278] Because of the dire necessity of water in summer, the boycott was to be ended on July 29, 1938. Socialists in the Amritsar *Bandobast* Committee toured the villages and advocated agitation over the remodelling of canal outlets, on the lines of the Lyallpur agitation.[279] It will not be out of place to cite some more instances of *Kisan morchas* and conferences here in regard with the Lyallpur *Kisan* agitation.

There had been series of meetings organised by the *Zamindar Sabha* in the Lyallpur district, cultminating in a *Zamindara* Conference on the 24th and 25th of June, 1932. The principal resolutions passed demanded; *(i)* reduction of land revenue by 60%; *(ii)* the realisation of land revenue on the basis of income-tax and *(iii)* the re-assessment of the Lyallpur district on the basis of the rates of agricultural produce during the last four year only.[280] Another *Zamindara* Conference was held on the 7th of July, 1932, A resolution was passed that *Zamindars* should not pay more than 50% of their land revenue.[281] A *Zamindara* Conference was held at a village in the Lyallpur district from 9th to 11th December, 1933, in regard to the resettlement of the Lower Bari Doab Canal.[282] Thus, there had been intense activity in rural central

278. *Kirti Lehr,* July 10, 1938, Nurpuri Chanan Singh, *The Great Morchas of Lahore and Harsa Chhina* (An Article in *Punjabi*) published in *Souvenir* issued by the CPI on January 26, 1976.

279. File No. 18/6/1938, Home Department-Political, NAI : New Delhi; (Rehmatullah, Khadam Hussain, Kulbir Singh, Ram Raksha, Sher Gulkhan and Kartar Singh were prominent workers of the PKC in this district).

280. File Nos. 18/5/1931, 18/6/1932 and 18/7/1932, Home Department-Political, NAI : New Delhi.

281. File Nos. June 4, 13, 18, 23, 25; November 24th, December, 13, 1931; File Nos. 18/10/1932, Home Department-Political, NAI : New Delhi. Wadhawa Ram, 'Some Memoirs of Nili Bar-*Banne-Utte-Adho-Adh, Souvenir,* issued by the CPI, January : 1976; *The Tribune,* Lahore, April 9, 24; May 1, 10, 20, 21, 23, 24, 26 & 29, 1931.

282. File No. 18/14/1933 and 18/2/1934, Home Deptt.-Poll., NAI : New Delhi.

Punjab districts and series of small meetings had been held by the District *Kisan* Committee in the Lyallpur district with a view to stirring up disaffection among the peasants against the system of land revenue and other cognate form of taxation. In the Montgomery district also, the Kisan Committee had been trying to exploit differences between the lessees and tenants.[283] It is important to note that in all forms of rural agitation, the chief agitators had been Communist Sikhs, many of them members of the *Ghadr* Party, trained in Moscow.[284]

In July 1938, *Kisan* processions and demonstrations at Amritsar had overshadowed all other forms of agrarian agitations. Leaders of *Kisan* Committees and *bandobast* brought out a poster stating that the Government planned an addition of 4 lacs per annum to the land revenue of the district, that the canal outlets of a number of villages in the Raya area had been reduced and that the peasants were groaning under the burden of *Malba, Chowkidara,* Chahi and local taxes.[285] The peasants who, in this province of scanty rainfall depended upon the supply of adequate water from canals, were threatened with utter ruin. Members of the *Bandobast* Committee and allied bodies decided to stage a big demonstration on these issues in July 1938, in the civil lines outside the canal and settlement offices. On July 20th, after a big peasant gathering in the Jallianwala Bagh, five hundred peasant volunteers under the leadership of S. Udham Singh, marched through the city to express their grievances before the public and to make them known to the Government.[286] When they defied Section 144, the police lathi charged to disperse them. Many received injuries and 144 prominent

283. File No. 18/8/1938, Home Deptt.-Political, NAI : New Delhi.

284. *Ibid.,* File No. 18/9/1938.

285. Home Department-Political, File No. 18/7/1938, NAI : New Delhi; The Tribune, Lahore, June 23, 1931, July 15, 1937.

286. *Ibid; Kirti Lehr,* July 31, 1938 (They also demanded action against water logging caused by the construction of canals) Vide *The Tribune,* Lahore, May 23, June 7, 1931; May 20, 1939; April 5, 1936, April 16, 1937.

workers were arrested.[287] A war council consisting of two members of the district *Bandobast* Committee (Akalis), two members of the *Kisan* Committee (Socialists) and one member of the Congress was formed to intensify the peasants struggle. It was decided to send out *Jathas* of 25 men every day to defy the order 144 Cr.P.C.[288] A huge meeting of the people declared support to the *Kisan* cause and condemned the repressive policy of the Sikandar Hyat Government.[289] Dr. Kitchlew assured the Kisan Committee of Congress support.[290] On 21st July, a *hartal* was observed in various *bazars* of Amritsar in sympathy with the victims of the police Lathi charge.[291]

A *Zamindara Sabha* had been formed in Amritsar district, but it had not yet given evidence of its intentions. Besides, the Ludhiana Akali *Jatha* was proposing to hold a series of meetings in October to protest against the Canal rates.[292] Similarly, the Punjab Provincial *Zamindara* League held meetings at Nankana Sahib on the 2nd and 3rd November, some two thousand persons attending on each day. Resolutions were passed demanding reduction in land revenue and water rates, the extirpation of bribery in the Irrigation Department, and relief in respect of those crops which had suffered severely from the heavy rains.[293] The Punjab National *Zamindar* League had organised various meetings in Amritsar district. The activities of the League appeared to have aroused the jealousy of the Local Communists who were contemplating the

287. *Kirti Lehr,* July 31, 1938 (about 20,000 peasants participated in the Jallianwala Bagh gathering); File No. 18/7/1938, Home Department-Political, NAI : New Delhi.

288. *National Front,* July 31, 1938.

289. *Ibid.,* August 7, 1938.

290. *Ibid.*

291. *Ibid.*

292. File No. 18/10/1933, Home Deptt.-Political, NAI : New Delhi.

293. File No. 18/13/1933, Home Deptt.-Political, NAI : New Delhi.

establishment of a *Kisan Qarza* League with the eventual object of preparing the peasants for refusal to pay taxes.[294]

Kirti Kisan agitation continued in Amritsar inspite of the prosecution under section 108 C.P.C., of some of its more extreme exponents, and was beginning to obtain a footing in the Sheikhupura and Gurdaspur districts.[295] In these and several other central districts there were now various forces at work the Congress trying to exert its influence by conducting enquiries into the condition of the agriculturist, the *Zamindar Sabha* calling itself the *Kisan Sabha* and only less extreme than the *Kirti Kisan Sabha* in that it repudiated Communism; the *Zamindar* League, also advocated extreme views and number of constitutional and semiloyalist bodies of agriculturists, held meetings to pass resolutions about their hard lot.[296] A series of rural meetings by the *Kirti Kisan* in the Amritsar district,[297] were organised. In fact, in Amritsar Socialists and Communists held almost daily meetings in some villages and rural propaganda was almost continuously carried on in the Batala *tehsil* of Gurdaspur and efforts to spread Communist views were made.[298] Akali Bandobast Committees had been busy, ostensibly agitating against the settlement of the district,[299] and remodelling of Canal outlets on the lines of the Lyallpur agitation.[300] The Akali *Bandobast* Committee had further decided to stage a demonstration on July 20th outside the Canal and Settlement Offices and the houses of the Revenue Minister and Deputy Commissioner. By July 20th, about 4,000 villagers had collected in Amritsar with a view to

294. File No. 18/2/1935, Home Deptt. Political, NAI : New Delhi.

295. File No. 18/V/1931, Home Deptt. Political, NAI : New Delhi.

296. File No. 18/V/1931, Home Deptt. Political, NAI : New Delhi.

297. File No. 18/VIIp 1931, Home Deptt. Political, NAI : New Delhi.

298. File No. 18/3/1939, File No. 94/2/1940 (1), Home Department,—Political, NAI : New Delhi.

299. File No. 18/6/1938 & 18/4/1939, Home Deptt.-Poll., NAI : New Delhi.

300. *Ibid.*, Sir Henry Craik-Governor of the Punjab, D.O. No. 83, F.L. No. 52a, July 8th, 1938, p. 115-a; NAI (Microfilm-Private Paper).

taking part in the demonstration.[301] However, the Government took every possible step to curb this agitation. It is noteworthy to state that the early months of the year 1941 had seen a revival of restlessness in labour circle in Amritsar. There had been some trouble among the workers in the Khewra salt mines in the Jhelum district. In brief, the various strikes which took place in various factories kept alive the peasants agitation in Amritsar area.[302]

Regarding the role of socialists in these agitations, a state police report concluded; 'There has been intense rural activity on Communist lines in the central Punjab district. *Kisan* Committee in the Lyallpur district with a view to stirring up disaffection among the peasants against the system of land revenue and other cogent form of taxation. In the Sikh villages affected by the recent agitation and by the peasants' propaganda, land revenue has not been collected with the usual promptitude. In the Montgomery district also, the *Kisan* Committee has been trying to exploit differences between the lessees and the tenants. In all forms of rural agitation, the chief agitators have been Communist Sikhs, many of them members of the *Ghadr* Party trained in the Communist Schools in Moscow.[303] However, it must be kept in mind here that what the state police refers to as Communist activity was basically the record of successful radical nationalist activity embodied in the activities of C.S.P. which of course included Communists in it.

From the above discussion, it become clear that the Peasants' agitation was not confined to any particular district or area. It was spreading all over the province. In Jullundur and Hoshiarpur districts, the propaganda tours of *Kirti Kisan Sabha* agitators were much less disturbing in their effects than

301. File No. 18/6/1938 & 18/4/1939, Home Deptt.-Poll., NAI : New Delhi.

302. File No. 18/1/1941; File No. 94/2/1940 (1), Home Deptt.-Political, NAI : New Delhi.

303. File No. 18/8/1938, Home Department-Political, NAI : New Delhi.

seemed probable.[304] Several prominent leaders, such as Sardar Vallabh-Bhai Patel were invited to attend a peasants' Conference which was to be held in June at Bilga in the Jullundur district. *Kirti Kisan* agitation continued in Amritsar region inspite of the prosecution under section 108, C.P.C. of some of its more extreme exponents and was beginning to obtain a footing in the Sheikhupura and Gurdaspur districts. *Zamindar* League also advocated extreme views and number of constitutional and semi-Loyalist bodies of agriculturists were holding meetings and passing resolutions about their hard lot.[305]

The Provincial *Kirti Kisan Sabha* held a Conference on November 12th at Nankana. All the active workers of the *Sabha* participated in it except Dasundha Singh and Santa Singh Gandiwind.[306] A red flag was hoisted, followed by speeches in which capitalists were accused of exploiting the poor. A Gurmukhi pamphlet, headed "Manifesto of the Kirti Kisan Party" was also distributed.[307] In the meeting some resolutions were passed emphasising the agrarian nature of their grievances. In 1933, a new *Zamindara Sabha* had been formed in order to take up the cause of the suffering peasantry. At this time, the Ludhiana district Akali *Jatha* decided to hold meetings in October to protest against the canal rates.[308]

Similarly, the Punjab Provincial *Zamindara* League held meetings at Nankana Sahib on the 2nd & 3rd November.

---

304. File No. 18/V/1931, Home Department-Political, NAI : New Delhi.
305. File No. 18/VII/1932, Home Department-Political, NAI : New Delhi.
306. Dasaunda Singh and Santa Singh were the most important leaders of the *Kirti Kisan Sabha,* who were recently accused of misappropriating funds. Vide. File No. 18/14/1932-Home Department-Political, NAI : New Delhi.
307. File No. 18/14/1932, Home Department-Political, NAI : New Delhi, (Such pamphlets were distributed from time to time such as *Gurmukhi* leaflet entitled "The Donkeys of the white Government", Vide. File No. 18/9/1932, Home Deptt.-Political, NAI : New Delhi.
308. File No. 18/10/1933, Home Department-Political, NAI : New Delhi.

Resolutions were passed demanding reduction in land revenue and water-rates, the extirpation of bribery in the irrigation Department etc.[309] At the same time, a *Zamindara* meeting was held at Raiwind in Lahore district on the 5th November. Another *Zamindara* conferences was arranged at Kot Radha Kishan, a town in the Lahore district, from 6th to 9th February, 1934. Resolutions were passed demanding the levy of land revenue on the basis of income tax and suggesting various methods of alleviating agricultural indebtedness.[310] A little later, in the same district, a *Gurmukhi* pamphlet advocating non-payment of land revenue was distributed in the rural area. In March 1934, the PKC organised an agitation in Lahore district against the land revenue increase under a new settlement. A demonstration was staged on 23rd March and a Satyagraha by batches of peasant volunteers defying Section 144 was initiated. This agitation was actively supported by the Congress and the Akalis.[311] This had been followed by a Congress bulletin of a similar nature, openly preaching of refusal to pay land revenue.[312]

In the beginning of 1935, the Punjab *Zamindara* League had organised various meetings in the Amritsar district. Resolutions passed at these meetings had been on the whole unobjectionable in that they aimed at the redressal of grievance by the Government rather than at direct action against the Government, which was a feature of the *Kisan Sabha* meetings of the year 1934. The activities of the League appeared to have caused apprehensions among the local Communists who were contemplating the establishment of a *Kisan Qarza* League with the eventual object of preparing the peasants for refusal to pay taxes.[313]

309. File No. 18/13/1933, Home Department-Political, NAI : New Delhi.

310. File No. 18/14/1933; File No. 18/2/1934, Home Department-Political, NAI : New Delhi.

311. File No. 18/12/1938, Home Department-Political, NAI : New Delhi.

312. File No. 18/3/1934 & 18/4/1934, Home Department-Political, NAI : New Delhi.

313. File No. 18/2/1938, Home Department-Political, NAI : New Delhi.

A *Kisan* Conference was also held at Anandpur in the Hoshiarpur district,[314] where leading Communists made speeches and attacked the agrarian policy of the Government. Another *Kisan* Conference was held at Kamalpura in the Ludhiana district on the 1st & 2nd January under the Presidentship of Master Kabul Singh. It attacked the atrocities of the Police on the peasants at the time of the collection of land revenue. Some members of the *Zamindara* Committee recently formed by non-officials to combat socialism and communism attended the Conference and one of the members made a speech, but did not get a good hearing. Sohan Singh Josh made a bitter attack on this speaker, pointing out that the Congress Governments had proved, at least in two ways, better than the Unionist Government, as the latter had banned the publication of *'Kirti'* and had been making efforts to suppress the peasants' agitation in the Punjab.[315]

Rural agitation was still on the increase, particularly in Amritsar, Montgomery and Lyallpur. The Socialist *Bandobast* Committee had arranged a propaganda tour of the villages and they were advocating agitation over the remodelling of canal outlets on the lines of the Lyallpur agitation.[316] At this time, the Congress made use of an annual fair at Abianwala in the Sheikhupura district to hold a few meetings. In these meetings, threats were made that the agitation over the remodelling of outlets would be extended to the whole district.[317]

In the month of November, 1938, the Jullundur Akali *Jatha*

314. File No. 18/1/1938, Home Department-Political, NAI : New Delhi.

315. File No. 18/1/1938, Home Department-Political, NAI : New Delhi, Personal interview with S. Sohan Singh Josh (Ajoy Bhawaṇ—New Delhi).

316. Nurpuri, Chanan Singh, *'The Great Morchas of Lahore & Harsa Chhina' Souvenir,* issued by the CPI, January : 1976; Wadhawa Ram (Some Memoirs of Nili Bar : *Banne-Utte-Adho-Adh' (Punjabi), Souvenir,* issued by the CPI-January : 1976; File No. 18/6/1938, Home Deptt.-Political, NAI : New Delhi; P.L.C.D., Vol. XXIV, 1934, 345.

317. File No. 18/6/1938, Home Department-Political, NAI : New Delhi; P.L.C.D., Vol. XXIV, 1934, 358-59.

arranged to demonstrate before the new Assembly Chamber in Lahore, ostensibly to ventilate the grievances of the peasants of the Doab. But the demonstration was forbidden. However, a deputation met the Premier and it was assured of the Governments' interest in peasants' affairs and of its desire to remove their grievances. The Jullundur demonstration took place on the 20th December. About fifteen thousand peasants took part.[318]

In the Hoshiarpur district there was friction of long standing between tenants and landlords. It was in January, 1939 that the tenants now declared their intention of not paying a single *Pie* to the landlords. At this time, in the Montgomery district, there occurred an incident on 15th February, 1939 and the workers of the *Kisan* Committee took advantage of it and gave rise to the idea that tenants who remained in a particular plot of land for over six years became entitled to proprietary rights.[319] To safeguard their own interests, a few landowners of village Suchan arranged for some of their tenants to exchange plots of land. The action by the landlords led the tenants to believe that the agitators were correct and so they refused to change their plots. The relations between the parties became strained and the landlords eventually attacked their tenants, the few policemen present being unable to prevent the clash. Ten tenants received injuries and one of them died later. The *Kisan* agitation got further momentum from it.[320]

The Sikh Akali Party had also been taking close interest in the peasants' demonstration. Most of the demonstrators had been Sikhs and the party feared that it might lose prestige if it did not lend a hand in the agitation. In the hope of taking over charges of the agitation, the Akalis offered to produce at

318. File No. 18/11/1938; 18/12/1938, Home Department-Political, NAI : New Delhi.

319. File No. 18/2/1939, Home Department-Political, NAI : New Delhi.

320. File No. 18/2/1939, Home Department-Political, NAI : New Delhi, Master Hari Singh, *'Punjab Wich Kirsani Laher (Punjabi), Souvenir,* issued by the CPI, January : 1976.

least five hundred persons to court arrest.[321] The Lahore district *Kisan* Committee resented the interference of other bodies because it too did not wish to lose the doubtful prestige that attached to the leadership in such a demonstration.[322] However, a few of the leaders of the *Kisan Fauj,* recently organised by the Akali Party, sought and were granted an interview by the Premier. He explained the details of the Lahore settlement scheme to them. But, there was still a certain amount of unrest among the tenants and *Kisan* Conference was held in that region to demonstrate their grievances.[323]

A new development occurred in the Kasur Sub-division of the Lahore district and the Dipalpur *tehsil* of Montgomery. A committee was formed to instigate peasants to refuse canal water as a protest against the enhancement of revenue under the new settlement in Lahore and against the refusal of the Government to accept the familiar socialist demands which included reduction of the revenue and water rates.[324] The *Kisans* also decided to continue the civil-disobedience until their demands were met.[325] The peasants' agitation had also spread to the Ferozpur district where a Water Rate Reduction Committee had been formed. Forty outlets had been closed by the agitators and their dupes.[326]

The running of the administration in Lahore had been taken over by the Provincial *Kisan* Committee and volunteers had been summoned from other districts. Groups of *Kisans* had left the Ambala, Ferozpur and Jullundur districts, and on their way to Lahore they did propaganda work in villages. In brief,

---

321. File No. 18/4/1939, Home Department-Political, NAI : New Delhi.
322. *Ibid.*
323. File No. 18/4/1939, Home Department-Political, NAI : New Delhi.
324. *Ibid.*
325. *Ibid.*
326. *Ibid.*

the agitation in Lahore, Montgomery and Ferozpur to get peasants to refuse canal water had made much headway.[327]

Because of the increase in assessment rates, the majority of the farmers in Muzaffargarh district refused to accept water from the new Haveli project. Stoppages and delays in the same canal system also caused some dis-satisfaction in the Multan district.[328] Besides, the Provincial *Kisan* Committee decided to organise a series of propaganda meetings in the central Punjab districts. At this time, the old standing trouble between landlords and tenants in the Una *tehsil* in the Hoshiarpur district gave rise to the peasants' agitation, an agitation that was designed to ventilate the grievances of the peasants of this district.[329]

The Punjab *Kisan* Committee had been formed in March, 1937 in pursuance of a decision reached at Faizpur during the session of the INC by the All India *Kisan* Committee to which it had since been affiliated. In 1938, it claimed to have atleast on paper, membership of 75,000. Its objects were briefly :

> Complete freedom from economic exploitation and full economic power for the peasants and workers.[330]

The Working Committee represented all bodies wth Communist leanings, the Congress Socialist Party, the *Desh Bhagat Qaid Parwar Sehaik* Committee, *Riyasti Paraja Mandal,* the Radical League and the Institute of Agrarian Reform. The central Punjab and colony districts had regularly constituted *Kisan* Committee between which and the Punjab *Kisan* Committee at Amritsar,[331] there was a close liaison.

---

327. File No. 18/5/1939-Home Department-Political, NAI : New Delhi; Master Hari Singh, *'Punjab Wich Kirsani Laher' (Panjabi) Souvenir,* issued by the CPI, January : 1976; Nurpuri, Chanan Singh, *The Great Morchas of Lahore and Harsa Chhina, Souvenir,* issued by CPI, January : 1976.
328. File No. 18/5/1939, Home Department-Political, NAI : New Delhi.
329. File No. 18/6/1939, Home Department-Political, NAI : New Delhi.
330. File No. 25/1924-June, Home Deptt.-Political, NAI : New Delhi.
331. File No. 18/9/1939, Home Department-Political, NAI : New Delhi.

Thus, the various Political associations exhorted the poor peasants to rise up against injustice and exploitation. District *Kisan* Conferences and local fairs were made the occasions for disseminating communist and revolutionary ideas. There had been a strong current in evidence at *Kisan* meetings, of anti-British feeling, opposition to war and enlistment in the army and condemnation of the Unionist Party. The benefits to the peasantry in general of the agrarian policy of the Unionist Party might in time restrict the growing influence of the Punjab *Kisan* Committee, but the irresponsible nature of its leaders and organisers at present held out little hope of its activities becoming either useful or even reasonable.[332]

Despite all this, the Punjab *Kisan* Committee tried to organise a volunteer corps in every district where a Committee existed and in conjunction with the Congress Socialist Party arranged a *Kisan* provincial delegates' Conference at Lyallpur. It had also given support to the Ferozpur district *Kisan* Committee in their agitation. The Punjab Congress Socialist Party also instigated the Ferozpur district *Kisan* Committee to defy an order issued by the State authorities, forbidding processions and meetings in the state.[333]

In the Montgomery district, there had been considerable activity and efforts were being made to make a projected *Kisan* Conference and to disturb relations between *Zamindars* and tenants. In the Ludhiana district, the Institute of Agrarian Reform had been holding *Kisan* Schools to propagate socialism. These schools represented a studied attempt to train rural Communist propagandists, and it was probable that their number would increase soon.[334]

After studying the activity of the *Kisan* Committee and the history of the *Kisan morchas,* demonstrations, Conferences etc., one cannot deny the fact that the peasants waged a long struggle against exploitation and oppression. Almost all the

332. File No. 18/9/1939, Home Department-Political, NAI : New Delhi.

333. File No. 18/9/1939, Home Department-Political, NAI : New Delhi.

334. *Ibid.*

political parties and groups, big and small, tried to involve the peasantry in the independence struggle. Undoubtedly, the peasants' struggle was a part and parcel of the anti-imperialist struggle since the beginning of the 20th century. The peasant movement succeeded in acquiring a wide social support in central Punjab by taking up demands which affected wide sections of the rural population.[335] The extent of involvement of different sections of the peasantry in action programme of different political parties is an issue which we have discussed in more detail in chapter V and the concluding chapter.

335. *Ibid.*, Wadhawa Ram, 'Some Memoirs of Nili Bar : *Banne-Utte-Adho-Adh', Souvenir,* issued by the CPI, January : 1976; Nurpuri, Chanan Singh, *'The Great Morchas of Lahore and Harsa Chhina,* Souvenir, issued by the CPI, January : 1976; Master Hari Singh, *'Punjab Wich Kirsani Laher' (Punjabi), Souvenir,* issued by CPI, January : 1976.

3

Factors Leading to Agrarian Unrest in the East Punjab States

After Gandhi's emergence on the political horizon of India much enthusiasm was evinced by the Indian masses all over the country for the struggle for national independence. Although the main centre of the Indian National Congress which had been directing the Nationalist struggle was confined to what was known as British India, the people of the Indian States did not lag behind. They also contributed towards the achievement of this goal. In the states, the struggle was, however, two-fold and more complex. In the states the rulers were autocratic and they had denied even those elementary rights which the citizens of British India as a rule enjoyed. The struggle in the East Punjab States was against autocratic princely as much as against British imperial power. As far as the struggle in the Punjab native states is concerned, it was the product of internal and external factors which are discussed in Section I of this chapter. A brief history of the Punjab *Riyasti Praja Mandal* is cited in the second section. However in Chapter V, a detailed account of the peasants' movement is given.

If we take the country as a whole in respect of internal developments, there are great variations among the native states of India. While some like Baroda and Mysore had made remarkable progress in the fields of industry and education, others like Patiala, Hyderabad and Bahawalpur lagged behind.[1] Historical factors and the economic and administrative policy of the Government in each state had bearing on the political attitudes and movements associated with it. Let us now examine the situation in the East Punjab States.

Since 1809, after the treaty of Amritsar signed between the British and the Maharja Ranjit Singh, the relations of these states with the British continued to be friendly, and he unbroken record of loyal and faithful service reached its zenith in 1914 when the states mobilised their total resources in support of the war effort. Their contribution in cash and material was 1.2 crore rupees or a sum nearing its total revenue for a whole year. More than 28 thousand recruits were supplied by the *Phulkian* States merely which gave a staggering proportion of one out of every ten male persons of the fighting age.[2] But the Punjab came to be very harshly treated during war and harsh methods were applied by the British bureaucrats in the matter of conscription and forcible realization of war funds.[3]

The Government of the state (Patiala) was not a popular

---

1. Home Department, File No. 18/6/1939-Political, NAI : New Delhi; The *National* (Lahore), 13th April, 1923; *Reports on the Native Newspapers Panjabi :* 1923, 267; File No. G-35 AICC (A letter from Mr. R.S. Azad to Mahatma Gandhi), 3.
2. *Some Confidential Papers of the Akali Movement*—Ganda Singh (ed.), Amritsar : *Sikh Itihas Research Board,* S.G.P.C., 1965, 175-89. (The services which the Malerkotla rendered to Great Britain during the Great War can never be forgotten. From 1914 to the last days of the war this force was constantly on active service and suffered heavy casualties which were made good by reinforcement from the state. The total number of subjects who served during the war was over 31 per cement of the eligible male population, surpassed only by two British districts). Vide. File No. 32 AICC (Indian States and Round Table Conference), NMML, Teen Murti, New Delhi.
3. File No. 32, AICC, NMML, Teen Murti, New Delhi; Ramesh Walia, *A Study of the Praja Mandal Movement in the East Punjab States,* Panjabi University, Publication Patiala : 1974, 56.

and responsible one.[4] The personal style of functioning of the Rulers and the concentration of the authority in a single individual or at best a clique made decision-making either too protracted or too rough and ready and abrupt a process. Again, the administration in most of the states lacked the bureaucratic efficiency of the Government in British India, allowing situations to reach a crisis point much oftener than in the latter. There were areas of Mohindergarh, Bawal and Dadri possessed by Patiala, Nabha and Jind respectively bordering on united Provinces, Rajasthan and Delhi, where people as well as the lower officials were subject to harassment from the Palace administration. The farmers living in these areas were subjected to an arbitrary and oppressive administrative machiner of the Punjab States.[5]

While the Haryana and Hilly areas were predominantly Hindu with a sizeable number of Muslims, they had practically no Sikh population except some men in the Government service.[6] These states were, on the other hand, mainly inhabited by Sikhs, which was a matter of special significance to these states. Sikhs were generally agriculturists and they

4. File No. 60, State Proceedings of the second Conference of the *Punjab Riyasti Praja Mandal* held at Ludhiana on 11, 12 and 13 October, 1930, (For further detail see File No. G-35, AICC (Long unheeded and unbearable *Zulum* by the Maharaja Patiala); Basta No. 13, Proceedings of the 4th Patiala Conference held at village Tungwali, P.S., Nathana, District Ferozpur; Serial No. 595, Case No. 485/13 of 1929; Serial No. 138, File No. 25 of 1938, *Records of the Kalsia State*; Punjab State Archives, Basta No. 18, Case No. 224 of 1928.

5. File No. G-35 (A letter from Mr. R.S. Azad to Mahatma Ji dated 25th September, 1938); Ramesh Walia, *A Study of the Praja Mandal Movement in the East Punjab States, Patiala;1974,* 56; Handa, R.L., *History of Freedom Struggle in Princely States,* Central News Agency : Delhi, 1968, 138-39; File No. 565/C of 1939-PSA; Patiala; Basta No. 179, Case No. 133/C (Welcome address made by Harnam Singh of Dharmgarh—Kisan Conference held at Village Chau near Mansa); Serial No. 138, File No. 25 of 1938—*Kalsia State Records*; Case No. 377/C of 1930; PSA : Patiala.

6. Census Reports of Patiala State : 1931 (Printed at Civil and Military Gazette Limited : Lahore).

had a larges share of the jobs in the armed forces. Sikhs were also dominating among the landed aristocracy particularly in the states of Patiala, Nabha, Kalsia and Faridkot.

To all intents and purposes, the economy of these states represented all that was backward and conservative in India as a whole. Practically no effort was made to assess and evaluate the mineral resources or to set up any industry. A vast majority of the population lived in villages. According to the 1931 census, only 10.4% of the total population in Patiala state lived in urban areas.[7] Agriculture was the main-star of the people. Out of a population of 16,26,520, more than 10 lakhs directly depended on agriculture. A large majority of about 2.5 lakhs of artisans and about a lakh of traders also indirectly depended on it.[8] The Government was, however, callous and careless and did absolutely nothing for the progress of agriculture; while in the Punjab the situation was changing fast with the colonisation of vast areas in the Bari-Doab districts, provision of relief against rural indebtedness, popularisation of better methods of cultivation and consolidation of holdings; in the states agriculture continued suffering under the dead weight of an unchanging exploitative system. But for the provision of certain irrigational facilities which too came as a byproduct of the development of the canals system in British Punjab the princes did nothing for ameliorating the lot of the peasants.[9]

The rulers and their courtiers were concerned only with the revenue of the states and the chief criterion of efficiency of an administrator was the state of revenues under his control.

7. *Ibid.*

8. *Ibid.*

9. Handa, R.L., History of Freedom Struggle in Princely States, Delhi, 1968, 271; Nehru, Jawaharlal, *An Autobiography*, p 13; Ramesh Walia, A Study of the Praja Mandal Movement in the East Punjab States, Patiala : 1974, 58; File No. 60-Prime Minister Office files, PSA : Patiala; Personal interview with Master Hari Singh, Communist Office, Chandigarh on December 19th & 20th, 1978, File No. 139, AISPC—Papers : Part I; *Partap* (Lahore), Jine 26th, 1921; Report on the Native Newspapers, 1921, 69, NAI : New Delhi.

The states existed for the pleasures of the princes. The Kapurthala *Maharaja* for example, had a reputation of spending most of his time abroad and was rarely available in the his own state.[10] Every thing was done to satisfy the whims of the individual ruler. The people at large suffered utter neglect. A glance at the budget of these states is industructive. Let us take for instance, the situation in Patiala. The first administration report was published in 1920-21 which showed an annual income of Rs. 1.35 crores which continued rising despite the steep fall in the prices of agriculture produce, till it stood at Rs. 1.59 crores in 1929-30. Out of this, commerce and industry contributed a meagre sum of Rs. 1 lakh. The report for 1932-35 admitted the effect of the abnormal fall in the prices of agricultural produce on the agriculturists, but did not suggest any relief measures. Instead it treated the whole matter as simple law and order problem which had led to decoities and other crimes. According to the official report, "political unrest, economic depression and heavy unemployment combined to promote the spirit of lawlessness and various gangs of dacoits sprang up.[11] The Revenue Department with the help of police[12] on the other hand was resorting to more and more coercive measures in realizing the land revenue. The following figures speak for themselves.[13]

10. The *Liberal*, 22nd June, 1921; *Bande Mataram*, 28th June, 1921; Dewan Raj Kumar, *Modern Kapurthala and Its Maker*, A Kapurthala State Government Publication; For more details see Fortnightly reports of the year 1921 to 1932, Home Department-Political, NAI : New Delhi.

11. Patiala State Administration Report for 1932, PSA : Patiala, Sr. No. 138, File No. 25 of 1938, State Kalsia, PSA : Patiala.

12. Memorandum submitted by the members of the Patiala War Council, Patiala, Patiala State Records : Prime Minister's Office, File No. 565/ C-1939 (*Biswedar Hakumat De Namuna*—an article in Panjabi); Dewan's letter dated 20th November, 1938, Kalsia State to Records, File No. 164; File No. 182; Ramesh Walia, A Study of the Praja Mandal Movement in the East Punjab States Patiala, 1974, 69.

13. Patiala State Administration Report for 1929-30 and 1932-33 Patiala (Reference Section : Central Library, Patiala).

	1929-30	1932-33
No. of Writ Demands or Dastaks :	870	1250
Warrants and Arrests issue :	117	479
Cases of imprisonment :	3	118

While the state was extracting every penny due from the peasant, it was doing absolutely nothing for him. No *taccavi* advances were granted in the years 1929-30 and 1932-33. The outstanding of the old *taccavi* at the beginning of the year was Rs. 2158.[14] Similarly, the disposal of the cases for compensation for land acquired by the state had been much in arrears. There was a balance of 201 cases of the previous year and fifty new cases were instituted in the year report. There was thus a total of 251 cases and seven out of these had been finally settled.[15] There were only 7 co-operative societies working in the Patiala State, four of them were agricultural and three non-agricultural. There total working capital was just Rs. 75,000/-.

The report of 1920-21 admitted that no new road had been built since 1907-08. There could be no expansion of irrigational facilities because of the stringency of funds caused by the financial equilibrium having been seriously disturbed during the first world war. In 1924, even Nabha town had no metalled roads.[16] About any out being applied to the privy-purse of the prince or any economy affected in his lavish expenses, the reports are completely silent.

The budgetary policies, heavily loaded in favour of the ruler, attached little importance to the welfare of the people and the expenditure on public welfare agencies was negligible.

14. *Ibid.*

15. Typed copy of an article by Singh, G.B. of Nabha, Vide Library, S.G.P.C., Amritsar; Home Department, File No. 79/1931-Political, 19, NAI, New Delhi; Sr. No. 1546, Prime Minister's office Files, PSA : Patiala.

16. Patiala State Administration Report for 1920-21, PSA : Patiala : Vaid, Chhajju Mal, *'Pepsu Ch. Muzarian Da Ghal Ten Communist Party'* (in Panjabi), *Souvenir,* issued by the Communist Party in January, 1976.

It was, therefore, quite natural for any political movement to demand restrictions on the privy-purses and to have more funds shifted to the construction of roads, hospitals and schools in the countryside.[17]

Another important aspect of these policies was that they were not at all conducive to increase in agricultural production or reduction of rural indebtedness.[18] Though Banking institutions made their appearance quite early, yet it was more or less a Government department and its main function was to provide short term credit grain dealers and other traders. It did nothing practically for the economic advancement of the state. To rural co-operative Societies, for example, the bank advanced a sum of Rs. 20.8 thousand in the year 1926-27, in Patiala state. Moreover, the bank was merely co-operative in name; actually it was a joint stock concern with effective control in the hands of the Government. Consequently, peasantry in the state was not benefited by this institution at all.[19]

All the state services were monopolised by the landed artistocracy or the urban Hindu traders and immigrants from

17. File No. 138, Part-I, AISPC-Papers, NMML, New Delhi. 42.2% was being spent on administration and army and just 2.7% on education and 2.5% on medical facilities in Patiala State. The same was true of Kapurthala and Faridkot. In Faridkot in 1910-11, the state spent 5 lakhs out of 12 lakhs on the ruler's marriage. Vide, Joginder Dayal, *'Riyasti Lokan Da Ghal Ten Communist'*, Souvenir issued on 26th January, 1976 by the CPI; Handa, R.L., *History of Freedom Struggle in Princely States*, Delhi : 1968, 70; Ramesh Walia, *A Study of the Praja Mandal Movement in the East Punjab States*, Patiala : 1974; For more details about the expenses of the rules see "India Princes as the People see Them".
18. File No. 138, Part-I, AISC-Papers, NMML, New Delhi; Ramesh Walia, *A Study of the Praja Mandal Movement in the East Punjab States*, Patiala : 1974, 63; Vaid, Chhajju Mal, 'Tenant Struggle in Pepsu Area', *Souvenir*, issued on the eve of 21st National Conference, All India *Kisan Sabha*, Bhatinda : 1973; Sr. No. 4756, Case No. 1025 of 1892 Sambat/611-C PSA : Patiala : Basta No. 51, File No. 565/C and 1017/C, PSA : Patiala.
19. Ramesh Walia, *A Study of the Praja Mandal Movement in the East Punjab States*, Patiala : 1974, 67-68.

British India. Only the army had a handful of jobs to provide to the common village folk. It was purely through the favour of the prince or his ministers that one could get a job or retain it. Corruption was rampant and in some states, posts were openly auctioned.[20] Efforts were made to recruit only such persons as were close relatives or co-religionists of the state officials or favourites of the *Raja*. An aggrieved employee could hardly secure justice if he had no influence over some *Ahalkar*.[21]

With the introduction of Minto-Morley reforms in 1909 a strong people's movement represented by the INC, backed the cause of legislative assemblies in British India. The steadily growing political consciousness of the people never allowed the British rulers to retracts a step once it had been taken, but in the states, the people were deprived of such assemblies, reforms and political awareness.[22] Moreover, the local-self Government institutions which became in British Punjab an effective instrument for the spread of political ideas and provided training facilities for budding leaders, did not play any such role in the states. Another agency which could have played a positive role in imparting consciousness amongst the people was the village school, but educationally the states were very backward. In 1933, Patiala, the biggest of the east Punjab

20. Personal meeting with Giant Kartar Singh of Village Chak, Malerkotla : January 15-16, 1976; Interview with Sewa Singh Bapla, Malerkotla : January 17-18, 1976; Interview with Ishar Singh Majhail at Patiala on July 20-21 1976; Basta No. 20, Case No. 485, PSA : Patiala.

21. Puri, Sahib Chand, *Ahlkari Sazshen*, Phulkian Samachar Publication : Patiala. Every minister had his own clique and there were plote and country plots to gain access at the ruler. Vide. Diwan Jermani Dass, Maharaja *(A number of interesting incidents have been related by the authors of* Ahlkari Sazshen.)

22. The Kapurthala State Assembly, for instance, never met after 1931 as some of the members were putting embarrassing questions to the Ministers. Vide. Sr. No. 639, His Highness Government : Patiala, Home Ministry Case No. 347 of 1930/1987, PSA : Patiala (See this file also for the detailed information regarding the denial of elementary political rights. This view is also supported by Master Hari Singh- Personal meeting at Chandigarh.

States, was sending 1.24 students to school per one hundred of population as against 4.44% in the Punjab.[23] It was no wonder then that the average literacy rate in the states was 4.1 per cent as compared to the average rate of 6.2 per cent in the neighbouring districts of Ludhiana, Hoshiarpur, Jullundur, Ferozepur and Ambala.[24] Further the states followed a policy of insulating their people from the influence of the press in British Indian territory. Undesirable printed matter was not allowed entry and political literature was often confiscated.[25]

Before tracing the history of the relationship between the tenants and *Biswedars* in the Phulkian States, which in the history of exploitation of the tillers of the soil by a group of people, who happened to be favourites of the rulers of these states, it would be relevant to define the terms of tenant and *Biswedar.* Tenant means a person who holds land under another person and, but for a special contract, is liable to pay rent for that land. The *Biswedar* (the local term for landlord) lay between these tenants and the state with his vague rights of middlemanship. He was essentially more for a ruler for the purpose of collection of the state revenue and for supporting him in all other matters. In other words, the *Biswedar* who with the local *Ahlkar,* wielded the biggest stick, is the direct ancestor of the present landlord.

The origin of the problem dates back to at least the First Regular Settlement of Patiala made in the first decade of the

---

23. Basta No. 50, File No. 565/C—Prime Minister's Office Files, PSA : Patiala; Vaid, Chhajju Mal, 'Tenants' Struggle in Pepsu Area', *Souvenir* issued on the eve 21st National Conference, All India *Kisan Sabha,* Bhatinda; 1973; Ramesh Wala, *A Study of the Praja Mandal Movement in the East Punjab States, Patiala :* 1974, 72.

24. The literary rate have been derived from the 1931 Census figures. For more details see Basta No. 22, Case No. 66 of 1931/1988-Patiala Sate Records, Prime Minister's office, PSA : Patala.

25. For detail see a report of the District Magistrate of Faridkot State, Confidential diaries of the district of Magistrate No. 2920-21, Faridkot State Records File No. 23, PSA : Patiala; Pattabhai Sitaramaya, (*History of the Indian National Congress,* Vol. I, 10).

20th century.[26] It, however, claims that the dispute over proprietory right existed prior to the commencement of Settlement operations.[27] It seems that when the Biswedars who earlier had some *Mafi* claims or revenue collecting rights, due to their growing influence in the administration, proprietory status, the tendency was for the courts to grant them this status and relegate the entire body of cultivating proprietors to the position of occupancy tenants.[28] But the effect of the Settlement, too, was to create causes for dispute where non-existed before, and to aggravate ill-feeling where they did exist.[29] And, it is interesting to note that the Settlement Commissioner was aware of this fact.[30] Thus far from remedying the inequitable court decisions, the Settlement merely accepted and gave further sanction to the status-granting full proprietory status to *Biswedars;* and the not very great benefit of the Punjab Tenancy Act of 1885 to the tenants.[31]

With the passage of time, the exploitation of the tenants grow. Whereas, in the adjoining British territory, there were the peasants, who enjoyed ownership of land which they cultivated. This made the tenants of the Phulkian States strive for a recognition of better status, which would entitle them to

26. AISPC-Papers, File No. 133A, 1945-48; Folio, 253-257-Patiala State Records, Prime Minister's Office File No. 556, 1929-30.

27. Final Report of the Settlement of the Patiala State A.D. 1909-8 (hereafter Settlement Report), 26. "The relations between *Biswedars* and *Muzaras* were strained and bitter, long before the settlement commenced". Vide. *Ibid.*, 26.

28. The tendency was for the small proprietors, who happened to be share holders in a village in which some one connected with the official class was an assigen of revenue or the owner of a predominant interest therein, to become occupancy the level of mere tenants-at-will, *Ibid.*, 26.

29. Settlement Report, 26-27.

30. *Ibid.*, 27.

31. *Ibid.*, 28 (This Report also pointed out that "the great majority of the 17,706 cases, which have been fought in the appellate courts of the Settlement, have been concerned with tenants' rights and tenants' liabilities").

own their land and pay revenue direct to the state and thus get rid of the *Biswedars,* whose dominance was imposed on the cultivating community, by the will of the ruler. It was indeed ironical that a tenant, after hard toil of the whole day, could not make both ends meet.[32] He had to depend upon the village moneylender to take loan from him for emergency needs. The rate of interest was so high that generation after generation, he could not get rid of the money once taken on loan and the moneylender always sacked their blood.[33]

The peasantry had been suffering ruthless repression and hardships at the hands of the *Biswedars.*[34] During the second half of the 19th century the land was under the cultivation of occupancy-tenants known as *Muzara Murusi.*[35] As the states of Patiala, Nabha and Jind were not under the direct control of the British Government, the problem of the land was different from the one in the other parts of India. The rulers enjoyed a free hand in regard to the distribution of land and they always preferred to give the lands to their own proteges. So the landlords got the land from the state. When the land was allotted to the *biswedars* they were not in a position to cultivate whole of the land. So they had to get help from the tenants who cultivated the land. The *Biswedar* was to take profit which was due to him.[36]

32. File No. 2193, PSA : Patiala, 39; Poster published in October, 1938 and Janga Singh's pamphlet *'Dukhee Janta Ka Ubaal'*, Ferozpur City, Amrit Electric Press : 1939.

33. File No. 138, Part-I, ASPC-Papers, NMMI, New Delhi; Salana Sahib Singh, *Aaop Biti* (Panjabi), 134; File No. 2193; File No. 135 of 1931- Prime Minister's Office Files, PSA : Patiala.

34. Patiala State tenants File No. 6, PSA : Patiala, 151; File No. 565/C-Basta No. 50-Prime Minister's Office Record; AISPC-Papers, File No. 138, NMML, New Delhi; Gieni Kehar Singh, *Praja Malekotla Di Dard Kahani,* Printed and published by Joga, Jagir Singh, Amritsar; *Desh Dard Press,* introduction, 1,2.

35. Rajomajra Equity Committee Report, PSA : Patiala, Wala, Ramesh, *A Study of the Praja Mandal Movement in the East Punjab States,* (Ph.D. Thesis), Panjabi University, Patiala : 1974, 58.

36. Patiala State Administration Report for the year 1929-30, PSA : Patiala; Patiala State Records, Prime Minister's Office File No. 135, 54-55.

There was another type of *Biswedars* also. They were from the persons who were playing the role of middlemen between the Government and the peasantry. They collected the land revenue like *batai* from the peasants and deposited it with the Government. The peasantry was exploited by these middlemen.[37] With the passage of time, the absentee landlords began to dominate and according to the law prevailing at that time in the state, the land belonged to the absentee landlord, but not to the occupancy tenant.[38] The latter had to pay share of the crop *(batai)* at every harvest to the former. If the tenant failed to pay the *batai* he could be evicted out of holdings. The occupancy tenants who had been attached to the land for many generations were resentful of their position as such. The fact was that many of them were the landlords and real proprietors, but had been deprived of their rights by the cunning landlords at the time of land settlement of 1904.[39]

In 1901-03, through quinquennial land settlement the *Biswedari* system was further strengthened.[40] The *Muzaras* were further differentiated into occupancy tenants and tenants-at-will. Moreover in the same village some land was recorded as *Maurusi* and some *gair-maurusi*.[41] In this land settlement, the occupancy-tenants even when they had enough documentary evidence in their possession in support of their claim as proprietors, failed to establish their rights. The occupancy tenant deemed himself the proprietor and protested against all inequalities. Hence, there arose a struggle against the cruel *biswedari* system. The occupancy tenants now wanted to get rid of the vicious system of landlordism.[42] But the

37. Patiala State Records, Prime Minister's Office File No. 578, PSA : Patiala; Also File No. 595.

38. Patiala State Administration Report for the year 1924-25, PSA : Patiala.

39. Popham Young, Settlement Report, 1904, 26-28.

40. Vaid, Chhajju Mal, *Pepsu Muzarian De Ghol Ten Communist Party* (An article in Punjabi), published in a *Souvenir*, issued by the C.P.I. On January 26, 1976, 73).

41. Patiala State Administration Report for the year 1904-05, PSA : Patiala; Popham Young, Settlement Report, 1904, 29.

42. Patiala State Records, Prime Minister's Office File No. 710, PSA : Patiala; Interview with Sardar Hari Singh, Chandigarh.

tenants of Patiala state were very much conscious of their rights to the land. They made many attempts to get rid of the yoke of the absentee landlord.

Forced by the agitation and clamour for reform, the state appointed an official commission on 24th July, 1939, to enquire into the respective position of the tenants and the landlords on the basis of evidence and to suggest reforms. The Commission completed its report in 1942.[43] But the Report never saw the light of the day as it had hinted at certain reforms in favour of the peasants.[44] Thus the position of the tenants remained the same.

Further, it was not as if their position as occupancy tenants was specially privileged and secure, since all they got was fixity of tenure, but no protection against rack-renting. The Settlement Report noted that "the capacity of the tenants to resist extortion, and maintain their hold on lands which they had brought under cultivation, rested upon their own strength or obstinacy and upon the weakness or the good feeling of their landlords, rather than upon any legal basis", (emphasis added).[45] The landlords had also succeeded in getting a *'Hidayat'* in 1872 making it incumbent upon all occupancy tenants to pay rent in kind.[46] Besides, the amount of *Batai* or share rent was decided by the *Kankut* system, which meant that standing crops were assessed before each harvest by a *Kankut* Committee consisting of State functionaries and the amount to be given to the *Biswedars* fixed accordingly.[47] The

43. Patiala State Records, File No. 2177, PSA : Patiala.

44. Patiala State Records, File No. 100, *Patiala Union Raj Aur Navin Lehran* (Poster in Panjabi), PSA : Patiala.

45. *Settlement Report*, 27-29.

46. *Ibid.*, A similar shift from cash to kind rents occurred in the British held Punjab as well. In a period of rising prices, which came in the way of commercialisation, landlords wherever they could, insisted on a share of the produce as rent as this secured to them an automatic increase in rents. Calvert, H., *Wealth and Welfare of the Punjab*, 1925, 198.

47. AISPC-Papers, File No. 139, Part-I, 1937-42, Folio-295-303.

grievances of the *Muzaras* of roughly 800 *Biswedari* villages (comprising about 1/6th of the total number in the state), therefore, related to three major issues : *(a)* the loss of proprietory right and reduction in their position in the tenurial structure; *(b)* the consequential increase in their obligations to the *Biswedars;* and *(c)* the Kankut system, in which over assessment of Crop was a constant cause of complaint coupled with the uncertainty of the exact amount to be paid to each harvest. The occupancy-tenants, as a result, felt greatly aggrieved and agitated against the callousness of the state. The only means left with them was to refuse the share of the crops *i.e., batai* to the *biswedars.* They demanded abolition of the *biswedari* system, meaning thereby that the status of these occupancy tenants must be raised to the level of proprietors. It was reliably reported that the state had promised to crush the tenants and all those who supported them.[48] Even the police force was used to take *batai* from the tenants.

The state share in the produce varied in different *parganas.* It was mostly 1/3rd, but 1/4th and 2/5th was also taken. There were a large number of extra dues called *abwabs.*[49] A cash rate per *bigha* called *Zabti* was charged on crops that could not easily be divided. The state share of the grain was realised either by actually dividing the produce or by appraisement,[50] *Kankut, Kan* or *Kachh Batai* was, with rare exceptions, usually resorted to in *rabi,* and appraisement, as a rule in *Kharif.* The officials who made the *batai* were called *Batwas* and those who made the appraisments were known as *Kachhus.*[51] In brief, there was no definite pronouncement of any theory of

48. Patiala State Records, File No. 6133, PSA : Patiala.

49. Popham Young, *Settlement Report of 1904;* Vaid, Chhajju Mal, Pepsu *Muzarian De Ghal Ten Communist Party* (An article in Panjabi) published in a *Souvenir,* issued by the C.P.I. on January 26, 1976, 73.

50. Popham Young, *Settlement Report of 1904;* Vaid, Chhajju Mal, *Pepsu Muzarian De Ghal Ten Communist Party* (An article in Punjabi) published in a *Souvenir,* issued by the C.P.I. on January 26, 1976, 73.

51. Patiala State Records, Prime Minister's office File No. 655; Young, Popham, *Settlement Report of 1904;* Basta No. 50, File No. 565/C (Confidential weekly report), PSA : Patiala.

land revenue assessment which limited the state demand to share of the landlords profits.[52] Under the system then prevailing in the *Phulkian* states, the tenants could never expect a better deal at the hands or either the state officials or the *biswedars* who could use all sorts of repressive measure to extract from the peasants whatever they wanted, with means not always fair. The poor tenants could lodge no protest against their high handedness and had to resign themselves to their lot. The peasants who constituted 70% of the population were still downtrodden and they groaned under the yoke of the *biswedars.* Their produce was taken by the *biswedars* and the state officials. Majority of the peasants had either no land or their own or the holdings they had were very small. The landowner peasants were at the mercy of the *biswedars.* Any movement aiming at the liberation of the peasants from the yoke of the *biswedars* or for the reduction of the land taxes was suppressed by the Government with iron hand.[53]

Because of the special concessions which the *biswedars* received at the hands of the state authority, they were like feudal lords of the medieval European Countries. They had plenty of lands at their disposal and were not to bother about the cultivation of the land. Moreover, the *biswedars* dominated both in the village affairs as well as in the state administration. They could manipulate the laws of the state to suit their own ends. There were also no well defined rules of ownership or the rate of revenue to be paid.[54] Such an arbitrary system governing the biswedar-tenant relationship was bound to contain grams of future trouble.

The villages were divided into different *pattis*[55] according to the tenants' shares as proprietors. This system continued

52. *Ibid.*, Patiala State Records, Prime Minister's Office File No. 655, PSA : Patiala.
53. Punjab State Records, File No. 2193; File No. 135 of 1931, PSA : Patiala (For further detail regarding the peasants condition see A.I.S. PIC. Papers, File No. 138, Part-I; Salana, Sahib Singh Aap Biti *(Panjabi)*, 134.
54. *Punjab State Records, Prime Minister's Office File No. 135, of 1931.*
55. *Rajomajra Enquiry Committee Report, PSA : Patiala.*

to prevail till 1929. On the basis of evidence furnished by a report of the Committee which went into the enquiry of Rajomajra, we learn that after 1882, partition was made not only of the land but it was also made tenant-wise. Whatever dignity the tenants' ancestors had enjoyed in the early days ended with the forfeiture of their *jagir* in 1882 in the village Rajomajra. The land now remained freeholding of one who was in possession of it, and it was with a view to ascertaining the area and the name of the owner of the land that charts were prepared by the Patiala State first in 1890-91[56] styled as *Pemayash Arazi Kachh Batai* and then in 1916[57] under the appellation of *Hissa-Kashi*. The relations between the *biswedars* and the tenants in the structure continued becoming strained and bitter because of the rising tide of consciousness among the peasantry of their being exploited. The people thought that the Settlement Committee appointed to go into their difficulties and redress their grievances would greatly help.[58] But according to Popham Young, the Settlement Commissioner of the state, "the effect of the settlement has been to create causes for disputes where none existed before and to aggravate ill feeling where they did exist".[59]

The cause of these strained relations was the conversion of proprietory into tenancy rights; the pre-settlement proprietory rights received recognition both from the state and public opinion. But there was no clear understanding either as to how their rights were acquired or what they amounted to. In many cases, the proprietary title had been in dispute between the main body of the cultivators resident in a village on the one hand and on the other some individuals who claimed the entire *biswedari* right on the basis of inheritance from the founder. Sometimes the latter alleged that their admitted rights as *mafidars* covered the proprietory title also. In such cases, the court of law would often allot to the main

56. *Ibid.*

57. *Ibid.*

58. *Ibid.*

59. *Ibid.*, Popham Young, Settlement Report of 1904.

body of cultivators the status of occupancy. The tenancy was for the small proprietors, who happened to be shareholders in a village in which someone connected with the official class was an assignee of the revenue or the owner of a predominant interest therein, to become occupancy tenant and for old tenants in a *biswedar* estate to sink to the level of more tenants-at-will.[60]

Moreover, the influence of the landlord class led to the issuance of the *hidayat* in 1873 from the state authorities making in incumbent upon all occupancy tenants to payments in kind.[61]

The first step to ameliorate the conditions of tenants was the introduction of the Tenancy-law in the State.[62] But it is to be noted that the principal objective of the tenancy reform was to appease the disgruntled tenants and to avert the agrarian unrest, which could harm the interests of the *Rajas* and *Biswedars* to a large extent. However, the Punjab Act XVI was very useful, though certain modifications were, of course, necessary and these were embodied in a Patiala Supplement to that Act. The tenants as a class were very happy when they learnt that their claims were being sympathetically considered by the state officials who now supposedly regarded landlords and the tenants with equal impartiality. The tenants jumped to the conclusion that their turn had come. At the time of the rent attestation, the whole tenant body affirmed that they had never paid rent which was customary for generations. On the other hand, it was found that the landlords were asserting that their tenants had always paid to them rackrents, made up largely of a number of impositions known as ceasses quite regardless of the actual facts. But to ascertain the fact, when there was no reliable record to refer to, was exceedingly difficult. A brief period of anarchy set in. Landlords refused to receive rents which did not include every

60. Punjab State Records, Prime Minister's Office File No. 756, PSA : Patiala.

61. File No. R-11-2003/P.24, PSA : Patiala.

62. *Ibid.*, Popham Young, Settlement Report of 1900-08.

sort of imposition which had been forced upon the weakest tenants by the strongest landlords in the neighbourhood and the tenants declined to pay rent at all, unless the landlords accepted the lowest share of the province,[63] which the most privileged tenants paid to the most considerate landlord. Though the action was justified, very serious crises took place which threatened to develop in the direction of murder and arson; but agrarian outrages were averted. The conflict between the landlords and the tenants took another form. Now the *biswedars* took recourse to criminal courts in order to put pressure upon the tenants with whom they had disputes of a civil nature.[64]

Eventually on 15th July, 1894 the *batai* system was abolished but a cash rent of 6 *annas* per rupee as the land revenue was fixed. The tenants did not accept it and decided to carry on the struggle and thereafter even this rent was abolished and the tenants were accepted to be the full owners.[65] But the *Biswedars* did not accept this settlement proposed by the state authorities. Thus the struggle continued between them and the tenants.

To put an end to the struggle of the tenants, the Council of Regency ordered in 1903 a regular settlement and as a consequence, divided the tenants into different categories, such as, tenants-at-will and different standards of rent were fixed for different categories of tenants.[66] A reign of terror was let loose by the *biswedars* for the realisation of rent in kind. The tenants then approached the Civil Courts for redress against the decision of these settlements but to no avail, as there too, they had to cope with the biswedars who held authority.[67]

63. Settlement Report, 1904, by Mr. Popham Young, Settlement Commissioner Patiala State.

64. *Ibid.*, Mr. Popham Young wanted to check them from doing so and also he wanted to protect the *biswedars* against exploitation by their tenants.

65. Patiala State Records, File No. 6157/6-2155, PSA, Patiala.

66. Mr. Popham Young, Settlement Report of 1904.

67. Patiala State Records, File No. 50, Case No. 1560, 5, PSA : Patiala.

Being disappointed by the courts of law the tenants again resorted to the non-payment of rent. The state openly came out to the help of the *Biswedars,* who knew no morality and who appeared no means of oppression. Thousands of tenants were put behind the bars and several were wounded or shot dead as a result of the firing. Cash, Cattle and Grain were forcibly taken away from their houses and the women insulted.[68] But, inspite of all this, the enthusiasm of the tenants did not abate and the movement acquired greater momentum. A group of five hundred tenants approached the Resident for the Punjab states at Lahore in order to appraise him of the situation. A Commission, of course, was appointed to enquire into the condition of the peasantry. The Commission submitted its report, which being in favour of the tenants, never saw the light of the day, despite persistent demands for its publication. Thus the position of the tenants remained the same.

The main grievances of the agriculturists, which were responsible for the peasant movement in this region, are detailed below :[69]

(i) The Agriculturists were grooming under crushing land revenue rates which were double, in some cases triple of, or even higher than those prevalent in the adjacent British districts.

(ii) The land cesses mounted to Rs. 21/15/4 in contrast to Rs. 17/8/4 per Rs. 100/- of land revenue in the adjacent British districts the former including Rs.

68. Patiala State Records, File No. 2177; File No. 100 (Poster in Panjabi entitled—"Patiala Union *Raj Ten Navin Laheran*"), PSA : Patiala, Supported by Master Hari Singh (Personal interview at Chandigarh, December 19, 1978).

69. Basta No. 13, Police (C.I.D), Scare Abstracts of Intelligence (2001); Office of the Faridkot Government, Case No. 360 of 1938; S.No. 538, Basta No. 18, Case No. 386/C of 1925; Basta No. 20, Case No. 485 of 1929; Basta No. 22, Case No. 135 of 1931/1988-*Sambat*; S.No. 653, Basta No. 22, Case No. 66 of 1931/1988-*Sambat*; Case No. 565/C-Part-II of 1939; Report for the week ending 28.2.1938 and 26.9.1938—Patiala State Records, Prime Minister's Office Files; File No. Part B-569, Re : Land Revenue Kapurthala State, PSA Patiala.

3/10/- of *Abwabi Khidmatguzari* which was a disguised name for *begar* cess.

(iii) Though *begar* (forced labour) had been declared illegal, yet it continued.

(iv) As in British India, Punjab peasantry were involved in huge accumulated debts from which there was no hope of escape, as has been shown no relief was offered either through Government agencies or co-operative Societies.

(v) Most of the officials were not only unsympathetic but positively hostile to the interests of the agriculturists and had been taking an active interest in anti-*Zamindar* propaganda, and the woes of the *Zamindar* Community owed, in no small measure, to their apathy and machinations.

The *Muzaras* Committees of various states, had been publishing *Gurmukhi* posters, from time to time, containing the alleged grievances of the *Muzaras* which were stuck on the walls of the houses in the villages to incite the tenants against the *biswedars* and the mal-administration of the *Maharajas* of the various states. The tenants gradually began to attend their meetings enthusiastically and participated in deliberations actively.

We shall now turn to certain movements in the East Punjab States—like the *Praja Mandal,* the Akali movement, the *Kisan Sabhas* etc. which had influenced the peasants.[70]

In 1921, the non-co-operation movement, launched against the British Government by the INC, was at its height. At the same time, the Sikhs started a religious struggle for the *Gurdwara* reforms known as the Akali movement. After a constant struggle for five years against the *Mahants* as well as the British Government, the Akalis succeeded in their mission

70. Quarterly Register, April 1924; Patiala State Records, Prime Minister's Office File No. 747; File No. 737; File No. 750, PSA : Patiala; Personal meeting with S. Jagir Singh Joga and Master Hari Singh on November 25, 1975 and December 19, 1978 respectively.

for freedom in governing *Gurdwaras* by its own elected and responsible body by the passing of *"Gurdwara"* Act of 1925. Now came a split in the Akalis and they were divided into two groups. The leaders of the first group continued their activities for the religious and educational cause while the other groups which consisted of progressive Sikh leaders like Gopal Singh Qaumi, Master Tara Singh, S. Sewa Singh Thikriwala, Jathedar Teja Singh and may others, associated the leaders of the Sikh community with the leaders of the National Movement struggling for National independence.[71] The Akali *Morchas* at Jaito and the Akali *Jathas*, often passing through Patiala territory sent a wave of enthusiasm which permeated the Sikh peasantry at the time.[72] However, the Akalis fought as an independent body against the imperialism and the tyrannical policy of the *Maharajas* of the states. Their role in connection with the peasant struggle is discussed at length in the fourth Chapter of this thesis.

In the twenties of this century, the struggle for national independence launched against the British imperialism by the INC was at its apex in British India. At that time, as has already been discussed, the condition of the native states was even worse than that of the subjects of the British India. The people were not free to launch struggle for freedom in the states openly.[73] In Patiala State, it was rather more troublesome to launch such a campaign because the *Maharaja* was one of the favourite stooges of the British. But of brave men of the states, inspired by the INC, Indian States' People Conference, the Akali Movement and other forces, felt that it was necessary to form some organisation which could bring consciousness in the states' people whose spirit had been paralysed under

71. Singh, Jagjit Aulakh, *Ikk Jiwan—Ikk Itihas*, 55 (The Akali leaders and the people of the states were determined to win Swaraj and put the *Maharajas* and *Nawabs* rights and said that they would not rest until they turned the British out of India) Vide. Basta No. 18, Case No. 224 of 1928, 96, PSA : Patiala.

72. *Ibid.*, 96 (Letter No. 110), Singh, Ganda, Some Confidential Papers of the Akali Movement, 190.

73. Singh, Jagjit Aulakh, *Ikk Jiwan—Ikk Itihas*, 67.

long slavery and to redress their political and economic grivencer. Hence, the outcome was the formation of *Praja Mandal.*

Possessing a *sanad* of recognition of his sovereign-rights or a treaty of alliance with the British power, every prince considered his big or small state at par with any other independent state of the world. But the British treated them as feudatory or subordinate states and did not accord to any Indian State, not even Hyderabad, the same political status or rank with diplomatic usage guaranteed to the smallest state in Europe.[74] If at all the sovereignty of the prince had any meaning, it was in relation to his own subjects. He could approach his counterpart, the ruling prince of another state, but only through the officer of the political department of the Government of India. According to Gandhi, one of the princely rulers confessed that they were no better than *Khansamas* of the British rulers.[75]

The rulers of the native states were doing great service to the British power. They were maintaining well-equipped armies, generally British trained and often British officered, read for use by the Paramount power against political unrest and seditious anti-British propaganda.[76] Time and again the Princes were referred to as helpers and colleagues in the great task of imperial rule[77] and were characterised as "a possible counterpoise to Congress aims."[78]

Under British protection, the princes enjoyed security not only against warring chieftains but also against their own

74. Majumdar, R.C. (ed.), *British Paramountcy and Indian Renaissance,* Bombay : Bhartiya Vidya Bhawan, 1963, 258.

75. Gandhi, M.K., *The Indian States Problem,* Ahmedabad : Navjeevan Press, 1941, 3.

76. Report of the Indian States Committee, 12; Dutt, R.P. *India Today,* (He has also quoted the view of Prof. Rushbrook William), 359-60; Dr. Walia, Ramesh, Study of the Praja Mandal Movement in the East Punjab States, Patiala, 1974, 6.

77. Diwan Jermani Dass, *Maharaja,* 296.

78. *Ibid,* 297.

subjects. They were bestowed with unbridled power and authority over their subjects. They had full control over their life and the only way the subjects of a despot could put an end to his oppression—had made the position really worse.[79] Jawahar Lal Nehru described the majority of these states as "sinks of reaction and incompetence".[80] The complete lack of civil liberties and the ruthless suppression of individuals and confiscation of property had reduced these states to nothing better than prison houses.[81]

The states' people were bound to raise their voice of protest against such conditions and demand a change. They could not remain unaffected by the dynamic changes that were taking place in the political and constitutional life of British India. Warnings to this effect had been sounded quite early by some British statesmen, and the princes were asked to introduce constitutional and administrative reforms.[82] But they turned a deaf ear to them. The states remained socially and politically backward, but still they were bound to accept influences from British Punjab, as there was a close identity of religious faiths among them and they cherished memories of common past.[83]

---

79. Dunber, Sir George, *India and the Passing of Empire,* London Nichalson and Watson, 1951, 150; Report of the Indian States Committee, 12; Sir Karnanith, Fitz also notes down this point very sharply in the back, *Twilight of the Marathas,* 175-76.

80. Nehru, Jawahar Lal, Presidential address to the Sixth Session of the All India States People's Conference, Ludhiana, 1939, (For more details also see, Sir Karnanith, Fitz, *Twilight of the Marathas,* 28).

81. Johan S. Hoyland, *India Crisis—The Background,* London : George Allen and Unwin, 1943, 92.

82. Chudgar, P.L., *Indian Princes under British Protection,* London, William and Norgate Limited, 1929; (Author of the Montague Chelmsford Report in para 157 said Hopes and Aspirations may overlap Frontier Lines like sparks across a street. Similar was the warning of Lord Curzon), Lord Irwin speech delivered to the Chamber of Princes in the period 1926-31 also contains such piece of advice.

83. The *Tribune,* dated 2nd September, 1945, Pattabhai Sitaramayya, *"Problems of the States".*

Despite all this, the process of politicalisation in the states was delayed because of the backwardness prevailing there. Their industrial backwardness negated any active participation of the working class. So it was left to the peasantry to assume the responsibility for unleashing a political movement. With the mass of the Indian people getting drawn into the freedom movement and larger section of the peasantry undergoing a radical transformation, the people in the states also experienced their first political awakening in the twenties. The visit of the Montague Chelmsford Mission in 1918, the establishment of the Princes' Chamber in 1921 and the growing expectation regarding constitutional reforms were some of the causes that aroused in intelligent and keen interest among the people in the affairs of the Indian States.[84]

All India States Peoples' Organisation had been organised earlier in 1922 but it could assume a concrete shape only in 1927. The Chief reason for this delay was the Congress policy of Mahatma Gandhi. The Gandhi-Irwin Pact, the failure of the second Round Table Conference and the withdrawal of the non-co-operation movement created a climate of despondency and despair. The left-wingers in the Congress were broken in heart and considered Gandhian leadership thoroughly inadequate and regressive.[85] However, as compared to Gandhi's attitude, there was Jawahar Lal Nehru's, that clearly displayed his interest in the Akali agitation of 1921-24.[86] Gradually in all provinces, Congress Committees started lending a helping hand especially after the All India States People's Conference was born. But generally the Congress extended only moral support leaving practically every thing to the people in the states where civil liberties

84. Report of the Bombay Session of the Indian States People's Conference, Published by Prof. Abhyankar, G.R. and Manishankar S. Trivedi, 1928, Reference Section of the Central State Library, Patiala.

85. Pattabhai, Sitaramayya, *History of the Indian National Congress,* Vol. II, 79. *Indian National Congress, Report of the 51st Annual* Session, 203-04.

86. Mitra, ed., *Indian Annual Register : 1924,* Vol. II, 187; Nehru Jawaharlal, *An Autobiography,* 183-84.

were non-existent and rule of law quite unknown. One may note the words of Lala Duni Chand Ambalvi,[87] "I have always felt that the Indian National Congress failed in its taking up the cause of the people of Indian States and tackling the problems affecting them. I have never been convinced of the wisdom of the letting along policy of earlier years of the Congress regarding the Indian States".

Though, opposed strongly by the princes,[88] the states' peoples' movement in about 10 years' time succeeded in focussing the attention of the people in British India on the problems of the state subjects. It withdrew the movement soon after the establishment of the *Praja Mandal* movement at the national level which would have otherwise remained a local affair. The voice of the *Praja Mandal* in the Punjab attained a special significance and it could successfully involve the peasantry in the freedom struggle[89] that had started in the Punjab States.

In order to grasp fully the genesis of the States' People's movement, attention must be paid to the various socio-religious movements which went a long way in imparting political consciousness, to the people of both British India and Indian India. K.P. Karunakaran has rightly written that, "Social and Religious reforms movements were often precursor to the political awakening in the country".[90] Pattabhai Sitaramayya regarded the socio-religious movements as, "so many threads

87. Patiala State Records, Prime Minister's Office File No. 655, PSA : Patiâla : Sharma, Jagdish, *Indian Struggle for Freedom,* (Selected documents & Sources). New Delhi. S. Chand & Co., 598-605.

88. Iyer, C.S. Ranga, *India Peace or War,* 156; (Documents and Resolution of the All India States' People's Conference available in the original in the References Section of the Central State Library, Patiala and quoted by Sharma, Jagdish, in his book, *India's Struggle for Freedom*; Handa, R.L., *History of Freedom Struggle in Princely States,* 70-75.

89. Chamber of Princes Records File No. CAS/L-9, PSA : Patiala.

90. K.P. Karunakaran, *Religion and Political Awakening in India,* Meerut; 1965, 22.

in the strand of Indian nationalism".[91] In the Punjab, there were three, not two, religious communities : Hindus, Muslims and Sikhs. The political scene here therefore always remained a little more complex than in other parts of the country. The Sikhs and their own specific Socio-religious movements running parallel to the *Arya Samaj* and the Aligarh movement. Not every movement was, however, relevant for the native states of the Punjab. The princes being jealous of all sorts of extra-territorial loyalties and affinities, always took care to seal their frontiers against potentially dangerous ideas. But some of these influences did percolate and affect their subjects. The *Arya Samaj* with all its aggressiveness and militancy in the initial stages attracted many Sikhs to its fold, but disenchantment soon set in when the *Samaj* believing in militant Hinduism started attacking the Sikh religion.[92] Despite all this, for a long time, the *Arya Samajists* dominated the Congress movement in the Punjab. The single factor was enough to drive Sikhs and Muslims away from it. But Hindus being quite advanced in the fields of trade and education were drawn into the freedom movement in the fields of trade and education were drawn into the freedom movement quite early. These factors were not very operative in the states. Both educationally and economically the East Punjab States were backward. So Hindus could not take the lead in the political field there. It were the religious reform movements among the Sikhs which really created stir among the states' people. The *Kooka* (Namdhari) movement of the Sixties of the 19th century and the *Singh Sabha* movement which was born about

91. Pattabhai Sitaramayya, *History of Indian National Congress?* Vol. I, 14.

92. Singh, Khushwant, *A History of the Sikhs*, Vol. II, Princeton, New Jersey : Princeton University Press, 1966, (Dayanand, the founder of *Arya Samaj*, was contemptuous of Sikh theologions because of their importance of Sanskrit, his favourite for any one who did not measure upto him was *Maha Murakh* ('Great Fool') Nanak he denounced as a *Dambhi* (Hypocrite). Dayanand set the tone, his zealous admirers followed suit), 166; Dr. Ganda Singh, (ed.), *The Punjab Bast and Present*, Department of Punjab Historical studies, Panjabi University, Patiala, Vol. VII, Part-I April, 1973.

a decade later gave a big jolt to the Sikh masses. The latter is particularly important because it did the spade work for the more significant movement for the reform of Sikh shrines which gripped Punjab in 1920-25.[93]

All castes of Hindus, Sikhs and even Muslims could become *Kookas* but generally it were the Sikh peasants and artisans who were drawn towards the movement. It spread rapidly in Ludhiana and Ferozpur districts of the Punjab and the *Phulkian* States of Patiala, Nabha and Jind. The British were alarmed by this new movement because its activities soon posed a grave law and order problem for the Government, as the Kookas started attacking Muslim butchers, either to gain popularity among the Hindus and the Sikh masses or out of fanaticism.[94] In due course of time, the British had received countless reports about the political design of the *Kookas.* Their independent *dak* system, their whispering campaign about the divine powers of the *Satguru* who would banish all *Firangis* and would himself become the ruler, their effective boycott of every thing foreign—all this was enough for the Government to take action but they were waiting for a convincing argument and this they could get when the Kookas attacked Malerkotla and a pitched battle was fought between them and the troops of Malerkotla. Baba Ram Singh, their leader, was arrested and finally transported to Burma. Now the *Maharaja* of Patiala and the Chiefs of other states ordered the arrest of all *Kookas* in their states.[95] Consequently, temporarily this movement was blasted out of existence on the grounds of Malerkotla episode.[96] The movement, however, left a deep impact on the consciousness of the people of the

93. Bajwa, Fauja Singh, *Kuka Movement,* Delhi : Moti Lal Banarsidas, 1965, 108.

94. Ahluwalia, M.L. *Kookas, The Freedom Fighters of the Punjab,* Bombay : Allied Publishers Private Limited, 1965, 55-56; Dr. Bhagat Singh, *The Kuka Movement, The Punjab Past and Present,* Vol. VII, Part-I, 1973, 152.

95. Bajwa, Fauja Singh, *Kuka Movement,* Delhi : Motilal Banarsidas, 1965, 109.

96. Singh, Kushwant, *A History of the Sikhs,* Vol. II, 136.

states. The repression of the *Kookas* generated great bitterness against the Princes and the *Kookas* later became the standard bearers of all progressive movements. They assisted the Congress and the *Praja Mandal* movement in the states.[97]

All activities of the *Singh Sabha* movement remained mainly confined to the Punjab. Its leaders paid little attention to the states' people. If at all it reached the states' people, it always remained in the loyalist hands. In brief, if the Singh Sabha movement in Punjab created a thunder, the people in the states felt its mild vibration. For example, a splinder group of the Chief *Khalsa Dewan* named the Punjab *Khalsa Dewan* started functioning from village Bhasaur (Patiala State) in 1906 under the leadership of Babu Teja Singh. But it could not make much headway; the atmosphere in the states was not so congenial as in Punjab where there was at least some progress in education and cultural field.[98] Hence, its impact in the states was only indirect and very weak.[99]

The Kamagatamaru episode followed by the 'Budge Budge Ghat Massacre' does not require detailed statement as the students of history are aware of it. However, a few lines in connection with the impact of this event may be called for. The harsh treatment acted out to those sikh emigrants, and the callous attitude adopted by the British rulers towards them dealt a badly blow to the prestige of the British Empire among the Sikhs who had served the crown so loyally. Out of desperation and anger, hundreds of Punjabis living in the

97. Dr. Walia, Ramesh, A Study of the Praja Mandal Movement in the East Punjab States, Patiala : 1974, 95.

98. *Singh Sabha,* Bhasaur, *Gurmate Ate Faisle,* Bhasaur, 1904, 1-4; (For more detail see *Khalsa Samachar,* Amritsar from 1901 to 1905); Gurdarshan Singh, Origin and Development of Singh Sabha Movement Constitutional Aspects, *The Punjab Past and Present,* Vol. VII, Part-I, 1973, 58; Memorandum submitted by a Sikh deputation to Lord Chelmsford in 1917, quoted in Sahani's Ruchiram, *Struggle for Reforms in Sikh Shrines,* Amritsar : Sikh the Research Board, S.G.P.C. 47-48.

99. Singh, Harbans, *The Heritage of the Sikhs,* Bombay : Asia Publishing House, 1964, 147.

U.S.A. and Canada, joined the *Ghadr* party of Indian emigrants. They were naturally receptive to revolutionary ideas and the policy of the *Ghadr* Party which advocated the forcible over-throw of the British rule in India. In 1914, many *Ghadrites* came to India to stir up rebellion against the British. They also tried to establish contacts with terrorist groups in other parts of the country and spread their activities in the whole Punjab. However, on the states, the impact of the *Ghadr* movement was negligible. The *Ghadrites* could set up only one centre for arms manufacture at *Lohat Badi* in the Nabha State. Harnam Singh Chamak of this village later became active in the Akali movement. Dala Singh of Jaladiwar in the Patiala State in this area and Karam Singh of Kapurthala state joined the *Ghadr* Party abroad. They went to the University for the Toilers of the East in the U.S.S.R. and on their return, took active part in organising the first Communist groups in the states of Nabha, Kapurthala and Patiala.[100] After some time, Sewa Singh of Thikriwala village in the Patiala State founded *Praja Mandal* movement. There were reports that Gurdit Singh of Kamagatamaru fame had stayed in this area for some months and had occasional meetings with Sewa Singh Thikariwala.[101] The latter may have received inspiration from Gurdit Singh and this led him to organise the peasant movement in the states.

The *Babbar Akali* movement rose in the form of terrorist groups functioning in the *Doab* region. Some of the Babar Akalis belonged to the Kapurthala state. After its suppression however, some of them degenerated and started playing in the hands of the *Maharaja* of Patiala who utilised them for his

100. *Ibid.*

101. Personal interviews with Sardar Ujjagar Singh Bawa, a close associate of S.Sewa Singh, He tells, "I was quite young at that time and accompanied Sewa Singh to a number of such meetings. Sardar Gurdit Singh was present at the Lahore session of the Punjab *Riyasti Praja Mandal* which elected Sewa Singh as its present".

own purposes.[102] Besides, the *Akali Dal* became quite active after the passage of *Gurdwara* Act in 1925 and this *Dal* launched the *Gurdwara* Reform Movement vigorously. In fact, this movement was born out of the *Singh Sabha* movement and the *Ghadr* Movement. The former proved so powerful that even the British Government bowed before it, when the keys of *Nanakana Sahib Gurdwara* were given to Kharak Singh. The first decisive battle, in the words of Gandhi Ji, was thus won.[103] After this, the Akalis held morchas at various places such as, Jaito for the liberation of *Gurdwaras.* In brief, the *Gurdwara* Reform Movement left a great impact on the politics of the Punjab,[104] as it imparted to the Sikh Community great political and communal consciousness. The sweep of the movement was so great that its anti-imperialist and anti-feudal character led to the dissemination of militant nationalist and democratic ideas, and brought the people of the States in connection with Political currents existing in British India. It exploded the loyalist policies which the Sikhs had been pursuing uptill then and drew them straight into the stream of National politics.

The changes in India, no doubt influenced the attitude of the people in the East Punjab States, but they were only indirect influence. However, all political activities in the neighbouring British territories found a direct echo in the East Punjab States. It was only in the twenties when the political scene warmed up enough that the people in the states also became politically conscious. But this awakening was, in a large measure, due to the *Gurdwara* Reform movement. The Freedom Movement

102. The case of Bijla Singh and his companion who worked against Nabha *Maharaja* Ripudaman Singh in Nabha Patiala dispute. References to their services are available in State files as also in some confidential papers of the Akali movement, edited by Dr. Ganda Singh, published by S.G.P.C., Amritsar, 182.

103. File No. 914/II-1922, Home Political (National Archieves of India, New Delhi); The *Tribune,* (Lahore), January 26, 1922; Sahni Ruchi Ram, *Struggle for Freedom in Sikh Shrines,* Amritsar Sikh *Itihas* Research Board, S.G.P.C., 160-162.

104. File No. 565/C of 1939, Prime Minister's Office Files, PSA : Patiala.

in India did not inspire the East Punjab States' People's movement, it only helped it. The shape, character and the dimensions of the tenants' movement was determined directly by the Akali movement.

In November, 1917, the Great October Revolution was successful in Russia. A big dent was made in the armour of Imperialism which could never again be mended. Imperialism had already raised a signal of alarm. On 12th December, 1917, *'The Statesman',* the chief organ of the British Capitalism in India had declared, "In substance, the activities of the revolutionary leadership in India are but almost powerful and wide-ranging movement of sabotage that has ever been launched against a historical state".[105] After a few months the Montague Chelmsford Report clearly felt that "The Bolshevik revolution in Russia has given inspiration to political consciousness in India".[106] To substantiate, no wonder the Chairman of the Reception Committee of a Communist *Kisan* Conference could, in 1943, after extending the 'Red Salute', ask his audience—"Is there any reason that Patiala and other States must remain in the 12th Century? Why can it not become like Russia or California"?[107] (The comrade quoted above, had in the same breath asked for the setting up of factories). Russia was highly developed and so too was California.[108] So where was the anamoly? In fact the Conference wished that every

105. File No. 41/C, PSA : Patiala.

106. C. Rajeshwara Rao, *The Decade after the Split*: The Part's Policy and Programme proved right, *Souvenir,* issued by the Communist Party, January 26, 1976.

107. Poster announcing a *Kisan* Conference at village Chaumar Mayscim October 1943. It contains the address of the Chairman of the Reception 14-15, 1943, Poster attached in Patiala State Records, Prime Minister's Office File No. 2193.

108. California occupied an important place in the hearts and lives of *Kirti* group of he Punjab Communists who had come to communism *via* the *Ghadr* Party with its headquarter at California and who still maintained close links with the Ghadr organisation in the united states and Jealously guarded their organisational and financial autonomy vis-a-vis the CPI communists.

peasant must own and cultivate his own plot of land. This was already an article of faith with the Punjab Communists, with their roots in the self-cultivating peasant proprietors of central Punjab. The Russian experience, too, had been seen through the eyes of the small holding peasant—early Bolshevk slogans (such as 'land to the tiller') and policies, especially those of the N.E.P. period.[109] Hence, this revolution also inspired the people in the Punjab. The following note which was reported to the higher authorities in 1920, gives an insight into the kind of sensitivity displayed by the CID to check the Bolshevik influence in the Punjab, because of its geographical proximity to Soviet Russia. "A Durani Pathan was recently found at Amritsar station talking Bolshevism and praising the Bolsheviks, representing that if they came to India, all wealth would be divided and there would be no more poor. He gave his name as Sardar Gulam Haider Khan and said that he was a horse dealer and going to Bareilly. It appears that there is a man of this name, resident of Kohat; enquiries are in progress".[110]

The impact of the external factors as has been shown above was not very potent in the beginning. But as time passed and political movement in India gained intensity, the people of these states also started agitation under the banner of the *Praja Mandal* Movement and had an active support of the Punjab *Kisan Sabha*.

Unlike many other native states, *Praja Mandals* in the East Punjab States were not formed by enlightened state subjects living in the British Indians cities directly under inspiration from the Congress movement. Instead, these were the

109. For details see Josh, Bhagwan, *Communist Movement in Punjab*, Delhi (1979) 96-99.

110. Roy, Subodh, Communism in India (1919-1924), unpublished documents, 1971, 135 (For more detail, see G. Adhkari, *Documents of the History of the Communist Party of India*, Vol. I & II.

handiwork of Akali workers[111] who themselves were the product of the *Gurdwara* Reform Movement.

The *Praja Mandal* was first formed in the Patiala State. The election of the office bearers was held at Village Saikha (Barnala Tehsil), in February, 1928. It was conducted under the Presidentship of Bakeshish Singh Kattu.[112] Similar *Praja Mandals* were formed in other states of the Punjab quite soon.[113] When *Praja Mandals* sprang up in the states other than Patiala it was felt absolutely necessary by the founders of the State *Praja Mandals* to establish a central body of this organisation for the smooth development and planning of a united struggle in a common cause in the various states of the Punjab.

Thus was formed the Punjab *Riyasti Praja Mandal* on July 17, 1928 at villages Mansa, with the avowed objectives of fighting for the establishment of a representative government and safeguarding the people's rights and liberties.[114] The *Praja*

111. Dr. Joginder Dayal, 'Struggle of the States People and the Communists' (An article in Panjabi), published in Souvenir issued by the CPI on 26th January, 1976; Personal meeting with Shri British Bhan, Chandigarh (The Akalis gave this movement a well determined and separate carder); Bhawa Ujjagar Singh, *Amar Shaheed Sewa Singh Thikriwala* (Panjabi), 4; (For details regarding the factors led to its formation see Aulakh, Jagjit Singh, *Ikk Jiwan—Ikk Itihas* (Panjabi), 67; House, Nemi Sadhan, *The Indian National Movement—An Outline,* 76.

112. To launch a struggle against the autocratic rule of states which was the root cause of their miseries and troubles; the unwarranted arrest of the beloved leaders of the Sikh community—Sardar Sewa Singh Thikriwala, which agitated the minds of the people of the states and the advise of Shri Amrit Lal Seth, the then General Secretary of the All India States People Association etc. kindled the fire towards the formation of the *Praja Mandals* in the States. Bhawa Ujjagar Singh, *Amar Shaheed Bewa Singh Thikriwala* (Punjabi), 4.

113. Giani, Nahar Singh, *History of the Freedom Movement in India,* 219; Ghudgar, P.L., *Indian Princes under British Protection,* London, William and Norgate Ltd., 1929, 92-93.

114. For more detail about its formation see Inspector General of Police Report dated 15.8.1928, given in File No. 224, PSA : Patiala; The Jagriti, (Punjabi Monthly), August, 1965, 24; Aulakh Jagjit Singh, *Ikk Jiwan—Ikk Itihas,* 68.

Mandal, as it has already been stated, was formed to work in tune with the ideals of the I.N.C. and the Akalis, who were struggling for independence. However, in view of the nature of this organisation, it was not possible to set up these *mandals* of the Punjab States in the vicinity of the state territories. This is why the head-quarters of the Central Organisation were established at a far off place like Amritsar and later on at Lahore in 1930, from where the working committee could guide more easily the activities of the *Praja Mandals* of the States.[115]

The Punjab *Riyasti Praja Mandal* adopted its own constitution on August 10, 1928. In this constitution, it was provided that the activities of the Punjab *Riyasti Praja Mandal* would be extended to the following states :[116]

(1) Dujana; (2) Kalsia; (3) Loharu; (4) Pataudi; (5) Simla Hill States; (6) Nahan; (7) Bilaspur; (8) Mandi; (9) Saket; (10) Kapurthala; (11) Malerkotla; (12) Faridkot; (13) Chamba; (14) Patiala; (15) Jind; (16) Nabha; (17) Bahawalpur; and (18) Kashmir.

But the activities of this organisation remained mainly confined to the following states :[117]

(1) Patiala; (2) Nabha; (3) Jind; (4) Malerkotla; (5) Faridkot; (6) Kalsia; (7) Kapurthala; (8) Nalagarh; (9) Pataudi; (10) Simla Hill States; and (11) Loharu.

Each State *Praja Mandal* had different objectives but the following were the common objectives of all of the states' *Praja Mandals,* under the control of the central body :[118]

115. Bhawa, Ujjagar Singh, *Amar Shaheed Sewa Singh Thikriwala,* (Panjabi), 181 (*Praja Mandals* were set up in the following adjoining important British Towns and cities by the Patiala State *Praja Mandal :* Raikot, Budhtada, Ambala, Khanna, Boota Singhwala, Khandiala, Dodar and Bhatna).

116. Bhawa, Ujjagar Singh, *Amar Shaheed Sewa Singh Thikriwala,* (Panjabi), 181.

117. *Ibid.*

118. *Ibid.,* Punjab State Records, Prime Minister's File No. 595, PSA : Patiala; Presidential address of Chhatar Singh Maur, printed at the Mitter Press, Amritsar.

Rajas/Nawabs should be given fixed salary/allowances out of which they should manage their household and personal expenses :

Establishment of Councils for law making and District Boards;

To improve the working of the law courts by lessening influence of the *Rajas/Nawabs;*

To agitate for removing the grievances of the people;

To attain freedom of speech and expressions; and

To attain constitutional form of Governments in the states to work for the welfare of the state.

In addition to the above common objectives, the Patiala State *Praja Mandal* stood for these objectives :[119]

Nazul system prevailing in the state should be done away with. It was the system under which the land of the owner was attached to the state if the former did not leave behind a descendent for five generations to inherit; *Begar* system (forced labour) should be done away with in the state;

Loans taken from the state people on the eve of the first world war should be returned to them immediately;

Due justice should be done to the tenants of the Patiala State;

Adequate scheme should be drawn up for the development of education in the state;

Birds (Forests) preserved by the state for hunting should not be maintained as the animals caused damage to the crop;

The confiscated properties, titles and pensions etc., should be restored to the Akalis or other political prisoners of the state.

---

119. Dr. Joginder Dayal, *Ryasti Lohan Da Ghol Ten Communists* (Panjabi), *Souvenir,* issued by the CPI on January 26, 1976; Bhawa Ujjagar Singh, *Amar Shaheed Sewa Singh Thikriwala,* (Panjabi), 181; Patiala State Records, Prime Minister's File No. 746, PSA : Patiala.

Similarly, the *Praja Mandals* in different states had objectives specific to each state. But it is to be remembered that in the initial stages the *Praja Mandal* Movement was primarily the movement of the Sikh peasants and raised its voice for the grievances of the farmers in its very first Conference,[120] which was held at Mansa. The activities of this organisation have been briefly discussed here.

As already stated, the first sign of unrest among the people in the states of East Punjab appeared in the twenties. The soldiers from the states, who were on active duty abroad became carriers of enlightened political ideas in the countryside after securing release from the army.[121] The people in the states got their first lesson in politics when the Sikh community as a whole came into clash with the British power in the Punjab. Hundreds of the simple-minded, god-fearing peasants participated in the *Gurdwara* Reform Movement, courted imprisonment and faced lathi blows in the *Guru-Ka-Bagh* and other *morchas*.[122] Though the *Gurdwara* Reform Movement ended with the passage of the *Gurdwara* Act in 1925, but the peasants were now ready to make any sacrifice at the bidding of their leaders.[123] For the first time, the Princes' monopoly of

120. *Ibid.*, Kapurthala State Records File A/5-1-45.

121. Personal interview with Gujjar Singh of Dhanetha (Jind State), "Ex-soldier and former Akali *Praja Mandal* Worker"; He stated, "We were then in Egypt and the news from Punjab were disturbing all of us". (The agitation against the Rowllat Act, non-co-operation movement, the episode of Jallkanwala massacre, forcible realisation of war funds from the peasantry and brutal and barbarous British policy). Our officers were very much concerned over the signs of unrest among us. They held out meetings and told us that there was nothing to worry about. (in connection with the wide spread Punjab disturbances, see Sinha, Sardhar, *Indian Independence in Perspective*, Bombay, Asia Publishing House, 56.

122. Dr. Ganda Singh (ed.), *Some Confidential Papers*, XXVI—of the introduction, also 138, 141, 142; Quarterly Register, April, 1924, Dr. Joginder Dayal, *Riyasti Lohan Da Ghol Ten Communist* (Panjabi), *Souvenir*, issued by the CPI, January 26, 1976.

123. Dr. Ganda Singh (ed.), *Some Confidential Papers*, 138-142; Master Tara Singh, *Meri Yaad* (Panjabi), Amritsar : Sikh Religious Book Society, 1945, 92.

leadership was being effectively challenged. If injustice in religious affairs was intolerable, so was political and economic high-handedness.

At the heels of the wave of mass politicalisation came the world economic crisis of 1928-39 which had a deep impact on the agrarian economy of the country in general and of the states in particular. Thus, the storm had been gathering for long in form of peasant unrest, and the movement for reform of Sikh shrines had accentuated the situation. It is to be noted that the *Maharaja* of Patiala was not in the state when the agitation was launched by the Punjab *Riyasti Mandal* and the Akalis.

When *Maharaja* of Patiala came back in January, 1929, he was determined not to give a free hand to the agitators. But he did not follow the policy of arresting the leaders of agitation. He instead followed the policy of isolating the deputationists.[124] But the movement was gathering power day by day. The state authorities mobilised all their resources to counteract the agitation.[125] It, therefore, became easy for the agitators to impress upon the ordinary villagers the tyrannical nature of the princely rule and the need for a struggle for civil rights. The leaders were now demanding the release of all political workers[126] and for this a petition was submitted to the district authorities on July 15, 1929;[127] it was rejected.

124. *Maharaja's* (Patiala) interview with Associated Press Representative dated February 6, 1929; Patiala State Records, Prime Minister's Office File No. 547 and 548, PSA : Patiala.

125. Prime Minister's office File No. 547 and 548, PSA : Patiala, (These files contain a detailed account of the steps taken by the State authorities to meet the situation).

126. (Some of the Political workers were—Bhawan Singh, Hazura Singh and Harnam Singh of Village Katran, Sham Singh of village Kanjala and Gian Singh of village Chhangli) Vide Prime Minister's office File No. 578, PSA : Patiala.

127. Patiala State Records, Prime Minister's Office File No. 578, PSA : Patiala; Vaid Chhaju Mal, *Pepsu Muzarian De Ghol Ten Communist Party,* An Article in Panjabi, published in a *Souvenir* issued by the CPI, on January 26, 1976.

Now the *Praja Mandal* Movement made a bold start in the East Punjab States. The leadership and cadre were provided by the Akalis. The main aim as stated earlier, was to win political rights for the states' peasantry and to get their grievances redressed.[128]

In the Malerkotala State, the movement was being organised by Giani Kehar Singh of the village of *Chak,* Sri Sewa Singh of village *Bapla* and Talib Hussain of *Sharwanikot.*[129] The main demands of the Malerkotla peasantry were to end corruption and illegal extraction of money by the *nawab,* the safeguarding of their rights in land and the bringing down of land revenue to the level of Ludhiana district in the Punjab.[130] These demands were published in the form of a poster termed "Malerkotla Indictment" by the State *Praja Mandal.* The people were asked to supply their grievances to the *Praja Mandal* workers. A demand was also made of the Paramount Power to hold an enquiry into the state administration and remove the *Nawab* in case the charges were proved. The annual observance of the *Kothala* day in memory of the persons who had fallen to police bullets in 1927, became a rallying point for the state peasantry. The responsibility for the observance of the day was now taken over by the Punjab *Riyasti Praja* Mandal and workers from neighbouring states who participated in the conference held in the Malerkotla State. The annual fair of Chhapur (Ludhiana district) provided another occasion for the *Praja Mandal* Workers to meet and chalk out their programme.[131]

---

128. Patiala State Records, Prime Minister's Office File No. 595, PSA : Patiala; Dr. Joginder Dayal, *Riyasti Lokan Da Ghol Ten Communist Party,* published in *Souvenir,* issued by the CPI on January 26, 1976.

129. Talib Hussain rose to an important position in the Punjab *Riyasti Praja Mandal.* He edited the official organ of the Punjab *Riyasti Praja Mandal "Riyasti Duniya".*

130. Giani Kehar Singh, *Dard Kahani* (Panjabi).

131. This fair was held in July-August at *Chhapar* which was near Ahamedgarh railway station Ludhiana-Hissar railway line. Thousands of peasants from states also attended it. Political parties held groups on the occasion to propagate their programme and policies. Vide File No. 1/5-1-45, Kapurthala State Records, PSA : Patiala.

In the Kapurthala state, the villages in the Bunga pocket surrounded on all sides by the Hoshiarpur district, became a centre of *Praja Mandal* activities. The *'Dhut Group'* of political workers, as it was called by the Kapurthala administration after the name of their village, was actively associated with the Punjab *Riyasti Praja Mandal* since its very inception. The group was led by Master Hari Singh. Here also the main demand centred round the reduction of land revenue, abolition of regressive and repressive taxes, and to corruption, more road and hospitals in the rural areas and a responsible Government.[132]

In the Jind State the *Praja Mandal* launched a morcha against the state administration. Sikh peasants in the Jind State had their grievances against the state administration which went unheeded at the hands of Dr. Rihari Lal Dhingra, the Prime Minister. Their grievances related mainly to the Judicial and revenue administration of the State. The land revenue had been enhanced and corruption prevailed all round.[133] It was alleged by the *Praja Mandal* that choicest land in two Sikh dominated villages had been gifted to Dr. Dhingra by the Maharaja and cultivating owners were being dispossessed by him. Then there were grievances concerning the *begar* system and forcible supplies of fodder and other provisions for the guests of the *Maharaja* and his hunting parties. The Jind *Maharaja* had little time for state affairs. He had left every thing to the care of his Prime Minister who was brought from

---

132. Personal meeting with Master Hari Singh, Communist Office, Chandigarh; (Master Hari Singh was an elected member of the Kapurthala State Assembly. He always took active part in its proceedings and put searching questions on grievances of rural people. He remained an office bearer of the Punjab *Riyasti Praja Mandal* for a number of years. Another leading light of the *Dhut* Group Baba Karam Singh was Chairman of the Reception Committee of the Ludhiana Session of the All India States' People's Conference held in 1939 under the Presidentship of Pt. Nehru) Vide Kapurthala State Records File A/5-1-45, Punjab State Archives, Patiala.

133. Longawalia, Bhagwan Singh, *'Maladministration in Jind State'*, Patiala State Records, Prime Minister's Office File No. 595, PSA : Patiala.

British India. The Sikhs, though in minority in the state, were not ready to accept Dr. Dhingra as Prime Minister as they considered. Jind to be a Sikh State.[134] Here again it was the Sikh peasantry that became the mainstay of the *Praja Mandal.*

The character of movement in the smaller states was not in any way different free that in the Patiala State. Akalis formed the hard-core of the *Praja Mandal* workers everywhere and their main demands were concerned with the redressal of peasant grievances. The only difference was that in smaller states the movement always remained on a low level. It neither attained the sweep it did in Patiala State nor could it attract the attention of the All India State People's Conference.

In the East Punjab States, the five months preceding the Lahore session of the Indian National Congress witnessed is tremendous growth of the *Praja Mandal* Movement. The local units of the *Praja Mandal* were set up in smaller states.[135] Now, the anti-Bhupinder Singh campaign was stepped up. Sewa Singh Thikriwala undertook an intensive tour of the Patiala State excepting the Hindi speaking and the Hill areas. The terrories of Patiala, Nabha, Jind and Malerkotla were contiguous to one another and the message which Sewa Singh carried reached not only the Patiala state but the rural folk in the adjoining states also.[136] Besides, on their return from Lahore, the *Praja Mandal* workers started making preparation for observance of the first Independence-day. On 23rd January, 1930, Sewa Singh Thikriwala led a procession of Kisans from his village to Barnala, where a public meeting was held. The Importance of the day was explained and a pledge was taken to liberate the people living in the states from the double slavery of the British and the princes. Processions and public meetings were also organised at *Sunam* and *Mansa,* two other strong-holds of the movement. The success of the various public meetings and processions gave new fillip to the *Praja Mandal*

134. *Ibid., Quarterly Register,* April, 1924.

135. Bose, Nema Sadhan, *The Indian National Movement—An Outline,* 76.

136. Patiala State Records, Prime Minister's office File No. 555, PSA : Patiala.

movement.[137] The people's discontent was so wide-spread and so intense that the Government had to take note of it. In 1937-38, the Prime Minister was reported to have drawn the attention of the subordinate officials and asked them to tour villages and redress the general grievances of the peasantry.[138]

It was after the death of Sewa Singh Thikriwala that dissensions in the Punjab *Riyasti Praja Mandal* leadership came to the surface. Soon two clear out factions took shape. One was led by Harchand Singh Jeji,[139] while the second faction led by Bhagwan Singh Longowalia and Jagir Singh Joga. The members of the latter group came under the influence of Marxist ideology, although many of them might not have been enrolled as regular members of the Communist Party.[140] From 1936 onwards, Punjab Socialist and Communist leaders were to be seen addressing *Praja Mandal* Conferences in and outside the Punjab States.[141] At these Conferences peasants were asked to enroll themselves as members of *Kisan* Committees in response to the call of the All India *Kisan Sabhas*.[142] In fact,

137. Patiala State Records, Prime Minister's office File No. 613, PSA : Patiala.

138. Patiala State Records, Prime Minister's office File No. 750, PSA : Patiala. (For more detail regarding the peoples discontent see File Nos. 700, 710 and 730, Patiala State Records, Prime Minister's office, PSA : Patiala.

139. Harchand Singh Jeji never occupied any office in the Punjab *Riyasti Praja Mandal* but his behind the scene activities made no less contribution to the movement. When we talk of his being the leader of one group, it only means that he had the de-facto leader of the faction.

140. Personal meeting with Sardar Jagir Singh Joga and Sardar Isher Singh Majhail, Arjun Nagar, Patiala (the latter expired last year).

141. Confidential Report (Weekly) from I.G.P. Patiala, dated 13.8.37, Patiala State Records, Prime Minister's office File 1546, 1937; Copy of report dated 20.4.93 (August 1936) from Inspector CID, Patiala, on the proceedings of a *Praja Mandal* meeting held at Khanna on 2.8.1936 under the Presidency of Sohan Singh Josh; B.P.L. Bedi, Arjan Singh Gargaj, Karam Singh, Mann and Baba Rur Sir.gh were the most prominent leaders invited to speak.

142. Confidential Report (Weekly) from I.G.P. Patiala dated 13.8.37, 21.10.37, 1.1.1938, 15.1.1938 etc. Patiala State Records, Prime Minister's office file 1546 and 1547; also see Walia, Ramesh, *A Study of the Praja Mandal Movement in the East Punjab States,* Patiala : 1974, 131-32.

the Communists were then working in the Congress and in the Punjab *Riyasti Praja Mandal* and they were mainly responsible for organising the *Kisan* Committee and encouraging new peasant struggle. The *Praja Mandal* workers who belonged to the peasant class gradually turned more and more to the Communists for help and guidance.[143] It has been said that the impact of the Communist ideology on the National Movement expressed itself on three fronts :[144]

(a) Complete independence as opposed to dominion status;

(b) Complete abolition of feudalism;

(c) An Organisation of peasants, workers and the youth into their distinct class organisation.

This latter impact had a particular significance for the states. Well known Communist workers from the Punjab frequently lectured at public meetings organised by the *Praja Mandal.* Sohan Singh Josh, Arjun Singh Gargaj, Karam Singh Mann and Baba Rur Singh were some of the prominent Communist leaders who were often invited to address the *Praja Mandal* Conferences in and outside the Punjab States.[145] The Presidential address of the *Praja Mandal* Conference held at Mehlan (Jind State) as a fine specimen of the secular and

143. Walia, Ramesh, A Study of the Praja Mandal Movement in the East Punjab States, Patiala : 1974, 79; For more details see Balabshevish, V.V., and others (ed.) *Contemporary History of India.* New Delhi : People Publishing House, 1963, 153-54.

144. *Ibid.*

145. Report of a Public Meeting at Khanna held on August 2, 1936, Vide Patiala State Records, Prime Ministers' Office File No. 747; The Poster (in Punjabi) of Longowal Conference scheduled for 7th & 8th November, 1936, Patiala State Records, Prime Minister's Office File No. 737, PSA : Patiala. (For details see Patiala State Records, Prime Minister's Office File 1544 and 1946 & 1937. The I.G. Police Patiala issued a circular order to all *Nizama* and S.Ps. to submit regular weekly reports in view of the recent activities of the *Praja Mandal,* their identification with communist and socialist tendencies, and plans to form *Kisan* Committees and *Praja Mandals* branches, Circular No. 15 dated 28.8.1937, *Ibid.,* File No. 1546).

radical approach of the organisation in this period as compared to the early emphasis on religious issues under Akali influence. The address discussed the political situation in the country in 1937 and exhorted people to organise *Kisan Sabhas* and seek affiliation with the Congress Socialist party; fight for reduction in land revenue and abolition of excessive taxation and demand more roads, schools and hospitals.[146] Another representative document of this period was *Praja Mandal Amli* programme (Praja Mandal programme of action) which could be termed as the Communist menifesto for the East Punjab States.[147] Its language was clearly Communist oriented, showing no influence or religion. It was proscribed by the Patiala State Government vide their Gazette notification dated 9th June, 1937. That the Communists were not dominating the organisation became clear at Anandpur Sahib where a *Praja Mandal* Conference was held on 25th and 26th March, 1937.[148]

The Conference had originally been announced by the Jeji faction of the *Praja Mandal,* and Bhagwan Singh Longowalia and Jagir Singh Joga had not been invited to lecture. But the stage was captured by the supporters of the latter group on the very first day and the Red *Kirti* Flag hoisted in the *Pandal.*[149] During the course of their speeches, the speakers demanded true rule of the peasants and workers in the states, jobs for the unemployed, proprietary rights for peasants and establishment of representative Government. The most significant aspect of the Conference was that the slogen of 'Long Live Revolution' was frequently raised and a frontal attack launched against Jeji and his group.[150] According to

146. Presidential address of Sri Chhatar Singh Maur, Printed at the Mittar Press, Amritsar.

147. Patiala State Records, Prime Minister's office File No. 744, (Programme published by Jagir Singh Joga), PSA : Patiala.

148. Patiala State Records, Prime Minister's Office File No. 747, Proceedings of the Conference, PSA : Patiala.

149. Personal interview of S. Jagir Singh Joga; *Ibid.*

150. Proceedings of the Conference, Patiala State Records, Prime Minister's Office File No. 747, PSA : Patiala; Dr. Joginder Dayal, *Riyasti Lokan Da Ghal Ten Communists, Souvenir,* issued by CPI on 26th January, 1976.

Jagir Singh Joga, his *Praja Mandal* was a party of the poor and that of Jeji a friend of capitalists.[151] Giani Kehar Singh of Malerkotla openly declared that, "we have now come under the *Kirti* Flag which symbolises freedom".[152] On the second day two separate *Diwans* were held. While the Communist leaders' speeches continued in the Longowalia and Joga Conference, whose ideological shift towards the left and their growing hold over Praja Mandal workers was no doubt influenced by their disillusionment with the Akali current and Master Tara Singh's pact with the Maharaja,[153] the second conference was addressed by Kartar Singh Nagal, Rulia Singh of Faridkot and Ujjagar Singh Bhaura who concentrated merely on personal issues and side-tracked the basic economic and political issued. In brief, it was under the banner of the Punjab *Riyasti Praja Mandal* that the peasants had held conferences, organised demonstrations, led deputations and submitted memoranda.

While these changes were taking place in the Punjab *Riyasti Praja Mandal,* the movement in other parts of the country was taking rapid strides. Pt. Nehru called 1938 the year of "mighty awakening among the people of the state".[154] As a result of the general elections held in 1937, in nine provinces of British India, Congress ministries were formed under the Government of India Act of 1935. These ministries were not taking any action against the *Praja Mandal* workers operating from their areas. They were instead rendering positive assistance to them in their work. The Princes were much disturbed over these new developments. The Chamber of Princes held protracted discussions on the question of

151. Patiala State Records, Prime Minister's Office File No. 747, PSA : Patiala (Proceedings of the Conference). Also confirmed from personal meeting with Master Hari Singh who was present in the Conference.

152. *Ibid.*

153. *Ibid.*

154. Presidential address of Pandit Jawahar Lal Nehru to the Ludhiana Session of the All India States' People's Conference, PSA : Patiala.

subversive movements from across the borders of the states and consulted legal luminaries whether the Grown representative should be pressed to take action against the state people's movement being directed from bases in British Provinces.[155] However, their nervousness subsided only with the declaration of war in 1939 when the Congress ministries resigned. Under Rule 26 of the Defence of India Rules, all agitations and propaganda against the rulers and their administration was prohibited. The amendment to rule 26 was carried out in the light of the opinion given by Sr.B.L.Mitter and the Chamber of Princes Standing Committee expressed its satisfaction over this.[156]

The condition in the Punjab, however, was quite different. The *Unionist* ministry here under Sir Sikander Hyat Khan had adopted a totally hostile attitude towards the Congress and the States' People's movement.[157] This hostile attitude of the Unionst Ministry figured in the address of Baba Karam Singh Dhut at Ludhiana Session of the All India States' People's Conference who severely condemned the Ministry's policy of persecuting the workers of the *Praja Mandal* movement in the Punjab.[158] Had there been a Congress Government at the helm of affairs in the Punjab, the story would have been different. This was proved in the post war period when the Congress Government in Punjab rendered all assistance to the *Praja Mandals* in the states of Jind, Faridkot and Nabha and the movement there touched new heights.

Another factor that affected the movement was the death of *Maharaja* Bhupinder Singh in 1938. The death of this controversial figure resulted in significant changes in the *Praja*

---

155. Chamber of Princes Records file No. CRS/3/45—PSA : Patiala.

156. *Ibid.*, Proceedings of the Standing Committee meeting dated January 16, 1941.

157. Sir Sikander's address at the Patna Session of the Muslim League vide the Bombay Chronical dated 28th December, 1938 and the Bombay Sentinal dated 27th December, 1938.

158. Patiala State Records, Prime Minister's office File No. 369, Baba Karam Singh Dhut's address, PSA : Patiala.

Mandal movement in Patiala and other neighbouring states. The new *Maharaja* Yadvindra Singh wedded the daughter of Harchand Singh Jeji, the arch-enemy of his father, and thus won a section of the *Praja Mandal* cadre to his side.[159] The withdrawal of Jeji and his group from the *Praja Mandal* left the field clear for the Communists who soon captured the organisation.[160] This section of the *Praja Mandal* leadership included Jagir Singh Joga and Harnam Singh Chamak, Sardara Singh Yuthup and Hardit Singh Bhattala all from the Nabha State, Kaur Singh Maur, Jaswant Singh and Gujjar Singh Dhanatha from the Jind State, Master Hari Singh, Basawa Singh and Chanan Singh from the Kapurthala State, Sewa Singh Bapla and Giani Kehar Singh from the Malerkotla State and Sunder Singh, Atma Singh and Shamsher Singh from the Kalsia State. They supplied the Communist Party in the East Punjab States with its first cadre.[161]

Under the guidance of this radical wing of the Punjab *Riyasti* Praja Mandal, the political scene warmed up further. In addition to the sharpening of the tenant movement, unrest among the peasant proprietors of Patiala, Faridkot, Jind, Malerkotla and Kapurthala continued. It rapidly mounted in the tiny state of Kalsia which witnessed a regular peasant revolt in 1938. However, the *Praja Mandal* in Kalsia was set up in February 1940. It was a direct result of the Charik *Morcha*[162] which is to be discussed at length in the third section of this chapter. The *Kisan* Committee and the *Praja Mandal* had common office bearers.[163]

An official report about Patiala State listed Dhuri and Sunam as the two places where the Hindus were becoming

159. *Ibid.*, Personal interview with Sardar Jagir Singh Joga.

160. Patiala State Records, Prime Minister's office File No. 369, PSA : Patiala.

161. *Ibid.*, Personal Interview with Sardar Jagir Singh Joga.

162. Kalsia State Record, File No. 164 (Dewan's latter dated November 20, 1938), PSA : Patiala.

163. Kalsia State Record, File No. 132, PSA : Patiala.

Congress minded.[164] But the draconian state laws prevented people from participating in these activities. The *Hidayat-88* in the *Phulkian* States and the Society Registration Act in the Faridkot state directly attacked people's right of association and free expression. The *Praja Mandal* organised a *Satyagraha* at Sunam in 1938 demanding the repeal of the *Hidayat.* The *Satyagraha* with its head-quarters at Ludhiana, continued for some days and some arrests were offered. It was suspended on Gandhi's advice and on the reported assurance of the *Maharaja* of Patiala that the *Hidayat* would be withdrawn in due course of time. The *Praja Mandal* leaders later alleged that the *Maharaja* had gone back on his assurances. They also complained that the *Maharaja* had used threatening language against a *Praja Mandal* deputation.[165] In the Faridkot state, the *Raja* was administering similar warnings to political workers against their seditious activities. Organisers of an Akali Conference held at Kotkapura, Giani Zail Singh, Gurbax Singh, Janga Singh and Sandhura Singh were called by the *Raja* and told bluntly to desist from holding political conferences in the garb of religious *dewans.* Therefore, all efforts were made that no *dewan* of this kind should be held at all in the states.[166] But the events were moving fast. A *Zamindar Sabha* was set-up on 24th July, 1938 and all the above named workers were associated with it. Through posters and pamphlets the committee put forward the most progressive demands ever made by the *Praja Mandal* in the states of East Punjab.[167] The emphasis, however, was chiefly on the peasants' demands, such as the auctioning of *shamlat* lands should be stopped and the peasants should be allowed to sell their crops in any market or town they liked and not necessarily inside the state.

164. Patiala State Records, Prime Minister's Office File No. 756, PSA : Patiala.

165. Gandhi, M.K., Indian States' Problem, 368.

166. Faridkot State Records, File No. 336, PSA : Patiala (The Conference was an Akali Religious Conference but the demands voiced were all concerned with grievances of the peasantry.

167. Poster published in October 1938, Janga Singh's Pamphlet *"Dukhee Janta Ke Dili Ubal",* Ferozpur City, Amrit Electric Press, 1939.

With the passage of time, two demands came to the forcefront, namely repeal of the Registration of Societies Act and full proprietory rights for the Kisans through the abolition of the *Ala Malik* system.[168] Public meetings were organised by the *Praja Mandal* in favour of these demands in 1938. But the State authority employed all possible means to disturb the meetings.[169] *Praja Mandal* activities, therefore, remained restricted.

In the Kapurthala State, too, the *Praja Mandal* Movement was very active. *Praja Mandal* workers captured the stage at a Public Meeting held in the city under the auspices of the National League,[170] and delivered speeches alleging police complicity in the death of one Shankar Singh in suspicious circumstances and demanded a judicial enquiry into the affair. A demonstration was later staged in the city.[171] In Nabha State, *Praja Mandal* workers were being arrested in 1938 for hoisting the Congress Flag and indulging in anti-state activities.[172] In May 1939, Kala Singh of Palasaur, President of the *Praja Mandal,* was challanged under provisions of the *Hidayat-88.* Similar was the fate of the *Kisan* Conference held at Chhapar fair in September, 1938.[173] Hardit Singh Bhattal who was to have presided over the conference, was arrested from his Presidential procession and people were dispersed by force by the police of the Malerkotla State. Sangat Singh, who presided over the conference, in the absence of Bhattal, was taken into custody. Some days later, all leading *Praja Mandal* workers of Malerkotla State, including Sahib Singh Salana from

168. According to this system the name of the *Raja* was entered in the revenue records as super owner of all agricultural lands in the state.

169. Avtar Singh, *Din Dihare Raatan* (Panjabi), published by the author; Faridkot State Records, File No. 357, PSA : Patiala.

170. The National League was a local organisation formed by some liberal minded citizens, but it was favouring the state Government as against the *Praja Mandal.*

171. Kapurthala State Records, File No. M/3-14-39, PSA : Patiala.

172. The *Tribune* (Lahore, August 24, 1938).

173. Salana, Sahib Singh, *Aap Biti* (Panjabi), 134.

the Nabha State, were arrested and a case of murderous assault under Section 307, Indian Penal Code was launched against them.[174]

As the above noted account shows the *Kisan* workers of the Punjab *Ryasti Praja Mandal* were everywhere actively carrying on their agitational work but some of them were coming under Communist influence. The State of Faridkot, however, was an exception. Here a group of workers under Giani Zail Singh and Sandura Singh were nearer to the Congress ideology and still maintained their links with the Akali leadership in Punjab. Alongwith these activities of the *Kisan* cadre of the *Praja Mandal,* work was also being undertaken in urban areas of the East Punjab states by groups of Hindu workers under inspiration from the Indian National Congress in general and Pandit Jawahar Lal Nehru in particular. This gave a new dimension to the movement and also created new problems for the *Praja Mandal* organisation, giving birth to the urban-rural question.

All the rural leaders who started their political work in this period did not adopt an identical line of activities. Each one was pursuing his own independent line without any co-ordination with others.[175] The sixth session of the All India States' People's Conference was held at Ludhiana in February, 1939 under the presidentship of Pandit Jawahar Lal Nehru in an atmosphere of peasant struggle and agitations for the repeal of repressive laws. It was for the first time that the session was being held in Punjab and it showed the significance that the All India States' People's Conference and the Indian National Congress attached to the movement in this part of the country. Pandit Nehru's participation drew thousands of villagers, among whom many were from the states. "I went to Ludhiana mainly because of Pt. Nehru but my participation in the session proved to be a turning point in my political career. From there I started working in the *Praja Mandal".*

174. *Ibid.*

175. Personal interviews with Sunder Lal, Harbans Lal, Des Raj, Brish Bhan and Tirath Singh.

This is what a prominent leader of the movement told me.[176] Pandit Nehru was then at the zenith of his political career and was considered to be the most out-spoken champion of the state people's cause.

The Punjab *Riyasti Praja Mandal,* which was playing host to the Ludhiana session, was now effectively under the control of the Communists. The conference Pandal was named Sewa Singh Nagar and the conference was attended by delegates from nearly all the East Punjab States including Patiala, Kapurthala, Kalsia, Malerkotla, Faridkot and Nabha and thousands of state people thronged to see and hear Jawahar Lal Nehru. The rulers already expected this and they tried their best to thwart the preparations of the Conference and counter the intensive propaganda being carried on by peasant workers in the countryside. The Malerkotla administration was particularly concerned as this state was very close to Ludhiana. According to an official, report, the near famine conditions prevailing in the Patiala State and the shortage of canal water furnished good grounds to the *Praja Mandal* agitators for their work. Instructions were issued by the Inspector General of Police to all District Officials to devote their whole-hearted attention to anti-conference work.[177]

The issue of civil liberties in the states was naturally discussed at the Ludhiana session. Pandit Jawahar Lal Nehru, in his presidential address, treated this as the focal point of the *Praja Mandal* activities. It was, according to him, the immediate objective of the *Praja Mandal* while their ultimate aim was a responsible government.[178] The Conference adopted two resolutions on the subjects one on a responsible Government and the other demanding an end to the repressive policies of the State and restoration of civil liberties. Baba Karam Singh Dhut demanded the repeal of the oppressive

176. Personal interview with Sunder Lal Advocate.

177. Patiala State Records, Prime Minister's Office File No. 756, PSA : Patiala.

178. Pandit Nehru's Presidential Address, Faridkot Records File No. 369, PSA : Patiala.

measures and made a special mention of the Faridkot Act, which he termed as *"Kala Kanun"*[179] or Black Act.

The Punjab *Riyasti Praja Mandal* was now a purely political organisation leading a movement for economic and political reforms and was firmly aligned with the All India States' People's Conference. But the movement had a new setback with the starting of the Second World War in September, 1939. Most of the front ranking workers including Baba Karam Singh Dhut, President of the Punjab *Riyasti Praja Mandal,* Master Hari Singh M.L.A. Harnam Singh Chamak, Hardit Singh Bhattal, Seth Ram Nath, Brish Bhan, Harbans Lal and others were arrested. In July 1940, Sahib Singh Salana[180] took over Presidentship of the *Mandal* but against him also arrest warrants were pending. He toured some of the states and tried to activities local *Praja Mandals* but was soon arrested on 20th January, 1941, while attending a meeting of the Praja Mandal workers at Ahmedgarh (Malerkotla State). So the war years proved to be a period of slackness so far as the agitational activity of the *Praja Mandal* is concerned.

During the war years, the Communists and the Congressmen remained in jail or were interned in their villages. The *Praja Mandal* movement remained a leaderless movement functioning in a vacuum. The only exception can be made in the case of the tenant movement in the Patiala State which continued unabated throughout the war years. In early 1939, a *Kisan Muzaira* Committee had been formed with Narain Singh Bahadur as President, Chand Singh as General Secretary and Dharam Singh Dalel-Singh-Walia as Joint Secretary.[181]

179. His address in Urdu, Vide Faridkot State Records, File No. 369, PSA : Patiala.

180. Sahib Singh Salana started his political career with the Ahmdgarh Train Dacoity case in 1929, an already seen. He was occupying important position in the District Ludhiana Congress Committee, was secretary of the Ludhiana District Communist Party and was President of the Punjab *Riyasti Praja Mandal.*

181. Report of the Inspector General of Police, Patiala State Dated 7th February, 1939, Vide Patiala State Records, Prime Minister's Office File No. 756, PSA : Patiala.

Tenants had long been nursing grievances against the Akalis and the Congress leadership that their case was not being adequately attended to.[182] The new committee gave a new direction to their movement and at a largely attended tenants' conference at Jetheka held a few months later, a call was given for total stoppage of payment of *Gotai* (Landlord's share of the produce). Tenants removed total crops to their homes. The State Government taking it as a challenge to its authority let loose police repression but the movement continued spreading to the village after another. About four hundred tenant villages were affected by the new movement. Clashes took place between the landlords and their men and the police on one hand and tenant men and women on the other. To protest against the wave of repression, a deputation of 101 persons was taken to Simla. The repression subsided to some extent but tension survived throughout the war years.[183] In 1945, a new twenty-one member *Muzara* War Council was set up. Under its leadership, armed guards were mobilised to defend gains of the movement. The gravity of the situation was recognised by the *Maharaja* of Patiala in one of his communications to the *Maharaja* of Jind, dated the 10th August, 1945.[184]

As already noted, some of the urban leaders of the *Praja Mandal* movement had been quite sympathetic to the tenant movement and lent it their support. But very soon a rupture took place between the Congress minded cadre and the *Praja Mandal* and the Peasant Cadre owing allegiance to the Communist Party. Trouble had been brewing since 1942. Whereas Congress men had been busy creating disturbances, the Communists had been aiding the war efforts. In 1945, the Communists were expelled from the Congress and so the Communists in the states also put an end to their conflicting loyalty. The All India States' People's Conference set up a

182. Personal Interview with Dharam Singh Fakkar.

183. *Ibid.*

184. A copy of the letter was sent to the Nabha Government also, Nabha State Records, Prime Minister's Office File No. 82-83, PSA : Patiala.

Regional Council for the Punjab States with Brish Bhan as Chairman and Harbans Lal as General Secretary. At the end of the war, therefore, there were three distinct political groups working in the East Punjab states : Akalis under the leadership of Master Tara Singh with Pritam Singh Gojran and Jagir Singh Phaguwalia as their local leaders; the Congress-led *Praja Mandal* under Brish Bhan and Harbans Lal; and the Communists with their *Kisan* Organisations under the leadership of Jagir Singh Joga, Master Hari Singh and Harnam Singh Chamak. As a result of these new developments, the character of the *Praja Mandal* had completely changed. The tenant movement, led by various political groups, particularly the Communists and the Akalis factions, in the East Punjab States, is discussed at length in next chapter.

4

The Peasant Movement in the East Punjab States

The first sign of agrarian unrest among the people in the states of East Punjab appeared in the twenties. However, stray cases of politically active individuals were reported in some of the States (Patiala, Faridkot and Kapurthala) earlier also but prompt action by the authorities forestalled any organised movement.[1] The real reason for the absence of any notable activity in the states in the post war period was the absence of any numerically significant middle class intelligentsia such as the one leading the movement in the Punjab cities, like Amritsar, Lahore and Ludhiana. It was from these centres of intense political work at a very early stage that politics travelled to the countryside. But in the states, the position was absolutely different. There it was the peasantry which was getting impoverished that provided the nucleus. The Semi-feudal rule was oppressive and the burden of rural debts excessive. The movement for the reform of Sikhs shrines in Punjab (1920-25) showed the way to Sikh peasants in the States.

The Sikh peasants got their first lessons in politics when the Sikh community as a whole came into clash with the British power in the Punjab. Hundreds of simple-minded, God-fearing peasants participated in the *Gurdwara* Reform Movement, courted imprisonment and faced *lathi* blows in the *Guru-Ka-Ghar* and other *morchas.* The movement ended in 1925, with the passage of the *Gurdwara* Act, which gave

1. Faridkot State Records File No. 23, and 37; Confidential Diaries of District Magistrate No. 2920-21, PSA : Patiala.

official recognition to the S.G.P.C. Now the peasants were ready to make any sacrifice at the bidding of their leaders. For the first time, the Princes' monopoly of leadership was being effectively challenged. If injustice in religious-matters was intolerable, so was political and economic high handedness.

A powerful agrarian movement started with great enthusiasm and vigour. The payment of *Batai* was stopped in all the villages throughout the states. Now the *Praja Mandal,* the *Kisan Sabhas,* the progressive elements in the Akalis and the other patriotic organisations extended their sympathy. It was on their return from Lahore that the *Praja Mandal* workers started making preparation for observance of the first independence day. On 23rd January, 1930, Sewa Singh Thikriwala led a procession of *Kisans* from his village to Barnala, the District Head-quarters, carrying the Congress flag in front. After covering the distance of four miles on feet, the processionists reached the town where a public meeting was held. The importance of the day was explained and a pledge was taken to liberate the people living in the states from the triple slavery of the British, the Princes and the *Biswedars.* Processions and public meetings were also organised at Sunam and Mandi, two other strongholds of the agrarian movement.[2] At the former place, a clash took place between the processionists and the police leading to the arrests of some leaders including Harnam Singh of Dharmgarh, a tenant and Akali leader of the area. These arrested were later tried on charges of rioting and sentenced to various terms of imprisonment.[3] Observance of the day was an unprecedented success which gave new fillip to the agrarian movement under the leadership of *Praja Mandalists.*

Inspite of the set backs which the movements had received from the death of Sewa Singh Thikriwala, unrest among the

2. Patiala State Records, Prime Minister's office File No. 555, Punjab State Archives, Patiala.
3. Patiala State Records, Prime Minister's Office File No. 613, Punjab State Archives, Patiala.

peasantry of the Patiala State remained mounting. Even in 1934, when both Sewa Singh and Bhagwan Singh were in jail, peasant agitation for redressal of their grievances had continued. The enhancement of water rate in sub-*tehsil* Bhadaur and the Ghaggar area created great dis-satisfaction among the peasants. *Abiana* in the Patiala State in 1934-35 was rupee one and *annas* eight as compared to fourteen *annas* in the British Punjab. Failing to receive any reply from the *Tehsildar* and the *Nazim* to whom they had been submitting petitions, the peasants of villages Chamaru, Rampur, Kapoori, Soutapur, Mandi, Sarala, Mehru, Atwana, Khalaspur, Majhali and Hadana were reported to be preparing to go to Delhi to submit petitions to the Viceroy against the administration of the State.[4] Besides, a public meeting was held at Bhudhlada on 25th-26th September, 1935, where resolutions were adopted condemning the enhancement of land revenue and *abiana* and demanding relief of taxes.[5] A demand was raised that the peasants would be permitted to sell their produce in the *mandis* of the Punjab as the prices there were higher. It was pointed out that the price of cotton was Rs. 4 and Rs. 6 per *maund* at Bareta (Patiala State) while it was Rupees 5 and *annas* 4 at Budhlada (British Punjab), the distance between the two *mandies* being hardly six miles. The mood of the peasantry will be clear from a speech delivered by an evicted tenant at this meetings :[6]

> "In the *Birs* (Forests), there are wild animals which ruin our crops. On the marriage of the *Tikka Sahib* we were forced to pay *neonda*[7] (Gift in Cash) at the rate of 5% of the land revenue. What relations do we have with the *Maharaja?* If he considers us his relatives, then why does he not pay *neonda* to us"?

At a political Conference held at Chhapar on 11th-13th September, 1935, the issue of the enhanced water rate and the

4. Patiala State Records, Prime Minister's Office File No. 700, PSA : Patiala.
5. *Ibid.*
6. *Ibid.*

higher rates of land revenue in the state was raised by Bhagat Singh Dhatagal. Quoting facts and figures, he demanded that these should be brought down to the level of the Punjab.[8] The people's discontent was so widespread and so intense that the Government had to take note of it. The state Finance Minister, Sir Fredric called for a report from the Chief Engineer of the Irrigation Department, Patiala State. On November 21, 1935 the latter confirmed that there were wide disparities in the rates prevailing in the Patiala State and in the Punjab. It, however, took a whole year for the Chief Engineer to explain the reasons and author three years for the state Government to grant a minor reduction (less than 3 *annas*) and that too only in the case of fodder.[9] This shows how unreasonable the administration was. But the point here is not the reduction but the recognition of the peasants' grievances. In 1937-38, the Prime Minister was reported to have advised the subordinate officials to tour villages and redress the general grievances of the peasants.[10]

The movement was now spreading to newer areas and the peasants were gradually getting vocal. A Jatha of *Dhukhee-Zamindars* was organised by Lal Singh of village Chamaru, Sub-*Tehsil* Ghanaur. According to a poster published by him as the Secretary of the *Jatha,* the peasants were called upon to organise themselves and represent their grievances to the *Maharaja.* The demands put forth in the pester included the followings :[11]

---

7. Neoda is a payment which relatives of the bride of bridegroom make at the time of marriage. A pays Rs. 21/- at the marriage of B's son or daughter, so B is expected to pay the same amount at the time of the marriage of A's son or daughter. In case he falls to reciprocate, it is considered to be a sign of bad manners.

8. Proceedings of the Conference Vide Patiala State Records, Prime Minister's office, File No. 730, PSA : Patiala.

9. Proceedings of the Conference Vide Patiala State Records, Prime Minister's Office File No. 730, PSA : Patiala.

10. Patiala State Records, Prime Minister's Office File No. 750, PSA : Patiala.

11. Patiala State Records, Prime Minister's Office File No. 746, PSA : Patiala.

Land Revenue should be brought at par with the British territories;

Nazool System should be abolished;

Steps should be taken against the high-handedness of some *Lambardars, Zaildars* and *Patwaris;*

There should be a legislative assembly in the State;

There should be more schools, hospitals and roads in the villages.

A meeting of the peasants from different villages was convened at Sil, a village six miles from Patiala. Lal Singh[12] distributed posters of his *Jatha* at the *tonga*-stand at Bahadurgarh to the outgoing and incoming passengers. Hence, in the late twenties, a new organisation was making its appearance in the countryside. It was the community led by the *Kisan* Committee.[13] At *Praja Mandal* Conference, peasants were asked to enroll themselves as members of the *Kisan* Committees. A poster issued by the *Praja Mandal* called upon the *Kisans* to set up their own committee in response to the call of the All India *Kisan Sabha.* "Form *Kisan* Committees, get affiliated to the *Tehsil Kisan* Committee, so that you may join the All India *Kisan* movement.[14]

Compelled by the ever-increasing struggle and the moral pressure of the public, the state authority issued *Farman-i-Shahi* No. 6 dated March 11, 1937. This failed to appease the tenants and the decision was viewed as one in favour of the landlords. The State anticipated that there would be wide spread agitation against it in the state.[15] So two days earlier

12. (He was a clerk in the Patiala High Court who was suspended on 15th July, 1937 and later dismissed from service) Vide File No. 746; File No. 710, Patiala State Records, PSA : Patiala.

13. Patiala State Records, Prime Minister's Office File No. 710, PSA : Patiala.

14. (This poster was issued on 13th Magh 1994 Bikrami) Vide Patiala State Records, Prime Minister's office File No. 750 (Copy of the Poster is preserved—Panjabi Version). PSA : Patiala.

15. File No. 100, *'Patiala Union Raj Ten Navin Lahran',* PSA : Patiala.

i.e. on 9th March, 1937, in order to suppress the anticipated agitation, they promulgated the Patiala Public Safety Ordinance and itself started propaganda in the press. It was claimed that the Patiala state had also abolished *biswedari* system and the tenants had been made full proprietors. They succeeded in their aim of duping the press and the out side public, who were ignorant of the true state of affairs in the state. The Public Safety Ordinancy was enforced in the state in order to crush the voice of the tenants, this was done on the pretext of quelling communal disturbances, and its provisions were used against the tenants and the organisations supporting them. At the same time the *biswedars* were also trying to crush the tenants' resistance, with the help of *Goondas.*[16]

It will not be out of place to cite a few cases of the high handedness of the *biswedars* here. Nirpal Singh, a *biswedar* attacked the tenants of the village Banjupura with the help of armed *goondas* and police. Having frightened the tenants, he extorted a sum of Rs. 4000/-. In Khatriwala village, the *biswedars* injured two tenants with gun shots and burnt their unthrashed crops. At Kalbanjara village, ten *biswedars* alongwith twenty five *goondas* attacked the tenants who were working in the field of Budh Singh; 5 tenants died on the spot and 7 others were badly injured. The police arrested 7 *biswedars* and 2 *goondas* but let them off without any punishment. They, therefore, grew bold and were out to terrorize the tenants and forcibly took possession of 400 *bighas* of land. On the contrary, on the report of the *biswedars,* the police arrested 40 tenants under section 10 Cr. P.C. and under the Public Safety Ordinance in village Naiwala without any reason. The police finally put the *biswedars* in possession of their land. The *biswedars* resorted to firing on the tenants and as a result thereof two tenants were shot dead while six others were wounded. When the tenants took the injured and the dead to the hospital they, too, were arrested there. Only

16. Memorandum submitted by the members of the Patiala War Council, Patiala; Patiala State Records, Prime Minister's Office File No. 565/C-1939 (*Biswedar Hakumat De Namune*—in Punjabi). Panjab State Archives, Patiala.

two of the *biswedars* were arrested. One of them was soon let off on bail while 50 tenants remained behind bars. In village Kasaiwala on the 3rd of June, 1947, at night, 6 *biswedars* alongwith 15 *goondas* attacked the tenants to frighten them into submission and belaboured them. Two were injured with gun-shots and two with lathi blows. The police refused to entertain the report loged by them. The *biswedars* of village Munshiwala put two tenants leaders to death with the help of *goondas.* At village Jarkian, the *biswedars* murdered a tenant leader.

As a result of such activities of the *biswedars,* about 15 tenants were murdered and 40 injured in villages, Benjupura, Khatriwala, Kalbanpura, Naiwala and Kasaiwala and no *biswedar* or the *goonda* was punished by the state.[17] Under the Public Safety Ordinance and under Section 107 Cr. P.C. about 1000 tenants were put behind the bars of Central Jail, Patiala. The *Praja Mandal* and the *Kisan Sabha* workers were also arrested and tortured.[18]

The War Council of the tenants put forward the following demands :

(a) Occupancy tenants under Section 5*(a)* should be made proprietors of their holdings and an Anna-per-rupee of land revenue be fixed in lieu of rent.

(b) In case of tenants with *Zabri Lagan* (Cash rent for various crops) As. 2/- per rupee be fixed.

(c) Other occupancy tenants under section 5 be required to pay As.-/4/- per rupee.

(d) For the tenants under Section 6008, The rate should be As.-/6/- per rupee.

(e) For tenants-at-will who were in possession of the land since the settlement, be fixed As.-/12/- per rupee.

(f) In case of other tenants-at-will, the ejectment of rules be abrogated and rent rates reasonably decreased.

17. *Ibid.,* also Dewan's letter dated 20th November, 1938, Kalsia State Records, File No. 164, PSA : Patiala.

18. Kalsia State Records, File No. 132; File No. 164, PSA : Patiala.

(g) The arrears of rent should also be realised on the above rates.

(h) The ejected land in the course of struggle be returned to tenants. Their arrears of rent should also be realised according to above rules.

(i) The prisoners be released and cases be withdrawn.[19]

In the section above we have discussed the general peasant unrest in the period under study. We shall now turn to that section of the agriculturists who were tenants and submitted to the exploitation by *biswedars* (refer to Section-I of Chapter IV). The relations of the tenants and the *biswedars* continued to deteriorate with the passage of time. It makes an interesting study as to when and why this movement started. The *biswedars* and the tenants were in conflict for preservation but the tenants united themselves against the *biswedars* only in the beginning of the 20th century. The main reason was the growing consciousness among the peasantry of their rights. The peasants of the British territory, who were enjoying a free life and paid only a fixed revenue to the state established contacts with the peasantry of the Patiala State in particular and other *Phulkian* states in general. The peasants of Patiala state had begun to realise their rights. The rising tide of nationalism in the country and the movement connected with it were also destined to have their influence on the movement of the tenants, and the peasantry in the East Punjab States organised itself in the form of *Kisan Sabhas*.[20]

In the Patiala State, the tenant movement started from a village near Dhuri, called Rajomajra.[21] Apart from Rajomajra, there were other places where the disputes of the *biswedars* and the tenants existed. The foundation of this dispute was

19. Memorandum submitted by the members of the tenants War Council, Patiala (A copy of this memorandum is preserved), Patiala State Records, Prime Minister's Office File No. 750, PSA : Patiala.

20. Patiala State Records, Prime Minister's Office File No. 101, PSA : Patiala; Rajomajra Enquiry Committee Report, PSA : Patiala.

21. Personal meeting with Sh. Chhejju Mal Vaid at Fazilka on September 18, 1979 and Master Hari Singh at Chandigarh, March 17, 1979.

laid by the system of *batai,* which was changed from cash to kind and it was to be 1/4th of the harvest and the *biswedars* were made the owners of the land while the tenants were declaring themselves as the owners of the land just like *biswedars.*[22] Before the establishment of these villages the biswedars took-away the lands from the tenants.

Many *Kisan Sabhas* were held in different places to get the demands of the tenants accepted by the Government. *Kisan* Conference were held where these parties also participated. A *Kisan Sabha* held at Chao in Ludhiana district, demanded the amelioration of the sufferings of the tenants.[23] Similarly, another Conference was held at Shehna village (District Ludhiana) under the Presidentship of Rattan Singh Mangali on 7th and 8th July, 1945.[24] About 300 persons attended it. A procession was also taken through all the main streets of the village of Shehna.[25] The processionists carried posters bearing the inscription.[26]

Be-Dakhal Hoiyan Zamina Vapis Deo,

Jagirdari Dhakka Band Karo.

Many political slogans were raised among which the slogan 'Stop *Batai* System' was enthusiastically repeated. Thereafter Jagir Singh Joga performed the flag hoisting and made a short speech wherein he pointed out that the red flag represented the poor labourers and peasants to whichever community and nationality they belonged. The labourers and *Kisans* should therefore rally round the red flag.[27]

22. Vaid, Chhajju Mal, *'Pepsu Muzarian Da Ghol Ten Communist Party',* (An article in *Panjabi*) published in *Souvenir,* issued by the CPI in January, 1976. Patiala State Records, File No. 2077, PSA : Patiala.

23. *Ibid.*

24. Vaid, Chhajju Mal, *'Pepsu Muzarian Da Ghol Ten Communist Party',* (An article in *Panjabi*) published in *Souvenir,* issued by the CPI, January, 1976.

25. Patiala State Records, File No. 2077, PSA : Patiala, 75.3

26. Patiala State Records, Basta No. 13, Secret Abstracts of intelligence, July 28, 1944.

27. Patiala State Records, File No. 2077, PSA : Patiala, 76.

There was another Conference attended by over seven hundred men held in the village Gujarwal. The Conference commenced with recitation of the following poem :[28]

Uth Jag Kisana Sutian Hoiya Lal Sawera Hoy,
Utter Dakhin Pachhim Jhulian Lal Phurera Hoy.

The *Kisan* Conference expressed its resentment against the organised looting of Patiala State *Muzaras* by the state officials and the *biswedars.* It requested the *Maharaja* of Patiala to stop action against *muzaras* and also to abolish the *batai* system. It also requested the state authorities to publish the *muzara* Commission Report which had duly been completed for seven years.[29] Finally, the conference assured *muzaras* that the *Kisan* Committee would support them if they made any effort to secure their rights. It will not be out of place if some more *Kisan* Conference as also the issues discussed there by the leaders are cited here. For this purpose a table is prepared which is given below :[30]

Date	*Place—Where the Kisan Conferences Held :*
July, 1938	Ludhiana and Abdullapura (Jagadhari)
April, 1939	Jethuke
May, 1939	Penchhat (Jullundur)
June, 1939	Ludhiana and Takhtpura, P.S. Nihalsinghwala, Ferozpur
July, 1939	Garangan, P.S. Kharar (Ambala), Chak Bhai Ram Singh (Ferozpur), Budhalada (Distt : Hissar), Sangrur, Assarpur, P.S. Ghula (Karnal)

28. Patiala State Records, Basta No. 13, A Secret Abstract of intelligence, July 28th, 1944, PSA : Patiala.

29. Prime Minister's Office, File No. 2077, PSA : Patiala, 79.

30. The above data is based on the Phulkian States Records Files—File Nos. 6157, G-2155, 541, 542, 547, 548, 549, 552, 553, 555, 556, 563, 564, 566, 567, 568, 569, 578, 608, 609, 613, 623, 624, 630, 639, 642, 644, 654, 655, 667, 669, 670, 672, 675, 689, 690, 692, 697, 700, 702, 703, 710, 713, 715, 724, 727, 729, 730, 733, 734, 737, 742, 744, 745, 746, 747, 750, 756, 772.

August, 1939	Budhalada (Hissar District)[31]
September, 1939	Kalan, P.S. Budhalada, Alampur Mandran, P.S. Boha, Narur (Jullundur)
October, 1939	Bhabeli, P.S. Sahena (Ludhiana), Khamonon-Kamli, P.S. Bassi
November, 1939	Jallianwala Bagh (Amritsar)
December, 1939	Gurdwara Khadial (Karnal)[32]
June, 1940	Mauli Bedwan (Ambala)
February, 1941	Shehna (Ludhiana)
April, 1942	Jethuwal P.S. Shehna (Ludhiana)
April, 1943	Bhakna (Amritsar)
July, 1943	Rar (Tehsil Mansa) and Ambala
April, 1944	Barnala (Patiala)
August, 1944	Kuleri (Hissar District)
September, 1944	Bhugwali (Patiala), Tungwali (Ferozpur), Barnala (Patiala)
October, 1944	Bhadaur; Ugrajan, P.S. Sunam; Malerkotla; Sangrur (Jind State)
January, 1945	Bhadaur
March, 1945	Dhanaula (Nabha State); Mandauli Kalan, P.S. Morinda (Ambala); Gujjarwal (Ludhiana); Kakrala (Ludhiana); Maur (Jind State); Dialpur, Haryal, P.S. Lehra
December, 1945	Mehmudpur (Malerkotla); Kotkapura; Goriana; Jaito (Faridkot); Aaspur (Karnal); Dwali; Rampuraphool; Logowal; Phaphra, Juwaharke, Mathiasar; Anandpur; Amritsar and Lahore. 33

31. Conference was held on 14th, 15th and 16th August, 1939. *Muzaras* of Sunam, Dhuri, Barnala, Bhatinda and Mansa participated in it. Similarly, almost all the *Kisan* Conference were attended by the leaders of various political groups. The *Kisans* and the *Kisan* leaders went from their native places to participate in these conferences even after waling a distance of 10 to 15 miles. Vide. Records of Patiala, Kalsia, Faridkot, Kapurthala and Jind States.

32. Though the *Dewan* was religious, it was held with political purposes and was not only by *Muzaras* and their leaders but the leaders of other political parties also participated. It is to be noted that during this period under review, such *dewans* were political in nature.

In these conferences, the *Kisan* leaders fired the zeal of the tenants against *biswedars.* To cite an example, the tenants-at-will of village Dhanoli Khurd, P.S. Dirbha were so aroused that they rioted and injured the police party under the D.M. Sunam, who had gone there to help the revenue officers to aid the *biswedars* in taking over possession from the tenants. Similarly, the occupancy-tenants of Bakshiwala, P.S. Sunam were reported to have taken possession even since *bandobast.*[34] The *Kisan* leaders criticised the *batai* and the *Kankoot* system and exhorted the *muzaras* to follow the example of the Bardoli.[35] The state policy of *mamla, Abiana* and *hasiyat* tax was also condemned and the high-handedness of the states' authorities and the *biswedars* was attacked.[36] In each conference, a few resolutions were passed in which the *Muzaras* were directed as follows :

(a) No *muzara* should have any sort of association with the *biswedars.* Even if a *muzara* was found calling 'taeh' to a *biswedar* he would be fined Rs. 5/-;

(b) No *batai, 'Kankoot'* or *'Girdawari'* be paid at all. A *biswedar* who accompanied the *Girdawar* or *'Kankoot'* Officer, was to be resisted or attacked, if necessary;

(c) In case the state authority ordered the forcible payment of *batai,* the crops be laid waste before any officer visited them to effect the *batai.* Corn was not to be kept in the houses for the state employees may seize it.

---

33. The *muzaras* Conference held in January, 1945 was attended by approximately 4000 *muzaras,* who came from villages—Kishangarh, Kartarsinghwala, Bhadaur, Damdamasahib, Dipgarh, Qasaiwala, Talwandi Sabo and Many others. Similarly, all other conferences held in 1945 were attended by large number of *Kisans.* The prominent leaders who organised and participated in these conferences can be seen in Appendix No. IV in the end of the thesis. Let it be noted the above data is collected from the records files of different Phulkian States, preserved by the PSA : Patiala.

34. Basta No. 15, CBI-I-Z, Pol. CID, 1945-46, PSA : Patiala.

35. Basta No. 50, S.No. 1546, File No. 565/C-1939, PSA : Patiala.

36. *Ibid.*

(*d*) The menials (*Kamins*) were asked not to continue their relations with the *biswedars*. A recalcitrant *Kamin* would be compelled to leave the villages;

(*e*) The orders issued by any court should not be complied with. If a *muzara* was sentenced to fine, he should not pay it but undergo imprisonment in default of payment of fine;

(*f*) The *biswedars* be put to trouble by every means and they should be compelled to leave their villages;[37]

(*g*) The *muzaras* who had not received reply to their petition to the state authorities, were exhorted to conduct propaganda from village to village;

(*h*) Rupee one per head be raised from every *muzara* by way of subscription;

(*i*) The posters, which were published for the *muzaras* should be kept by themselves and not handed over to any *biswedar* or his employee. They should be distributed among the public in time.

(*j*) The tenants were urged to organise themselves to get their alleged grievances redressed.[38]

While tracing the genesis of the tenant movement, it will not be out of place to cite here the following main demands of the tenants which were placed before the state authorities :

(*i*) The objection of the *muzaras* from land should cease;

(*ii*) The land which was lying useless for want of cultivation should be given to the *muzaras*;[39]

37. In every *biswedari* village there lived only one or two *biswedars* families and the remaining were *Muzaras*. It was therefore, easy for them to tease the *biswedars*.

38. S.No. 1563, File No. 565/C-1939, PSA : Patiala.

39. Demanded from the state authority to give away the state *Birs* (Forests) to the state *Kisans* in order to strengthen the grow more food campaign and to improve their economic condition, Vide Patiala State Records and the records of Malerkotla and Kapurthala States, Basta Nos. 13, 50 & 85.

(iii) Sufficient water supply should be arranged in the canals and the canal tax should be at the same rates as it was in the British territory;

(iv) *Batai, Malba* and *Nazool* systems and the *Girdawari* should be abolished in all the states of East Punjab;[40]

(v) *Begar* (forced labour) and *Thikri Pehra* (duty of a night watchman) should be abolished;

(vi) Remission in or reduction of revenue be made and the increased taxation in Nabha and Malerkotla States be abolished;

(vii) All the tenants of all the 784 Patiala villages, many of who had paid *batai* since before the year 1918 and who had been declared *'ghair maroosi'* for unknown reasons be declared *'Maroosi'* and thus the discrimination between *'maroosi'* and *'ghair maroosi'* be removed;

(viii) The land be restored to the *muzaras* from which they had been dispossessed and the revenue be assessed on the same scale on them as it was levied on the land of the general public or at the rates prevalent in the neighbouring partitions of the Patiala state;

(ix) The action against *muzaras* under section 424 I.P. and also the looting of *muzaras* by the state officials and *biswedars* be stopped;

(x) The non-occupancy tenants be recognised as occupancy tenants and the system of assessment in cash be introduced also; The land revenue should be realised by tehsil authorities;

(xi) The tenants (evidently occupancy tenants) in 784 villages of Patiala state declared themselves to be landlords and wanted the existing record land

40. File No. M/3-22-40 (File contains various Pamphlets in *Panjabi*) PSA : Patiala; AISPC Papers, File No. 138 (Part One). Private Papers Section, NMML : New Delhi.

owners to be altogether eliminated and the settlement of the revenue to be made with them;

(xii) The confiscated property be restored and the execution of decrees be stopped;

(xiii) *Hidayat* 1988 (Samabat) should be annulled;

(xiv) Responsible Government should be set up in the states; the right of franchise should be given to the tenants to elect the *Zaildars* and *Lumbardars* from the terms of three years; freedom of speech and press was also demanded;

(xv) The punitive police posts should be removed;

(xvi) The price of grain should not be allowed to fall lower than in the British *ilaqa;* the Government agencies to buy grains in the market should be established;

(xvii) Cases running against the anti-fascist comrades (Communists) should be withdrawn; the officers should be stopped from concocting false cases against the tenants;

(xviii) *Kisan Sabhas,* the student unions and the *Praja Mandals* should be acknowledged as lawful organisations.[41]

The demands of the *Kisans* were thus voiced and the state was urged to stop their exploitation at the hands of the *biswedars.* A deputation of the *muzaras* met the *Maharaja* of Patiala to get their grievances redressed and when they were ignored, they started taking possession of the *biswedars'* lands forcibly. They also decided in a conference at Anandpur Sahib not to pay *batai.* Consequently, the *muzaras* of various villages (*e.g.*, Bir Khurd, Jangiana, Karamgarh, Bassi, Dipgarh,

41. Memorandum submitted by the members of the Patiala War-Council, Patiala State Records, File No. 565/C-1939; Kalsia State Records, File No. 164, PSA : Patiala. (The various demands of the peasants can be gathered from various posters, pamphlets distributed in the villages and the memorandum submitted to the rulers. For this one has to see the Records of all the States of East Punjab).

Alampur, Madran, Satika, Mallsinghwala, Moolasinghwala, Khiwa, Shehzada Singhwala, Talwandi-Sabo, Chinarthal, Teona, Pujarian, Jarkian, Bhadaur, Kot Duna, Jeonda, all the villages of Bhudhalada) refused to pay *batai*. At the same time a large number of posters both in *Panjabi* and *Urdu* were published and circulated among the rural masses. Though these posters the *Kisan* Committees and other political organisations continued their war against the state authorities. It was made clear through these pamphlets that the *Jathas* of *Kisans* would go and attack the palaces of the *Maharajas* and *Nawaba* and soon there would be the rule of the peasants in the Punjab.[42] Similarly, many *Jathas* of *Muzaras* were sent to Lahore to meet the British Resident and also to Simla to place their grievances and demands before the higher authorities of the British Government.[43]

There were, actually, four political parties active in the *Kisan* front—the *Kisan* Committees, the Communists, the Ridha Singh party and Col. Raghbir Singh Akali group—which were of the view that it was an imperialistic war.[44] At this time, the All India *Kisan Sabha* demanded the imposition of ceiling on land holding and distribution of surplus land to agricultural labourers and poor peasants. In their conference of 1945, it was stressed that the question of taking concrete action to impose ceiling on land holdings had become a burning issue and its significance was all the more in view of the Government of India schemes for higher agricultural production and organisation of agricultural economy.[45]

In brief, various bodies of the tenants demanded from time to time that the poor peasants who received land in distribution should be allowed to pay rent direct to the Government and in no case the rent be more than one sixth of

42. Kalsia State Records, File No. 132, PSA : Patiala.
43. Patiala State Records, Prime Minister's Office File No. 750, PSA : Patiala.
44. Patiala State Records, File No. 2077, PSA : Patiala; Basta No. 13, File No. 2001, PSA : Patiala.
45. Patiala State Records, File No. 2077, PSA : Patiala, 81.

the gross produce. If the existing rent was less than that, it should not be increased. The Government after deducting charges should pay the rent as compensation to the landlord. This compensation to the landlords was in no case to exceed a period of 10 years and after that the Government should collect only land revenue. The person receiving land should be made full owner immediately after the first year's rent was paid.

The peasants' unrest culminated in two violent incidents. The firing cases of Rajomara and Quilla Hakim are the best examples of the ruthless persecution of the state peasantry at the hands of the *biswedars* who dominated the state Government.[46] A brief summary of these two cases would not be out of the place here :

This case provides an interesting study of the tenants' Movement in the Patiala State. According to the judicial enquiry Commission, which investigated the happenings at Quilla Hakim in 1937[47] (on the 11th Maghar, 1944), an incident happened at Raipur Quilla Hakim, Tehsil Dhuri, district Bassi, in which firing was reported to have been ordered. As result of this firing, 11 persons received injuries and 2 out of them subsequently died. The state issued orders on 29th of November, 1937 to the Commission to proceed immediately to hold a judicial enquiry into the incident.[48]

The Commission headed by the Judicial Magistrate reached Quilla Hakim on the morning of the 30th November, 1937. The village people were informed about it so that those who wanted to say something might appear before the Commission and give their statements. On that day the tenants of the village were reluctant to come and help the enquiry. However, the magistrate explained to them the purpose of the enquiry and

46. Dr. Joginder Dayal, *'Riyasti Logon Ka Ghol Ten Communists'*, (An article in *Panjabi*), published in a *Souvenir*, issued by the CPI on January 26, 1976, 91-95.

47. File No. 6175, Report of Judicial Enquiry into the happening at Raipur Quilla Hakim, Patiala State Records, PSA : Patiala.

48. *Ibid.*, Copy of the poster preserved in Patiala State Records, Prime Minister's Office File No. 750, PSA : Patiala.

that there was nothing to be afraid of. Next morning regular enquiry began. Statements of over 49 witnesses were recorded. The Statements of the tenants, *biswedars*, their agents, *Lambardars, safedposhes* and *Zaildars*, were all taken at the village. Instead of discussing the evidences recorded it would be more appropriate to give a brief history of the case, given in the revenue records.

Raipur Quilla Hakim was a *biswedari* village and its tenants were given the status of occupancy-tentants under sections 5 and 8 of the tenancy Act, paying *batai* to the landlords. The landlords, regularly received the share of the produce since the regular settlement, with a few exceptions on some occasions when some tenants now and then refused to pay rent; and the tenants reportedly admitted the status of the landlords and acknowledged themselves to be tenants.

But gradually due to non-payment of rent the *biswedars* were obliged to institute suits for the recovery of the rent and apply for ejectment. Though the *biswedars* obtained decrees against the tenants, some remained unexecuted and this fact emboldened them to withhold the payment of *batai* altogether and they posed themselves as owners of the lands. The tenants under the circumstances expressed their inability to pay the land revenue to the landlords. This state of affairs continued till 1930 when the tenants again began to pay the land revenue. The landlords took proceedings against the tenants to the law courts and some of them were ejected. The tenants there upon began to submit petition after petition to His Highness contesting the landlords. The *Maharaja* asked the Minister of law and justice to hold a thorough and exhaustive enquiry into the matter. Diwan Bahadur S. Pindi Dass Sabharwal submitted a detailed report on the 11th June, 1933. When the final orders on this report were still awaited, the *biswedars* submitted another petition. The case was finally decided by the *Ijlas-i-Khas* committee that the tenants' claim to ownership was frivolous and so their claims were rejected and an order was passed that action be taken accordingly by the revenue authorities.

However, the tenants were not prepared to give *batai* to the *biswedars* inspite of the above orders. On this the *biswedars* applied to the revenue authorities for the division of the produce. The revenue authorities also favoured them. But the tenants were determined not to allow *batai* under any circumstances.[49] The tehsildar alongwith the Mukhtiars of biswedars and some policemen went to collect *batai*. Some 120 villagers including male and female persons reached *Chhaur* and openly refused to obey and the *tehsildar* failed in his mission. Now the *Zamin* accompanied by the Superintendent of Police, Sunam, 4 head constables and 11 constables out of whom 11 had guns went to the village. H had with him some licence holders, *Safedposhes* of the *ilaqa* and some *lamberdars*.[50]

But the tenants did not listen to any advice and they refused to come to him. Rather, they gathered near the *Mosque* and did not allow the *bata* even at the cost of their lives. 3 tenants were taken into custody. As soon as they were arrested, some 300 to 400 people came to the land in front of Hattai. The *Nazim* seeing this attitude of the tenants, proceeded to the *Chhaur* of *Bhanga Singh* where the *batai* was stopped. Hence, the tenants succeeded in their agitation.[51]

It was really on of the most important cases in the Patiala State and was destined to serve as a precedent to solve the disputes between the tenants and the *biswedars*. The case arose out of a century old dispute between the tenants and the *biswedars*. It not stood the span of more than a generation but also resisted the colossal labour and energy of several enquiry committees appointed off and on by the Patiala State. From the records of this case now preserved in the Punjab State Archives, Patiala we learn that the limitation was sent to the Commission on the 7th of September, 1945. The first open siting of the Commission however, came up on 13th of September, 1945, in which both the parties were directed to appear before the Commission on September 23, 1945. They

49. Patiala State Records, Prime Minister's Office File No. 6157/6-2155, Punjab State Archives, Patiala; Personal meeting with Chhajju Mal, who took an active part in almost all the *morchas* in the East Punjab States.

50. Patiala State Records, File No. 6157/6-2155, PSA : Patiala.

51. Prime Minister's Office File No. 6157-6-2155, PSA : Patiala.

were also directed to file a list of the biswedars and tenants respectively. The second sitting was fixed for 9th October, 1945. On this date the representatives of the *biswedars* filed a list of all the *biswedars* but the representatives of the tenants pleaded their inability to cope with the work entrusted to them but submitted that the number of the tenants was about four hundred. Consequently, the enquiry was fixed for October 18, 1945 and on this day the statements of both the parties were recorded. The next sitting was fixed for 25th October, 1945, when the statement of the *Daftar-Qanugo,* Dhuri was recorded. This case was now adjourned to 14th November, 1945. The *Sadar-Qanugo,* Bassi, was also summoned with all the relevant records previous of the settlement of 1905.

The Commission was, however, not satisfied with the production of the old records and felt the necessity of making a searching enquiry into all relevant previous records besides the one that had already been brought before the previous Enquiry Committee of 1931. So, the Commission visited Bassi and ransacked the whole record pertaining to the dispute. Both the parties engaged counsels, who addressed the Commission at a considerable length for 4 days. The *biswedars* explained that the village was founded by their ensestors, Kaula Singh, Balla Singh and Daula Singh and the defendant tenants had been cultivating the land and paying *batai.* A dispute, however, arose regarding the right to receive *batai* and some of the tenants submitted to the *batai* rights of the *biswedars* while others denied that claim to them. But generally the land remained with the tenants. This led the Commmission to the conclusion that if the position of the *biswedar* was that of *"ala-malak"* or *'Taluqdar',* which in the state terminology, was equal to *biswedar,* the tenants' ancestors were a sort of *'adnamalaks'* and were entered in the old records as *'Zamindars'.* In the Punjab, the one was termed as 'superior owner' or *'ala-malak'* and the other was described only as *'adna-malak'.* The rights of the inferior proprietors some times extended over the whole estate including the waste land and in other cases they were confined to their separate holdings and the waste was at the disposal of the superior or *'ala-malik'* subject to certain rights of use enjoyed by the village community. In such cases the *'ala-Malik'* continud to receive a share in some districts in kind and in other districts it was commuted by the collectors into a fixed percentage of the land revenue. The Financial Commissioner had declared that both-*'ala-Malik'* and *'adna-Malik'* would be liable for the land revenue, but he laid down no specifications. But in actual practice only the inferior landlords who were actually in cultivation were held to be liable for the land revenue.

Occupancy tenants, holding on privileged rents were in possession of a part of proprietory rights but they differed from inferior owner in as much as their rents were, within certain limits and circumstances, liable to enhancement and their rights of transfer were subject to limitations based on the superior rights or another person who was recognised as landlord. Because of the circumstances it was felt that the occupancy tenancy could get nothing beyond the land revenue and it was to be deposited in the State Treasury. The tenants, moreover, had not yet submitted to that position ether on account of obduracy or as they alleged, on account of the justification of their case.

It would be interesting to point out here that in the course of this enquiry, the representative of the tenants asserted that in the preparation of this record of enquiry, they should not be referred to and recorded as tenants but only as a party. But the *biswedars* claimed that the defendants be declared as tenants and that rent would be equivalent to the land revenue. Apart from this consideration, the Commission was satisfied with the documentary evidences and by the analogy prevailing in other districts of the Punjab that the plaintiff were *biswedar 'ala-malik'* and the defendents were *'adna-malik'*. The Commission recommended to the Patiala State Government that Revenue record be amended accordingly. The above findings brought the Commission to the other part of the issue as to what relief the parties were entitled to. In this respect, it goes without saying that in the cases of divided ownership of the proprietors, profits were shared between the two classes and following the precedents of other districts of the Punjab as well as of he United Provinces, it was thought advisable that the claim of the superior owner of a share in the *Batai* over the inferior proprietor, be converted into a cash levy as a surcharge upon the land revenue calculated at a certain percentage or a fraction in a rupee without, of course, the imposition of ceases which was thought to be an anachronism and no case would be made out of it. This method as stated above, could be enforced either by framing a rule or by some special order or legislative measure by the Sate Government. In this arrangement the defendants were to have the status of a *'malak-Qabza' i.e.* that of an inferior proprietor with the right of letting, a mortgaging, selling their lands as they pleased and having their own tenants if they so liked and the *biswedars* as superior proprietors were to get a certain share in the land revenue without coming in conflict with the defendants in any manner. The surcharge or the addition in the land revenue was termed as *Haq-malkan*. In regard to the rate of this surcharge the point was not free from difficulty. However, the Commission submitted that the rate in other places varied with the locality and on the terms of mutual contract. In this controversy the Commission could see no scope or room for mutual agreement and if the parties were left to strike mutual agreements, there was a danger of the whole matter again being shelved and thrown into cold storage. The Commission took note of the fact that fund the tenancy law, this surcharge could go to the extend of two *annas* in a rupee but the equities of the case in Rajomajra village demanded that it should not, in any way, exceed one *anna* in a rupee on the land revenue. It also pointed out that in case the defendants did not again submit on the point of surcharge on the land revenue, two ways were open to the Government. One was that of the enforcement of the rule of law and the other of conciliation. Finally, the Patiala State agreed that the land revenue in comparison with the rates prevailing outside the state, might not come down very much; the other via media would have been that the ascertained land revenue might be accepted by the Government including the surcharge rent payable to the *biswedars*. Under this system of fixed surcharge of a fraction with or without the land revenue, the *biswedars* were enabled to hold their former position and the right of superior proprietorship while the tenant class was to find itself to be in an elevated and privileged position by this division of ownership into superior and inferior one.

Thus, these two incidents showed that the tenant movement which started in 1928 had now reached a decisive stage. As will be shown in later sections, it was an indication of the growing Communist influence on the *Kisans* struggle in general and the tenant movement in particular.[52] It also symbolises the impatience leading to desperation which had overtaken the general peasant masses of the state. It was in these circumstances that *Maharaja* Bhupinder Singh announced the setting up of a Constitutional Reforms Committee which was wholly consisted of officials. The Committee was to recommend changes in the Constitution of the State "with a view to giving the subjects a definite voice and share in the making of law and the administration throw in the state."[53] It was to submit proposals within six months. The Maharaja, however, died within a fortnight of the appointment of this Committee and so it went into cold-storage. But the appointment of the Committee provided a fit climax to the ten year old *Praja Mandal* movement which had been guiding the *muzaras* movement in the state. Consequently, the tenant struggle against the state's authority continued more

52. Well known Communists workers from Punjab were the most frequent speakers at Public meetings organised by the *Praja* Mandal. Sohan Singh Josh, Arjan Singh Gargaj, Karam Singh Mann, and Baba Rur Singh were some of the prominent communist leaders. Vide (Report of a public meeting at Khanna held on August 2, 1936), Patiala State Records, File No. 747; (The poster of Longowal Conference scheduled for 7th & 8th November 1936), Patiala State Records, File No. 737, PSA : Patiala.

53. The Committee was consisted of *Nawab* Liyakat Hiat Khan, Prime Minister of the Patiala State—as Chairman; Raja Hari Krishan Kaul, Revenue Minister; Major K.M. Panikar, Foreign Minister; Capt. H.N. Raina, Law Minister; Major S. Ajmer Singh, Accountant General. Vide, *The Tribune,* Lahore, January 23, 1938, *Ibid.*

vigorously. Now the tenants' movement was assuming the shape of a mass movement.

Let us now have a look at the *muzaras'* agitation in states other than Patiala. In the Malerkotla and Faridkot states, peasants did not have full proprietory rights on the land held by them. They were treated as occupancy tenants, and in the revenue records it was the prince or some landlord who was known as *'Ala-Malik'* or the super-lord. The peasant in the Malerkotla state never accepted this position as there the situation was worse than in Faridkot. The reason for such a situation was clear, the Muslim were mainly the landlords, while the cultivators were mostly sikhs. An enquiry had been conducted into their claims but its findings and recommendations were never seriously accepted by the *nawab* or his *biswedars*.[54] The peasants had continued their struggle. One of these was the agitation launched by the peasant proprietors of Malerkotla state against encroachment on their rights by the *Khawanin* (muslim landlords), who did not permit them to dispose of their land according to their will.

The *Nawab* was accused of taking undu benefit of the *nazool* laws and taking possession of lands when there were legal heir alive and who had a legitimate claim.[55] Nothing else can make the peasant more agitated than a danger to his proporietory rights in land. The peasants therefore, met in a Convention at Khottala on 10th January, 1927 and decided to set up a *Zamindara* Association for the safeguard of their rights. They also decided to lead a mass deputation to Simla that summer and present a petition to the Viceroy. The proposed move and widely publicised and people were asked to send their grievances to this newly formed body to be incorporated in the petition. This greatly irked the state authorities and made the *Nawab* and *Khawanin* quite panicky. A campaign of vilification was let loose against the *Zamindara* Association

54. Giani, Kehar Singh, *Praja Malerkotla Di Dard Kahani,* printed and published by Jagir Singh Joga, Amritsar : Desh Dardi Press, Introduction, 1-2.

55. *Ibid.*, 39, 43 and 49.

and a puppet National *Zamindara* Association was set up with loyalist aims and objectives. But nothing could check the advance of the agitation. As the news of the proposed *morcha* to Simla spread, the anxiety of the *Nawab* mounted. In utter desperation, a meeting of the association was attacked by the state police and the armed forces on 18th July, 1927, killing 14 men, women and cihildren.[56] Hundred of peasants were arrested including many on their return from Simla and a conspiracy case was launched. One of the office bearers of the Association Talib Hussain turned approve and the accused were sentenced to long terms of imprisonment. Talib Hussain later retraced his steps and publicly apologised for the misconduct and became a leading advocate of the tenant movement in the state.[57]

Khottala episode symbolized the general peasant unrest in the state and it was also the beginning of the powerful movement for defence of the peasants' interests. It took hardly two years for the tenant agitation to raise its head in other states. This episode would have remained an isolated affair, had it not taken place at a time when the general tide of freedom movement in the country was rising high.

In the thirties, in Malerkotla state, the movement was being organised by Giani Kehar Singh of the village of Chak, Sewa Singh of village Bapla and Talip Hussain of Sharwanikot.[58] The main demands of the Malerkotla peasantry were to end corruption and illegal extraction of money by the *nawab*, the safeguarding of their rights in land and the boinging down of land revenue to the level of Ludhiana district

56. Giani, Kehar Singh, *Praja Malerkotla Di Dard Kahani*, Printed and published by Jagir Singh Joga, Amritsar : Desh Dardi Press, 67.

57. Walia, Ramesh, A Study of the Praja Mandal Movement in the East Punjab States, Patiala : 1974, 82-83.

58. Hussain Talib rose to an important position in the Punjab *Riyasti Praja Mandal*. He was a forceful writer and an effective speaker. He also edited *"Riyasti Duniya"* Vide File No. 578; File No. 595; PSA : Patiala.

in the Punjab.[59] These demands were published in the form of a poster termed 'Malerkotla Indictment' by the state *Praja Mandal* and people were asked to supply their grievances to the *Kisan* leaders. A demand was also made of the paramount Power to hold an enquiry into the state administration and remove the *Nawab* in case the charges were proved. The annual observance of the Khottala day in memory of the persons who had fallen to police bullets in 1927 became a relaying point for the state peasantry. The annual fair of Chhapar, district Ludhiana, provided an other occasion for the peasants to meet and chalk-out their programme for further agitation.[60]

In Jind State, the peasants launched a *morcha* against the state administration. The Sikh peasants in the Jind State had their grievances against the state administration which went unheeded at the hands of state officials, particularly the Prime Minister, Dr. Bihari Lal Dhingra. These grievances were mainly related to the judicial and revenue administration of the state. Land revenue had been enhanced and corruption prevailed all round.[61] It was alleged by the *Kisan* leaders that the choicest land in two sikh dominated villages had been gifted to Dr. Dhingra by the *Maharaja* and the cultivating owners were being dispossessed by him. Then three were grievances concerning the *begar* system and forcible supplies of fodder and other provisions for the hunting parties of the *Maharaja* and his guests. Again it was the peasantry that became the mainstay of the agitation in the state.

The character of the tenant movement in the Jind State was not in any way different from that in the Patiala State.

59. Giani, Kehar Singh, *Praja Malerkotla Di Dard Kahani,* Amritsar, 90-93.

60. Chhapur is near Ahemedgarh railway station on Ludhiana-Hissar Railway Line. Thousands of peasants from states also attended it. Political parties held conferences on the occasion to propagate their programme and policies.

61. Longowalia, Bhagwan Singh, *'Mal Administration in Jind State'* Patiala State Record, File No. 595; A personal interview with Gujjar Singh Dhanetha village also confirmed the material published in the booklet.

The Akalis formed the hard core of the peasant workers everywhere and their main demands were concerned with the redressal of the peasant grievances. The only difference was that here the movement always remained on a low level. It neither attained the sweep it did in Petiala for could it attract the attention of the Indian States' People's Conferences.

Unrest among the peasants rapidly mounted in the tiny state of Kalsia which witnessed a regular peasant revolt in 1928. This state was consisted of two chunke of territory : One, the main block of villages round Chhachhrauli, the Capital Town bordering on the Ambala District, and the second, a small twenty square mile seven-village pocket of Charik in the Ferozpur district. The Charik pocket was more than a hundred miles away from the capital and was beyond any effective administrative control from the state headquarters.[62] The peasant movement in the Ferozpur district had made rapid strides in the thirties and Baba Rur Singh had emerged as an influential leader having been elected to the Punjab Assembly in 1937.[63]

It was mainly under his inspiration that the Charik peasants set up their own *Kisan* agitation in early 1938 and presented a charter of demands to the Kalsia ruler.[64] The charter contained 28 demands and some of the most important are as follows :[65]

(a) The land revenue of Rs. 2-8-9 per *Ghumaon* was very high which the *Kisan* could not afford in those days of comparative cheapness and it must be reduced and

62. Kalsia State Records, File No. 25 of 1938, PSA : Patiala.

63. (Rus Singh was an able organiser leading the *Kisan* Committee, a Communist controlled organisation of the peasants) Vide. Shamsher Singh Gill, *The Woeful Tale,* published by the author as Secretary of the *Ilaqa Charik Kisan* Committee.

64. Kalsia State Records, File No. 25 of 1938, PSA : Patiala; Gill, Shamsher Singh, *The Woeful Tale,* published by the author as Secretary of the *Ilaqa Charik Kisan* Committee.

65. Charter published in the *Tribune,* Lahore, dated 12th June, 1938; The copy of this Charter is also available in Kalsia State Records, File No. 25 of 1938; PSA : Patiala.

brought in level with the rates current in the adjoining British *Ilaqa*, which was between 0.12.0 and Rs. 1.0.0 per *Ghumaon* in different places;

(b) *Begar* was too heavy and must be done away with altogether;

(c) Indebtedness Bill should be brought in force;

(d) Necessary arrangement for the timely and adequate supply of canal water should be made in agreement with the Canal authorities and the revenue rates be reduced so as to be sompatible with the current economic conditions;

(e) All the lands of *Zamindars*, now held by the *Shahukars* or other *Zamindars* under twenty years agreement, should be restored to the *Kisans* without any payment.

The people of the *Ilaqa* Charik were bent upon getting their grievances redressed and were fully prepared to undergo any amount of suffering for their just and lawful demands.[66] So, they launched an agitation in support of their demands, held public meetings and sent *Jathas* to the state Capital. They raised slogans like, "Redress our grievances", "Grant us our legitimate rights". "Give us the desired protection of a good Government and make friendship with us as ever". But all their appeals had fallen on deaf ears. Now the local peasants came out with a firm determination to demand their just rights and enrolled themselves in a Committee entitled, "The *Ilaqa* Charik *Kisan* Committee". The Committee had held some open air meetings in the villages and had also affiliated itself with the provincial *Kisan* Committee of Punjab.[67] The Committee had resolved to get the demands of the peasants fulfilled at any cost by all non-violent means.[68]

The Charik movement had full co-ordination with the agitation of the people of Chhachhrauli and the surrounding villages in support of similar demands. However, Moga was

66. Kalsia State Records, File No. 25, of 1938, PSA : Patiala.

67. *Ibid.*

68. *Ibid.*

generally the centre of their activities but the tenants were reported to have held a meeting at Ludhiana, with a view to launching their movement in the state of mass scale. Now a *Jatha* of the *Kisan* Committee held a big red flag demonstration in front of the Diwan's residence and the police station on 29th July, 1938 but no arrest was made. Getting no response from the state administration, the Committee decided to boycott the annual cattle fair at Charik which was to be held in the month of September 1938. All entrances to the site of the fair were blocked by women volunteers and prospective buyers and sellers were dissuaded from participating in the fair. There were reports of earthen even *(Tandoors)* at the fair site having been snatched b the volunteers of the *Kisan* Committee.[69] Nails were spread on the roads to puncture the tyres of the vehicles. The boycot of the fair proved a big success.[70]

About the agitation, a police report said[71] that the agitation was increasing day by day. Open defiance was being preached, the prestige of the police was being lowered, bad and indecent speeches were being made in every part of the state and feelings of hatred against the ruler and the administration were being created. Repressive policy would have to be adopted. This might lead to further trouble but there was no other way out. But the state authority lacked police force to curb this agitation.

The cumulative effect of this situation was that the agitation continued unabated. Conditions were getting worse as no *lambardar* cared for the *Tehsildar* or any other state official. *Jathas* continued marching to the state capital throughout the

69. *The Tribune,* Lahore, September 17, 1938 (Statement of the Dewan).

70. (The total income to the state upto 19th September, 1938, penultimate day of the fair was a paltry sum of rupees one thousand as compared to rupees eight thousand of the previous years. Total number of the cattle sold in the fair was 789 as against 4861 in 1937, their total value being rupees 28, 488 and Rs. 2, 07, 625 in 1938 and 1937 respectively) Vide. Report of the Superintendent of Police dated 25th Sept., 1938, Kalsia State Records, File I & II, PSA : Patiala.

71. Report of the Superintendent of Police dated 30th August, 1938, PSA : Patiala.

months of October and November. State officials apprehended difficulties in the realisation of land revenue in December 1938 because of the ruffled feelings of the *Kisans* over the Charik Morcha.[72] A *Jatha* of 20 tried to force their entry into the fort on 12th November, 1938 but only five arrests were made. To the earlier demands of the *Kisan* Committee now was added another on for the release of the arrested workers. The Kalsia ruler was forced to come to terms with the agitators. A public *durbar* was held at Charik on 27th November, 1938 where the ruler of Kalsia state promised to fulfil all the main demands of the peasants.

The Charik *morcha* was indicative of the new mood of the state's people. It brought into bold relief the total bankruptcy of the administration in the smaller states. The *Morcha* also underlined the effective help which the movement at some places was receiving from the British territory. The formation of the *Praja Mandal* in Kalsia in Feb., 1940, was a direct result of this *Morcha*.[73]

In the Faridkot state, the ruler was administering similar warnings to political workers as well as the *muzaras'* leaders. *Raja* called all the important workers[74] to his palace and told bluntly to desist from holding political conference in the garb of a religious *Diwan*.[75] But the events were moving very fast. A *Zamindar Sabha* was set up on 24th July, 1938. The state Government promulgated the Registration of Societies Act in 1938, on the lines of the *Hidayat* 1988 enacted six years earlier by the Phulkian rulers. However, the political parties put forward the most progressive demands.[76] The emphasis,

72. Kalsia State Records, File No. 164, (Diwan's letter dated 20th November, 1938), PSA : Patiala.

73. Kalsia State Records, File No. 132, PSA : Patiala.

74. The main organisers of a political conference held at Kot Kapura were Zail Singh, Gurbax Singh, Jang Singh and Sandhura Singh, Vide. Faridkot State Records, File No. 336, PSA : Patiala.

75. Faridkot State Records, File No. 336, PSA : Patiala.

76. Poster published in October 1938, and Janga Singh's *Urdu*-Pamphlet *'Dukhee Janta De Dili Ubal'*, Ferozpur City, Amrit Electric Press, 1939. Preserved in PSA : Patiala.

however, was chiefly on peasants' demands, like the one that the auctioning of *Shamlat* lands should be stopped and the peasants should be allowed to sell their crops in any market they liked and not necessarily inside the state. They also demanded full proprietory rights for the *Kisan* through the abolition of the *Ala-Malik* system.[77] Public meetings were organised by the *Praja Mandals* at Kot Kapura in favour of these demands in 1938, but heavy brick-batting was done by loyalists and squads of drum and *Cannister* beaters were employed by the administration to disturb the meetings.[78]

Another *Kisan* Conference was held at Wadanikala on 10.10.1938. The leaders who addressed the Conference referred to the evils of the administration. Evils like *begar, Malba, Chowkidars* were condemned and the *muzaras* and other people were asked to unite and fight against the *batai* system, corruption in the revenue department and highhandedness of the police and *biswedars*. They were exhorted to continue this struggle till the state authorities yielded.[79] Another big conference was held, at Muktsar on October 30, 1938, under the presidentship of Sardar Lal Singh, an advocate of Ludhiana. The demands, discussed above appeared in almost all the speeches delivered there.[80] In brief, this struggle continued till their demands were met.

The seed of the agrarian unrest and disturbance of peace had been sown in the Kapurthala state since the beginning of the thirties. Begowal, Talwandi, Chaudharian and some more were the villages where the unrest had its origin but the activities of the tenants' leaders had also inspired the tenants

77. Faridkot State Records, File No. 4, PSA : Patiala; Avtar Singh, *'Din Dihare Raatan', Panjabi*—a booklet—published by the author, Faridkot State Records, File No. 357, PSA : Patiala.

78. Faridkot State Records, File Nos. I & II (Material given in *Panjabi*), PSA : Patiala; File No. 108, PSA : Patiala.

79. Faridkot State Records, File No. 3, PSA : Patiala; File No. 108, PSA : Patiala.

80. Faridkot State Records, File No. 4; File No. 357, PSA : Patiala.

of the surrounding villages.[81] The fact that the cultivators of other places in the tehsil of Phagwara, Bhunga and Sultanpur had not joined their fellow-cultivators in this agitation, establishes that their demand was ill conceived. But this version given by the state officials does not appear true, because later on it was admitted by the state authorities that the petty officers of the state such as *Numberdars, Zaildars, Patwaris* and school teachers had a hand in strengthening and directing the agitation.[82] For instance, Sardar Abdul Haq, Revenue Minister of the state (and brother of the Chief Minister) took a prominent part in the agitation through the agency of his subordinates in the villages. Some of his subordinates who openly took part in spreading the disturbances were given undue promotions.[83]

It was the *Zamindars,* League (non-communal and anti-communal) that made sincere efforts for the attainment of its objects like *(i)* the amelioration of the economic condition of the agricultural classes and their social and political advancement; *(ii)* Constitutional reforms—like the welfare, prosperity and the progress of the agriculturists in other directions. Let us first of all have a look on their grievances. The main grievances of the agriculturists are detailed below :[84]

(a) They were groaning under crushing land revenue rates which were double, in some cases triple of, or even higher than those prevalent in the adjacent British districts, while the measurement scale was smaller.

(b) The land cases amounted to Rs. 21/15/4 in contrast to Rs. 17/8/4 per Rs. 100/- of land revenue in the adjacent British districts, the former including Rs. 3/10/- of *Abwahi Khidmatguzari* which was a guided name for *Begar* cess :

81. Kapurthala State Records, File No. 556-J/3/15-37.

82. *Ibid.*

83. *Ibid.*

84. Kapurthala State Records, File No. M/3-37-37 Part B No. 569 Re. Land Revenue, PSA : Patiala (many grievances of the agriculturists are given in this file).

(c) Their economic condition was pitiable. They were involved in huge accumulated debts from which there was no hope of escape except through Government (State help; etc.).

During the course of their struggle the Zamindars demanded that :[85]

(i) The land revenue should be assessed on the principles and rates prevalent in the adjacent British districts and steps should be taken to place the land assessment on an equitable basis;

(ii) Measures should be devised to emancipate the agriculturists from huge indebtedness and afford them economic relief otherwise beneficent activities should be extended to the rural areas on an increasingly liberal scale;

(iii) *Begar, Malba, Batai* and *Nazool* systems should be immediately abolished; etc.

When the state Government did not care for their just demands the agriculturists sped up their agitation. Now a big demonstration was staged in the city. With this, the Muslim tenants refused to pay the customary rent to the landords.[86]

In 1938-39, there was a peasant agitation against *malba* tax which was being charged at the rate of six percent of the land revenue.[87] The people refused to pay the tax and the *landlords* expressed their inability to do any thing in the matter. The situation became quite grave at village Narur which was described as a storm centre of the agitation. The state Government held the extremist political workers led by Master Hari Singh and Chaman Singh Dhut. The agitation won a partial victory when the *Maharaja* granted relief of the tune of a total sum of rupees sixty five thousand.

The agrarian agitation in Nabha state was led by the *Praja*

85. *Ibid.*, (Many more demands put forward by the *Zamindara* League are also cited in one of the pamphlets which are given in this file).

86. Kapurthala State Records, File No. 556-J/3-15-37, PSA : Patiala.

87. Kapurthala State Records, File No. M/3-14-39, PSA : Patiala.

Mandal workers in 1938. Many of the workers of this organisation were arrested because they were, according to the state authorities, indulging in anti-state activities. Notable among those arrested were Sahib Singh Salana, Hardit Singh Bhattal, Hira Singh Bhattal and Hardial Singh of Nabha. Even the state Government admitted that certain, "malcontents had been arrested for their defiance of some of the state's existing laws".[88] Similar was the fate of the *Kisan* Conference held at Chhapar fair in September, 1938.[89] Hardit Singh Bhattal who was to have presided over the Conference, was arrested from his presidential procession and the tenants were dispersed by force by the police of the Malerkotla state. Sangat Singh who presided over the Conference, in the absence of Hardit Singh Bhattal, was taken into custody. Some days later, all leading workers of Nabha as well as of Malerkotla states, including Sahib Singh Salana were arrested and a case of murderous assault under section 307 of the Indian Penal Code launched against them.[90]

It was under the leadership of the Punjab *Kisan Sabha* that a *Kisan Sabha* was set up in Patiala. The tenants' movement went on during the second world war also. In 1946, a tenants' convention was held at the village Dalel Walah.[91] The Convention formed a 'Tenants' War Council' and it provided war leadership to the movement. In almost all the villages of the tenants, the payment of *'Batai'* was stopped. The *stop-batai* movement had to bear with limitless atrocities. Even the firing at Kishangarh could not suppress this movement. Many leaders attained martyrdom in this movement.[92]

---

88. *The Tribune,* Lahore, dated 24th August, 1938.
89. Salana, Sahib Singh, *Aap Biti,* 134.
90. *Ibid.,* 136; AISPC Papers, File No. 138 (Part-I) 1933-48 (Private Papers Section, Nehru Memorial Museum and Library, New Delhi) 911.
91. Personal interview with Master Hari Singh, Chandigarh. Masterji was at that time the General Secretary of the Punjab *Kisan Sabha,* also took part in the Convention. This is also supported by Vaid Chhajju Mal and Sardar Ishar Singh Majhail.
92. Master Hari Singh, *'Punjab Wich Kirsani Laher'* (The Farmers' movement in Punjab—Before and after Independence), in *Punjabi,* published in a Souvenir issued by the CPI on January 26, 1976, 36.

Like Patiala, in Una *Tehsil* also, the tenants had been fighting against the exploitation of the owners right since the first *Bandobast*. In 1936-37, this movement acquired war proportions. The tenants refused to get the standing crops assessed. But in 1946, this movement gained still greater momentum. In 84 villages, the payment of *'batai'* discontinued.[93] The movement continued even after independence. In 1952, the *Marusi Muzara* law was passed in the Punjab *Vidhan Sabha*. According to this law, all the *Marusi* tenants were made owners and some compensation was charged from them. This law came into force all over the state.[94]

Similarly, the tenants' movement continued against the exploitation of the state authorities in the Malerkotla, Faridkot, Kapurthala and Nabha states. The state sucked their very blood. Therefore, in 1948, they took an active part in the upcoming movement for ending royalty *(Raja-Shahi)*. As a result of the upsurge among the people of the state, in 1948, all the states of the Punjab merged and the Pepsu was formed.[95]

The *Jagirdars* of the Patiala state particularly appeared to be exceedingly perturbed. They anticipated that the final decision of this long standing controversy was going to be made in favour of the *Muzaras* by the Commission appointed by the *Maharaja* of Patiala, a reference to which has already been made earlier in this Chapter. Some big *biswedars* concluded that if the decision resulted in favour of the *Muzaras* it would ruin the *biswedars* altogether and would mean another great trouble for the state administration because the *muzaras*[96] movement in the states formed a part and parcel of *Kisan* Party in the British Punjab which was essentially

93. Master Hari Singh, *Punjab Wich Kirsani Lehr* (Panjabi) published in a *Souvenir* issued by the CPI in January, 1976.

94. *Ibid.*

95. *Ibid.*, Vaid, Chhajju Mal, *'Pepsu Muzarian Da Ghol Ten Communist Party'*, see *Souvenir* issued by the CPI in January 26, 1976.

96. Patiala State Records, Prime Minister's Office, Case No. 565/C of 1939; PSA : Patiala.

Communistic in character.[97]

Since the beginning of the peasants' movement, the *biswedars* had been standing like a rock in their way, as a result of which the peasants' agitation could not succeed in extending its activities in every region of the state. The *biswedars* also held that the Patiala Government ought not to have taken up this question, at least, during the war period. They further argued that since the same law pertaining to the rights of regents was in force in the British Punjab and no special concessions were being allowed to the *muzaras* there, why then any such steps should be taken in the state.[98] Moreover the *biswedars* requested the *Maharaja* of Patiala not to accede to their (tenants') demands. Firstly, the tenants wanted rights from the *biswedars* and then they would refuse payment of revenue to the state. They also stated that in case the state Government did not concede to their rights, the *biswedars* would send a deputation to wait upon the Viceroy.[99]

Just as the tenants were organising attacks on the landlords, the *biswedars* thought of organising attacks on them. The *biswedars* felt that they should recruit strong youths for this purpose. Their names would be kept secret and they would be expected to be on duty for all the 24 hours. The landlords, being the friends of police and other officials, since they were rich men, could very easily win over them, and used this force against the tenants' agitation.[100]

When the campaign for non-payment of *Batai* was launched by the tenants, the *biswedars* sought to eject them with due formality.[101] However, this rather strengthened the agitation

97. *Ibid.*

98. File No. 1564, Basta No. 50, Case No. 565/C of 1940 (Part-III), Basta No. 173, Case No. 41/C of 1939, PSA : Patiala.

99. Patiala State Records, Basta No. 15, PSA : Patiala.

100. Patiala State Records, Basta No. 25, S.No. 740, Case No. 773/C of 1936; Basta No. 15, CBI, I-2, Pol. CID, 1945-46, PSA : Patiala.

101. Patiala State Records, Case No. 565/C of 1939 (When the tenants absolutely stopped to pay our proprietors' share, some of the *biswedars* approached the law courts and got decrees for arrears or rent and ejected some from non-occupancy holdings), PSA : Patiala; S.No. 6157, Basta No. 135, Case No. 120, PSA : Patiala.

because the tenants were not ready to accept this treatment.[102] Even if the *muzaras* of some villages promised to pay *batai* according to the *Girdawari* rule, the agents *(Mukhtiars)* of the *biswedars* did not like this attitude of the *muzaras* and they approached the state officials and the latter always favouring them ordered payment of *batai* to be made according to the *Girdawari.* The landlords on the contrary forcibly took away the crops (unthrashed) from the fields of the tenants with the help of the police or the hired *goondas.*[103] All sorts of atrocities were inflicted on the poor peasants. In fact, the landlords did not treat the *muzaras* as human beings, nor did the state Government have any soft corner for them.[104] Thus the poor farmers were badly tyrannised over by the jagirdars but the latter failed to crush their agitation.

The landlords too had their association to meet the challenge of the tenants' agitation. Its leaders always sided with the state Government. They always poisoned the ears of the *Maharajas* and also of the officials against the tenants' movement in the state.[105] It will not be out of place to cite some of the suggestions given by the landlords to the states' authorities against the tenants' agitation. These are as follows :

(a) The *Zamindar Sabha* requested the state Governments to direct the police authorities to recover unlicenced and unauthorised arms from the villages of *Biswedars.* The tenants had already launched attacks upon *biswedars.* If no immediate action was taken there was every possibility of widespread lawlessness. The *Sabha*

102. The tenants fought their cases from the lowest to the highest courts when they failed they either offered resistance or absent themselves and let the landlords take nominal possession of the land but as soon as the Government official had departed, they resumed possession. Vide Patiala State Records, S.No. 6157, Basta No. 135, Case No. 120; File No. 1560, Basta No. 50, Case No. 565/C of 1939, PSA : Patiala.

103. Patiala State Records, S.No. 1553, File No. 565/C of 1939, PSA : Patiala.

104. *Ibid.*, Patiala State Record, Basta No. 51, S.No. 1574, Case No. 565/C/1017-C, PSA : Patiala; Basta No. 50, Case No. 565/C of 1939, PSA : Patiala.

105. Patiala State Records, T.I. of 2001, PSA : Patiala.

had already been informing the State Officials of the intentions of the tenants and all the information had proved to be correct.

(b) The *Zamindar Sabha* viewed with great concern the speedy increase of dacoits, and murder cases due to the influence of Communists and therefore called upon all its members to help the authorities in getting the dacoits arrested. The natural result of their help would be that the increased power of the Communists and the leaders of the tenants' movement would be smashed in a few days for ever;

(c) The *Zamindar Sabha* requested the State Government to issue orders to district officers to carry out the provisions of *batai* under the existing law because the *Sabha* found that the steps so far taken by these officers were inadequate and unsatisfactory;

(d) The *Zamindar Sabha* considered the murderous attack upon some of the *biswedars,* like Sardar Jaswant Singh Jeji, as the direct outcome of a deep rooted conspiracy by the tenants. The *Sabha* therefore, had started collecting a fund called 'Gobindgarh Relief Fund' which was to be utilised to fight the oppression by tenants and Communists against the *Zamindars* during the course of the peasants' struggle;

(e) The *Zamindar Sabha* considered the question of restoration of the properties of those wards who had attained the required age, and recorded its surprise that so many wards who had attained the age were not getting their estates. The *Sabha* requested the states' authorities to take immediate steps in this direction;

(f) The *Zamindar Sabha* expressed their resentment against the settlement report, submitted by the Settlement Commissioner, Popham Young. All the tenants of the villages in Patiala State were, upto the last settlement, tenants-at-will. But for the first time, the tenants were raised to the status of occupancy-tenants, never before known in the Patiala State. This too was resented by the *biswedars*.[106]

However, the *Zamindar Sabha* in question had been existing for a long time. For some time its activities had become slow, but it did not become an inactive body. It was loyal to the Government. Keeping in view their position, it could not be suspected that the *Zamindars* would oppose the administration at any time.[107] The State Governments, therefore, were supporting the states' *biswedars* against the rightful cause of the *muzaras*.[108] Moreover, there was throughout the states a strong offensive and defensive alliance between the official *(Ahlkar)* and landlord *(biswedar)* classes. The *Ahlkar* who was not a *Biswedar* generally contrived to become one, and the *Biswedar* found that it was necessary to obtain a footing in the official camp. It was the influence of the landlord class which led to the issue of a *'Hidayat'* from the supreme authority in the Patiala State making it incumbent upon all occupancy tenants to pay *kind rents*.[109] Thus, the *biswedar* class always tried to crush the mounting peasants' agitation through constitutional or unconstitutional ways.

Any movement for the liberation of suffering masses was described by the state as treason and its advocates were punished through all means. No wonder the tenants' movement was described by the authorities of East Punjab as an open challenge and against the law. The tenants wanted to introduce the progressive principles in the Government by the elimination of the landlords entirely from the village polity in contravention of their recorded and traditional rights.

When the movement reached its climax the situation became vary serious and it could not be trifled with. The landlords in the state were as much the bulwark of administration as the tenants. The latter were, however more

106. *Ibid.*, Patiala State Records, Case No. 41/C of 1939, PSA : Patiala.

107. Patiala State Records, Basta No. 51, Case No. 565/C, PSA : Patiala; Kalsia State Records, File No. 35, of 1938, PSA : Patiala.

108. Kalsia State Records, File No. 25 of 1938, PSA : Patiala.

109. Kalsia State Records, File No. 35 of 1938, PSA : Patiala.

dependable and thoroughly loyal and any movement to crush them could only lead to very serious dislocation of administration. The state wanted to curb the rising movement and had given powers to the police even to resort to firing if and when it was necessary. Firing was resorted to at various places at the time of the *muzaras'* agitation.[110] It was ordered that all the ring leaders must furnish heavy security. The Government policy was to take hold of the ring-leaders, who were instigating and also leading their *morchas* against the *Biswedari* system and the states' authorities as well. But the Government was helpless in taking hold of them.

Now stray cases of politically active individuals were reported in Faridkot, Kapurthala and Kalsia States, but prompt action by the authorities forestalled any organised movement. The entry of news papers was banned in time and suspected characters were ousted from the states.[111] *Kisan* Conferences were not allowed to take place and even the *Jathas* of the tenants bound for the Conferences were checked at the place of starting by the Government.[112] Those who resisted were thrown into jails and the police even registered false cases under section 424 IPC against the tenants, thus causing them unnecessary harassment.

The state Government, if at all was compelled to probe into some clash between the landlords and the tenants, it instead of ordering a judicial enquiry under the Government of India Act, appointed some personal friends of the ruler.[113]

110. Patiala State Records, Basta No. 50, File No. 1565; Basta No. 18, Case No. 386; Basta No. 85, File No. 221/4-7775, PSA : Patiala.

111. Faridkot State Records, File Nos. 23 and 27; Confidential diaries of district magistrate No. 2920-21 (on June 29, 1939, the tenants of Kishangarh had reached Patiala and were bent upon to *Khandaghat*. The revenue minister instructed the IGP to see that these people were sent back to their village at every cost). Vide, Patiala State Records, Basta No. 13, Police CID, CB-I-2 (2001), PSA : Patiala.

112. File No. M/3-22/40, PSA : Patiala; Basta No. 85, S.No. 1263, File No. 221/4-7745, Patiala : 7775, PSA : Patiala.

113. All the *Biswedars* in the states had become *biswedars* by having given the hands of their daughters to the *Rajas* and the real owners of land had become *muzaras* and slaves, Vide. Patiala State Records, Basta No. 13, Police-CID, CB-I-2 (2001), PSA : Patiala.

Consequently, the tenants boycotted the enquiry and the problem remained unsolved. It is interesting to note that new taxes were levied and old taxes enhanced according to the whims and fancies of the land revenue authorities and that several other hardships were caused to the *riyots* in this connection.[114] The state Government in connection with the tenants' movement decided :

(i) Legal action should be taken against those who were inciting the tenants for the non-payment of *batai* to the *biswedars* :

(ii) Such persons as were visiting the tenants and might thereafter visit them with the intention of inciting them not to pay *batai* due from them should be stopped from doing so and counter propaganda should be started by the district authorities, police and revenue officers with the help of such biswedars as could be depended upon for the purpose;

(iii) When any peasant refused to pay *batai,* although it was a rightful due according to the revenue records and the past practice, action should be taken against him under the Tenancy Act;[115]

(iv) Revenue, Civil and Criminal laws should be promptly and strongly enforced and sections 107/151 Cr.P.C. might be freely used against the agitators and the tenants;

(v) Efforts should be made to arrest the professional agitators and a list of such tenants should be drawn up;

(vi) Punitive police posts in the villages affected by this movement were set up and it was to be watched by

114. What happened in Sunam? Fire was opened, females were dishonoured and even were asked to loosen their *Nalas.* (This was a kind of *Zulum*). The *Maharaja* ordered that the tenants should yield *batai,* when the poor fellows were starving. When they refused to pay *batai,* they were prosecuted under Section 424, Vide. Basta No. 50, File No. 1565; File No. 19281-23-C, PSA : Patiala.

115. File No. 41/C of 1939, PSA : Patiala.

the district officials that the tenants' movement must be stopped.[116]

The tenants, who had fled for life into the British territory, were arrested by the state police with the assistance of the British police. If any one resisted the police, he was prosecuted and subjected to so much torture that he became unconscious. Besides, the administration had so far refused to acknowledge the *Kirti Kisan* people as a representative body and held that they represented only a very small minority of mischief-mongers.[117]

The position, in brief, is that it was for the *Darbar* to take all necessary measures to deal with the situation within the state. As for the situation in British India districts surrounding the states, the Punjab Government was being kept informed of the position as reported from time to time by the *Darbar* and it was for the Government to decide upon the action to be taken.[118]

Now, as the Government of the state was afraid of the influence of the political department of the British Government, it thought of satisfying the rising tide of the tenants' movement. So, rights of the tenants were conceded; but at the same time to save the honour of the *biswedars,* they were declared *Malik-ala,* the tenants being *Malik-adna.*[119]

116. Patiala State Records, Confidential 17, Case No. T-I of 2001, PSA : Patiala.

117. Patiala State Records, Basta No. 85, S.No. 1263, File No. 221/4-7775, PSA : Patiala; Basta No. 50, File No. 1565, PSA : Patiala.

118. Final Report of the Settlement of Patiala State (1900-1908), submitted by Popham Young; Patiala State Records, Basta No. 180, Case No. 189/C, PSA : Patiala.

119. Vaid, Chhajju Mal, *Pepsu Muzarian Da Ghol Ten Communist Party,* see *Souvenir* issued by the CPI on January 26, 1976 (According to this system the name of the *Raja* was entered in the revenue records as Super Owner and all agricultural lands in the State); Master Hari Singh, *The Tenants' Movement in Punjab—Before And After Independence.* (An article in *Panjabi*) published in a *Souvenir,* issued by the CPI on January 26, 1976.

The Government had to take some more steps and the Patiala Government passed some laws. One legislation was also passed by the Government of Patiala and East Punjab States Union department. The important Acts passed by the state were the following :

(a) The Patiala Alienation of Land (Amendment) Act, 1999 B.K.;

(b) Pepsu Alienation of Land (Repeal) Act, 2008 B.K.;

(c) The Pepsu Abolition of *Ala-Malkiyat* Rights Act of 1954.

The State Government wanted to pacify the tenants, so it adopted some measures. It will not be out of place to state here that it was just after one year of our liberation from the British imperialism *i.e.*, in 1948 that the peasants, who were restless and miserable took an active part in the upcoming movement for ending Royalty *(Rajashahi)*. As a result of this upsurge among the people of the states, in 1948, all the states of the Punjab merged and Pepsu was formed. In 1952, actually the farmers in the states were relieved from the supreme ownership *(Ala-Malik)* of the *Rajwaras* (Princes) of Malerkotla, Faridkot and Kapurthala and the tenants became owners of their lands.[120] However, it was in 1955 that the most important Act was passed, known as Pepsu Tenancy And Agricultural Land Act of 1955.[121] According to Section 9 of this Act, the tenants were relieved from exploitation by the landlords in demanding or taking exhorbitant or excessive rent from them. A land-owner was not competent to claim rent at a higher rate than one-third of the produce of the land or the value thereof.

The tussle between the landlords and the tenants was increasing day by day. The tenants were being influenced by the movements like the *Kisan Sabhas,* the Communist Party, the Akali Movement and the *Praja Mandal.* They were

120. Master Hari Singh, '*Punjab Wich Kirsani Lehr* (in *Punjabi*), see *Souvenir,* issued by the CPI on January 26, 1976.

121. The Pepsu Tenancy and Agricultural Land Act, 1955, Section 9, 15; Vaid, Chhajju Mal, *Pepsu Muzarian Da Ghol Ten Communist Party,* published in a *Souvenir* issued by the CPI on January 26, 1976.

exploiting the tenants for their own selfish motives. Some of the leaders wanted followers and they could easily get hold of the village tenants. The tenants were not willing to become their tools. These movements soon exploited their position as the tenant and they made them realise their status vis-a-vis that of a *Biswedar.*

For these reasons the tenants were agitating against the policy of the Government. They wanted to get their right for undisputed ownership of land, while the Government was helpless before the tenants as they could go to the British Resident and would explain the attitude of the Government towards the tenants.

As all the previous legislations had failed to satisfy the tenants, there was the need of a final workable settlement, which was at last achieved by the passage of the Pepsu Tenancy and Agricultural Lands Act of 1955. Its purpose was to protect the tenants against unjust and abrupt termination of the tenancy. This aimed at amendment and consolidation of the law relating to tenancy of agricultural lands and to provide for certain measures of land reforms. Thus with the passage of this Act ended the period of struggle of the peasantry in the East Punjab States in general and the peasant movement in the Patiala State in particular.

5

Various Political Parties and the Agrarian Unrest

This chapter has two main objectives, firstly, to present the facts about the activities of the major political parties and the interest they displayed in connection with agrarian problems, and secondly, to measure the strength of each political organisation in the province. The chapter is divided into two sections, Section one deals with the activities of the *Ghadr* Group, the Akalis and the *Babbar* Akalis, the Communists, the Indian National Congress and the Unionist Party. References have also been made to the part played by other political factions in the agrarian agitation in the province. Section two covers the development of party-politics and the involvement of the major political parties in this region of the country. Attempt has also been made to highlight the impact of party-politics on the rural masses in particular.

We are concerned about *Ghadr* party only to the extent in contributed to the formation and growth of the *Kirti Kisan* movement in the province. Although, the *Kirti Kisan* party was not merely in extension of the *Ghadr* Group,[1] it owed much of its initial impetus to the *Ghadr* Group in the United States. The idea of the formation of the Punjab *Kirti Kisan* Party originated with the *Ghadr* Group.[2] In the party meeting

1. Williamson, The., *Communism in India*—1935 (Compiled in the Intelligence Bureau, Home Department : Government of India revised upto 1935), 271.

2. Home Department File No. 233/II/1926, 26; Williamson, H., *Communism in India*—1935, 261 (Also see Section II of Chapter II of this thesis).

held towards the end of 1922, it was decided to send Bhai Santokh Singh and Bhai Rattan Singh to India for organising workers and peasants. Both the leaders entered into India in May 1923 but they were arrested in the tribal territory of the North Western Frontier Province and released on security towards the end of the year. Now Bhai Santokh Singh, who had stayed back in India, got in touch with the radical minded workers of Amritsar, Lahore and Dhariwal. As a result of his efforts the plan of organising workers and peasants in the Punjab took shape.

The presence and an active participation of Bhag Singh 'Canadian' a Ghadrite emissary at the first meeting of the Punjab Workers' and Peasants' Party on April 12, 1927[3] indicated the earnest desire of the *Ghadr* Group to establish links with the radical minded workers in the Punjab. The *Kirti Kisan* Party was formed with the primary object of organising workers and peasants. The immediate aim of the party was to accomplish a thorough democratisation of India,[4] leading to political economic and social emancipation of the masses.[5]

It is a fact that the *Kirti Kisan* leadership had grasped the anti imperialistic ideas and absorbed the militant spirit of the *Ghadr* Group in abundant measure. However, it may be stated that the strategy of the *Kirti Kisan* Party was to mount a simultaneous offensive against imperialism as well as revolutionary groups as the *Babbar* Akalis.

In the late 1920's, *Ghadrites* had come under the influence of the economic and social theories of Marx; they began to look upon the British Government as something more than a

3. *Meerut Conspiracy Case* Sessions Judgement, 1930, Vol. I, Pt. XXIX, 594, NAI, New Delhi.
4. *Meerut Conspiracy Case Papers :* Sr. No. 167, Exhibit No. P. 344 (T), 771-Aims & Objects and Rules and Regulations of the Punjab *Kirti Kisan* Party; Also Sr. No. 19, Vol. XIV, Joint Statement of Nimbkar, A.S. and Others, 4892.
5. *Meerut Conspiracy Case Papers,* Sr. No. 167, Exhibit No. P. 344(T), 771; also Sr. No. 161, Exhibit No. 549 (15), 922-26.

predatory organisation maintained by coercion and terrorism.[6] If it was to perform its bourgeois democratic task *i.e.* the overthrow of imperialism, the abolition of landlordism etc., it must fight not only imperialism and landlord class but the bourgeois as well.[7] The same task was adopted by the workers' and peasants' movement. But it should be clear here that the *Ghadr* leaders disapproved of individual terrorism, because it had very little social significance.[8] However, they did not, in principle, condemn the assassination of public officials. The urgency of dealing with the traitors and informers, who obstructed the progress of the *Ghadr* movement at every step, compelled the *Ghadr* leadership to revise their views. Various aspects of this problem were discussed at length in a number of articles, published in the *Ghadr*.[9]

Concentration on the elimination of sycophants and traitors practically consumed energies of the members and resources of the *Ghadr* Party. It may be pointed out that the problem of dealing with the *Jholichuks* (loyalists), which had assumed gravity and urgency for the *Ghadrites* did not figure in the programme of the Punjab *Kirti Kisan* Party. The *Kirti Kisan* Party contemplated and prepared itself for the use of force for bringing about national revolution and disbanding reactionary elements.[10] In short, the *Ghadr* Party had chosen the method of armed rebellion.[11] As opposed to the *Ghadr*

6. *The Bulletin* (San Franscisco), October 20, 1913, Quoted in Brown, Emily C., *Hardayal : Hindu Revolutionary and Nationalist* (New Delhi : 1976), 142.

7. Joint Statement of Nimbkar and others, 5415; Latila, Kartar Singh, *'Kirti-di-Unati-de-Sadhan'* published in the *Kirti* (Amritsar), September : 1927, 27.

8. Quoted in Brown, Emily C., *Hardayal : Hindu Revolutionary and Nationalist*, 160-61.

9. *Ibid.*, 146 (For details see the *Ghadr* of November 29, 1913).

10. *Joint Statement of Nimbkar*, R.S. and Others.

11. Bala, Shastri Hardas, *Armed Struggle for Freedom : Ninety Years of Independnce, 1857 to Subhash*, translated by S.S. Apte (Poona Kal Prakashan : 1958), 252-53 (Hardas quotes at large from Khan Khoje's Diary which recorded the details about the Ghadr plan of action).

methods, organisation of peasants' and workers' was the watchword of the policy of the Punjab *Kirti Kisan* Party, at had a two fold strategy : mass movements on the one hand and red terrorism on the other.

The Punjab *Kirti Kisan* Party owed special debt to the *Ghadr* Group for its role in founding the *Kirti*, a journal in *Panjabi*, designing the party's pattern of growth and guiding its policy. Expertise of Bhag Singh 'Canadian' and Bhai Santokh Singh in the *Ghadr* techniques of propaganda was an asset for the *Kirti Kisan* agitation in the province. Realising the importance of propaganda in organising the workers and peasants on the basis of economic principles,[12] Santokh Singh pubilicised the principle of Socialism and created class consciousness among its readers.[13]

The *Kirti* fulfilled its role of moulding public opinion. It exhorted its readers to give a befitting reply to the official repression by promoting its sale and thus contribute towards the campaign for revolution.[14] It was similar to the appeal which appeared in the Ghadr of November 8, 1913.[15] Being the potential precursors and vanguard of revolution,[16] they were the most suitable recipients of the *Kirti's* message of Socialism, class struggle, freedom of the press and complete independence.[17] Above all, the main theme of fighting against the British imperialism and capitalism remained the focus.[18] Being fully appreciative of the contribution of the *Ghadr* Group, the *Kirti* ever since its appearance in 1926, followed

12. *The Kirti* (Amritsar), July, 1927, 13-15; also of June, 1929, 17-19.
13. *The Kirti,* April, 1929 (Mahatma Karl Marx), 7; also of May, 1929 (Comrade Karl Marx), 56-63.
14. *The Kirti, 'Firangh Shahi Da Takhta Dul Giya',* December, 1929, 1-2.
15. Karr, J.C., *Political Trouble in India,* 1907-17 (Indian reprint, Calcutta : 1973, 173.
16. *The Kirti* (Amritsar), December, 1929, 1-2 (Meerut Jail Wich Dake do Kirti Augun da Zabani Suneha).
17. *The Kirti* (Amritsar), August, 1929, 50 *(Kirti Lehr Nahin Dabegi)* 126-27.
18. *The Kirti* (May Day), May, 1929, 5.

the consistent policy of expounding their ideas of egalitarianism and complete independence.[19] Publication of autobiographies, biographies and photographs of *Ghadrites* continued to inspire the readers of the *Kirti*.[20] Even after the death of its founder, there was no change in the policy of the *Kirti*. It remained an effective medium of propaganda and instruction for the potential militant nationalists. It advised them to avoid lapses in the *Ghadr* plan of action and to strength mass organisation.

The *Kirti* also got financial help from the *Ghadr* Group when it was in danger of being forced to suspend its publication.[21] It is significant to note, while the *Kirti* fought the battle in India itself, its editors kept in close touch with the *Ghadr* Party in the United States. It served as an effective channel of communication between the *Ghadr* Group and the Punjab *Kirti Kisan* Party. A letter dated June 1, 1927, published in the *Kirti*, revealed how the *Ghadr* Group had helped the organisers of the *Kirti* in the formation of its policy. While this particular letter had hailed its inception and acclaimed its mission of creating awakening among the *Kirtis*, it emphasised the need of organising and enlisting the support of large numbers of peasants in the Punjab whose needs and potentialities had so far been ignored. It further stressed the need of widening the scope of the programme of the Kirti Kisan Party so as to include the benefits and privileges the peasantry would obtain in a free India of the future. This party had surely realised the value of their advice for its leaders and its mouth-piece, the *Kirti*, proclaimed that the success of the freedom struggle depended upon the extent of involvement of the *Kirtis* and *Kisans*.[22]

---

19. *The Kirti* (1914-15 de Shahidan Ton Sikhia), May, 1929, 7-8.

20. *The Kirti*, March, 1930, 43-52.

21. Home Department, File No. 44/36-1934—Political (Statement of Harjap Singh—A member of the *Hindustan Ghadr* Party), 4; also File No. 6/10/1928, 39, NAI : New Delhi; For details also see File No. 235/II/1926, 30; *The Kirti*, February, 1926, 77-78; March, 1926; July, 1926, 20.

22. *The Kirti* (Amritsar), *'Zamindar Sabha'*, February, 1928, 77-78; *The Kirti*, March, 1930, 1930 (Brij Narain's *'Zamindar Te Kisan)*, 16-19.

Redesigning of the *Kirti* and modification of its motto, in response to the suggestion of some important leaders of the *Ghadr Group*,[23] and to the favourable reaction of the working class readers in Europe and other countries and the immediate implementation of their suggestions, further indicated the extent of its ideological appeal.

The *Kirti* of August, 1927, carried an appeal from the *Ghadr* Party to the Chinese nationalists to guard their right of asylum by protecting Desunda Singh, from being arrested.[24] The writings of Harjap Singh notably "Lenin and Kisan, "Hindustan and Terrorism"[25] and "Arrest of Santa Singh at Madras",[26] in this magazine highlighted the different faces of the *Kirti Kisan* movement in the Punjab and its ideological stand on various issues such as the official policy of arresting the *Ghadrite* emissaries in India. The members of the *Ghadr* Group valued highly the work done by the *Kirti* for the dissemination of anti-imperialists and anti-capitalistic ideas. Rattan Singh visited India second time in August 1927 with the specific purpose of assessing the role of the *Kirti* group in the country.[27] Similarly Harjap Singh visited India in 1930[28] with the object of helping the growth of the *'Kirti Lehr'* in the Punjab.[29] In the course of his stay in India, his concentrated efforts for the renewal of contacts with the returned emigrants helped in increasing the number of active workers of the *Kirti Kisan* struggle in the Punjab. Besides, he, alive to the need of being conversant with the growth of the *Naujawan* as well as the Congress movements, attended their respective sessions, which

23. Home Department, File No. 44/26/1934, 15, 18; *The Kirti*, July, 1927, 50.
24. *The Kirti* (Amritsar), August, 1927 (Desaunda Singh was an Indian National in China).
25. For details see *The Kirti* (Amritsar), February, 1930, 3-13.
26. Home Department, File No. 44/36/1934, 14 (Its text is not traceable).
27. Patric, D., *Communism in India*, 1924-27 (Compiled in the intelligence Bureau, Home Department, Government of India), 263.
28. Home Department, File No. 44/36/1934, 15, 18.
29. *Ibid.*, 16.

coincided with those of the All India *Kirti Kisan* Party at Karachi in March, 1931.

To sum up, from 1926 onward, the *Ghadr* Group had shown a good deal of initiative in spearheading the movement for organising peasants and workers in the province. Their activities were especially noticeable in connection with the founding of the *Kirti*, its growth and sustenance. Their contribution to the rise and expansion of the *Kirti Kisan* movement in the Punjab was not limited to their successful early efforts for the formation of the Punjab *Kirti Kisan* party in April, 1927. Association of Bhag Singh 'Canadian' with the *Kirti Kisan* organisation exercised a decisive influence in the evolution of its ideology. It accounted for its devotion to the *Ghadrite* ideals of equality and complete independence. Moreover, the militant spirit of the *Ghadrites* and the example of their fight against national bondage, injustice and inequality—social, economic and political—enabled the *Kirti Kisan* party to evolve their own genre of militant nationalism. Mass action was given priority and terrorism was put aside as the last resort to be used against the imperialists and reactionaries.

In the later half of 1930's, when the party embarked upon its programme of action, the *Ghadr* emissaries had, perforce, to shet the role of mentors.[30] Another reason for the gradual eclipse of their influence was the increasing indifference of the International to the workers' and peasants' parties in India; the *Ghadrite* emissaries, who had trusted the Communist International as a guide, felt bewildered over its change of policy. Furthermore, forcible cessation of the publication of the *Kirti*, the stronghold of the *Ghadr* Group, eroded their control over the peasants' and workers' movement in this province. Moreover, the emphasis shifted to peasants' agitation between 1935-39 and this agitation threw up new leaders known as *'Babas'*, during this period.

30. The important among them such as Santokh Singh, Bhag Singh 'Canadian', Rattan Singh 'American' and Harjap Singh were either dead or behind the bars.

It will not be out of place if some more facts about the *Ghadr* Group in connection with the freedom struggle are cited here. There existed a significant difference between the Friends of Freedom for India League and the *Ghadr* party. It was that the League was ready to accept the help of Russia, but it would not tolerate any Communist propaganda while the latter was in favour of Communist work.[31] The *Ghadrites* were convinced that the British rule could only be overthrown with the help of arms and there was no other possible way to do so. They had already reached the conclusion that the failure of the *Ghadr* movement in 1915 was due of the mistake of not carrying the masses alongwith them. Despite its failure, the formation of the *Ghadr* Group was credited to have produced the greatest political change as it had come up with the purpose of destroying the British in India and establishing a peoples' Government in its stead.[32] This aspect has already been discussed.

It is also not out of place of state that the *Ghadrites* are mostly the sons of the families with small proprietory holdings who, because of economic distress went to the U.S.A. to work as labourers so that they could improve their living conditions.[33] It is significant to state that the Punjab *Ghadrites* were maintaining links with the third International Organisation through Rattan Singh.[34] The information which is available proves that Rattan Singh was collaborating with the Communist International.[35] In March 1926, a batch of five *Ghadrites* left for Russia to be trained in Communist

31. File No. 1929, Part-I, 1920—India Office Library (Archives on Contemporary History of India, J.N.U., New Delhi).
32. Home Department, File No. 9-B, 1921, NAI, New Delhi.
33. They were peasants as well as workers. They organised themselves to defend the rights of the workers. In India they sought to organise the peasants while sympathising with the labour class.
34. Petrie, David, Communism in India : 1924-27 (Compiled in the Intellegence Bureau, Home Department, Government of India), 142; Home Department, File No. 41/1926-Political, NAI : New Delhi.
35. *Ibid.*

propaganda.[36] They maintained contact with the *Kirti* in the Punjab through Kabul Centre. Another important fact which is to be noted is, the *Kirti* also tried to maintain its links with the Red Peasants' International, and the League against Imperialism.[37]

Going through documents, we get the impression that there were different groups within the *Ghadr* Party which had links with different circles in Punjab who were preaching militant nationalism through militant papers like—*'Desh Sewak', 'Akali-te-Pardesi'* and *'Punjabee'*.[38] Though the *Ghadr* Group and various emigrant societies were sending money to all these papers, only the *Kirti* emphasised the Communist ideas and ideology. It is to be noted that the members of the *Naujawan Bharat Sabha* derived inspiration from the courage, self-sacrifice and dedication of the *Ghadr* heroes.[39]

To what extent the *Ghadr* Group had succeeded[40] in propagating the leftist ideology is yet to be answered. This aspect will be discussed in this chapter under two heads—The Akalis and the Communist. However, it is clear from the above stated facts that the *Ghadrites* and their leadership not

---

36. *Ibid.*
37. Petrie, David, Communism in India : 1924-27 (Compiled in the Intellegence Bureau, Home Department, Government of India), 83-87; Williamson, H., Communism in India : 1935 (Compiled in the Intellegence Bureau, Home Department, Government of India issued upto 1935), 20.
38. For details see Adhikari, G., Documents of History of the Communist Party of India, Vol. I, 8; Home Department File No. 235/II-1926; Kaye, Sir Cecil, Communism in India : unpublished documents from NAI, 1919-24, ed., by Subodh Rai (Calcutta : 1971), 167.
39. For ideological evolution of its leaders see Ghosh, Ajoy, *Article and Speeches,* Moscow : 1962; Chandra, Bipan, "The Ideological Development of the Revolutionary Terrorists in Northern India in the 1920", in Socialism in India, edited by Nanda, B.R., 1972; Josh, Sohan Singh, *Hindustan Ghadr Party,* P.P.H. Delhi : 1977, 17.
40. For its success or failure see Khushwant Singh, *History of the Sikhs,* Vol. II, 183; Josh, Sohan Singh, *Hindustan Ghadr Party* PPH : Delhi-1977, 32.

only propagated the leftist ideology, rather they successfully involved the masses (rural masses in particular) in large in the arena of freedom struggle.

The Sikh peasants, in the Punjab, lashed out at the *Mahants* or heads of temple and *Gurdwara* establishments, who had become virtual owner of their estates and appropriated their yields as their private incomes. These *Mahants* like other moneylenders and *Zamindars* exploited the peasantry and supported the British administration. Hence, they became the target of the masses no less than the British administration. Therefore, the masses, mostly workers and peasants, joined the Akali agitation and began to seize the properties of the temples. Naturally, there were clashes between the Akalis and the *Udasis*, as the *Mahants* were called. In 1921 there was a big encounter between the two parties at Tarantaram; in February the temple guards killed about 200 unarmed Sikhs at *Nankana Sahib*. Next year *Guru-Ka-Bagh* near Amritsar was the scene of arrests and shooting. Public opinion was aroused. But differences arose among the Akalis as to whether they should continue to observe non-violence or take to violent means. Whereas the main body adhered to the policy of non-violence the *Babbar* Akalis indulged in terrorism. Unnerved by these bickerings the Akali movement gave way, but in course of time, its gains were appreciable.[41] In brief, it is clear that the Akali movement had assumed a religious complexion which muffled its agrarian or economic character. It is important to note that the Congress lauded this movement but disliked its communal overtones. In fact, by this time,

41. This account is based on the material collected from various files of Home Department Political, NAI : New Delhi; Prime Minister Office records, PSA, Patiala; Sahni, Ruchi Ram, *Struggle for Reforms in Sikh Shrines,* S.G.P.C. Amritsar : 1964; Teja Singh, *The Gurdwara Reform Movement and Sikh Awakening,* Desh Sewa Book Agency, Jullundur : 1922-23; Giani, Partap Singh, *Akali Lehr Da Itihas,* Singh Bros., Amritsar : 1951; Singh, Niranjan, *Akali Lehr Dian Kujh Yadan,* Singh Bros., Nai Sewan Amritsar; Josh, Sohan Singh, *Akali Morchian Da Itihas,* Navying Publishers, Delhi : 1972; *The Indian Annual Register : 1922-26;* Some issues of *Akali-te-Pardesi;* Mohinder Singh, *The Akali Movement,* Macmillon : Delhi : 1938.

under the impact of the Congress programme of non-co-operation, the religious *Diwans* arranged by the Akali leadership became the centres of religious and political propaganda among the rural classes of the Sikh Community. British bureaucracy noticed this sudden change with great consternation.[42] A little later, the Akalis gradually began to take keen interest in the peasants' agitation particularly in the East Punjab States.

Since the very beginning of their struggle against British imperialism, the Akalis held that there was no Government, and no justice.[43] They did not have any regard for the then Government because they thought that the Government was intoxicated with power.[44] During the course of its struggle against the autocratic rule of the British on the one hand and the highhandedness of the *Mahants,* who were loyalists, on the other, the Akalis could win over the sympathy of the spirited Sikh peasantry of *Malwa* region in particular.[45] Let it be clear that the *Rajas* of *Phulkian* States as well as the British bureaucracy left no stone unturned to crush the Akali movement. However, they failed to check the Akali activities, and on the contrary, lent further impetus to the anti-Government and anti-ruler feelings and activities among the people.[46] In fact, the Akali activities assumed wider ramifications after the *Praja Mandal* and the *Muzaras* agitation joined hands with the Akalis.[47]

The Akali *Fauj* (on of the Akali *Jathas*) worried the

42. File No. 628-3-P-1924, Foreign-Political, NAI : New Delhi; *The Civil and Military Gazette,* August 22, 1924.

43. *The Civil and Military Gazette,* December 4, 1922 (Court Proceedings in the Case Crown V. Sardar Kharak Singh and others).

44. *Ibid.*

45. Home Department, File No. 914/1922-Political, NAI : New Delhi.

46. File No. 100, PSA : Patiala (It contains the names of about a dozen villages which organised and held the Akali *Diwans*).

47. For details see Walia, Ramesh, A Study of the *Praja Mandal* Movement in the East Punjab States, Punjabi University, Patiala, 1974.

authorities the most. It had the solid backing of the extreme left-wing Sikh League, and was constituted along the lines of the volunteer movement of the Congress and the *Khilafat* whom the Akali volunteers might join. What terrorised the authorities most was, 'the spirit of fanaticism' among the Akali volunteers.[48] Other factors which added to the worries of the authorities were the reports from the Army sources of attempts of the Akali *Fauj* to temper with the loyalty of Sikh soldiers in the Indian Army,[49] and its increasing popularity with the Sikh peasantry.

Let it be noted that the Sikh peasantry constituted the backbone of the Akali movement and was mainly responsible for the struggle's spectacular success. The Sikh peasantry, which was growing increasingly discontented with the Government for a number of reasons, with their ranks swelled by soldiers discharged at the end of the First Great War, quickly responded to the Akali propagandists' contention that the bureaucracy was bent upon destroying the Sikh religion.

While the bulk of the Akali volunteers came from the Sikh peasantry, the leadership was provided by the educated middle class nationalsits.[50] This leadership was acceptable to the Sikh masses (rural people especially), because of their educational background, their environment, their political consciousness as a result of their association with the nationalist organisations of the time, and above all their ability and boldness to expose the evil practices of the hereditary *Mahants*, and the acceptance of such leadership meant rejection of their

48. Home Department, File No. 459-II/1922-Political (Confidential Memorandum), For details regarding Akali *Fauj* also see File No. 235/26-Political (1923-26), NAI : New Delhi.

49. Home Department, File No. 455-II/1922-Political, NAI : New Delhi, (General Staff's note on 'The Military Aspect of the Present Situation in the Punjab).

50. Middle Class supporters consisted of Barristers, *Vakils,* Teachers both from the schools and colleges, Headmasters, Military prisoners and middle-level landlords. Vide Confidential Memorandum, File No. 459-II/1922-Home Department-Political, NAI : New Delhi.

so called natural leaders who were loyal to the Government.[51] On the other hand, it was alleged by the Government that, generally speaking, it was only the good-for-nothing men who had nothing to lose, who joined the Akalis, and 95 per cent of them were composed of Tarkhans, Lohars and the Resser ats...........[52] But such official statements were attempts on the part of the British bureaucracy to weaken the movement and o alienate from it the sympathy of the middle-level Sikh griculturists. It is significant to note the contrast between he figure of 95 per cent manilas in the Akali *Jathas* as given ut by the Government to the public and 15% admitted in the onfidential report prepared for use by the higher authorities.[53]

During the period under review, the Akali agitation was n full swing. It was being focused on the *Maharaja* of Nabha, vho had abdicated in order to support the Akali movement. esides, the Akalis were waging a militant struggle to oust he autocratic control of the *Mahants* in order to assert the emocratic right of the community; on the other hand it anted to set up the autocracy of the *Maharaja* of Nabha. onsequently, the illiterate rural masses were faced with the ilemma of taking an ideological stand vis-a-vis this dual ndency projected by the Akali movement. In fact on this sue the Communist were prepared to take side of the people nd they condemned the section of the Akalis, as the mmunist could not support the Nabha *Maharaja's* etensions. Moreover, they wanted to abolish landlordism d old feudalism.

Here, it will be significant to place the Akali movement in e broader frame-work of the non-co-operation movement the Punjab started by the Indian National Congress. In the st half of 1921, Congress workers were holding meetings in hore, Amritsar and a few other towns. But Gandhi was

1. *Ibid.*; Mohinder Singh, *The Akali Movement,* Macmillion, Delhi : 1979, 98.

2. Confidential Memorandum, File No. 459-II/1922-Home Department-Political, NAI : New Delhi.

3. *Ibid.*

dissatisfied with the pace of the movement in the Punjab and sent Maulana Abul Kalam Azad to organise boycott activities. During the course of non-co-operation and other activities of the Congress, the Akalis always co-operated.[54] The Punjab countryside was stirred because of the Akali movement. It tended to embrace the various sections of the Sikhs into its fold. It, however, affected a section of the peasantry *i.e.* the Sikhs in the central districts, because of the limited nature of the programme of reforms in Sikh shrines.[55] Let it be noticed that it embraced the members of the *Ghadr* Group which gave the Akali movement its dogged tenacity, sharp anti-imperialist edge and rural orientation.

After the moderate faction set-up by Mehtab Singh had made compromise settlement with the Government in 1926, the cleavage along the rural-urban lines became obvious among the Akali ranks. The other faction was set-up by Bhag Singh 'Canadian' as President and Mangal Singh as General Secretary. The *Khatri* and *Arora* Akalis from Rawalpindi and the Malwa region supported Mehtab Singh, while the other group was mainly drawn from the Jats of Lahore, Amritsar, Gurdaspur, rural Sialkot, the Doab and Lyallpur regions.[57] Many members of this faction later on came under the banner of the Punjab *Kirti Kisan* Party.

In her article "The struggle of the Akali Sikhs in the Punjab", Evelyn Roy expressed that "The Akali revolt in the Punjab is but one manifestation of the widespread spirit of unrest that has seized very part of the Indian people........and which expresses in numerous and prolonged strikes on the part of the industrial proletariat in all big cities, and on the part of the Indian peasantry from Madras to Punjab......in riots

54. *The Tribune* (Lahore), September 16, 1921.

55. Home Department, File No. 112/1926-Political, NAI : New Delhi.

56. Home Department, File No. 235/1926-Political, NAI : New Delhi; Adhikari, G., Documents of History of Communist Party of India, 528; also see Kay Sir Cecil, Communism in India, published documents from NAI, 1919-24, ed., by Subodh Rai, Calcutta-1971, 140.

57. *Ibid.*

and risigns, in non-payment of rent and taxes and, in frequent bloody conflicts with the armed forces of the States."[58] She further wrote, "The Akali movement produces a monumental revolution which will not be a mere expression of resurgent nationalism but a vast social and economic upheaval as well".[59] She drew the picture of an exceptionally revolutionary situation in the Punjab ending with the statement : "The years from 1918-20 are filled with official reports about the looting and burning, rioting and killing, on the part of the Punjab peasantry, such lawless action form stepping stones on the road to an open agarian revolution, and the Government sees the danger ahead."[60]

It will not be out of place to state that the *left* in the Punjab before the Meerut Conspiracy Case was constituted by the individual drawn from *Muhajirs*, nationalist youths, Akali militants and members or sympathisers of the *Ghadr* Group. What brought them together was their desire to organise the oppressed section of the society in an uncomprimising struggle against imperialism and communalism.[61] In the beginning, many of the militant Akalis were simultaneously the supporters of the *Kirti Kisan* movement.[62] They conceived of complete independence as the establishment of a workers' and peasants' Government in the country. Moreover, of these four currents, individuals from the latter two currents were not only the larger in number but also played an important part in the organisation of the Punjab *Kisan* organisation. Here, it is worth nothing that the districts of the Central Punjab—Lahore, Amritsar, Jullundur and Ferozepur—where the small holding peasantry predominated—were precisely the areas

58. Inprecorr, Nos. 75 and 88/1922.

59. *Ibid.*

60. *Ibid.*

61. The Communist International. "Between 8th and 6th World Congress : 1924-28" (A Report on the Position in all sections of the world Communist Party); ACHI/JNU, New Delhi (also quoted by Bhagwan Singh Josh in his M. Phil thesis : *Communism in the Punjab.*

62. *The Kirti* (Amritsar), February, 1929.

which had a tradition of militant British struggle in the Akali movement which had consisted primarily of Sikh peasantry. The leadership of the Punjab *Kirti Kisan* Committee was also drawn from these areas and most of it had matured through the Akali and the *Ghadr* struggle.

A change began to come over the political ideas of the Sikhs, as the year rolled by. The motive force behind this phenomenon was the rise of powerful Indian nationalism from the start of the 20th century. From a community centred world-view, the Sikh made a gradual transition to a wider nationalist out look. They thought of their community. From the beginning of 20th century, particularly during the second decade, the Sikhs involved in the *Ghadr* agitation, began to think in terms of Indian Nation and not their own community.[63]

The Akalis strongly condemned the Sikh Sabhaites for their pro-British ideas and activities. They wholeheartedly espoused the ideology of the national movement and did what they could for its speedy triumph.[64] They played a significant role in the non-co-operation movement of 1921 and the Civil Disobedience Movement of 1931-33.[33] They stood aloof from the Quit India Movement of 1942 on account of certain differences with the Congress. But this does not mean that they were opposed to the demand for independence. The occasional demands made by them for a separate Sikh State were more a move to counter the Muslim demand for Pakistan than a serious proposition.[66]

From the middle-thirties it was feared that the Akali movement would die out if the Communist were not checked.

---

63. Khushwant Singh, *The Sikhs,* 134; Bajwa, Fauja Singh, 'Political Ideas of the Sikhs during the 18th to 20th Centuries', *The Punjab Past and Present,* Vol. X-II, October, 1976.

64. *Ibid.,* also see, Home Department, File No. 112-IV/1926-Political, NAI : New Delhi.

65. *Ibid.*

66. Khushwant Singh, *The Sikhs,* 152; For details see Kirpal Singh, *The Partition of the Punjab,* Punjabi University : Patiala, 1972.

The Akalis had chalked out an elaborate programme to do anti-communists and pro-Akalis propaganda. But the effect of the Communists continued on the public mind.[67] Besides, the Communists had detailed their workers to undertake tours in the rural areas and persuade tenants there to rise up and join the *Kisan* Party. Above all, the hold of the Communists was so strong over the minds of the villagers that no body cared to listen to their (Akalis) propaganda and thus the Akali agitation ended in fiasco.[68] The reason for their failure was that the Communists had started criticising the section of the Akalis, which wanted to set up the autocracy of the *Maharaja* of Nabha, as the communists could not support the *Maharaja's* pretensions, and that the ruralities had understood by this time that the Akalis were either loyal to the British bureaucracy and if at all they fought the British imperialism, they liked Congress, adopted the weapon of non-violence which was not acceptable to the militant nationalists.

The Progressive Akali Group led by Durlab Singh, the Servants of Sikh Society led by Kartar Singh of Cambellpur, Lahore and the Communist party were the strongest among their opponents.[69] The Communist Group, especially, would chalk out their own programme of holding a conference when the Akali party would have decided the date and place of their own *Diwan*. Above all the internal dissension in the party led to its failure.[70] The Akali movement also failed because it had brought into existence such dangerous revolutionary Organisations as the *Babbar* Akali gang of the Punjab.[71] The

67. Home Department, File No. 18/10/1944 *(i)*-Political; File No. 232/1940-Political; File No. 18/2/1941-Political, NAI : New Delhi.

68. Patiala State Records, Basta No. 13, Case No. 535/C (Abstract of Intellegence); PSA : Patiala (Pb). For details also see Patiala State Records, Basta No. 51, S.No. 1577, PSA : Patiala (Pb).

69. *Ibid.*, Case No. 565/C, Basta No. 50, PSA : Patiala, Punjab.

70. Patiala State Records, Basta No. 18, Case No. 386/C of 1925; Basta No. 50, Case No. 565/C of 1939, PSA : Patiala, Punjab.

71. Home Department, File No. 200/1926-Political (For details regarding the activities of the *Babbar* Akalis—The Babbar Akali Movement see Home Department, File No. 1/10/1924-Political, NAI : New Delhi; also see various issues of the *Desh Bhagat* (Amritsar) for the year 1926.

activities of the Akali in the states met with strong resistance. There it was a complete failure. The Chamber of Princes' resolution in 1925 made it clear that the Indian states would like to remain under the British even on the attainment of *Swaraj*.[72]

It will not be out of place to state that Sikh ruralities in the Punjab (who readily provided recruits for the *Jathas*) lost faith in the leaders who were openly accused of treachery, corruption and misappropriation of public funds. The relatives and dependants of those who underwent sufferings and who died were left uncared. This was one of the reason why the *Jats* in the villages refused to listen to the leaders. The most important factor was that the Akali agitation had brought no gain to the peasants. The force of religious conviction which lent the Akali Movement impetus and impelling force and motive, was altogether absent after 1926 onward. The reform of the Sikh shrines was no longer a live issue with the masses in the villages.[73] It was also alleged that the Akali policy was built on the shifting sands of opportunism and changed with the political tides[74] which at a later stage resulted in its failure.

Despite its failure, the Akali movement, though itself a product of the general awakening and growing political consciousness in the country, seems to have greatly strengthened the forces of nationalism in the Punjab by rejecting the *Mahants,* the landed aristocracy and other pro-British and vested interests in the Sikh community who had been declared the natural leaders of the Sikhs by the official machinery. The movement provided the Sikh community in general and the peasantry in particular with a new type of

72. Patiala State Records, Basta No. 18, Case No. 386/C of 1925; Basta No. 50, Case No. 565/C of 1939, PSA : Patiala.

73. Home Department, File No. 132/III-1927-Political, NAI : New Delhi.

74. Home Department, File No. 18/10/1944 (1)-Political; File No. 232/1940-Political, NAI : New Delhi.

middle-class nationalist leadership,[75] which preferred to join the main stream of nationalism in the country.

Further, the progressive elements in the Akali ranks, who seemed to have imbibed a Marxist bias during their early contacts with the Ghadrites and other revolutionary elements in the province as well as abroad, started turning towards the left-wing extremist groups in the country and finally joined the ranks of the *Naujawan Bharat Sabha* and the Punjab *Kirti Kisan* party, both of which had a strong *Marxist* bias.[76]

The data available on the Akali movement and personal interviews with some of the activities and the so-called *Babas* indicate by then that the Sikh peasantry formed the backbone of the Akali movement.[77] That the movement was able to achieve a large measure of success was primarily due to this class of people involving itself whole-heartedly in the Akali struggle. Out of the total number of Akali volunteers from different regions, roughly 66% belonged to the *Jat* Sikh peasantry,[78] the majority of them hailing from the districts of Lahore, Sheikhupura, Lyallpur, Amritsar, Jullundur and

75. Josh, Sohan Singh, Akali Morchian Da Itihas, Navyug Publication, Delhi, 1972, 473 (However, the leadership was provided by middle class Sikh nationalists such as : Niranjan Singh, Bawa Harkrishan Singh, Mehtab Singh, Teja Singh, Bhag Singh, Gurcharan Singh, Sunder Singh, Mota Singh, Tara Singh, Hira Singh Dard, Sujan Singh and Sohan Singh Josh and several others).

76. Mittal, S.C., *Freedom Movement in Punjab,* Concept Publishers, Delhi : 1977; Chandra Bipan, 'The Ideological Development of the Revolutionary Terrorists in Northern India in 1920's, *Seminar on Socialism in India,* 1919-39 (Second Session), October 8-10, 1969; Josh, Bhagwan Singh, Communism in the Punjab, *Anupam* Publication, Delhi : 1979; Rai Satya, 'Evolution of the Heroic Tradition in Punjab in Modern Times', *The Punjab Past and Present,* Punjabi University, Patiala.

77. Mitra, M.N.,The Quarterly Ragisters, Calcutta : 1923, 1924, 1925 and 1926.

78. This figures are taken from Mohinder Singh's, *The Akali* Movement; For details also see Confidential Memorandum, Home Department, File No. 459/II/1922-Political, NAI : New Delhi; Patiala State Records, Prime Minister's Office Files, PSA : Patiala.

Hoshiarpur. Similarly, in the case of the Akali movement in the Sikh states the majority of the participants again belonged to the peasantry. If we study the aims and programme of the Akalis during the course of their struggle, it becomes clear that they had undertaken the issues which were being supported by the Punjab *Kirti Kisan* party, the Communists, the Congress and many other political organisations in the province.

The most important and lasting contribution of the Akalis was that their movement brought about political awakening among the rural masses, particularly the Sikh peasantry. It was only during this struggle that the pro-British feudal leadership of the Sikhs was replaced by the educated middle-class nationalists and the rural and urban classes united on a common platform during the two-pronged Akali struggle. The Akali leaders had made this fact clear that their liberation from hereditary priests was not possible without the political liberation of the country and it became a vital factor in the politicalization of the Sikhs. It was thus the idea of the liberation of the country, that united all the sections of the Sikh community and brought the Hindus, the Sikhs and the Muslims of the Punjab, together. Another significant factor in connection with the Akali movement is that the Congress found an opportunity to further its own programme of non-co-operation and Civil Disobedience movement in the province. Through the Akali leadership they could influence a large section of the Sikh masses, particularly the peasantry, who had till then remained aloof from the Congress programme.[79] In brief, the Akali movement gave rise to militant nationalist elements and prepared the ground for the formation of the Punjab *Kirti Kisan* Organisation. The Akalis were united with all the *Kisans' morchas* in one form or the other. Undoubtedly, the revolutionary terrorist activities of some of the political organisations were the direct result of the influence of the Akali movement on these organisations.

79. For details see Report of the 38th Session of the Indian National Congress held at Cocanada on December 28-31, 1927, NMML; *The Tribune* (Lahore), January 1, 1924.

Hence, the Akali faction was closely connected with the peasants' problems and agrarian agitation in the province.

When the Akali movement was passing through a crucial stage, the *Babbar* Akali agitation began to gather momentum. The radical section of the Akali reformers, dissatisfied with the Gandhian method of non-violence, organised themselves into separate militant groups popularly known as the *Babbar* Akali *Jathas*.[80] With this, the militant spirit of the *Punjabees* which had died since the suppression of the *Ghadr* movement was once again revived. Mostly, the emigrants, *Ghadrites* and retired and demobilised soldiers constituted this militant group which was bitter at the imperialist policies of the British bureaucracy of openly backing the *Mahants,* the landed aristocracy and their repressive policy against popular movements. They considered the Gandhian policy of non-violence an attempt to bridle the struggle of the peasants against imperialism. They, now, rejected the peaceful struggle for reforms in the shrines and decided to organise a militant struggle of their own.[81]

In their programme, they decided to slay those who were responsible for the measure of the Akalis during the course of various Akali *morchas.* They also wanted to demonstrate to the Government.that self respect and militant spirit was very much alive in the Sikh Community.[82] However, the sphere of their activities was confined primarily to the two districts of

80. Mukhsuspuri, Sunder Singh, *Babbar Akali Lehr,* 39 and 88; Home Department, File No. 134/II of 1923-Political, 25, NAI, New Delhi.

81. Home Department, File No. 268/1922-Political (CID Report in the File); File No. 134-11/1923-Political; Mukhsuspuri, Sunder Singh, *Babbar Akali Lehr* (Second Edition, *Punjabee*), 50.

82. *The Civil and Military Gazette* (Judgement by P.J. Rust in the Akali Conspiracy Case), June 6, 1922; Mohinder Singh, *The Akali* Movement, Macmillian, Delhi : 1979, 114. For details regarding the attitude of the *Babbars* towards the supports of the Government and the *Mahants* also see Mukhsuspuri, Sunder Singh, *Babbar Akali* Lehr, (Second Edition, Punjabee), 70-71; Mohan, Kamlsh, *The Babbar Akali Movement and Its Ideology, The Punjab Past and Present,* Punjabi University, Patiala, April, 1975.

Jullundur and Hoshiarpur like that of the *Ghadrites.*[83] Another point worthnoting is that their leadership as well as the organisation received large sums of money from their counterparts still in America and Canada.[84] Like the *Ghadrites,* they moved from place to place in the countryside and appealed to the martial instincts of the Sikhs. They urged the people to resort to arms.[85]

The Babbar Akali leadership created a degree of discontent among the ruralities of the Jullundur Doab area, through the medium of religious *diwans* and by distributing articles and leaflets. They also appealed to the Hindus and Muslims to join them in their struggle against the exploitation of landed aristocracy and British imperialism. They also appealed to them to adopt the creed of violence if they wanted to see their country independent.[86] However, the Akalis did not approve of the *Babbar* plan of violence and their programme of assassinations. They exhorted the Sikhs not to associate themselves with the activities of the *Babbar* Group as the latter programme clashed with the policy of non-violence adopted by the Akalis.[87] However, inspite of this opposition, the Babbar leadership continued their movement in their own way.

On the contrary, the Babbar Akalis claimed that they knew the cause for the failure of the *Ghadr* movement and that was the lack of support by the masses. They felt that it was necessary to awaken the rural masses and to enlist their support

83. Home Department, File No. 134/II of 1923-Political (History of the Babbar Akali Movement), NAI : New Delhi.

84. *The Civil and Military Gazette* (*Babbar* Akali Case), June 10, 1923.

85. *Ibid.*, October 5, 1923 (Babbar Leaflet reproduced for further details).

86. *Ibid;* also of Jun 6, 1922.

87. *The Civil and Military Gazette,* October 5, 1923 (Even Mahatma Gandhi had not approved of the *Babbar* Akali programme, for details see 'My Friend the Revolutionary', *Collected Works of Mahatma Gandhi,* Vol. XXVI, 487-89; also see Satya Rai, 'Evolution of Heroic Traditions in Punjab in the Modern Times', *The Punjab Past and Present,* Punjabi University, Patiala, April, 1975.

and sympathy for the *Babbar* cause. With this object, they sent *jathas* of the *Babbar* to different parts of the province to arouse the people to revolt against the Governemnt.[88] The moving spirit behind the *Babbar* movement was Sardar Kishan Singh.[89] After being inspired, they also decided to paralyse the supporters of the British by terrorising them through various forms of violent acts.[90] It was Kishan Singh who intensified revolutionary propaganda among the Sikh peasantry. Again, it was under his leadership, in August, 1922, that in a meting at Gojowal, the *Babbar* leadership decided to strengthen the propaganda machinery of the *Babbar* movement by starting a cyclostyled paper called *Babbar Akali Doaba Akhbar* in September, 1922. This paper highlighted the desperate economic condition of the agriculturists and their exploitation at the hands of the British bureaucracy. It too drew the attention of the rural masses, especially of the Sikh peasantry, to the *Kirti Kisan* movement and pointed out the futility of the Akali programme of passive resistance. The *Babbar* leadership, on the one hand insisted the Akalis and the Sikh soldiers to kill their English officers and on the other, they decided to paralyse the supporters of the British by terrorising them through various forms of violent acts.[91]

Several meetings of the *Babbar* Akalis were held in the month of December, 1922.[92] From the records of the

88. *Ibid.*, August 30, 1923.

89. For the activities of the *Babbars* and role of Kishan Singh, see Mukhsuspuri, Sunder Singh, Babbar Akali Lehr (Second Edition, Punjabee); Home Department, File No. 134/II-1923, NAI : New Delhi.

90. *The Civil and Military Gazette,* October 5, 1923; Home Department, File No. I/X-1924-Political; File No. 200/1926-Political, NAI : New Delhi.

91. A meeting was held at Jassowal on December 25, 1922 and other two meetings took place on Dec. 30 and 31st, 1922. Regarding the details of these meetings see Home Department, File No. 134/II-1923, NAI : New Delhi; Mukhsuspuri, Sunder Singh, *Babbar Akali Lehr* (Second Edition, *Panjabi*); 97-99.

92. *Ibid., The Civil and Military Gazette,* October 31, 1923; Home Department, File No. 200/1926-Political, 6, NAI : New Delhi.

proceedings of these meetings, it becomes clear that they seemed to have attracted a large number of adherents from the Sikh peasantry of the Jullundur *Doab* region.

As a result of the violent activities of the *Babbar*, the Peace Councils and *Sudhar* Committees, composed of the loyalists, were constituted, which diverted the attention of the villagers towards the blessings of the British rule in the Punjab. These associations further advised the villagers not to trust their propaganda and asked them to help the Government in effecting their arrests.[92] But, this was not a very successful move. Even the official account admitted that it was due to the help of the villagers that the *Babbar* members could create panic in the rank and fill of the loyalists. A number of village officials and other loyalists were in fear for their lives and many of them, in reality, expressed desire to resign their posts.[94] In 1923-24, therefore, the Government took certain special measures to meet the *Babbar* challenge. To restore confidence among the loyalists in the affected areas, the *Babbar Jathas* were proclaimed as an 'unlawful association' under the Criminal Law (Amendment) Act of 1908.[95]

Unmoved by the repressive policy of the Government,

93. For details see Home Department, File No. 134/II-1923-Political Punjab Government Communique dated April 24, 1923; Mukhsuspuri, Sunder Singh, *Babbar Akali Lehr* (Second Edition, Panjabi); Mohinder Singh, *The Akali Movement,* Macmillian, Delhi, 1979, 120 (Mohinder Singh's account is based on the Private Papers of Malcalm Hailey in the Indian Office Library Nos. MSS EUR. E 220/ 41 to 45); Seth, G.R., *Sikh Struggle for Gurdwara Reforms.*

94. For details about *Babbars* activities and the Government policy towards their Group see *The Civil and Military Gazette, July* 24, 1923; Home Department, File Nos. 234-II/1923-Political; File No. 134-II/1923-Political; Mukhsuspuri, Sunder Singh, *Babbar Akali Lehr* (Second Edition, Punjabee), 115-20.

95. *The Civil and Military Gazette,* August 9, 1923 (For more details regarding the measures adopted by the British to crush the *Babbar* leadership and *jathas* also see Home Department, File No. 134-II/ 1923-Political, NAI : New Delhi; Mukhsuspuri, Sunder Singh, *Babbar Akali Lehr* (Second Edition, *Punjabee*), 199, 229-30), Home Department, File No. 134/III of 1923—Political, 27, NAI : New Delhi.

they carried out their earlier programme of preaching hatred towards the British rule and continued their policy of arresting the loyalists and supporters of the British bureaucracy. Their struggle was greatly sustained by the response of the Sikh peasantry. However, the *Babbars* failed to organise the peasantry on the basis of their economic grievances against the feudal system and its protector—the British Government—and thus build a stronger and wider democratic front against British imperialism in the country. Nevertheless the contribution of the *Babbars* to the Akali movement, when we assess the Akali movement, cannot be ignored. They increased the bargaining power of the Akali leadership and the Akali Group by creating panic among the supporters of the British and also in the bureaucratic machinery in the Punjab and thus compelled the Government to come to terms with the Akalis.[96] Besides Kishan Singh Gargaj and Master Mata Singh, the masterminds behind this movement, tried their best to eliminate the causes which had led to the failures of the *Ghadr* in 1915. Its organisation, the method of propaganda, each move in the struggle against a foreign Government and the need of an efficient and inspiring leadership had been given a serious thought. In the final analysis, the achievement of the *Babbar* Akali movement was that by intensifying revolutionary activities in the Punjab, it quickened the pace of the Indian National Movement. Their martyrdom strenghtened the determination of the Indian revolutionaries to eject the foreign Government out of the country.

Our present purpose is not to trace the history of the *Naujawan Bharat Sabha* but to study its activities in connection with the agrarian agitation in the Punjab. The *Naujawan Bharat Sabha* was formed in March 1926 at the suggestion of Dr. Satyapal to educate youngmen in extremist politics.[97] It was declared in the year 1927 by the British Government to be an

96. Mukhsuspuri, Sunder Singh, *Babbar Akali Lehr* (Second Edition, Panjabi), 229-31; Mohinder, Singh, *The Akali Movement,* Macmillian, Delhi : 1979, 124-25.

97. Home Department, File No. 498/1930-Political, NAI : New Delhi.

unlawful organisation.[98] However, the *Sabha* was revived in April 1928, by the efforts of the Lahore Communists and the *Kirti* Group.[99] Let it be noted at the outset that the *Naujawan Sabha* stood for complete independence of the country from foreign yoke, which was only possible by mobilising all the workers, peasants and other anti imperialists forces, thereby over-throwing British imperialism and its allies by mass action and establishing a workers' and peasants' republic in India.[100] Thus, their first task was to organise labourers and peasants by means of newspapers and by setting up libraries of Socialists literature in certain villages. The All India *Naujawan Bharat Sabha,* at its Karachi session had decided that the *Naujawans* should totally boycott all foreign goods and the British made articles.[101] Besides, they were strongly agitating against communalism as well as feudalism.[102]

Within a short time, it was reported that a new society called the *Nau Jawan Hindu* had arisen which was similar to the *Naujawan Bharat Sabha.* Its objectives which were defined at its initial meetings, were precisely those of the *Naujawan Bharat Sabha.* The *Naujawan Bharat Sabha* was reported to have revived at Amritsar by the efforts of the Lahore Communists and the *Kirti* Group in April, 1928, as stated above also, but its revival resulted in the arrest of four of its leaders. It was also revived at Lyallpur and there too some of its leaders were arrested.[103] Meetings of the *Naujawan Bharat*

98. *Ibid* (It was active only for a short period from March 1926 to April, 1927). Vide Home Department, File No. 130 & K.W. 1930-Political, NAI : New Delhi.

99. Home Department, File No. 130 & K.W.-130, Political, NAI : New Delhi.

100. Home Department, File No. 24/15/1935-Political, NAI : New Delhi.

101. Home Department, File No. 39/9/1931-Political, NAI : New Delhi.

102. Home Department, File No. 18/4/1933-Political; File No. 18/1/1933-Political, (The *Naujawan Bharat Sabhas* of Lahore and Amritsar were more active and taking keen interest in the agrarian problems and peasants' unrest and their agitation in the countryside), NAI : New Delhi.

103. Home Department, File No. 130 & K.W.-1930-Political, NAI : New Delhi.

Sabha, Amritsar were held on 19th and 21st, 27th and 29th July, 1930. This *Sabha* was also reorganised in Hissar and it was made public in its meeting held on 27.7.1930. It was very active and held meetings at various places. The aim of these meetings was to arouse the masses, particularly in the rural tracts.[104]

Young revolutionaries both in the Punjab and U.P. were taking keen interest in Socialism,[105] and many were in touch with the Communist groups,[106] which were sprouting up all over the country,[107] particularly in the Punjab—but also in some parts of U.P. They maintained close contacts with the Communists.[108] During the year 1928-30, the revolutionaries and the Communists worked together in the *Naujawan Bharat Sabha*.[109] As we have seen in Chapter-II, the Russian Revolution had already made a great impact on the minds of the young revolutionaries.[110] We get even a clearer picture of this view in the statement of Bhagat Singh and Dutt of 6th June, 1929. In their opinion, socialism also represented a new state structure in which power then rested in the hands of the

104. Home Department, File No. 498/1930-Political, NAI : New Delhi.

105. Yashpal, *Singhavelokan* (Hindi), Lucknow : 1951, Vol. I, 96; Gosh, Ajoy, *Articles and Speeches*, Moscow : 1962, 36; (Lajpat Rai publicly described Bhagat Singh as a Russian agent and complained that he wanted to "make me into Lenin") Vide, Sandhu Virendra, *Yogdrashta Bhagat Singh* (Hindi), Delhi, 1968, 316.

106. Many of them might have been influenced by the Kanpur Bolshevik Conspiracy Case since they were present in Kanpur at that time. Vide. Chandra Bipan, 'The Ideological Development of the Revolutionary Terrorists in Northern India in 1920's, *Seminar* on Socialism in India 1919-39 (Second Session, October 8-10, 1969).

107. Sanyal, J.N., *Sardar Bhagat Singh* (Lahore : 1931), 26.

108. *Ibid.*

109. *Ibid.*

110. Home Department, File No. 130 & K.W.-1930-Political (The Philosophy of the Bomb), 10; also quoted by Bhagwan Singh Josh, *Communism in the Punjab*, Anupam, Delhi-1979.

workers and peasants.[111] Similarly, Bhagat Singh declared in 1931 that their main task should be the organisation of peasants and workers.[112]

The leadership of the *Naujawan Sabha* emphasised the importance of the role of the people in the freedom struggle. Its leaders were convinced that the capitalist and upper classes were showing a tendency to join the foreign power and were likely to abandon the freedom struggle half way through.[113] As Bhagat Singh put it : "The nation can wage a successful struggle only on the strength of organised workers, *Kisans* and the common people".[114] This emphasis on revolutionary work among the peasants and workers, and recognition of their revolutionary potentialities, was not new in the revolutionary terrorist movement. Earlier in 1924, the Hindustan Republican Association had decided that "to start a labour and peasant organisation, suitable men must be engaged on behalf of the Association to organise and control the workers and peasants.[115]

In practice, little headway was made in the organisation of the common people. The *Naujawan Bharat Sabha* did take part in one or two agrarian agitations in 1928 and issued a few exhortations to the peasants to organise themselves.[116]

---

111. *Rules and Regulations of the Naujawan Bharat Sabha* : Punjab May 1, 1928 Vide *Meerut Conspiracy Case 1929,* English translation of Urdu exhibits No. P. 205(T); Home Department, File No. 130 & K.W.-1930 (Reports on the *Naujawan Bharat Sabha*)-Political, NAI : New Delhi.

112. Sandhu, Virendra, Yugdrashta Bhagat Singh (Hindi), Delhi, 1968, 224.

113. Gopal, Thakur, *Bhagat Singh : The Man and His Ideas* (The Menifesto : Bhagat Singh), Delhi-1952, 39.

114. Quoted in Gopal Thakur, *Bhagat Singh : The Man and His Ideas,* 40-41; also see Sachin Sangal, *'Bandi Jiwan'* (Hindi), Delhi : 1963, 237.

115. Constitution of the HRA in Chatterji, J.C., *In Search of Freedom,* Calcutta : 1967, 342 (This seems to have been the result of Sachin Sangal's first hand experience of the effectiveness of labour as a political force). Vide Sachin Sangal, *Bandi Jivan* (Hindi), Delhi : 1963, 237.

The *Sabha* had only one village branch in Morinda in Ambala and two tehsil branches at Jaranwal and Talagang, and those were all inactive.[117] In practice, all the activities of the Sabha were confined to the cities and their lower and middle class sectors.[118] Nevertheless, the *Naujawan Bharat Sabha* tried to reach out to the workers and peasants who were yet passive, 'dumb' and 'voiceless'.[119] In reality, this *Sabha* failed to do any political work among the common people. It had hardly any contact or link with them. Not to speak of its organising their class and leading them in class struggles. It was virtually cut off from the classes which it had accepted in its programme as the social base of their movement. This was perhaps one of the most important weaknesses of the *Sabha*. The fact of the matter was that the main appeal of the *Sabha* was to the radical youth only and in practice the leadership of the *Sabha* placed its reliance for political work on the youth.[120]

Moreover, their ideas, and the prestige of their sacrifices

116. Home Department Political Proceedings, File No. 130 & K.W. (1930), 38-77 (And these may be ascribed to the *Kirti Kisan* Component of the Sabha).

117. *Ibid.,* 13 (In January, 1930, it was decided to intensify work among the workers, peasants and Students but no one was assigned to work among the peasants) Vide *Ibid.,* 36; *The Tribune,* (Lahore) December 7, 1929 (Lalit Kumar Mukherjee's Evidence in the Lahore Conspiracy Case); Josh, Sohan Singh, *Immortal Heroes : Lives of Communist Leaders,* Communist Party publication, 1975, 13.

118. Home Political Proceedings, File No. 130 & K.W. 1930-Political The Philosophy of the Bomb), 13.

119. *Peaceful and Legitimate,* a H.S.R.A. Pamphlet, *Copies of the Exhibits in Lahore Conspiracy Case (ii) History of the Freedom Movement,* Phase II, Region III, 6/3; Exhibit, P.N.; also see 6th June Statement of Bhagat Singh and Dutt quoted in Sandhu Virendra, *Yugdrashta Bhagat Singh* (Hindi), Delhi-1968.

120. *The Tribune* (Lahore), October 22, 1929 (Bhagat Singh's and Dutt's message to the students); Proceedings of the Delhi Conspiracy Case, Vol. I, (Kailashpati's Evidence), 229; Chandra Bipan, The Ideological Development of the Revolutionary Terrorists in Northern India in 1920's *Seminar on Socialism in India, 1919-39,* Second Session October 8-10, 1964.

behind those ideas, could perhaps become powerful instruments in the spread of revolutionary socialist consciousness in the later years if the leftist parties had so utilised them. But for some unknown factors, these parties failed to do so.[121] Above all, while in theory the *Sabha's* leadership wanted to base their movement on the masses—he workers and peasants, in practice they could only appeal to the lower middle class or petty bourgeois youth. While in theory they wanted to create and lead a mass movement, in practice they remained a small group of heroic youth. While in theory their small organisation was to serve as a cell around which would gather the rising revolutionary forces of the country, in practice they found it difficult and in the end impossible to maintain the integrity of the original group itself. Its rank and file remained disinterested in theory and functioned almost entirely at the level of revolutionary nationalist consciounsess.[122]

Let us now narrate a few facts related to its growth and activities. Bhagat Singh, the founder of the *Naujawan Bharat Sabha* met Sohan Singh Josh in the *Kirti* office and informed him about his association.[123] As a result of this meeting, both these groups joined hands to work together.[124] To organise workers and peasants, the prominent leaders of the *Naujawan Bharat Sabha* such as, Abdul Majid, K.N. Sehgal and Sohan

---

121. Chandra, Bipan, The Ideological Development of the Revolutionary Terrorists in Northern India in 1920's *Seminar on Socialism in India,* 1919-39, Second Session, October 8-10, 1964, 33, 34.

122. Yashpal, *Sinhavalokan,* Vol. II (Hindi), Lucknow : 1951, 282; *Second Lahore Conspiracy Case* (Inderpal's and Madan Gopal's Evidence); Bhagwan Dass Mahour in *Yash Ka Dharohar,* edited by Banarsi Dass Chaturvedi, (Hindi), Delhi : 1968) (Second Edition), 27-28; Vaishampayan, *Amar Shahid Chandra Sheikhar Azad,* (Benaras : 1967), 306-07.

123. *The Naujawan Bharat Sabha* had become inactive due to certain reasons. But now he promised to attend the Conferences of the *Kirti Kisan* Group. Vide, Josh, Sohan Singh, *Immortal Heroes : Lives of Communist Leaders,* C.P.I. publication, 1975.

124. *Ibid.,* 13.

Singh Josh visited various places, held meetings and helped them to organise local *Sabhas.*[125] A significant fact to be noticed here is that there was a deep imprint of the ideology of the *Kirti* Group on the leadership of the *Naujawan Sabha* which was noticeable in many directions. This can be noticed in the formation of the new executive elected on February 24, 1929. With the help of the *Kirti* and the Communist Groups, no participation in any future war and denunciation of communalism, imperialism and capitalism were the central themes of propaganda conducted by the leadership of the *Naujawan Bharat Sabha.*[126] The communalist press constantly carried on propaganda against the *Naujawan Bharat Sabha.*[127]

Another significant point to note here is that all the young revolutionaries held : "the action would arouse the masses and strengthen the movements"; and it became a pivot of their world view. The *Sabha's* leadership, as stated earlier also, derived inspiration from the courage, self sacrifice and dedication of the *Ghadr* heroes,[128] who were the guiding force to the *Kirti Kisan* leaders as well. The *Ghadr* heroes' unprecedented sacrifices and its ideology of armed struggle had a firm hold on their thinking.[129] Therefore, the militant attitude of the *Sabha* was a threat and could not be ignored by the imperialists authorities.[130] Consequently, the British

125. *Meerut Conspiracy Case : 1929-30*—Punjab and U.P. Speeches, ACHI/JNU (For the total strength of the NBS see Home Department File No. 130 & K.W.-1930. It also carries the names of all prominent leaders of the NBS and their link with the *Kirti Kisan Party*).

126. *Meerut Conspiracy Case* (Punjab and U.P. Speeches), NAI : New Delhi.

127. *Ibid.*

128. For ideological evolution of Bhagat Singh and his Comrades see Ghosh, Ajoy, *Article and Speeches,* Mascow : 1962; Chandra, Bipan, The Ideological Development of the Revolutionary Terrorists in Northern India in the 1920's", *Socialism in India-Seminar,* edited by Nanda, B.R., NMML, New Delhi.

129. For details see Ghosh, Ajoy, *Article and Speeches,* Moscow : 1962, 16-17.

130. Home Department, File No. 130 & K.W.-1930-Political, NAI : New Delhi.

bureaucracy followed repressive policy to curb the activities of this organisation.

It will not be out of place to state that after the Saunders' murder, the *Kirti Kisan* Group tended to publicly disassociate itself from the terrorist tendency represented by the leadership of the *Naujawan Bharat Sabha*. Sohan Singh Josh declared, on 6th December, 1928 in a meeting held at Jallianwala Bagh, "Our *Naujawan Sabha* does not believe in terrorism.......We can not change the system, nor can we remove injustice and oppression.....That is why we want to prepare for mass Civil-disobedience or mass no tax campaign. That is why we lay stress on mass organisation."[131] Besides, several meetings of the provincial *Naujawan Bharat Sabha* were held at different places. For instance, a meeting of the provincial NBS was held at Lahore from February 22 to 24, 1929. The proceedings of the Conference reflected the revolutionary communist, anti-British spirit of the NBS since its rival the previous year.[132] Another meeting of the NBS was held in Amritsar on the 9th and 10th August, 1929. It was attended by Pt. Nehru and a considerable number of returned immigrant extremists of the Doab members of the *Kirti Kisan* party also attended the Conference. The Conference considerably strengthen the position of the *Sabha*, vis-a-vis Congress.[133] Thus, the NBS was closely related to the problems of the peasants and workers and its leadership was helping the agrarian movement in the countryside, in their own way.

Lahore was one of the ideological centres which came into existence, in various parts of the country, in the early 1920's. M.R. Khan, Shammsuddin Hassan and Ghulam Hussain took a leading part in the formation of the Communist Party in

131. Josh, Sohan Singh, *Immortal Heroes : Lives of Communist Leaders,* CPI Publication, 1975, 22; For details see Josh, Bhagwan Singh, Communism in The Punjab, Anupam Delhi, 1979.

132. Home Department, File No. 18/2/1929. For details regarding Josh, Sohan Singh, views about the ideology of *NBS* also see *Meerut Conspiracy Case,* 1929-33, 207(T). NAI : New Delhi.

133. Home Department, File No. 18/8/1929-Political, NAI : New Delhi.

Lahore.[134] In the beginning, their work was primarily confined to rescruitment of members into their circles and dissemination of the Communist literature obtained from abroad. Ghulam Hussain came into contact with the Balshevist Centre,[135] when he visited Kabul. After his return to Lahore, the started a Communist newspaper—*'Inquilab'*.[136] The motive behind it was to promote Communism in Punjab and to obtain hold in the labour and the *Kisan* organisations of Lahore. However, the Lahore Group which had started crystallising around the *Inqilab* collapsed soon because of the arrest of its founder in June, 1923.[137] The work of Communist propaganda had been undertaken by the *Ghadrites* at the time of third international. The *Ghadr* Group was convinced that British rule could only be overthrown with the help of arms and there was no other possible way to do so. In March, 1921, the *Ghadr* Group published a pamphlet—*Inquilab-i-Hind,* which clearly stated its ideology.

It was through Rattan Singh that the Punjab *Ghadrites* were maintaining contacts with the third international organisation.[138] And, he himself was collaborating with the Communist international.[139] At this stage a batch of five

134. Adhikari, G. *Documents of History of the Communist Party of India,* Vol. I, 1972, 2-3; Home Department, File No. 103/IV-1923-Political (The Communist Party at Lahore was formed towards the end of 1922).

135. For details see Home (Political) Department, File No. 261, K.W. (I) 1924, NAI : New Delhi.

136. *Ibid.;* File No. 103/IV-1923-Political (Originally this paper was started in August, 1922 by Shamsuddin Hassan, but had stopped after a few issues. It was restarted as a bi-weekly by Ghulam Nabi on the advice of Ghulam Hussain). For details about *Inqilab* see Kay, Sir Cecil, *Communism in India : 1971,* 71-72; Adhikari, G., *Documents of History of the Communist Party of India,* Vol. II, 1974, 138.

137. For details see Home Department, File No. 261-K.W. (I)-1924, NAI : New Delhi; Kaye, Sir Cecil, *Communism in India : 1971,* 75.

138. Petrie David, *Communism in India : 1924-47,* 39. For Rattan Singh activities see *The Kirti,* February, 1926.

139. Home Department, File No. 41/1926, NAI : New Delhi.

Ghadrites left for Russia to be trained in Communist propaganda,[140] who maintained contacts with the *Kirti Kisan* organisation in Punjab through Kabul Centre, which was definitely of Communist leanings. In reality, the *Kirti Kisan* movement was merged in the Communists, who always thought in terms of helping the agrarian movement.[141] Similarly, the other political associations had always shown and were out to show their sympathies with the agrarian movement which shows that all these Groups were having left leanings to some extent and also had close contacts with the Communists.[142] For example, even before its birth, three Peshawar Conspiracy Cases (1921-22) were instituted against the revolutionary workers having Communist ideology.[143] To get a permanent hold and propagate their ideas among the peasants in the province, the Communists started a paper *Jang-i-Azadi.* Soon after this, the agrarian movement gathered momentum. Now, those who held Communist leanings, wanted to start agrarian movement enmass under the banner of the Communists. Similarly, the tenants of the states received a sufficient backing from the Communist leadership.[144] The so called *Kisan* Conferences were being organised by the tenants in league with the so called Communists in the States. Similarly, the Communists tried to take the tenants and small landholders in the organisation.[145]

---

140. *Ibid.*
141. For details relating to the relation and co-operation of the Communists, see fortnightly Reports of the Province from 1934 to 1937 in particular; also File Nos. 18/9/1941-Political; 226/1942(1)-Political of Home Department, NAI : New Delhi.
142. Malhotra, Avtar Singh, 'Fifty Years of Struggle of CPI', publishd in a *Souviner* issued by the CPI in 1976.
143. *Ibid.;* Zafar Iman, *The Rise of Russia and Socialism in India* : 1917-29, 22; Basta No. 18, Case No. 386/C-Patiala State Rcords, PSA : Patiala (Punjab).
144. Patiala State Records, Basta No, 13, Case No. 535/C, PSA : Patiala; Malhotra, Avtar Singh, 'Fifty Years of Struggle of CPI'.
145. Home Department, Fortnightly Reports-Political, years from 1934-41; Patiala State Records, Basta No. 50, Case No. 565/C, PSA : Patiala.

The *Kisan Sabhas* at first, were mistaken for Communist organisations. But to speak of any influence of the Communists' ideology over peasants' at this date is ridiculous, for, in the early days, the Communists thought that the peasants, with their conservative tradition-bound and superstitious outlook were anti-revolution.[146] But later on, as stated above, the Communists were the real leaders of the Punjab *Kirti Kisan* movement in the province and the tenants' movement in the Punjab states as well.

It was, however, this Group which exposed ruthlessly the dreadful reality of imperialism. It also advocated that total liberty could not be attained without eradicating it from social and economic fields. It equally exposed the stooges and the allied forces of imperialism, *Rajwarashashi, Jagirdari* and Capitalism and made their extinction an essential objective of the freedom struggle.[147] The Communist leadership also laid emphasis on the special role of workers and peasants in the freedom struggle and alongwith organising and marshalling them for the protection of their interests and rights, it too made them conscious and active to make maximum contribution in the national freedom struggle.[148]

In numerous revolutionary struggles, this group in the forefront. Its role in the *Ghadr Lehr*, the *Babbar* Akali *Lehr*, the *Naujawan Bharat Sabha*, the *Pepsu* tenants' movement was prominent.[149] As seen earlier, the young terrorist

146. Ramakrishan, T., '*Kisan* Movement in Andhra' : 1918-38, *Seminar on Socialism in India*, Part-II, No. 28-30, 1968, NMML, New Delhi; (For details also see Sarkar, B.B., *The Origin of the Social Movement in India : 1919-39)*.

147. Krishna Hathree Singh, *With no Regrets* (Bombay : 1943); Malhotra, Avtar Singh, 'Fifty Years of Struggle of CPI' published in a *Souviner* issued by the CPI in January, 1976; Zafar Iman, *The Rise of Soviet Russia And Socialism in India* (1919-29), 22-23.

148. Malhotra, Avtar Singh, 'Fifty Years of Struggle of CPI' published in Souviner issued by the CPI in January, 1976; Krishna Hathee Singh, *With No Regrets*, (Bombay : 1943).

149. *Ibid.*; also Personal interviw with Master Hari Singh (C.P.I. Office, Chandigarh).

revolutionaries also established contact with the small Communist Groups which were sprouting up all over the country.[150] Particularly in Punjab but also in Kanpur and Allahabad, they maintained close contact with the Communists.[151] During the year 1928-30, the Communists and the terrorist revolutionaries worked together in the NBS.[152] And, we have already noted that one of the major objectives of the *Sabha,* as laid down in its rules and regulations was the organisation of workers and peasants.[153] The NBS also decided to open branches in villages in order to emphasise the value of work in the rural areas and the Communists were always supporting them.[154]

Another significant fact worth mentioning is that the CPI was the first political party which applied the scientific principles of Marxism Leninism to the problems of the peasants and prepared its land programme on systematic lines. It also organised the Indian peasants at the grass-root level. It also advocated the right revolutionary policy of associating the peasants with the Workers' movement and National struggle for freedom. The Communists advocated a considerable reduction in *Malba* payable by the peasants; exemption (be given) from *Malia* for a period as long as it was necessary and relief (be provided) to small peasants to a reasonable extent in view of the decrease in the rent of land.[155]

150. Sanyal, J.N., *Sardar Bhagat Singh,* Lahore : 1931, 26.

151. *Ibid.*

152. *Ibid.*

153. Rules and Regulations of the *Naujawan Bharat Sabha,* Punjab 1 May, 1928, *Meerut Conspiracy Case,* 1929, Exhibit No. P. 205 (T); Home Department (Political) Proceedings, File No. 130 & .W., (1930), 35; Sanyal, J.N., *Sardar Bhagat Singh, 25;* Gopal Thakur, *Bhagat Singh : Man & His Ideas,* New Delhi : 1952, 39; Sandhu, V., Yugrashta Bhagat Singh (Hindi), Delhi, 1968, 224.

154. Home Department (Political) Proceedings, File No. 130 & K.W. (1930), 10.

155. For demands, aims and programme of the Communists in the Punjab see Home Department File Nos. 6/11/1924-Political; 10/V/1929-Political; 10/V/1929-Poltical; 12/3/1936-Political; 18/5/1936-Political; 6/8/1936-Political; 18/6/1940-Poltical; 18/8/1940-Political; P.L.C.D., Vol. XX, 1931.

It will not be out of place to state the fact that the Communists had been working within the Congress itself and had led a staunch anti-imperialists and leftist section of the party. They were to play a prominent and specific role, which was : to lay stress on the importance of revolutionary struggle against the British empire, to make efforts for the unity of all revolutionary and patriotic forces for this purpose; to get the demands and feelings of the working people reflected in the programmes of the Congress and to project Congress as a National *'Morcha'* against imperialism and feudalism and for national liberty.[156]

However, this fact can not be ignored that in 1930-31, the Communists started criticising the Congress. It was between 1928 and 1935, that the official Journals of the Comintern published a series of articles, statements and documents branding Congress leaders as treacherous anti-revolutionaries and exhorting the Indian Communists to launch a firm fight against the left section of the Indian National Congress particularly. The Communist leadership accepted this new line at once. The speeches at the various *Kisan* Conferences showed that the Punjab Communist Party was also following the political line of the Communist Party in India.[157] It is also important to state that the main socialist (Communist) activity centred round a number of conferences in the Amritsar district. The police reports vividly show that—in Amritsar district, Socialists and Communists held almost daily meetings and *Diwan* in some villages or other and rural propaganda was almost constantly carried on in the Batala *Tehsil* of Gurdaspur".[158] Though these conferences could not attract a large audience, this insistent and constant effort to spread

156. Personal Interview with Master Hari Singh (CPI Office : Chandigarh).

157. *The Kirti* (Amritsar), January : 1930 (For details also see the Fortnightly Reports of the year 1935—Home Department Political, NAI (Most of the *Kisan* Conferences were organised by the Commuists where they demanded cancellation of debts and assessment of Land Revenue on the basis of income-tax etc.).

158. Home Department, File Nos. 18/3/1937-Poltical; 18/7/1938-Poltical; NAI : New Delhi.

Communists views, of course, requires a careful attention, because the Communist workers had reached a stage where action by the Government was required.[159]

Another significant point worth mentioning is that the Communist enjoyed the support of the masses in the countryside and also of the *Jat* agriculturists. But it is very difficult to state clearly whether it were the poor or well-to-do *Jats* which provided them with shelter and organisation help in the rural areas. However, the inference which one gathers from the memoirs written in the later period tends to point out that the local leadership was mostly provided by the well-to-do section of the agriculturists.[160] However, despite its sincere efforts, the C.P.I. remained a narrow sectarian group between 1925 and 1935. Infact, it was the seventh Congress of the Communist International that enabled the Indian Communists to build for the first time a real All India Communist Party with provincial Committees in almost all provinces.[161]

At this stage, the Comrades in the Punjab had decided to form a provincial Communist Party and an open agitation was favoured by them.[162] Having this aim in mind, on July 30, three private conferences were held in Bradlaugh Hall, Lahore in which it was decided to form a labour party in the province; To organise the masses for economic uplift and for political work in the country.[163] Let it be noted that two of the three Conferences were held by the NBS and the *Mazdur Kisan Sabha*. The aim of the conveners was to bridge the gulf between the *Kirti Kisan* and the NBS as a preliminary to an extension of Communist activity throughout the province.[164]

---

159. Home Department, File No. 18/4/1937-Political, NAI : New Delhi.

160. For details see Jagjit Singh's Article published in the *Punjabee* daily, *Nawan Zamana*, December, 1975.

161. Dutt, R.P., and Bradly, *Inprecorr*, February 29, 1936.

162. Home Department, File Nos. 103/IV/1923-Political; 10/IV/1929-Political; 18/9/1932-Poll; 18/8/1933-Political, NAI : New Delhi.

163. Hom Department, File Nos. 18/8/1933-Political; 18/12/1933-Political; 18/13/1933-Political; 18/14/1933-Political, NAI : New Delhi.

Thus, the three bodies—The *Kirti Kisan* Party, the N.B.S. and the Communist Group worked in collaboration; Their efforts to amalgamate would not have met with much success[165] if these bodies had not worked together. For instance, when the Amritsar *Kirti Kisan Sabha* drew up an extensive propaganda tour from 29th May to the 17th of June in Villages of the Amritsar and Gurdaspur districts, many Sikh Communists had been announced to speak. Its object was to exploit the discontent over the prospective re-settlement of the district and to impress on the Government the necessity of reducing revenue and water rate.[166]

Some time in 1935-36, differences sprang up between the *Ghadr* Group and the Communists. But the latter were determined to continue their programme in villages and to create as much unrest as possible.[167] In brief, the real Communist agitation continued in the districts of the central Punjab under the auspices of the Punjab *Kirti Kisan* Party.[168] The Communists and the Socialists also continued to make use of all sort of meetings for the propagation of their particular cult.[169] As we have noted earlier also, the *Kirti*, the *Punjabee* journal was the organ of the *Ghadr*-cum-Communist Sikhs.[170] So, the above said differences between the two factions could not continue for long.

---

164. Home Departmnt, File No. 18/1/1934-Poltical, NAI : New Delhi.

165. Home Department, File Nos. 18/2/1934-Poltical; 18/3/1934-Political; 18/4/1934-Political; 18/5/1934-Politcal; 226/42(1) (The Punjab *Kirtis* and the Communists were united in their hatred of British Imperialism), NAI : New Delhi.

166. Home Department, File No. 18/6/1934-Political; 18/4/1937-Political, NAI : New Delhi.

167. Home Departmnt, File No. 18/2/1937-Political, NAI : New Delhi.

168. Home Department, File Nos. 18/6/1934-Political; 18/5/1934-Political; 18//1934-Political; 18/8/1934-Political; 18/10/1934-Poltical, NAI : New Delhi (For detail also see File Nos. 18/6/1936-Poltical; 18/7/1936-Political; 18/10/1936-Political).

169. Home Department, File No. 18/10/1937-Political, NAI : New Delhi.

170. Home Department, File No. 18/1/1937-Political, NAI : New Delhi.

The main activities of the Communist Group, however, centred round a number of Conferences in the districts of the central Punjab—particularly in the areas where the *Ghadr* and the *Kirti* leaders resided.[171] Their main objective was to interest all the peasants in the new settlement. The main cry was for the assessment of land revenue on an income tax basis and they also demanded the abolition of the *Khikri Pahera, Beggar, Malba* and *Abiana*, etc. Thus, they helped to create an impression of the growing strength of Socialism and Communism.[172] Now the Communists-cum-*Ghadr* Party held conferences in Jullundur district. They were determined to organise a country-wide 'no rent' campaign. The Punjab Communists also planned to take advantage of the war situation and the possible political unrest in the province to spread their doctrines and influence.[173] It was in October 1939 that the Punjab branch of the Communist Party brought out a fortnightly paper *Alan-i-Jang* and distributed it in the Punjab and the North West Frontier Province.[174] It contained anti-recruitment propaganda and also inciting material for the peasantry and troops.[175]

The well known Meerut Conspiracy Case (1929) was used by the English imperialists to declare the party illegal with the several organisations and fronts associated with it and this ban continued uptill 1942.[176] In reality, in the second half

171. Home Department, File No. 18/6/1937-Political, NAI : New Delhi.
172. Home Department, File Nos. 18/4/1937-Poltical; 18/7/1937-Poltical; 18/8/1937-Political (For details also see File Nos. 18/6/1936-Political; 18/9/1937-Poltical), NAI : New Delhi.
173. Home Department, File Nos. 18/7/1939-Political; 18/10/1939-Politcal, NAI : New Delhi.
174. Home Department, File No. 7/6/1939-Political, NAI : New Delhi.
175. *Ibid;* For more details also see File No. 18/6/1940-Political, NAI : New Delhi.
176. Zafar Iman, 'The Rise of Soviet Russia and Socialism in India 1919-29', *Mathon Socialism in India,* 1919-39, NMML, Delhi, 1964, 22; Malhotra, Avtar Singh, 'Fifty Years of Struggle of C.P.I., *Souvenir,* issued by the CPI in January, 1976 (Confirmed by Master Hari Singh in a personal meeting with him at Chandigarh on December 17, 1978).

of 1942, the Communists were very active in conducting propaganda and they organised as many as 7 rural meetings. They held that it was imperative to resist the Japanese aggression and stated that the support for the British was a matter of expediency. It was alleged that joining the Army in large numbers would transform it into a National Army paving the way for the seizure of power at the end of the war. Soon after this, the Communists belonging to the CPI and the *Kirti* Group joined hands for the first time with "mutual trust" and "full-faith".[177] The *Kirti* Group was also backing the Communists. During the month of August, twenty three meetings were held by the Communists at various places. Similarly, they had held Conferences throughout the month of July, but it was becoming increasingly difficult for them to conduct effective pro-war campaign in the face of the reports spread by the Akalis and the Congress that the Communists had purchased their release from jail on the understanding that they would back the war efforts of the Government.[178] The ban on the Communist Party was removed on July 23, 1942; with the removal of ban, the systematic organisation of the Communist Party began in the Punjab.

We may here add, however, that the *Kisan* and *Kirti* Movements were identified with the Communists but could not grow stronger after their leaders had been detailed. But no sooner did the Punjab Government release them, they started reorganising the Communist movement under the pretext of accelerating war efforts. And, there was possibility that the tenants might join this movement, as a body, sooner or later. Even the Superintendent of Intelligence, Patiala toured Lahore, Amritsar and Taran Taran and thereafter confirmed his assessment of the Communist danger.[179] According to him,

---

177. Home Department, File No. 18/7/1942-Political, NAI : New Delhi.

178. Home Department, File No. 18/7/1942-Poltical; 7/2/1942-Political—I. & K.W., NAI : New Delhi.

179. Confidential Note on Tour of Amritsar, Lahore and Taran Taran from June 8 to 12, 1942, by Superintendent, Intelligence, Patiala, dated 24.6.42, PSR., P.M's Office File No. 1577.

there were two strong rival political parties in the Punjab, the Communists and the Akalis and the strength of the former was larger than that of the latter, even after many important Communist leaders had been detained and that as the *Shiromani Akali Dal* had been making efforts at checkmating their advance. It was also reported that the Communist leaders had started reorganising Communists in the right earnest and were holding conferences in large number. Thus the *Kisan Kirti* movements were receiving a large support and the *Muzafar* of the state, too, had received a sufficient backing. It was expected by the British that this might result in the intensification of the *Muzara* movement.

To substantiate, the success of the Communists' efforts was reflected in the *Jathas* of 40 tenants that participated in the All India *Kisan* Conference held at Bhakna in Lahore district from April 12 to 14, 1943.[180] The rapid increase in Communist influence was also explained by their simultaneous attempts to struggle against the loyalist Akalis led by Master Tara Singh. In this effort, they Co-operated with the Akalis of the States' *Akali Dal* and who were consolidated under the name of the rival *Akali Jatha* Patiala State, and who were not happy over master Tara Singh's collusion with the Patiala Maharaja and over the communal character of his politics. The Communists participated in and were prominent in the religious *dewans* held by this group to condemn Master Tara Singh's anti national and communal politics.[181] Jagir Singh Joga, a prominent Communist leader, made it clear that though, out of expediency, the Communists were then co-operating with the Government of India,[182] however, he stated, when the right time came, they would make it impossible for the Government to function and shall favour the *Kisans* and

180. Patiala State Records, P.M.'s Office File No. 1573 (CIP Secret Abstract of Intelligence, dated 9.4.1943).

181. *Ibid.*

182. Patiala State Records, P.M.'s Office Case No. 565/C of 2000 (1943-44), C.I.D. Secret Abstracts of Intelligence, dated 13.3.1943 and 2.7.1943.

Muzaras.[183] This projection of the Communists as the militant upholders of the Akali tradition of relentless struggle against oppression—of therefore being 'better Akalis'—was valuable ideologically in mobilising the *muzaras.* The Communist plan of holding counter-meetings wherever Master Tara Singh's party held its conferences was reported to have seriously disturbed the Master Party and forced it to lie low, as it was suffering serious inroads into its popularity.[184]

Despite attempts to ban meetings and conferences, throughout 1943 and 1944 the Communist workers kept up a hectic pace of propaganda and mobilisation of tenants through ostensibly religious *Dewans.*[185] The administration referred to all such meetings and Communist conferences[186] and the Patiala authorities were seriously worried about the "daily increase" in the Communist influence on the *Muzaras.* The self-confidence of the Patiala Communists was expressed at Tungwali in the demand for the recognition of the Kisan and Communist organisation and the students Unions,[187] and thought that it could only be checked by the settlement of the *muzara Biswedar* dispute.[188] However, the Communists

183. *Ibid* ('Expediency' here obviously refers to the necessity to take the side of the Allies once the Soviet Union was attacked by Hitler).

184. Progressive Akali Party led by Durlab Singh, Servants of Sikhs Society led by Kartar Singh of Complellpur, Advocate, Lahore and the Communist Party were the strongst amongst their opponents, *Ibid.*, dated 4.6.1943.

185. Patiala State Records, P.M's Office Case No. 565/C of 2000 (1943-44), C.I.D. Secret Abstracts of Intelligence dated 4.6.1943 and 14.1.1944 and CB-1-2 of 2001 (1944-45).

186. From about Mid-1943, this term became increasingly common when reference was made to *Muzara* activities, or other Communist organised meetings.

187. Patiala State Records P.M's Office Case No. CB-1-2- of 2001 (1944-45) dated 8.9.1944, C.I.D. Secret Abstract of Intelligence.

188. *Ibid.*, 7.7.1944 (The note further said, "The programme which Communist Party propagates amongst the *Muzaras* appeals to the latter very much and the result is that the *(Muzaras)* have alliance

(Contd.)

continued to be in the lead of this movement, carrying on propaganda, holding meetings in villages where clashes took place, organizing armed guards to protect the seized lands, demonstrating their solidarity at various conferences, sending petitions, organising deputations, arranging for the defence of tenants involved in court cases, touring the villages and enlisting members and collecting funds.[189] A *Muzara* war council was set up in 1945 itself, consisting of 21 members, mainly communists, to co-ordinate the movement and especially to organise armed guards to defend the gains of the movements.[190]

Now the *Kisan* Committee and the Communists were using their influence to prevent anti-Government sabotage and violence. But there was a major shift in the nature of Communist political work within a few months. By October 1942, the Communists in the Punjab had almost abandoned the conduct of antifascist propaganda and were concentrating on strengthening and enlarging the party organisation.[191] In their open meeting, the main emphasis was on the

with the Communist Party, No effective measures are being adopted in the direction of preventing propaganda carried on by the Communist in the State, They are therfore, having an opportunity of strengthening their movment........when they intend holding conferences in the state, it is anned........but the proganada that hey do individually and surreptitiously can not be lawfully shocked".

189. CID Secret Abstracts of Intelligence, dated 27.7.1945, 25.8.1945, 21.9.1945, 23.11.1945, 22.2.1946, 29.3.1946 and 5.4.1946, Patiala State Records, P.M's Office Case No. CB-1-2 of 2002 (1945-46); Report sent in by *Biswedars* to Govt. dated 22.2.1946; Patiala State Records, P.M's Office Case No. T-1 of 2001 (1945).

190. Walia, Ramesh, *A Study of the Praja Mandal Movement in the East Punjab States, Punjabi University, Patiala*, 1974, 163; PUC dated 1.2.1947 from Secretary, *Zamindara Sabha*, reporting proceeding of Dalelsinghwala *Muzara* Conference at which at appeal was made for collecting Rs. 5 lacs required by *Muzara* War Council to form a powerful union against *Biswedars* and state police, File on Landlords' Association, Patiala, Patiala State Records, P.M's Office Case No. T-1 of 2001 (1945).

191. Home Departmnt, File No. 18/10/1942-Political, NAI : New Delhi.

establishment of a national Government. Surveying the political situation in the province, a police report observed : "The Communist influence was, no doubt, helpful in exercising a moderate effect on the Congress campaign during its critical phases; it now remains to be seen whether or not Communists have outlived their usefulness".[192] *Jung-i-Azadi,* the Communists' organ continued to conduct the propaganda in favour of National Unity, to critcise the Government, to demand the release of the Congress leaders and to issue appeals to resist the Japanese aggression.[193] After the end of the second world war, the Communist party gave a still more solid shape to its land programme and demanded that the land reforms should not be limited merely to the abolition of *Zemindari* (The demand which the Congress had already conceded in 1946). These should, on the contrary, go still further as a programme of the distribution of land.[194]

However, during the period under review, the Communist movement, in the Punjab, had always been a minority movement but not an insignificant movement. It was one of the smaller parties but the Communist movement was fast gathering popular support undoubtedly. The Communist Party in the Punjab was opposed by the other political organisation. But the Peasants' movement in the Punjab and the Tenants' struggle in the Punjab states was supported by all the political groups which had left leanings and believed in leftist ideology of the Communist International. Its role and place in the Punjab politics we shall study in the second section of this Chapter.

Punjab became an important centre of political and social activity during the Rowlatt Act agitation and non-co-operation movement. Undoubtedly, the failure of the method of the *Ghadrites* and the revolutionaries in the rural Punjab prepared

---

192. *Ibid.*

193. *Ibid.*

194. Malhotra, Avtar Singh, "Fifty Years of Struggle of CPI, *Souviner* issued by the CPI in January, 1976. (For complete detail see the Fortnightly reports Home Department-Political of the year 1945 and 1946.

the ground for the favourable reception of the Congress and Gandhi's non-violent technique for attaining *Swaraj.* Even the earnest members of the *Ghadr* and other revolutionary parties lost faith in their own methods and were drawn towards the Congress movement.[195] But it is to be noted that the Indian National Congress remained a hand-maiden of the urban classes in the Punjab till 1947;[196] and it could attract to its fold neither the peasantry—Hindu, Muslim or Sikh, nor the Muslim community of the province. We also know the fact that the political failure of the urban classes in making common cause with the rural classes, or in striking an alliance with the Muslim community, paved the way for the tragedy of the partition of the province.[197] Since the Indian National Congress in the Punjab was so closely identified with the urban classes, the peasantry of the region was not directly recruited into the congress led agitation, as was true for other parts of the country.[198] However, it is absolutely wrong to presume that the Indian National Congress did not have any hold in the village of the Punjab.

The Punjab politicians had renewed contacts with the Congress, the process culminating in the right attempt to link divergent sections in the province-wide politics, in the first

195. Lajpat Rai, *Writings and Speeches,* Vol. I, 328; *Gandhi Collected* Works, Vol. XVI, Appendix-III, 533-34 (See a letter of a follower of Hardyal to Lajpat Rai regarding the weak position of the *Ghadrites*); Malhotra, S.L., *Gandhi and the Punjab,* Chandigarh : Punjab University Publication Bureau : 1970, 13; Lajpat Rai, *Autobiographical Writings,* (Delhi University Publishers; 1965, 91.

196. For details see the Fortnightly Reports of the period under review as well as the Punjab Legislative Council Debates and the various issues of the *Kirti* and other vernacular newspapers and journals.

197. For details regarding the parttion of the Punjab and involvement of the Congress and also other political groups in this issue see Kirpal Singh, *The Partition of the Punjab,* Punjabi University Publication : Patiala : 1972.

198. Ravinder Kumar, 'The Two Revolution in the Punjab', Presidential address—Modern Section—Punjab History Confernec,e February, 28th and 29th, 1976, *Proceedings Punjab History* Conference, Tenth Session, Punjabi University : Patiala.

decade of the present century. Despite Government efforts to suppress urban and rural agitation under the Congress, the Punjab Congress proved successful in developing sustained organisation and contacts which might. The district organisations disintegrated, secular political activity outside a small elitist circle ended, and the Congress did not become prominent for another decade. The failure further marks out dominant themes in Punjab politics,[199] in the period 1930's.

Congress supporters were unprepared to capitalise an opportunity for mass mobilization. Surprised by the degree of unrest, they searched for a plan which would aid in focussing public sentiment. Lajpat Rai, for instance, attempted to secure books on Irish rural politics and Unions.[200] Other politicians suggested transplanting a modified form of the Shivaji festival to co-ordinate resentment and action. Only recently shaken in reliance on petition, the *Punjabees* had no experience with tactics which might have been successfully employed.[201]

Conflicts of interests added to the Congress predicament. The Lahore, Indian Association had just completed demonstration against amendment of the Land Alienation Act. A session of the Punjab *Jat Mahasabha* in Delhi, reflecting land owning interests, was quick to note the contradiction between that agitation and the newly found concern over land revenue rates and hardship in the canal colonies.[202] The agitation in

199. Barrier, N.G., 'Mass Politics and the Punjab Congress in 'Pre-Gandhian Era', *The Punjab Past and Present,* Vol. IX-II, October, 1975, 351 and 356.

200. Lajpat Rai's correspondence with Bhai Parmanand in Judicial and Public Files, IQL, 2273, 1911.

201. Barrier, N.G., Mass Politics and the Punjab Congress in the 'Pre-Gandhian Era', *The Punjab past and Present,* Vol. IX-II, October, 1975.

202. *The Tribune* (Lahore), February 15, 1907, 4; Notes by Charles Rivaz, in *The Tribune,* February 12, 1907 and Thomas Walker in *The Tribune,* February 2, 1907; Barrier, N.G., Mass Politics and the Punjab Congress in 'Pre-Gandhian Era', *The Punjab Past and Present,* Vol. IX-II, October, 1975, 336 (He quotes from keep-with to PRF 108-A, Punjab Revenue File, Board of Revnue Lahore).

the Punjab over the colonization Bill came to the notice or Gandhi in South Africa. He admired the *Punjabees* for carrying on their struggle against the bureaucracy heroically.[203] Later when he was back, the Congress under his guidance took keen interest in the problems of this province.[204] But in the beginning, unsure of themselves and concerned essentially with their own issues, Congressmen did not know how to proceed. Though barred from using the rick religious metaphors that previously had been a part of their political life, Congressmen made short tours to the canal colonies to preach a bland message of National unity and criticism of the British.[205]

The Congress in the Punjab could not obtain a strong footing. Why so? It was supposed to be a non-violent movement, but actually it was not. The old Congress, that loyal and constitutionalist institution, after all was then dead. Now forces had come into existence which wanted to attain independence at once.[206] The limited extent to which the non-co-operation movement had made progress in the Punjab again establishes the fact that the Congress was not strong in the Punjab.[207] However, the Congress Sub-committee had not abandond all hopes of an agitation in regard to the canal water rates; so far the Committee had achieved very little because

203. *Gandhi Colleced Works*, Vol. VIII, 1962, 6.

204. For details see Sedition Committee Report, 142; *Gandhi Collected Works*, Vol. VIII, 1962, 361.

205. *The Punjabee*, see all the issues of the year 1907 (Editorials and the Articles by Lala Lajpat Rai).

206. P.L.C.D., Vol. I, 1921 (Mian Muhammad Shah Nawaz's Speech), 508.

207. *Ibid.*, (Speech of the Hon'ble Sir John Maynard), 89-90 (For more details related to Non-co-operation movement in the Punjab see this complete Vol.; also see Native Newspapers of this period; Home Department, File No. 1920—Pros. 203-204 (A), October, 1 (Why did the Non-co-operation Movement fail see *The Punch* (Lahore), February 16, 1921; *Th Zulfiqar* (Lahore) February 24, 1921; *The Akhbar-i-Aam* (Lahore), June 4, 1921; *The Tribune* (Lahore) May 7, 1921; *The Bande Matram*, October 29, 1921; Home Department File No. 708/1922-Political, NAI : New Delhi.

the agriculturists, who led the opposition to the enhancement, supported the Government in practically all its demands.[208] But the Provincial Congress sub-committee[209] tried to explore the possibilities of agitation against the enhanced *abiana* rates. It also organised a meeting on 20th July, 1924 at Kana Kacha in the Lahore district, which was attended by 700 *Zamindars,* including a few Akalis. Resolutions were passed for the adoption of "all legitimate and peaceful methods" to secure the removal of the tax. A similar meeting was held in the Sheikhupura district, which was poorly attended, only protests were made and there was no mention of non-payment of land revenue or canal rates.[210]

The Congress Water-tax Committee held meeting at Raewind in the Lahore district on 31st August. It undertook a scheme for the organisation of *Zamindara Sabha* throughout the province chiefly for the purpose of agitating against the increased *abiana.*[211] Another meeting in connection with the *abiana* agitation was held at Tarn-Taran on 23rd March, 1925. The Congress water-tax Committee also made an attempt to extend its activities to the Amritsar and Lyallpur districts but failed to achieve success.[212] In brief, the prestige of the Congress appeared to be on the decline throughout the province. The main reason for this was the failure of the attack on the land revenue.[213] A public statement had been made at a Congress meeting in Ferozpur, that no payment of land revenue was no part of the programme in that district. In

208. Home Department, File No. 25/1924-July, NAI : New Delhi.

209. The Committee was composed of Dr. Satyapal, the Secretary and two agitators one of them a brother of S. Ajit Singh who was prominent in the attempts made in 1907 to incite the colonists to rebellion. Vide Home Department File No. 25/1924-Political, July, NAI : New Delhi.

210. *Ibid.,* File No. 25/1924-August-Political, NAI : New Delhi.

211. *Ibid.,* File No. 25/1924-September-Political, NAI : New Delhi.

212. Home Department, File No. 112/1925-February and also of March-Political, NAI : New Delhi.

213. Home Department, File No. 18/VIII/1930-Political, NAI : New Delhi.

1930's, the only noticeable centres of the Congress activities were the Hissar and Rohtak districts and here too it was at a but low level and defensive.[214]

Even in the Amritsar and Lahore districts, the hollowness of the movement was noticeable.[215] In Gurdaspur and Sialkot, the Congress meeting was broken up by the boys of Sikh school of the latter district. In Sheikhupura, though there was some rural unrest, the revenue realisations were well up to standard. Similarly, in Gujrat and Attock districts the Congress lost ground.[216] However, the year 1931 was a landmark in the political life of the Punjab because several political conferences[217] under the auspices of the Congress were held in different Ilaqas in the province. The main theme of the speakers, in almost all the Conferences, was the peasant and his difficulties and the necessity of being prepared for the coming struggle. Among the resolutions as one condemning the Government's alleged repressive policy in the collection of land revenue and another calling on the Government to remit the whole of the land revenue and *abiana.* Appeal was made to a rustic audience not pay land revenue and *abiana.*[218] And, Pt. Nehru who visited the province many times, always in his speeches stressed that the programme should not be to help the Government but to oppose it, culminating in the refusal to pay land revenue, *abiana* and other taxes.[219] However, when Pt. Nehru visited Khalra in Lahore district, Sirhali in Amritsar district, Tarn Taran, Sheikhupura, Jaranwala and Lyallpur, he

214. *Ibid.*

215. *Ibid.*

216. *Ibid*; Home Department, File NO. 17/1929-Political, NAI : New Delhi.

217. For the details of these Conferences see Appendix-III, Vide Home Department, File Nos. 35/50/1931; 18/11/1931 and 18/12/1931-Political, NAI : New Delhi.

218. *Ibid*; (The main item of Congressmen demands will be reduction in land revnue by 50% allround) Vide Home Department, File Nos. 33/9/1931-Political, 95-96 (Also see the address of S. Satwant Singh-President of a Congress meeting) Vide *Ibid*, 131; also 39/9/1931-Political, NAI : New Delhi.

219. Home Department, File No. 4/14/1936-Political, NAI : New Delhi.

spoke very simply and confined himself to a few subjects while addressing rural people. All his speeches dealt with the amelioration of the conditions of workers and peasants, the establishment of the socialist state and the attainment of freedom from British imperialism. The effect of his visits to the countryside was likely to be more dangerous, the peasants were eager to hear solutions of their economic difficulties. His visits proved the existence among the rural class of interest in such questions an socialism and independence and they stimulated this interest. It undoubtedly encouraged the numerous Socialists and Communists who were attempting to spread their programme in rural areas.[220]

Nehru's visit to Sirhali ubdoubtedly increased the risk of opposition to the new settlement; non-payment of rent or land revenue or other taxes were the weapons on which, more than on any other, he relied to bring the then Government to its knees.[221] He flattered his audience by insisting that the peasantry, if they acted together, could achieve every thing, and he had preached this heady stuff in the heart of the Majha, a tract of the province where already revolutionary views and socialist doctrines had a number of almost fanatical adherents.[222] He always tried to create a revolutionary mentality and atmosphere specially in the countryside.[223] Consequently, there had been a certain amount of agrarian agitation against the settlement operation.

The campaign to interest the villagers in the South-East Punjab also continued. In the South-West, a number of meetings were held in the districts of Montgomery, Multan, Lyallpur and Muzaffargarh to support the Congress candidate in the Punjab Assembly by-election. Similarly, a small party of Congressmen was touring the Gurdaspur district to enlist

220. Home Department, File Nos. 12/3/1936-Political; 18/6/1936-Political, NAI : New Delhi.

221. Home Department, File No. 4/14/1936-Political, NAI : New Delhi.

222. *Ibid.*

223. Home Department, File No. 12/3/1936-Political, NAI : New Delhi.

members.[224] There had been a revival of Congress activity through out the province especially in the central and eastern Punjab. Now the Congressmen made a bitter attack on the Unionists, imperialism and recruitment in the army. But in the Attock district, Congress activities had met with considerable opposition from the villagers.[225]

The Congressmen and Socialists stirred an unrest in the Multan district of the Punjab. Their speeches were anti-Government with the result that tenants in the area declared their determination not to pay any dues to their landlords. In *Majha* tract, small meetings were held, during the month of June, 1937, in villages at which the Communists were condemned and attempts were made to attract the *Kisans* towards the Congress.[227] Of course, there had been little activity at provincial headquarters but, in districts, the Congress reorganisation and election propaganda had proceeded space. More than 70 meetings were held during the month of June, 1937. But the Congress leaders did not discuss the merits and demerits of the scheme of reshaping but concentrated on their own election propaganda.[228] The Congress agitation against *Malba* had been partly successful in the Amritsar, Ludhiana and Hoshiarpur districts. But the elections to the Congress Committee, such as in Amritsar, Sialkot and Rohtak, displayed that internally the Congress was still torn by factional feuds.[229]

The C.S.P. renewed agitation for the release of political

224. Home Department, File No. 18/7/1937-Political, NAI : New Delhi.
225. Home Department, File No. 18/8/1938-Political, NAI : New Delhi.
226. See Zetland Collection.
227. Home Department, File No. 18/6/1938-Political, NAI : New Delhi.
228. Home Department, File Nos. 18/6/1938, 18/6/1939-Political, NAI : New Delhi.
229. *Nawan Zaman*, December 26, 19; Home Departmnt, File No. 18/9/1938-Political (Individual Congressmen; however, continued to promote agrarian unrest and to give considerable attention to pasant problems. These efforts and culminated in a series of *Kisans* Confrences throughout the province) Vide. File No. 11/1/1937-Political; *The Kirti Lehr* February 27, 1938.

prisoners. It arranged daily meetings in Lahore to support the demand for the release of political prisoners. September 4th was fixed as the "Army Recruitment Bill Day" and was observed throughout the province. A meeting of the C.S.P. was held in Lahore which condemned this Bill and reaffirmed the adherence of the Congress in its policy of non-participation in any imperialist war.[230] It is noteworthy to state here that the C.S.P. also was not without internal dissensions. Just after a few months of its formation, in February, 1938, the Radical League was transformed into the Punjab Socialist Party.[231] The two groups adopted a hostile attitude towards each other and joined hands with the rival group in the provincial Congress Committee.[232] The C.S.P. alongwith the *Kirti* group was closer to the Satyapal faction while the Radical League was close to Dr. Gopi Chand faction.[233] The 4th session of the All India Congress Socialist Party was held on 12th and 13th April, 1938. An attempt was made to mediate between the dissident and the provincial C.S.P. leadership.[234] After some time, the Punjab Socialist Party was dissolved and a statement was issued by Fazal Allahi Qurban an behalf of the party,

---

231. *Ibid*, File No. 18/2/1938-Political. (The Karam Singh Mann affair led to the separation of the Radical League from (SP) Vide *The Kirti Lehr* (Meerut), February 13th, 1938; also of December 18, 1938.

232. Harjap Singh, Kabul Singh, Sohan Singh Josh, Karam Singh Mann were the important membrs of the Punjab Socialist Party. Vide *Kirti Lehr*, April 29, 1938. (For details regarding internal dissension in the Congress and even Socialists Group in the Congress see—Report of the Select Committee of the Punjab Legislative Assembly on the Money Lending Bill, Published in *The Tribune* (Lahore), June 28th, 1938.

233. *Kirti Lehr*, February 13th, 1938 (For details see *Nawan Zamana* December 26, 1975); Home Department, File Nos. 18/7/1938-Political; 18/8/1938-Political; 18/12/1937-Political; NAI : New Delhi; File No. P-17-1937-38, Part-I-AICC (A letter from Bhagwan Singh Gandhi of Sialkot to Pt. Nehru). NMML, New Delhi.

234. Home Department, File No. 18/4/1938-Political (This Session was presided over by M.R. Masani. Ajoy Ghosh and Yusuf Meherally attended it.).

asking its members to come back to ranks of the C.S.P.[235] The dissension among the Socialists was one of the factors that the Congress and even its left wing failed to participate in the agrarian agitation in the province.[236]

It is the most appropriate place to discuss the Congress policy regarding agrarian legislations. The Punjab Legislative Assembly's summer session which ended on July 23, 1938, passed several Bills, such as the Registration of Moneylenders Bill, the Alienation of Land (Amendment) Bill, The Restitution of Mortgaged Lands Bill and The Agricultural Produce Market Bill. The Unionists introduced these agrarian legislations, because they were convinced that such a Legislation would be opposed by the Congress leaders and thus was the best means of weaning the peasantry away from the Congress.[237] As we have been in the second chapter, the Alienation of Land Act passed in 1900 did practically nothing to stop the steady impoverishment of peasant masses. It had instead created a new class of moneylenders from among those sections described as agriculturists in the Act.[238] The policy of the Congress party to oppose these bills had been adversely criticised in the press and at many meetings.[239]

On the other hand, even during the election campaign in the Punjab, the leaders of the National Congress never specifically mentioned any thing about the agrarian question,

235. *Kirti Lehr*, April 24, 1938 (For details see *National Front,* October 30, 1938.

236. For details see the *Kirti Lehr*, July 9, 1939; Home Department, File No. 18/1/1939; 18/3/1939-Political; 18/10/1939-Political, NAI : New Delhi.

237. File No. P.L. 10-1937-38 (Correspondence re-collection of funds from Punjab Legislative Assembly members, letters of Pt. Nehru to Gopi Chand Bhargav) AICC, NMML, Teen Murt House, New Delhi.

238. For details regarding Congress policy towards Agrarian Legislation see Sir Sikandr Hyat's speech quoted in the *Tribune* (Lahore), January 17, 1937; *National Front,* July 3, 1938; Home Department, File No. 18/7/1938-Political NAI : New Delhi.

239. Home Department, File No. 18/7/1938-Political, NAI : New Delhi.

the predominant problem of the province.[240] This was obvious and logical, one reason for which was the internal factionalism in the Provincial Congress Committee and its lack of preparations. Moreover, the urban moneylenders and trading section formed the bulk of the Congress.

Of course, at the rural meetings, non-payment of land revenue was advocated by the Congress workers and in certain villages attempts were made to resist the payment. When Chhotu Ram's *Zamindara* League and *Zamindara Sabha* sought to mobilise the peasants on the slogan of reduction in land revenue and water rates, the latter held series of meetings to protest against the proposed resettlement of the district, the Congress workers and the *Kirti Kisan* party backed the movement.[241] The Congress gave special attention to the intensification of the rural propaganda in the districts of Lahore, Amritsar and Lyallpur. In eastern districts, both the Congress and the *Zamindara* League led agitation had spread to a serious extent to many of the villages.[242] In brief, during the course of the peasants' agitation, the Congress urged the Government to take steps towards affording substantial relief to the agriculturists by giving effects to their demand.[243] It is enough to state that the Congress workers always backed the agrarian movement whenever launched by any political faction in any region of the Punjab. But it is interesting to note that the Congress did not enjoy high reputation and sound footing in the rural Punjab.

Why did the Congress fall in the Punjab, so far as the agrarian problems and peasants' movement were concerned? The answer is not so easy and simple, because it failed as a result of a combination of many factors. Some of the important factors are cited here :

240. It is true, much agitation in rural areas was fostered but little attmept was made to study the agrarian problem scientifically and at lengh) Vide. Home Department, File Nos. 6/8/1936-Political; II/1/1937-Political, NAI : New Delhi.

241. Home Department, File No. 18/11/1930-Political, NAI : New Delhi.

242. *Ibid.*

243. *The Tribune* (Lahore), June 23, 1931.

With the continuous and oppressive political stalemate leading to constitutional deadlocks in the Legislative Assembly and the deterioration of the economic situation in the province, a sense of despair had developed in young peoples' minds and they began to loss faith in the methods and the ideas of the Congress leaders. The only lead Gandhi gave was his programme of village reconstruction and the revolutionary youth of the province, impatient for action began to doubt whether the Gandhian method could ever succeed.[244] But this truth can not be ignored that the Congress successfully could bring the nationalist movement from Conference rooms to the streets and villages. It also brought about at once not only a spirit of rebellion in the country, it too made the Indian think, almost for the first time, about the nature of British exploitation and that of future India. And, Punjab did not remain exception to it.

Indeed, the Karachi programme of the Congress had laid down that, 'in order to end the exploitation of the masses, the political freedom must include real economic freedom of the starving millions', but this remained only a sentiment with the Congress leadership. In the light of this fact, it is clear that the Congress was not developing any consciousness for socialism. It could not push any scheme of agrarian reforms because of the domination of the *Zamindars.* In spite of being a peasant organisation, it failed to do any thing for the peasantry.[245]

Writing about the character of the Congress, Nehru wrote : "The Indian National Movement is obviously not a labour or proletarian movement. It is a bourgeois movement, as its very

244. Mokkerji, Girija K., 'Growth of Socialist Ideas in the Twenties', *Seminar on Socialism in India* (1919-39) Second Session, October 8-10, 1969, 3 and 8, NMML, New Delhi.

245. For more details regarding the Congress policy towards agrarian problems see Jawaharlal Nehru, *India's Freedom,* Unwin Books : London, 1962, 14; Dorothy Norman, *Nehru : The First Sixty Years* : Vol. I,, Asia Publishing House, Bombay, 1961, 47; Sitaramayya, P., *The History of the Indian National Congress*: 1935-37, Vol. II, Padma Publication Ltd., Bombay : 1947, 11, 12.

name implies, and its objective so far has not been a change of the social order, but political independence".[246] Nehru again wrote that the Congress as it was constituted could not become an instrument for agrarian reforms. In 1930, "there was an ideal opportunity for a 'no fax' campaign, as the part of the general civil-disobedience movement", but "if the tenants stopped paying their rent, the landlord suffered immediately........."[247] "..........gradually the lower middle class began to dominate the Congress, and later the peasantry made their influence felt".[248] But the Congress leadership firmly discouraged the move for affiliation of the class organisations of the workers and peasants, and Congress Committees were directed not to associate themselves with activities which promoted a spirit of violence in the countryside. The Congress workers were also advised to keep away from the *Kisan Sabha* movement. Consequently, the Congress party became unpopular among the peasants and labourers.[249]

It will not be out of place to state that the Gandhi-Irwin

246. Nehru, Jawaharlal, *An Autobiography*, Allied Publishers Ltd., Bombay, 1962, 365. (It was allegd that the middle-class political movement, as the Congress agitation hitherto had ben by then, more or less, a spent force, and that the national movement could become really 'national' and an effective movement only if the masses could be attracted by their social and economic programme to take part in it); Bose, A.C., 'The Socialists in the Indian National Congress', *Seminar on Socialism In India*, 1919-39, November 28-30, 1968, NMML, New Delhi; Home Department, File No. 18/11/1935-Political NAI : New Delhi; *The Kirti*, December 22, 1935 (Even Pt. Nehru admitted, while speaking to Lahore Journalists, on 3rd June, 1936, the Congress being dominated by middle-classes instead of upper classes, If they are able to bring Congress nearer to masses after conflicts in Congress ranks. It was inevitable that Congress should become peasant organisation in country like India which was essentially a peasant country) Vide Home Department, File No. 4/14/1936-Political, NAI : New Delhi.

247. *Ibid.*, 232.

248. *Ibid.*, 416; Gopal Krishan, 'Notes on Congress Response to Socialism', *Seminar on Socialism*, NMML, New Delhi.

249. *Indian National Congress : Report of the 51st Annual Session*, 213-14.

Pact, the failure of the Second Round Table Conference and the withdrawal of the non-co-operation movement created a climate of despondency and despair. The left wingers in the Congress were disappointed and considered Gandhian leadership thoroughly inadequate and repressive.[250] And, these factors did not remain un-noticed in the Punjab. Moreover, the Punjab leaders criticised the Congress for not clarifying to the people the notion of *Swaraj.* They told the people that the Congress was not interested in organising the peasants and workers and independence to the Congress meant independence of native capitalists to exploit the working masses.

They did not want to pursue the anti-imperialist movement vigorously to achieve complete independence.[251] Throughout the period (1930-47), this policy of criticism and denunciation of the Congress was vigorously followed. In April 1931, in Amritsar and Jullundur, the *Kirti Kisan* party, with the help of *Zamindara Sabha* and *Akali Dal* acquired some foot-hold and a dozen of meetings were also held. The peasants were advised to agitate for the immediate reduction of land revenue.[252] The Congress and capitalists' methods were attacked and many *Ghadrites* who sympathised with the *Kirti Kisan Sabha* tried to capture office in the Congress Committees. Thus, the activities of the other political groups gave a set back to the Congress party in the Punjab.

The strong opposition of the Unionists was another factor for the weakening of the Congress. They claimed that their ministry was a *Zamindara* Government, working for the welfare of peasantry.[253] Referring to the Congress stand on the agrarian legislations, this party claimed that the so called

250. Rai Prasad Akhilendra, 'Gandhiji and Socialism in India' *Seminar on Socialism in India,* 1919-39, November 28-30, 1968; For further details see Private Corresondence of Jayaparakash Narayan.

251. *The Kirti,* June, 1930.

252. Home Department, File No. 18/4/1931-Political, NAI : New Delhi. Also File No. 18/5/1931-Political; 31/III/1931-Political.

253. Home Department, File No. 18/9/1938-Political, NAI : New Delhi.

Congressmen in the Punjab were a gang of traders and capitalists, who were working not for the liberation of the country, but to grind their own axe........It was the Unionist faction which was following the Congress programme in practice.[254] Moreover, commercial and trading classes were the supporters of the Congress and enjoyed a powerful pull on the Provincial Congress leadership. Their vested interests pressurised the Congress leadership to defend the moneylenders from the attack of the Unionist Party. This lowered the prestige of the Congress in the eyes of the poor peasantry and indirectly helped the Unionists to project itself as the Government of the peasantry. Now only the left (many of whom were the members of the Punjab *Kirti Kisan Sabha*) was a politically organised faction which sought to mobilise the poor and small landholders, both against the moneylenders as well as the landlords.

It is equally important to state that the activities of the *Kirti Kisan Sabha* in 1931 and even after that were anti-Congress. Nevertheless it was in a sense doing the work which the Congress proper might have wished to do, but with its predominantly urban structure, could not succeed in most parts of the Punjab. In the eastern districts, the Congress was attacked because of its procapitalist policy and the methods of usurers.[255] On the other hand, the rural Sikhs vied with the urban Muslims in making the Congress a failure. Both of them spent their time and money in breaking the congress conferences as the Muslims believed that the Congress was in league with the *Dogra Raj* and instrumental in curbing the aspirations of the Muslims, while the Sikhs abhorred the Congress for not accepting the Sikh demands in the Round Table Conference. The *Zamindars* at large whether Hindus, Muslims or Sikhs—condemned the Congress for being responsible for the present depression in trade and the fall in

254. Gopal, Madan, *Sir Chhotu Ram : A Political Biography*, Sterling, 1977, 116.

255. Home Department, File Nos. 18/V/1931-Political; 18/XI/1931-Political, NAI : New Delhi.

prices.[256] In fact there was a strong indignation against the Congress in rural areas in the thirties.

It is significant to note that most of the Congress leaders did not support the demands of the *Kisans,* especially when they saw the *Kisan* movement in the hands of the socialists and Communists with drastic programme for debt repudiation and expropriation.[257] However, they believed that a healthy *Kisan* agitation could not grow up otherwise than under Congress tutelage. Nehru suggested further that though the Congress and peasants' movements must work together in harmony, the real solution to the *Kisan* demands was for more peasants to join the organisation.[258] But on the whole the Congress had achieved little success inspite of its wide spread and sustained efforts,[259] because, the Congress socialists apparently did not wish the villagers to improve their lot; rather they showed great hostility to the *Dehat Sudhar* or Rural Upliftment movement.[260] Hence, they were deprived of a fertile field for agitation.

The Congress also failed in the rural areas because its candidates and their supporters had throughout the election campaign preached violence freely.[261] For instance, on the 18th of February the Congress organised a conference at village Jandoli purely in order to terrorise the local *Zaildar* and other Government officials. It was against their creed of non-violence and it definitely made the Congress unpopular in the rural Punjab particularly.

The Congress was, of course, a much less important factor

256. Home Department, File No. 5/85/1932-Political (A Report of a CID Officer of the Punjab) 5; also see File Nos. 18/2/1933-Political; 18/9/1937-Political, NAI : New Delhi.

257. Home Department, File Nos. 11/1/1937-Political, (The attitude of the orthodox Congress leadership was not easy to define) Vide File No. 18/7/1937-Political, NAI : New Delhi.

258. Home Department, File No. 11/1/1937-Political, NAI : New Delhi.

259. Home Department, File No. 18/1/1938-Political, NAI : New Delhi.

260. Home Department, File No. 18/3/1938-Political, NAI : New Delhi.

261. Home Department, File No. 18/2/1930-Political, NAI : New Delhi.

in the Punjab than in other province. It was only a small minority in the Assembly and without akali support, which might not be accorded, would be almost insignificant. It did not include a single outstanding personality and as stated above, it was rent with internal dissensions. Moreover, the Congressmen and the Hindus generally were probably more alive there than elsewhere to the necessity of conciliating Muslim opinion and the danger to them of Muslim resurgence.[262] It will be appropriate to add here that Master Tara Singh expressed his willingness to take part in a Congress Civil Disobedience Movement, provided it did not extend to preventing the Sikhs from joining the army. But he was snubbed by Gandhi who pointed out that the Akalis had nothing in common with the Congressmen and that it would be better for both if they parted company. So, Master Tara Singh resigned from the All India and the Punjab Provincial Congress Committees and the possibilities of the whole of the Akali Sikhs parting company with Congress was now the subject of much speculation.[263] This further weakened the Congress.

Undoubtedly, the British bureaucracy from the very beginning started out with no less an ambition than to crush the Congress. Many Acts and Special Ordinances were passed and adopted to prevent the growth and spread of Civil Disobedience, Non-co-operation movement and other activities of the Congress particularly in the rural areas.[264] Finally, in 1937-38, the Punjab election dispute also led to the decline of

262. Linlithgow Correspondence—Microfilm—A letter from the Governor of Punjab to the Governor General, April 1st, 1940; Acc. 2335, M. SS. F. 125/28, (Linlithgow Collection—July 1939—December 1941—Official Telegrams between Viceroy and the Secretary), NAI : New Delhi.

263. Home Department, File No. 18/9/1940-Political (Many Hindu *Mahasabha* workers together with much of the Hindu Press were also encouraging the Akalis to withdraw from Congress), For more details also see File No. 18/7/1944-Political; 18/9/1944-Political, NAI : New Delhi.

264. File No. 35/1935-36-AICC (Private Paper Section) NMML, New Delhi.

the Congress in the province because during the election days opposition members or dissidents in the Congress party made propaganda against its own leadership. It was bound to leave somewhat effective influence on the minds of the people in the countryside and gradually, they began to lose faith in the Congress.[265] Before discussing the Congress participation in the Punjab politics let us have a brief account of the Unionist Party here.

It was just on the eve of elections held during the year 1923 that the agriculturists' movement, after a long struggle of two decades through the formus of *Jat Sabhas*, All India *Jat Mahasabha, Zamindara* Association and several other organisations, attained atleast in the Punjab, a concrete shape as a political organisation by the victorious emergence of the Unionist Party in the Punjab Legislative Council under the joint leadership of Sir Fazl-i-Hussain and Chaudhari Chhotu Ram.[266]

The factors that had brought closer the two leaders, one Muslim and the other Hindu, need explication especially since on April 4, 1923, Chhotu Ram had criticised the politics of Mian Fazl-i-Hussain. The main criticism was that Fazli was favouring the Muslims as a community and was not making

265. File No. P-17, Part I-AICC (1937-38); also Part II-AICC (1938-39); File No. P-17/P-936-AICC, 43-45, (For more details relating to internal dissidents in the Congress also see File Nos. G-16/1940; G-5/1940-Part-I; G-23, K.W.-I/1940; G-28/1940-Part-I (Private Papers Section), NMML, New Delhi.

266. Punjab Gazette for December, 1923, and January, 1924; Shastri, R.S., *Chaudhari Chhotu Ram : Jivan Charitra* (Hindi), Rohtak, 1965, 80; *The Tribune* (Lahore), 12/1/1939, 4; *Pioneer* (Allahabad), 12/1/1945, 5; P.L.A.D., Vol. XXII, March 10, 1944, 493; *Mitra's Annual Register*, Vol. I, 1944, 218; Hussain Azim, *Fazl-i-Hussain : A Political Biography*, Bombay : 1946, 156; Sharma, S.R., *Haryana-Ka-Itihas*, Rohtak : 1966, 84. (All India *Jat Mahasabha* set up by Unionist Party with its headquarters at Rohtak in the early years of the second decade of the present century, However, even Sikh and Muslim *Jats* (In border sense of the term agriculturists were allowed to be its members. Soon its activities were spread to the entire province) Vide. *Jat Gazette* (Rohtak), February 12th, 1918, 11.

any effort to safeguard the rights of the Muslim agriculturists much less of their Hindu and Sikh counterparts; it was alleged that, as a result, even the Government circular promising more employment to the agriculturists had remained unimplemented. At the same time, however, Chhotu Ram had limitations of his own. Even though he professed sympathy for the starving peasantry, he only led the group of the agriculturists, mostly ruralities, while the second group which comprised the non-agriculturists urbanists or well educated classes, was led by the *Arya Samaj*. However, the *Arya Samaj*, according to him, had by its remarkable role, set the agriculturists community on to the path of awakening and education in various parts of the province. There appeared firmness in the efforts of the *Arya Samaj*. There were two groups, one of the non-agriculturists urbanists or well educated classes, and the second non-agriculturists urbanists or well educated classes, and the second comprised the agriculturists. The latter had realised that the complete clavation of the agriculturists was possible only through their own organisations because an overwhelming majority in the *Arya Samaj* was not prepared to concede to them a preferential treatment in its educational and economic programme.[267]

Chhotu Ram's increasing efforts for organising the *Jats* of all the communities under the banner of the *Zamindara* Association set up in 1917 with its headquarters at Lahore, and *Jat Sabhas*, had annoyed most non-*Jat* Sikhs who opposed his movement as vehemently as they could with the plea that he was attempting a division in the Sikh community. In fact, all the local sections of the Hindus and the Sikhs in the Punjab had considered the *Zamindara* movement as anti-*Mahajan*, anti-*Brahmin*, anti-Sikh and anti-*Arya Samaj*. Despite this opposition, the Sikh-agriculturists had started joining the *Zamindara* Association with Kirpal Singh Mann and Kharak Singh Dhillon as its President and Secretary respectively but

267. Sharma, S.R., *Haryana-Ka-Itihas*, Rohtak : 1966, 86-88; Shastri, Y., *Kashtri Jation Ka Uthancpattan* (Hindi), Hardwar : 1956, 626-629.

it evoked little response from the Muslims.[268] It was at the close of 1923 that Chaudhari Chhotu Ram and Fazl-i-Hussain founded the National Unionist Party,[269] and thus brought the indebted and backward agriculturists of the Muslim community also into the fold of the *Zamindara* movement.

It will be most appropriate to write here that the Unionist Party was formed with the basic aim of improving the economic and political lot of the peasants of the Punjab. It was to provide equal opportunities of advancement to all, and to direct, in an increasing measure, the beneficient activities of the Government to backward classes with a view to enabling them to make up the beway caused by neglect in the past.[270] However, in the formation of the Unionist Party, the British authorities succeeded in creating an institution which not only become a bulwork against the Congress or left influence but also actively collaborated with the imperialism on issue of common interest.[271]

The formation of this party, popularly known among the

268. *Jat Gazette* (Rohtak), April 2, 1923, 2; 9.7.1923, 7-9; 3.1.1917 (*Jat* and Non-*Jat* controversy), 7; 23.3.1927, 3; 26.6.1917, 8; 18.12.1917, 7; 25.12.1917, 2-4; 11.1.1918, 8-17; 19.3.1918, 1; 2.4.1918, 3; 9.4.1918, 3; 16.4.1918, 8; 11.5.1918, 11; 28.5.1918, 3; Shastri, R.S., *Chaudhari Chhotu Ram : Jivan Charitra* (Hindi) Rohtak, 1965, 93-96.

269. Gopal Madan, *Sir Chhotu Ram : A Political Biography,* 1977, 69; *Punjab Gazette,* December, 1923 and January, 1924 (For more information also see Hussain, A., *Fazl-i-Hussain : A Political Biography,* Bombay, 1947, 150-160).

270. P.L.A.D., Vol. I, 1937; Hussain, A., *Fazl-i-Hussain : A Political Biography,* Bombay, 1947, 154-55; Bajaj, Y.P., 'Land Revenue Reforms of the Unionist Party', *Thee Punjab Past and Present,* October, 1976. (For its creed, aims and objects see Punjab Unionist Party Rules and Regulations (Published by the Punjab Unionist Party Headquarters' Secretariate, Lahore) Vide AIMMS-Papers, NMML, New Delhi; Hussain, A., *Fazl-i-Hussain : A Political Biography,* Bombay, 1947.

271. Madan Gopal, *Sir Chhotu Ram : A Political Biography,* 1977, 11, (The British policy, conceived with enough foresight in 1900, of driving a wedge between the countryside and the city to stem the tied of Nationalism in the countryside was thus crowned with success in the formation of the Unionist Party).

masses as rural or *Zamindara* party, by bringing the agriculturists of all the communities under the banner, tried to stem the tide of communalism.[272] Thus, it practically banished Muslim League from the Punjab at least for two decades, and liquidated the dominance of the urbanites both Hindus and non-Hindus. It is noteworthy to mention that it was held that the only remedy for the malady of communalism was the Nationalist Unionist Party formed on the basis of common economic programme.[273] Its leaders wanted to bring communal unity.[274] Special protection for the weak and special help for the backward was another aim of this party.[275] In other words, besides the agriculturists, it aimed at uplifting the tribes and areas which were backward in education as a result of which they failed in obtaining various positions in the Government, and benefits of the various departments of state activities. As regards the means, both Sir Fazli and Chhotu Ram, with a view to preparing the agricultural folk as full partners in the Government of the country when India became independent, persistently advised them to follow constitutional methods so that they could advance financially, educationally and socially and receive training in the art of self-government.[276]

---

272. *18 Months of Provincial Autonomy in the Punjab,* April 1, 1938, 3; Bajaj, Y.P., *Sir Chhotu Ram and His Work* (Unpublished Ph.D. Thesis, Kurukshetra University : 1972), 85 (The agriculturists were not divided into classes. The number of big landholders in the Punjab was very small-discussed in Chapter-I. For instance in 1929, those paying over Rs. 500/- as land revenue totalled 0.15% of the Punjab population) Vide. *Jat Gazette,* August 1, 1931, 1.

273. *Jat Gazette,* August 1, 1931, 1; Evidence before Simon Commission, cited in *Mitra's Indian Quarterly Register,* Vol. II, 1918, 122-23; *The Punjab Past and Present,* Vol. V, Part-I, April, 1971, 165; Bajaj, Y.P., *Sir Chhotu Ram and His Work* Appendix II.

274. *Jat Gazette,* June 15, 1927, 4; June 1, 1931, 1; December 5, 1941, 5; January 8, 1941, 5; January 29, 1941, 1; May 28, 1941, 6; *The Tribune* (Lahore), September 17, 1933.

275. File No. 19-Institution-III, *Chaudhari Chhotu Ram : Jivan Charitra* (Hindi), Rohtak, 1965, 3, NMML, New Delhi.

276. The Tribune (Lahore), January 11, 1945, 3; Shastri, R.S., *Chaudhari Chhotu Ram : Jivan Charitra* (Hindi), Rohtak, 1965, 124, NMML : New Delhi.

To secure the support of the Sikh landed aristocracy and small landed gentry who were already dominating Sikh politics, the Reforms Act of 1919 gave them a system of minority representation. The Common economic programme which united all the Unionists was to keep intact the Punjab land Alienation Act as a measure of protection to backward classes.[277] The ideology of this party claimed that it was set up to protect the small as well as the big landowners against the urban, largely Hindu moneylanding and commercial groups.[278]

Among the statutory agriculturists, *Jats* constituted nearly 50 per cent of the notified agricultural population of the Punjab.[279] However, the words *'Jats'*, 'agriculturists' and 'backward classes' became synonymous, and *'Jatism'*, which conjured up racial affinity became unifying ideology of all the *'Jats'* or *'Zamindar'* population irrespective of economic status and internal economic contradictions.[280] This *Zamindara* or agriculturist ideology took its living form in the establishment of a few institutions,[281] which alongwith weekly *Jat* Gazette,

277. For more details see Hussain, A., *Fazl-i-Hussain : A Political Biography,* Bombay, 1946, 154-55.

278. Karson, J. Henery, ex., *Contemporary Problems of Pakistan,* 7. (The Unionist Party was a party of the landed gentry, who sat in legislature and who dominated the political life of the districts. They were all conservative, most of them educationally backward, and practically all of them without any political tradition or aptitude) Vide Hussain, A., *Fazl-i-Hussain : A Political Biography,* Bombay, 1946, 318.

279. Prem Chaudhary, 'Social Basis of Sir Chhotu Ram Politics', *The Punjab Past And Present,* April, 1976—Sr. No. 19, 160.

280. The slogan *Raj Karega Jat* (The *Jat* shall rule) though raised only once by Chhotu Ram, betrayed the real nature of feelings and aspirations stirred by an ideology which rationalised the anger and distrust of the "collective unconscious" historically embeded in the psyche of Jat population.

281. Institution such as *Jat Mahasabha Samiti,* All India *Jat* Conference, and Jat Heroes Memorial School. Vide Gopal Madan, *Sir Chhotu Ram : A Political Biography,* 1977, 161; *Jat Gazette* (Rohtak), February 12, 1918, 11; Hussain, A., *Fazl-i-Hussain : A Political Biography,* Bombay, 1946, 156; Sharma, S.R., *Chaudhari Chhotu Ram-Jivan Charitra* (Hindi), Rohtak, 1965, 84.

not only repulsed the nationalist attack on this ideology, but also mobilised opinions to gather enough pressure in order to secure economic concessions and reservation of services for agriculturist classes.[282]

Chhotu Ram made it public that he had accepted ministership to serve and help the agriculturists. A series of articles entitled *Bechara Zamindar* (*i.e.*, helpless agriculturist) published in the *Jat Gazette* depicted his exploitation by money-lenders and corrupt officials. The need for the *Jats* to unite into one brotherhood of *Zamindar* community was also preached.[283] Before coming to power in 1937, the Unionists constantly pleaded that no land revenue should be charged from them who had either two acres of canal irrigated land, or five unirrigated acres, or who paid land revenue upto Rs. 5/-.[284] They also supported the demand of the agriculturists that the land revenue should be charged on income tax basis.[285] But once they captured the power, they refused to implement either of the two demands even when pressed by many Congressmen. The importance of these demands can well be understood when we find that 17.5 lac cultivators fell under the category of those paying Rs. 5/- or less as land revenue.[286]

A number of conferences were held, during the year 1937, by the Punjab *Kisans* Committee at various places such as Anandpur in Hoshiarpur district, Gobindpur in Gurdaspur, Chhajewal in Ludhiana, Daudhar in Ferozpur, Bhakna in Bhatinda and several other places. Now the Congress activities in the rural areas almost coalesced with the *Kisan* Committee activities. At this stage, the Unionists commanded a majority in the new Legislative Assembly and also enjoyed the support of the National Progressive Party and the *Khalsa* National

282. Gopal Madan, *Sir Chhotu Ram : A Political Biography,* 1977, 161.

283. *The Tribune* (Lahore), April 30th, 1938.

284. Bajaj, Y.P., 'Land Revenue Reforms of the Unionist Party'. *The Punjab Past And Present,* October, 1976, 345.

285. *Ibid,* 351; (The income upto Rs. 2000/- was exempted but in the assessment of land revenues no such exemption was alloted).

286. This point we have already noted in the first chapter of this work.

Party.[287] Besides, in one of the conferences held at Nowshera Punuan on September 28th and 30th, Munshi Ahmad Din declared that the idea of the Congress Socialist Party was to get a majority in the Congress and then oust from it the element which supported Gandhian principles and that it was satisfied with a few pieces of reforms.[288]

From the above discussion, we can have a clear picture of each political organisation so far as its participation in the agrarian movement was concerned. All the political factions, whether large or small tried their utmost to have hold in the rural areas of the province. In reality, due to the sincere and constant efforts of one political group or the other a wave of militant nationalism ran through the length and breadth of the province. The leftist ideology gradually started gathering momentum in the rural Punjab. All the political parties, irrespective of their place and strength, had acknowledged the importance of winning the support of the peasantry.

The purpose of this section is to assess the various political groups which were claiming to be the custodians of the agriculturists in the province, but in fact, it was not so. We shall see how different political parties were involved in the party-politics and how they ignored completely the welfare of the peasantry. In the first section of this Chapter, we have seen the contribution of the various political factions in regard with the agrarian problems and the peasants' movement in the Punjab. But, in reality, these groups, excluding the Punjab *Kirti Kisan* Party and the Communists, (These two parties launched the agrarian struggle and took part in almost all the *Kisan morchas* and *Kisan* Conferences held during the period

287. National Progressive Party, a semi-communal party, represented the interests of a section of the Urban Hindu Commercial Group and was led by Raja Narendra Nath : *Khalsa* National Party of the Sikhs aristocracy and the intellectuals having close ties with it. Vide AIMS Papers (Private Papers Section), NMML, New Delhi.

288. For more information regarding the *Kisan* Conferences (for Congress activities) see Home Department File Nos. 18/3/1937-Political; 18/4/1937-Political, NAI : New Delhi; also see details in Chapter II, Section II of this thesis.

under review), helped the peasants' movement and included their demands in their manifestoes, but they did all this just to have their hold in the rural areas, as it was clear that without the backing of the masses, they could not secure a sound footing in Punjab and survive for and long.

As mentioned above, the agriculturists' movement, at least in the Punjab, attained a concrete shape of political organisation by the victorious emergence of the Unionist Party in the Punjab Legislative Council in 1923,[289] under the joint leadership of Sir Fazl-i-Hussain and Chaudhary Chhotu Ram. It is a well known fact that the Unionist Party ministry stepped into power in 1923.[290] Though looking to all India Muslim politics, (the Muslim League had been speedily growing weaker during 1924-26),[291] the Unionist group assured of freedom from its pressure on the Muslim members of the Punjab Legislature who also formed a majority in the Unionist Party, should have comfortably implemented its aims and objects; however, the latter had to face heavy odds, right from the beginning due to two reasons. Firstly, the *Hindu Sabha* faction led by Raja Narendra Nath, which had been a political challenge to the urban vested interests in the formation of their ministry, mobilised all their energies to overthrow it.[292] British

289. For details see Hussain, Azim, *Fazl-i-Hussain : A Political Biography,* Bombay : 1946, 156; Shastri, R.S., *Chaudhari Chhotu Ram : Jivan Charitra* (Hindi), Rohtak : 1965, 80; Sharma, S.A., *Haryana Ka Itihas,* Rohtak : 1966, 84; *Mitra's Indian Annual Register,* Vol. I, 1944, 218, P.L.C.D., Vol. XXII, 10.3.1944, 493; *The Pioneer* (Allahabad), 12th January, 1945, 5; *The Tribune* (Lahore), January 12, 1939, 4; *Jat Gazette,* Rohtak, February 12, 1918, 11.

290. Rowlinson, H.G. and Garrettee, H.L.O. (ed.), *The Great Men of India,* 1939, 359; Khushwant Singh, *History of the Sikhs,* Vol. II, Bombay : 1944, 224, (Fazl-i-Hussain and Chaudhari Lal Chand replaced by Sir Chhotu Ram in September, 1924 as ministers for the Transferred Department) Vide Hussain, A., *Fazl-i-Hussain : A Political Biography* : Bombay, 1946.

291. Adhikari, G., *Pakistan And National Unity : The Communist Solution,* Bombay : 1944, 22.

292. Shastri, R.S., *Chaudhari Chhotu Ram : Jivan Charitra* (Hindi), Rohtak, 1965, 123-28.

bureaucracy was backing this faction against the Unionists. Secondly, the two leaders clashed with the Governor, Sir Malcolm Hailey who had desired and partly manoeuvred with the help of the above group, for the continuation of cases against the out-going President or the Provincial Legislature.

Finding that his machination had been foiled, the Governor tried to veer Fazl-i-Hussain and Chhotu Ram round to his view point. But the two leaders strongly held that the Government could not be allowed to usurp the rights of the Indians as they had. Abdul Qadir, a Unionist was elected the President. True to the principle of communal harmony, the Unionists elected Mohinder Singh, their Vice-President.[293] Before discussing the reaction towards this event, it will be appropriate to state the exact character and the ideology of this party. Its ideology claimed that the party was set up to protect the small as well as the large land owners against the urban (largely Hindu) money-lending and commercial groups.[294] But, in reality, it actively stood for furthering the interests of the large landlords. For example, the common economic programme which united all the Unionists was to preserve intact the Punjab Land Alienation Act as a measure of protection to the rich agriculturists class as opposed to backward classes.[295]

It will not be out of place to write a few lines about the Land Alienation Act of 1900. Undoubtedly, it had some effect in arresting the process of alienation. But it defined the agriculturist and non-agriculturist classes in quite an arbitrary

293. *Ibid.,* 129; Hussain, Azim, *Fazl-i-Hussain : A Political* Biography, Bombay, 1946, 160.

294. Karson, J. Henaery (ed.), *Contemporary Problems of Pakistan,* 7; (It was a party of the landed-gentry who sat in legislature and who dominated the political life of the districts. They were all conservatives, most of them educationally backward, and practically all of them without any political tradition or aptitude) Vide, Hussain, A., *Fazl-i-Hussain : A Political Biography,* Bombay, 1946, 318.

295. Hussain, A., *Fazl-i-Hussain : A Political Biography,* Bombay, 1946, 154-55 (For details also see AIHMS-Papers : Private Papers Section, NMML : New Delhi).

manner which left the poor peasantry entirely at the mercy of landlords and rich agriculturists. Secondly, it precipitated a long term fundamental split between the town and the country interests, and later on defence of rural interests became the hub of the programme of the Unionist Party, a party of the big *Zamindars.* No doubt, by carefully separating the *Jat Zamindars* and projecting the ideology of *"Jat* Brotherhood", the Unionists succeeded in isolating the moneylenders as the root cause of all evils. They also assured the British bureaucracy of their consistent opposition to the Indian National Congress as well as of their support in the shape of military and material help during times of crisis. Again, by focusing their attack on the money-lenders and carrying on practical legislation against them, the Unionists were able to rally behind them the whole of the Punjab countryside. However, they failed to bridge the gulf between the rich and the poor agriculturists. Moreover, the commercial and trading classes supported the Congress and exercised a powerful pull on the provincial Congress leadership. The Congress leadership defended the moneylenders from the attack of the Unionists. This definitely lowered the prestige of the Congress in the eyes of the poor peasantry and indirectly helped the Unionist Party to project itself as the "Government of the Peasantry". This further widened the gulf between the moneylenders on the one hand and the peasants on the other. This also intensified the political crisis in the province and as a result of it, the welfare of the peasantry was ignored to a great extent.

It will be appropriate to state the categories of the agriculturists and of the other sections of the people living in the countryside. Among the statutory agriculturists, *Jats* constituted a very large percentage. In Chhotu Ram's estimate, the *Jats* formed nearly 50% of the notified agricultural population of the Punjab.[296] The words 'backward classes', *'Jats'* 'Agriculturists', became synonymous, and *'Jatism',* which conjured up racial affinity became the unifying ideology of all

296. Chaudhary, Prem, "Social Basis of Sir Chhotu Ram's Politics", *The Punjab Past and Present,* Sr. No. 19, April, 1976, 160.

the *'jats'* or *'zamindar'* population irrespective of economic status and internal economic contradictions.[297] This *Zamindars* ideology took its living form in the establishment institutions such as *Jat Mahasabha Samiti,* All India *Jat* Conference, etc. All these organisations with an Urdu weekly the *Jat Gazette,* not only repulsed the nationalists' attack on this ideology, but also mobilised opinion to gather enough pressure in order to secure enough economic concessions and reservation of services for 'martial and agriculturist classes'.[298]

The event did not pass without a strong reaction. Retaliating soon, the Governor piloted two important bills—Regulaton of Accounts; the Land Revenue (Amendment), in spite of the fact that these bills had earlier been passed by the Punjab Legislative Council in 1925-26.[299] Besides, a number of steps were taken to suppress the activities of the *Zamindara Sabha* or League in the districts of Lahore, Ferozpur, Jullundur, Ludhiana and other places where these were growing very powerful. For instance, Mohinder Singh of village Mohi, District Ludhiana who was the principal organiser, was arrested just to reduce the influence of the *Zamindara* League. A news paper *Haryana Gazette* was

297. The slogan *Raj Kare Ga Jat* (*Jat* shall rule) though raised only once by Chhotu Ram, betrayed the real nature of feelings and aspirations stirred by an ideology which rationalised the anger and distrust of the "collective unconscious" historically embeded in the psyche of *Jat* population. *Punjabee* folk saying has given expression to this common experience of the exploited peasantry. In folklore *'Baniya'* or *'Kirar'* is always projected as a clever, treacherous, mean, dishonest and cowardly fellow.

298. Gopal, Madan, *Sir Chhotu Ram : A Political Biography,* Delhi : 1977, 161; *The Tribune,* Lahore, April 30, 1938; Bajaj, Y.P., 'Land Revenue Reforms of the Unionist Party', *The Punjab* Past and Present, Sr. No. 20, October, 1976, 341 & 351.

299. *Punjab Government Gazette,* Part I, 1928, 657; also of 29.11.1929, 51-64; Hussain, A., *Fazl-i-Hussain : A Political Biography,* Bombay, 1946, 147; Ram. T., *Sir Chhotu Ram : Apostle of Hindu-Muslim Unity,* Lahore, 1946, 7.

instituted under the leadership of Chaudhary Lal Chand who then had developed differences with Sir Chhotu Ram.[300]

In December 1926, with the nomination of Sir Fazl-i-Hussain as Revenue member,[301] it seemed that the Government opposition would relent. But, on the contrary, the Unionist Party and the peasants' movement received shocks. The system of majority party Government introduced in the Punjab in 1923 with great efforts of the Unionists, being unpalatable to the then Governor, Sir Malcalm, was put to an end.

Betraying his declared intention of making the Montford Reforms successful in the Punjab in accordance with the Convention and honour respectively of the British Parliament and nation,[302] he became obstructive. Inspite of the Unionist majority, the balance of power rested in the Governor's hands because in the transferred department, all the three ministers belonged to different communities and political parties. Thus, the provincial Government was not to run on such constitutional principles as were deducible from the Government of India Act of 1919, but the Government was to be guided by what, from time to time, the Governor declared to safeguard the British rule;[303]

It sharpened the rural-urban conflict, especially among the Hindus as is obvious from the articles[304] appearing under such titles as 'Punjab Politics, Rural and Urban Divisions', and

300. Shastri, R.S., *Chaudhari Chhotu Ram : Jivan Charitra,* (Hindi), Rohtak : 1965, 169-70.

301. Rowlinson, H.G. and Garvet, H.L.O. (Ed.), *The Great Men of India,* 1939, 359; *The Hindustan Times,* New Delhi, 16.12.1969; Shastri, R.S., *Chaudhari Chhotu Ram : Jivan Charitra* (Hindi), Rohtak : 1965, 126; Bhandari, Som Nath (ex.), *Eminent Hindus of the Punjab,* Lahore : 1943, 95.

302. Shastri, R.S., *Chaudhari Chhotu Ram : Jivan Charitra* (Hindi), Rohtak : 1965, 106.

303. *Ibid.,* 107 (For more details also see *Jat Gazette,* 22/12/1926, 8; also of 1/6/1927, 8.

304. *Jat Gazette,* December 22, 1926, 8; June 1, 1927, 8; June 8, 1927, 6-7; August 24, 1927, 32.

'Chhotu Ram and some other leaders'. These articles condemned preference for the rural tracts in developmental activities, proportionate representation in public appointments, due reduction in taxes from over the agriculturists and imposing them on the urban population, etc.

Consequently, the strength of the Unionists progressively dwindled in the Punjab Legislature for about a decade (1926-35). In 1927 Sardar Baldev Singh quit the Unionist Party.[305] In the subsequent legislature, the elections to which held in 1929, the Unionists' strength was reduced to 37,[306] whereas the strength of the *Hindu Sabhites* who had formed themselves as National Progressive Party, rose to 20 from 9 in 1926.[307] On the other side, the Governments machination of segregating Sir Chhotu Ram and some of his associates from the active politics of the Punjab in order to destroy the mass character and the strength of the *Zamindara* party, became apparent when Malcolm Hailey made a proposal to Chhotu Ram in early thirties offering him Kashmir's Prime Ministership, and the membership of the special Tribunal appointed to try the accused of the Lahore Conspiracy Case. However, this offer was declined by him.[308] In this context, Sir Fazl-i-Hussain's appointment to Governor General's Council in 1930 though regarded by the Unionists as a great opportunity to promote the cause of agriculturists[309] and others was also a part of the same manoeurving to unto the hold of Sir Fazli on the Punjab Muslims, and replace him by Sir Sikander who appeared more

305. *Jat Gazette* (Rohtak), 25.5.1927, 7.

306. *Ibid.*, February 26, 1930, 11.

307. Hussain, A., *Fazl-i-Hussain : A Political Biography, Bombay : 1946,* 162.

308. P.L.C.D., Vol. XVII, 16.1.1931, 243; Vol. XXIII, 20.3.1933, 590; Ram, T., *Sir Chhotu Ram : Apostle of Hindu Muslim Unity,* Lahore, 1946, 9-11 (For more details also see Shastri, R.S., *Chaudhari Chhotu Ram : Jivan Charitra* (Hindi) Rohtak : 1965, 201-05; Khushwant Singh, *History of the Sikhs*—Vol. II, Bombay : 1944, 225; *The Tribune,* Chandigarh, 25.2.1969, 1).

309. Rowlinson, H.G. and Garret, H.L.O. (ed.), *The Great Men of India,* 1939, 359; P.L.C.D., Vol. XV, 21.3.1930, 795.

amenable to the policies of the Governor. If the Unionist debacle was averted, the credit rested with the farsighted and vigilant leadership of Mian Fazli and Chhotu Ram, who had also steered clear their party on earlier occasions from communalism[310] while that was the end of which the Government desired because in that lay the irreversible clash of the Hindu and Muslim communalism and subsequent dissipation of their energies, ensuring the safety of the British interests because the Congress was not very strong in the Punjab. Continuing Hailey's policy, his successor Herbert Emerson, soon after his appointment, visited Rohtak to suggest Chhotu Ram to organise a party independent of the Unionists, to better serve the cause of the agriculturists. But he was disappointed by his flat refusal to oblige him.[311]

It is essential to take stock of the political stance of the Muslims resulting from the Government attitude. They were a majority community in the province but were not given representation in the Punjab Legislature proportionate to their population, because of the Lucknow Pact. This issue of the Muslims or Hindus, in their campaign for an era of communal harmony and prosperity advocated due representation for the Punjab Muslims in and outside the Punjab Legislature Council. For instance, Sir Chhotu Ram, speaking on the Punjab Reforms committee report regarding representation to different communities in the Punjab Legislature strongly advocated, "half and half should be the proportion between Muslims and Non-Muslims.........no majority should be reduced to minority........Thus, in different provinces communal tension would be replaced by love and unity.........and auspicious day of *Swaraj* would draw near".[312]

However, the communally minded could, as they did, try to take advantage of this grievance of the Punjab Muslims when the Unionists under the leadership of Mian Fazli and

310. Shastri, R.S., *Chaudhari Chhotu Ram : Jivan Charitra* (Hindi) Rohtak : 1965, 163-64.

311. *Ibid.,* 204.

312. P.L.C.D., Vol. XXIV, March, 1929, 243-44.

Sir Chhotu Ram fell into disfavour with the British Government. With a view to winning them over, the All India Muslim League through its Delhi proposal of 1927, demanded majority for the Muslims in the Punjab and Bengal Legislatures.[313] Muhammed Shafi and Sir Fazli sensing the danger, revived the Punjab Provincial Muslim League widening the Unionists' sphere in the Committee nominated by the Punjab Council with Sikander Hyat and Sardar Ujjal Singh respectively as Chairman and Secretary to assist the Indian Statutory Commission while the Muslim League had boycotted its deliberations.[314] Reacting strongly to the Punjab Muslims' independent course of action, Jinnah revived an earlier decision to hold the annual session of the All India Muslim League under Shafi's Chairmanship at Lahore.[315] It was unusually well attended. In their speeches in the session Nawab Zulfi-qar-Ali, Muhammad Iqbal Shafi and some more leaders criticised Mr. Jinnah and his supporters for ignoring the national cause and promoting the feelings of communalism and separatism instead of finding out solution to the Muslim problem particularly in Punjab and Bengal.[316]

Both the leaders gave another jolt by successfully organising the All Parties' Conference (from December 31 to January 1, 1929), with a view to bypassing Jinnah's League. The Conference also demanded a federation with autonomous status wherein the residuary powers should rest with the member states and separate electorate for the Muslims to wardoff communal tension during the elections.[317]

---

313. *Ibid.*

314. *Jat Gazette* (Rohtak), 1.1.1931, 1; Bajaj, Y.P., *Sir Chhotu Ram and His Works* (unpublished Ph.D. thesis, Kurukshetra University, 1972), Appendix-XX.

315. *Indian Annual Register,* Vol. I, 1927, 431; Shastri, R.S., *Chaudhari Chhotu Ram : Jivan Charitra* (Hindi) Rohtak : 1965, 172; Hussain, A., *Fazli-Hussain : A Political Biography,* Bombay : 1946, 358.

316. *Indian Annual Register,* Vol. II, 1930, 263; Khushwant Singh, *History of the Sikhs,* Vol. II, Bombay : 1944, 226.

317. *Indian Annual Register,* Vol. II, 1927, 408.

As regards the reaction of Sir Chhotu Ram, these demands were within the orbit of his ideas and these were to root out the political and social evil of communal tension and bring about and maintain unity amongst all sections of the Punjab population. He had been emphatically advocating that every community, agriculturists and non-agriculturists etc. should be accorded due representation in the Legislatures and Government services through out the country.[318]

Shafi refuted the alleged threat of a 'Muslim Raj' that might be set up in the Punjab in consequence of a Muslim majority in the Punjab Legislature. He argued, that the Punjab Muslims did not have any such ambition; even if such a possibility arose in future, it would be impractical because of its repercussions in the Muslim minority provinces; and thirdly, if an attempt in that direction could ever be made, he assured Dr. G.C. Narang and others, he would be the first to fight it in grim earnest. However, for establishing and consolidating a Government of the agriculturists in the Punjab, he added, every one irrespective of his creed would make all out efforts.[319]

Without being complacent at the success of the All Parties Conference, Fazli worked on the plan of the appointment of a Muslim who could adequately represent the Punjab Muslims' view point vis-a-vis Jinnah's. It was due to his efforts that Muhammad Iqbal was nominated as a delegate at the Second Round Table Conference in preference to Dr. Ansari.[320] These

---

318. For details see *Punjab Press Abstract,* 1920, 112; Home Department, File No. 26/6/1930—Ests.-Political, NAI : New Delhi; *The Tribune,* Lahore, 20.3.1920; *Jat Gazette* Rohtak, 12.2.1927, 1; 12.1.1930, 4; P.L.C.D., Vol. X, March, 1927, 355-56; Vol. XXIII, 1933, 176, 285, 559; Vol. XXV, 20.12.1934, 455; Vol. XXVIII, 19.3.1936 and 20.3.1936, 651-52; Bajaj, Y.P., *Sir Chhotu Ram and His Works* (unpublished Ph.D. Thesis, Kurukshetra University, 1972) 32-33 and Appendixes, XXII and XXIII.

319. *Indian Annual Register,* Vol. II, 1927, 410; P.L.C.D., Vol. XVIII, 20.3.1929, 243-46.

320. Hussain, A., *Fazl-i-Hussain : A Political Biography,* Bombay : 1946, 251 and 319.

endeavours did not bear fruit. Jinnah became aware of the importance of the Punjab Muslim leadership and their alienation, for Jinnah became quite tolerant towards them almost upto 1944. The Communal Award, though it did not come upto the expectations of the Unionist Party, held 49% Muslim seats in the Punjab Legislature. It was really a grand achievement because in Bengal with almost a similar Muslim majority, they were accorded 47.5% of the total seats.

The standing of the Punjab Muslims received a set back in Shafi's death in 1932. Soon the disintegration started and the Punjab Provincial League ceased to exist by the year 1934. In 1936, Muhammad Iqbal, who had started compaigning for a separate state for the Indian Muslims, breaking with the Unionist Party, joined hands with Jinnah. Simultaneously, the British hostility towards the Unionists increased because they had condemned corruption in the Government services, holding the senior Government officials responsible. The Unionists opposed the Punjab Municipal Executive Officers Bill, 1931, and the Punjab Municipal (Amendment Bill, 1932), and another similar Bill proposed by the Government in 1931 providing for the appointment of Executive Officers in the district Boards. They also opposed the Anti Picketing Act of 1932 and the Punjab Criminal Law (Amendment, 1935) Act, both of which were directed against the picketers. Many times, when the civil disobedience movements of the Congress were confronting the Government, they threatened the Government with peasants' movement if their demands were not acceded to.[321]

As narrated earlier, the Government with a view to weakening the Unionists, endeavoured to pull away Chhotu

321. P.L.C.D., Vol. XVIII, 25.3.1931, 385-86, 90; Vol. XIX, 7.5.1931, 220 and 225; Vol. XXI, 4.3.1932, 22; 10.5.1932, 1044; Vol. XXII, 7.11.1931, 84; Vol. XXIII, 28.3.1933, 883 and 961; 3.4.1933. 936; Vol. XXIV, 20.10.1934, 148; *The Tribune,* Lahore, 12.5.1932, 9; 28.8.1932, 5; 2.9.1932, 5; 14.1.1933, 7; Home Department, File Nos. 95/35-Poli.; 99/35/Poll; 44/13/35-Poll.; 23/25/35-Poll.; 6/12/35-Poll.; NAI : New Delhi; *Jat Gazette,* Rohtak, 13.4.1932, 3; Bajaj, Y.P., *Sir Chhotu Ram and His Works,* (unpublished Ph.D. Thesis, Kurukshetra University, 1972), 260.

Ram and supplant Fazli by Sir Sikander Hyat so that even if the former spurned the Government offers calculated to take him away from Punjab politics, there might be a contest for Premiership between him and Sikander Hyat.[322] But Fazli's calm mind and deep insight saw through the play of Herbert Emerson, the Governor of the Punjab and he came back to Lahore. His return in 1935 was a great relief to Chhotu Ram, especially when the elections under the proposed scheme of provincial autonomy, were in the offing.

Strengthening the Unionist Party organisationally, Sir Sikander Hyat, who had been recently appointed the Deputy Governor of the Reserve Bank of India, proved that the revolutionary ideas of his youth still inspired him. Inspite of his being ambitious, he clearly refused becoming a plaything in the hands of the party whosoever they were. He rather made it clear that he had accepted Sir Fazli as his leader and would gladly agree to serve as his lieutenant.[323] At this time *i.e.* in 1936, the Unionists declared their election manifesto. It included provincial autonomy; community of economic interest as the true basis of political parties, provision of equal opportunity and facilities for all with special solicitude for the backward classes and areas whether rural or urban.[324] The solidarity of the Unionists was proved when Jinnah visited Lahore four times, but could not break asunder the hold of Fazl-i-Hussain.

Had there been no stable and enduring convention of elective leadership infighting would have disintegrated the Unionist Party. In the unity achieved under senior Unionist leadership, and the Acts beneficent to the agriculturists enacted and supported by the party since 1923, lay significant clues to

322. Bajaj, Y.P., *Sir Chhotu Ram and His Works,* (unpublished Ph.D. Thesis, Kurukshetra University, 1972) 260-61 (For details see Hussain, A., *Fazl-i-Hussain : A Political Biography,* Bombay : 1946.)

323. Ram, T., *Sir Chhotu Ram : Apostle of Hindu Muslim Unity,* Lahore : 1946, 7.

324. Hussain, A., *Fazl-i-Hussain : A Political Biography,* Bombay : 1946, 344.

the land slide victory of the Unionist Party in the election to the Punjab Legislative Assembly in 1936-37. Beating all expectations, they captured 101 seats out of a total of 175, thus defeating convincingly the Congress (20 Seats), The National Progressive Party (15 Seats), The Khalsa National Party (16 Seats), The Muslim League (17 seats), The Mujlis-i-Alam (2 Seats), Mujlis-i-Itihad-i-Millat,[325] (2 Seats) and 2 seats remained vacant. By virtue of this majority, they could have all the ministers out of their own ranks, yet, true to their widely proclaimed principles of communal harmony and due representation, in the Unionist's ministry of six, there were three Muslims, two Hindus and one Sikh. Out of these, four including the Premier, belonged to the Unionist Party and one each to the *Khalsa* National Party and the National Progressive Party. It is worth noting that Sir Sunder Singh Majithia and Sir Manhor Lal belonging respectively to the *Khalsa* National Party and the National Progressive Party, contrary to the condition imposed by the Congress on he Muslim League members in U.P., were not asked to adopt the Unionist label in order to be able to join the Unionists' ministry.[326]

Though no agreement was entered into with these parties, the gesture giving special representation in the cabinet to the Sikhs and the non-agriculturist Hindu minorities did evoke goodwill, appreciation and general support of the Khalsa National Party for the Unionist Party.[327]

---

325. *18 Months of Provincial Autonomy in the Punjab,* 8-9; *Civil and Military Gazette,* Lahore, October 21, 1933, 9.

326. *Civil and Military Gazette,* Notification No. 470-P.G.-37/13,000 dated 1.4.1937; Singh, Khushwant, *The History of the Sikhs,* Vol. II, 234 and 251; Ram, T., *Sir Chhotu Ram : Apostle of Hindu Muslim Unity,* Lahore, 1946, 57; Lakhanpal, N.K., *Governor of the Punjab : 1937-47; A Constitutional Study,* (Unpublished Ph.D. Thesis, Punjab University, Chandigarh, 1972).

327. Sen, N.B. (Ed.), *Punjabs Eminent Hindus,* Lahore : 1943, 40, 101 and 106; Sharma, R.S., *Haryana Ka Itihas,* Rohtak : 1966, 87 (Except Dr. G.C. Narang, all the members of the National Progressive Party shifted to the ministerial banches).

That the Unionist leadership was genuinely working to win the confidence of the minorities was well borne out by the fact that Sir Manhor Lal continued as minister representing the non-agriculturist Hindus although during 1938, almost all the members of the National Progressive Party on account of their differences with the Unionist Government over the issues like relief to the agriculturist debtors and economic programme had shifted to the opposition banches. But the withdrawal of their support did not make much difference because by the middle of 1938, the policies of the ministry had been tested. About 120 members of the Punjab Legislative Assembly including approximately 40% to 50% of the total Hindu and Sikh members respectively, belonging to the constantly hostile opposition, voted for the Ministry's economic programme.[328] Thus, it may be observed that the economic programme tended to out across communal differences.

In the Punjab Legislature Congress was acquiring more strength with the help of the Akalis and at the cost of the National Progressive Party.[329] Besides, the Muslim League had not forgotten the raw deal it had at the All Parties Conference that had met on February 11, 1938 at Delhi, throwing overboard the resolution already passed by the Indian National Congress in December, 1937 at the Madras session and the All India Muslim League session, Calcutta in the same month, and the tough opposition to their demands by the Hindu leaders, especially the *Hindu Mahasabha* at the second and third Round Table Conferences inspite of a pre-election understanding. But the Congress refused to force coalition ministries in 1937 and thereby created resentment among the Muslim masses. The event by itself was remarkable in the history of India's struggle for freedom as also in the Hindu-Muslim relations because thereafter Jinnah or the All India Muslim League neither offered terms for co-operation with the Congress as done in the past; nor did they accept the concessions which the latter was prepared to concede.

328. *18 Months of Provincial Autonomy*, 10.

329. *Ibid.*, *Punj Darya (Punjabee)*, Lahore, October, 1940, 14.

This development was interpreted by the Communist Party of India as growing rivalry between the bourgeoisie of both the Communities and advancing nationalist and anti-imperialist consciousness among the Muslim masses. In a resolution passed at Mantanawari Pattam in 1938, they also advocated the right of self-determination for every nationality with a view to reviving mutual confidence and achieving the Congress-League unity by rallying different nationalities to fight shoulder to shoulder for India's freedom. Such a guarantee by the Congress, they held, would mean to Muslim people not separation but a more glorious, voluntary and lasting unity within a free Indian Union.[330]

In the present context, we have to note the fact that three Muslim majority provinces of Punjab, Bengal and Sind had then provincial parties which formed their Governments in 1937. However, the Muslim League did not have any share in these Governments, and the Muslims, in general, were broadly divided into two sections—communalists and nationalists. But since 1933, when after the three Round Table Conferences, the Muslim Majority provinces proposed to have greater autonomy, the separatists and communalists had been progressively pulling more weight.[331] That apart, Jinnah's status as the All India Muslim leader to conduct negotiations on their behalf had also been lowered by the results of the above mentioned elections to the provincial legislatures. To the Central Legislature, no fresh elections were held. No doubt, the Muslim League occupied secondary position, the Congress having been the chief opposition. The Congress leadership alleged that Jinnah did not enjoy the support of the Muslim majority provinces.

It was in these circumstances of stress and strain that the annual session of the Muslim League was convened at Lucknow on 15th October, 1937 and to which the Muslim Premiers Sir

330. Rowlinson, H.G. and Garrett, H.L.O. (ed.), *The Great Men of India,* 1939, 380-81; Adhikari, G., *Documents of the History of the Communist Party of India,* Vol. II, PPH, New Delhi : 1974, 28; Gwyer and Appadorai, *Speech and Documents on Indian* Constitution, Vol.I, Bombay : 1957, 422-23.

Sikander and Fazl-ul-Haq respectively of the Punjab and Bengal with the Muslim members of these legislatures were also invited. A day before the session began, Jinnah reached an understanding with them by virtue of which both declared allegiance to the All India Muslim League.[332] The understanding with Sikander, though a misnomer, because it was never signed by the two leaders, inspite of the draft having been prepared, is yet called the Sikander-Jinnah Pact, as reported by the correspondent of the *Civil and Military Gazette* detailed to cover the League session. Sikander agreed that on his return to Lahore he would persuade the Muslim members of the Unionist Party to join the Muslim League as well. But this arrangement was not to affect either the programme or objectives of the Unionist Party.

In arriving at this understanding with Jinnah, Sikander's bonafides was questioned. Critics argued that in October, 1937, the Muslim League had only one member, namely Barkat Ali, in the Punjab Legislative, but by making the pact, he ressurected that party. However, an answer to the charges call for an analysis of the following points :

(i) Did Sir Sikander enter into this pact without any necessity?

(ii) Did he and his successor Khizer become separatists and Camp followers of Jinnah after making this pact?

(iii) What was the reaction of the Hindu Unionist leaders?

(iv) Did the Muslim League become strong in the Punjab due to this pact, and had the pact not been concluded, would not the Muslim League have become so powerful in all India politics as it did?

As regards *(i)* besides the circumstantial compulsions discussed earlier, the Unionist Government right from the

---

331. Ram, T., *Sir Chhotu Ram : Apostle of Hindu Muslim Unity,* Lahore : 1966, 53; Khanun, K.S., *Inside India,* London : 1937, cit. in *The Amrit (Punjabee),* Taran Taran, August , 1938.

332. Ram, T., *Sir Chhotu Ram : Apostele of Hindu Muslim Unity,* Lahore : 1966, 54.

beginning faced a difficult communal situation. Due to lack of space, the incidents of communal riots are not traced here. However, to substantiate this point, it is enough to state that the *Shahid Ganj* Mosque agitation and Khaksar movement began to threaten then peace of the province.[333]

Now, coming to the reaction of Sir Chhotu Ram, it is worthwhile to note that Sikander had attended the Lucknow session of the League with his concent, but the development of the Pact under study came about suddenly. Sikander Hyat, considering that the pact neither authorised Jinnah to interfere with Punjab affairs, nor did it affect the programme of the Unionist Party, thought that he would persuade Chhotu Ram, but when he explained the reasons of concluding it, Chhotu Ram warned him against the complications that would arise in future. Although the *Hindu Mahasabha,* probably with a view to weaning away Chhotu Ram, did propagate though wrongly, that the pact would lesson the influence of Chhotu Ram, yet a relevant question as to why Chhotu Ram did not break away with Sikander Hyat needs explanation, because the pact, after all, was a compromise with communalism.[334] Was it for the sake of some material gains like ministership?

So far ministership was concerned, he had repeatedly declined the opposition's offers of 1930-35 of a ministerial berth, since these were motivated by communal feelings, with the remarks, "I am not prepared to give up my lifelong principles for any material gains and honours".[335] Similarly, he had rejected the Government's offer of the Premiership of Kashmir.[336] Besides, Jinnah had neither supported, to their

333. *18 Months of Provincial Autonomy,* 31, 36-37; Ram, T., *Sir Chhotu Ram : Apostle of Hindu Muslim Unity,* Lahore : 1946, 94.

334. For details see, Ram, T., *Sir Chhotu Ram : Apostle of Hindu Muslim Unity,* Lahore, 1946, 55; *Civil and Military Gazette,* Lahore, 23.10.1937.

335. P.L.C.D., Vol. XIV, 20.9.1939, 239; Bajaj, Y.P., *Sir Chhotu Ram and His Works* (unpublished Ph.D. Thesis—Kurukshetra University, 1972), 26-27.

336. *Ibid.*

great bewilderment, such interpretations of the pact as were made by men like Barkat Ali, Muhammad Iqbal and Gulam Rasool Khan that by virtue of this pact the Unionist Party was losing its independent identity and stood merged with the Muslim League, nor did he contradict Sikander Hyat Khan when he repudiated publicly, as also in the sessions of the Punjab Legislative Assembly, their assertion that the pact had set up Muslim League ministry in the Punjab.[337]

Let it be viewed from another, though purely hypothetical aspect; how could Chhotu Ram, who alongwith his supporters was doing much useful work for the rural, backward and downtrodden sections join or form another party? While launching another party would have added to the communal confusion in the province, the joining of the Congress (the party near to his ideas) with its policies of disobedience and non-payment of land revenue and taxes was unsuitable to his constitutional methods, (here, it is to be kept in mind that Chhotu Ram was an important member of the Unionist Party Government and always wanted that the income of the Government must be maintained at all costs), necessitated by the handicaps, difficulties, trials and tribulations of the backward agricultural community that urgently needed educational, economic, political and social awakening and upliftment.[338] He also warned the illiterate rural community against joining the Congress although the Unionist Party itself was following in the Punjab the economic programme of the Congress.

As regards joining hands with other parties like the *Hindu Mahasabha* and the National Progressive Party, he stood poles apart because they condemned the Unionist ministry as a Muslim ministry and branded Chhotu Ram as a communist.[339]

337. Letters of Muhammad Iqbal to Jinnah, 1943, 28-32; Ram, T., *Sir Chhotu Ram : Apostle of Hindu-Muslim Unity,* Lahore, 1946, 54.

338. Ram, T., *Sir Chhotu Ram : Apostle of Hindu Muslim Unity,* Lahore, 1946, 39; Bajaj, T.P., *Sir Chhotu Ram and His Works,* (unpublished Ph.D. Thesis-Kurukshetra University, 1972), 259.

339. *The Punjab Past and Present,* April, 1971, 164 (Chhotu Ram's speech at the Id festival organised by the Young Jat Association, Punjab, Lahore, on November 4, 1940); Ram, T., *Sir Chhotu Ram : Apostle of Hindu Muslim Unity,* Lahore : 1946, 39.

So far as joining the Communist Party was concerned, it was out of question; besides his disagreeing with its violent and terroristic methods, it had adopted the undertones of supporting the right of self determination for every community in its own way as discussed earlier.

After the election, however, the Unionists were lent support both by the Congress and the *Panthic Pratinidhi* Board, and Khizer again formed the Government. This event was significant as it reaffirmed that Khizer and the Unionist Party were following a policy of communal harmony. In the present context, reference may be made to an important resolution passed in 1942 in Delhi by the All India Jat Conference, primarily organised by the efforts of the Unionist leaders at Delhi. The resolution stated that Indians had no faith in the repeated assurances of the British to grant independence to India and demanded that the task of framing a constitution for an independent India should be taken in hand at once.[340]

As expected, the Muslim league did not take the formation of Khizer's ministry lying down. It so intensified its propaganda ultimately to lend to direct action. Consequently, communal passions rose high, and on January 24, 1947 Khizer's Government passed an order warning private bodies like the Muslim League, the National Guards, the Hindu R.S.S. and the Akali *Dal*, against their communal activities. But the Muslims successfully staged such a total defiance that the order had to be withdrawn which compelled Khizer to submit resignation of his ministry.

Sinkander Hyat was no camp follower of Jinnah. The latter did not interfere in the Punjab affairs till 1944. It appears that both the leaders adopted a policy of containing each other to strengthen their respective parties. It was with this end in view that Jinnah let the Muslim Unionists capture the Provincial

---

340. The Conference was held on 29.11.1972 (For details see Shastri, R.S., *Chaudhari Chhotu Ram-Jivan Charitra* (Hindi) Rohtak : 1965, 320; Bajaj, I.P., *Sir Chhotu Ram and His Works* unpublished Ph.D. Thesis (Kurukshetra University) 1972, Appendix, XX).

Muslim League despite the protests of its old guards like Muhammad Iqbal, Barkat Ali and Gulam Rasool.[341] In April, 1938, he allotted to the old Muslim League only ten seats on the Provincial Executive while the Unionists got the remaining 25 berths with Sir Sikander Hyat as the President.

On the other hand, Sir Sikander, as the leader of the Unionists continued his efforts for bringing about communal harmony. In this regard, his reaction to a proposal initiated in the Punjab Legislature by a Muslim member purporting to restore to the Muslims the site of the demolished Mosque of *Shaheed Ganj* is significant. On March 16, 1938, the Premier said on the floor of the House, "The Musoalmans of the Punjab owe a special responsibility not only to the minorities in the Punjab, but also to their religionists who constitute minorities in other provinces.................The issues before us are grave and call for the most anxious and careful consideration from all concerned............."[342] In July, 1939, he proposed a scheme of an all India Federation comprising seven regional Federations with a view to solving the communal and political tangle.[343]

However, soon after Sir Sikander realised the incompatibility of his dual position because on all important questions like the second world war, the communal problem, the future constitution of India, etc., Jinnah and he differed widely. Contrary to Jinnah's attitude, the Unionists extended support to the Government right from the beginning and concluded Sikander Baldev Pact on June 15, 1942, although the Akalis were the staunch opponents of the Muslims League's demand of Pakistan.[344] The *Hindu Mahasabha* had

341. Batalvi, A.M., *Iqbal Ke Aakhari Do Saal,* 623-28.

342. Telegram from Governor of the Punjab to Governor General, 1st April, 1940, Linlithgow Correspondence, Acc. No. 2355, M. ss. F. 125/28; P.L.C.D., Vol. III, 1939, 221; *18 Months of Provincial Autonomy in the Punjab,* 36; Home Department, File No. 18/5/1936-Political, NAI : New Delhi.

343. Gulati, K.C., op. cit., 113; *PunjaDarya,* Lahore, May, 1941, 7; *Indian Annual Register,* op. cit., 1939, Vol. II, 1; *The Tribune,* Lahore, 16.6.1942.

344. Home Department, File Nos. 18/2/1941-Political; 18/10/1944(1)-Political, NAI : New Delhi.

been backing the Akalis as well.

Inspite of the Lahore resolution of March 22, 1940 of the Muslim League demanding sovereign Pakistan, the Unionists continued, their efforts against the bifurcation of the country. For instance, 18 Muslim Unionists who sent a telegram to Jinnah during the Madras session of the Muslim League in 1941 extending their support for Pakistan, made it conditional that it should be a partner within the Indian Federation. The same year Sikander Hyat announced he would not accept Pakistan except in Union with India in some federal form.[345]

Similarly, the Sikander formula of 1942 which was approved by a senior Unionist Chhotu Ram for supporting Jinnah's stand conceded the same right of self determination to the minorities in the Punjab and elsewhere as Muslims claimed for themselves. Though censuring the formula of self-determination to every community was colossal, yet Sikander continued negotiations with the Hindus and the Sikhs. Expressing his dissatisfaction, he gave out in a private talk that either Jinnah would accept his solution or he would part company with the league leader. It is another matter that such a fateful occasion never came, because the Hindus, whom he had met on November 3rd at Lahore, and the Sikh leaders could not come to any settlement[346] and soon after, Sir Sikander died of a heart attack on December 26, 1942.

It was after his death that the circumstances began to grow favourable for Jinnah. Khizer Hyat's becoming new Premier of the Punjab created heart burning in Shaukat Hyat, the eldest son of the late Premier, mainly due to the reasons that there

345. *The Tribune*, Lahore, 16.6.1942; *The Punj Darya*, Lahore, May, 1941; Ram, T., *Sir Chhotu Ram : Apostle of Hindu Muslim Unity* (Hindi), Lahore : 1946, 56;

346. *Modern Review* (Calcutta), December, 1942, 449-50; IAR, Vol. II, 1942, 293-94; Singh, Khushwant, *History of the Sikhs*, Vol. II, 251; Ram, T., *Sir Chhotu Ram : Apostle of Hindu Muslim Unity*, (Hindi), Lahore : 1946, 45 and 57; Lakhanpaul, N.K., *Governors of the Punjab : A Constitutional Study*, unpublished Ph.D. Thesis, Punjab University (Chandigarh), 1972, 197; *Punjab Government Gazette*, (Extra-Ordinary), 28.12.1942.

had been a family rivalry between the two; secondly, Shaukat Hyat was very ambitious and had aspired to succeed his father as the Premier. But inspite of it, the Unionist leaders, to ward off open rupture in the ranks of the party, appointed Shaukat Hyat a minister. However, the policy of appeasement did not satisfy the party's unity. Rather, it whetted his ambition and he became a willing scape goat of veiled designs of the young ambitious Muslim Unionists who had been planning to replace Khizer's Government by the one in which they could find berth for the Hindus.[347] During the period reviewed, a considerable section of the Sikhs also revived its active opposition to the Unionist Government. For example, in an article in August, 1943, Master Tara Singh wrote, "The establishment of Azad Punjab is very essential for deliverance from the present communal Government of the Punjab". The three main points in his policy remained : *(a)* over-throw of the Unionist Ministry, which the Akalis held to be predominantly Muslim; *(b)* strengthening of the Sikh position in the Army and *(c)* exertion of pressure of Sikh states to make them accept the Akali demands for the appointment of officials from their ransk.[348] In view of the circumstances, Jinnah grilled Khizr for not making Muslim League an affective party in the Punjab and not carrying out the terms of Sikander—Jinnah Pact in the true sprit.[349]

While Khizr sincerely tried to work up the Sikander-Jinnah Pact, the latter had no ulterior motives even in the above mentioned threat. He progressively stepped up his demands as well as the condemnation of the Unionist Party in order to stage an open confrontation because he thought, as he did openly declare, that the Unionists stood between him and the phantom idea of Pakistan. As regards the strategy of attacks, Shaukat and his group had successfully schooled Jinnah to

347. Ram, T., *Sir Chhotu Ram : Apostle of Hindu-Muslim Unity* (Hindi) Lahore, 1946, 57.

348. Home Department, File Nos. 18/1/1942-Political; 18/6/1942-Political, NAI : New Delhi.

349. *Punjab Darya* (Lahore), August, 1943, 21.

appeal to the communal fanaticism of the Punjab Muslims and concentrate on Chhotu Ram who had the reputation of having repeatedly marshalled the Unionists against the Muslim League.[350]

Here, one may note some contemporary activities of some senior leaders of he Unionist party, which might have irked Jinnah. Since early 1941, the leadership of the Unionists had been preparing to give a mighty blow to the idea of Pakistan.[351] In August, 1942, when in return for condemning the Quit India Movement and offering co-operation, Jinnah asked the Government to concede the demand of Pakistan, Chhotu Ram especially, however, argued that any such declaration would certainly result in an extensive trouble in the Punjab, a view point that was lent support by the them Governor of the Punjab, Sir B.J. Glancy.[352] He discussed on September 13, 1942, a detailed plan of expelling the Muslim League from the Punjab with Jasdev Singh Sidhanti, a parliamentarian.

Under the plan, it was programmed to launch a campaign in which *Maulvis* were also to work for the political awakening of the masses especially the peasantry. *Zamindars* Leagues were set up and activated in all the districts. A daily to propagate the policies and programmes of the Unionist Party was to be brought out. An extensive tourising with a view to realising these ends was underaken by the Unionist leaders. More organisations such as the Young *Zamindars* and Young *Jats* Associations, founded in 1937 and 1940, were made very active. These two bodies opposing Jinnah's propaganda among the students and the Muslim masses of the Punjab organised numerous public meetings, many of which were addressed intrepidly and without and police protection by Khizr Hyat and Chhotu Ram.

---

350. IAR, Vol. I, 1943, 277-78; Ram, T., *Sir Chhotu Ram : Apostle of Hindu Muslim Unity* (Hindi), Lahore : 1946, 58 and 67.

351. *Jat Gazette,* Rohtak, 19.3.1941, 31; 2.4.1941, 3 (More details can be gathered from various issues of this paper of the year 1941).

352. Nicholas, M.N. (ed.), *India Transfer of Power,* 1942-47, 771-74, 834-35; *Quit India : Documents,* Nos. 598 and 640, London : 1971.

Besides, Jinnah also launched massive propaganda among the Muslims students and the masses during 1943 culminating on 19th March, 1943, in the threat that the Muslims would find another alternative if the Unionist ministry, from their view point, failed to work properly. It appears that Jinnah who then had gained so much strength that even the Congress was wooing him, was planning to mount an offensive on the Unionists in general and on its leadership in paticular.[353] Soon after the inevitable followed in the last week of April, 1944, when Jinnah coerced Khizr to change his attention towards the Muslim League and rename his Government as the Muslim League coalition ministry. But Khizr wrote back that after Sikander's death, Chhotu Ram was the most senior leaders, who should have filled the place, but it was a Muslim who succeeded Muslim and also refused to relabel the Unionist Ministry as the Muslim League coalition.

On May 1, 1944, Chhotu Ram also asked Jinnah to withdraw his press statement and abandon the idea of Pakistan.[354] Jinnah, now decided upon erasing the very name, 'Unionist', declared that the Sikander-Jinnah Pact was nothing more than an announcement made by a follower to give practical shape to the plans of his leaders. Consequently, Khizr might be expelled from the Muslim League formally, Khizr's stand was earnestly supported by most Unionists and his cabinet colleagues except Shaukat who had already been dismissed, yet Jinnah's cleverness did work its way, though on a small scale, when four parliamentary Secretaries resigned in protest against the hard attitudes of the prenior in not surrendering to Qaid-i-Azam, Jinnah.

Though this little success against the Unionists would not

353. *Time of India,* Delhi, 11.1.1945; *Civil and Military Gazette,* Lahore, 10.1.1945; Shastri, R.S., *Chaudhari Chhotu Ram : Jivan Charitra* (Hindi), Rohtak : 1965, 339-40; Ram, T., *Sir Chhotu Ram : Apostle of Hindu Muslim Unity* (Hindi), Lahore : 1946, 67-68; Home Department 74/1-A/1940-Political.

354. IAR, Vol. I, 1944, 210-11 (Khizr-Jinnah Correspondence from 24.4.1944 to 28.4.1944, Ram, T., *Sir Chhotu Ram : Apostle of* Hindu-Muslim Unity (Hindi), Lahore : 1946, 5960.

have been of much consequence by itself, yet combined with the prestige that the Muslim League was gaining every day in all India politics, it resulted in the increasing depletion of the ranks of the Unionists, Encouraged by it in December, 1944, the Muslim League tabled a no-confidence motion in the Punjab Assembly against the Khizr's Ministry. Even though the Muslim league failed in its main objectives of disolodging the Unionists' ministry, communal sentiments had gained grounds. As Chhotu Ram was unwell, Khizr all alone was to face the day to day worsending political situation for the Unionists.[356]

Soon, Jinnah scored another point by wrecking the Simla Conference because it was feared that Lord Wavel might nominate a Muslim Unionist to one of the five Muslim seats in the Reformed Executive Council. It had the effect as desired by Jinnah and in the elections held in 1946, only the Muslim League with its election manifesto of Pakistan carried 73 out of 85 Muslim seats. The Unionists managed to have only 19 candidates elected while it had put up 99.[357] In those elections, the Congress, the *Panthic Pratinidhi* Board and the independents carried 51, 21 and 11 seats respectively. In the present context the following facts are notable :

(a) In his electioneering, Master Tara Singh, on the one hand, high lighted the grievances of the Sikhs against the Unionist Government; on the other hand, he declared that the Sikhs who would vote for the Sikhs contesting on the Congress tickets would do great disservice to the *Panth*, because the Congress had accepted Pakistan in half of the Punjab[358] *i.e.*, in Muslim majority districts and

355. IAR, Vol. I, 1944, 222, 225-26; Ram, T., *Sir Chhotu Ram : Apostle of Hindu-Muslim Unity* (Hindi) Lahore : 1946, 60.

356. Shastri, R.S., *Chaudhari Chhotu Ram-Jiwan Charitra* (Hindi), Rohtak : 1965, 344 & 385; Ram, T., *Sir Jiwan Charitra* (Hindi), Rohtak : 1965, 344 & 385; Ram, T., *Sir Chhotu Ram : Apostle of Hindu-Muslim Unity* (Hindi), Lahore : 1946, 69-70.

357. *Ibid.*

358. For details regarding the Akalis opposition to the Congress at one time, see Home Department, File Nos. 18/9/1940-Political; 18/10/1944-Political, 232/1940-Political, NAI : New Delhi.

(b) Maulana Azad with a view to keeping the Muslim League out of power, gave all out support to the Unionists in quite a few constituences.[359]

March 2, 1947,[360] practically marked the end of the Unionist Party, though in the general elections held in 1952, some candidates did contest to the Punjab Assembly on the Unionist tickets, their number was insignificant.

Before coming to the last question, let us have an idea about the involvement of the Communists in the Punjab politics during the period of our study.

The Communists were not only critical of the Congress but also made all possible efforts to counter-act Akalis.[361] They also made propaganda by holding conferences. Mention was also made in the Conferences of the Sikander-Baldev Pact and the embazzlement of Gurdawara funds by the Akalis.[362] Efforts were also made to persuade Akalis of join Hindus and disgruntled members of the Muslim League to unite in order to over-throw the Unionist Party. In order to secure Muslim co-operation with the Communists, workers had been instructed to support the Muslim League and press for a resumption of the Gandhi-Jinnah Pact talks as a necessary preliminary to Pakistan.[363]

However, the most significant point to be noted is that when the *Azad* Punjab scheme produced no results, they then

359. *Punj Darya,* Lahore, September, 1945, 44-45; December, 1945; 29-30; March, 1946, 51; *Press Information Bureau Government of India,* Series No. 22, dated 5.3.1946, 5, 10, 12; Sayee, K.B., *The Pakistan : The Formation Phase,* 130; *The Tribune,* Chandigarh, January 12, 1972, 5.

360. *Punj Darya,* Lahore, April, 1947; Singh, Khushwant, *History of the Sikhs,* Vol. II, 270-71.

361. Home Department, File Nos. 18/8/1937-Political; 18/8/1942-Political, NAI : New Delhi.

362. Home Department, File Nos. 226/42(1)-Political; 18/2/1944-Political, (For more information also see File Nos. 18/4/1944-Political; 7/5/1944-Political, NAI : New Delhi.

363. Home Department, File No. 18/2/1943-Feb.-Poll., NAI : New Delhi.

decided on revising their view or policy towards the Akali Party with a view to using them as a weapon for their own ends. This policy, if adopted, would accept the Sikh demand for self determination and the previous communist slogan of Congress-Muslim League unity would be expanded to include the Akalis. The Communists' aim was to make the Akali Party, which they recognised as the most Sikh party in the Punjab into a strong democratic national organisation of the Sikh.[364] Despite all this, they had watched with pleasure the disunity creeping into the Sikh politics and Jinnah's attempts to disrupt the Unionist party. The replacement of the Unionist Government by a Muslim League Government would, in Communist opinion, substitute a more national and liberal form of Government for what they considered a reactionary and elite autocracy.[365]

It is interesting to cite that Jinnah discouraged the Communist offer of co-operation in over-throwing the Unionist ministry, but the Communists were still trying to penetrate into the League and their latest effort was the establishment of a branch of the League in Lahore.[366] The Communists, during the period under review, tried to unite the Muslim League, the Akalis and the Congress to over-throw the Unionist ministry. It was suggested that the Congress workers should be won over by the propaganda asking for Gandhi to be allowed to meet other Congress leaders and by a campaign for Congress-Muslim League Unity; that the Muslim League should be approached by helping them against the Unionists; and that the Sikhs should be united into a progressive nationalist body by suggesting that their Gurdwaras should be run on democratic lines and by encouraging their rights of self-determination on the basis of unity with the Muslim.[367]

Sajjad Zaheer's report on the Muslims was not very convincing. His main points were that Muslims should be

364. Home Department, File No. 18/2/1944-Political, NAI : New Delhi.

365. Home Department, File No. 18/3/1944-Political, NAI : New Delhi.

366. Home Department, File No. 18/4/1944-Political, NAI : New Delhi.

367. Home Department, File No. 18/5/1944-Political, NAI : New Delhi.

encouraged to join the Muslim League and turn it into a mass Muslim Organisation, that Muslim Communists should also join it, that control would eventually pass into the hands of the masses and that the Congress Muslim unity could then be achieved.[368] In fact, everything was to be done to undermine the strength of the Unionist Party. Hence, the Communists had been of some value as a check to the activities of the Congress and the Akalis in the Punjab. As we have seen earlier, they had openly and vehemently condemned the activities of the Congress Socialists, whom they described as fifth columnists, and to whom they attributed all the disturbances, which had taken place after August 1944.[369] They had consistently opposed the Akalis in Amritsar and Doab area and preferred to take advantage of the dissensions in the Akali Party caused by the resignation of Master Tara Singh in order it win over the extremists and in them in opposing the moderate leaders. They alleged that if they succeeded in their plans they would build up a dangerously strong Sikh revolutionary party in the Punjab.[370]

Their approach to the Muslim and the Hindus of the Punjab was no more helpful. They aimed at over-throwing the Unionist Ministry. They would prefer a Muslim League Ministry in its place which they would strive to influence through their contacts with the Progressive Muslims. As regards the Hindus, they saw in the *Rashtriya Swayam Sewak Sangh*, the most vigorous organisation likely to serve their purpose. They admitted its tendencies towards fascism, but maintained that they would expel all the pro-fascist elements once they had established their influence. Thus, the most important contribution of the Communists in connection with the political development in the Punjab during the period under review was to put forward a definite plan for bringing about unity among the Muslim League, the Akalis and the

368. *Ibid.*

369. *Ibid.*

370. *Ibid.*

Congress,[371] to over-throw the Unionist Ministry which the party regarded as a barrier removal was essential for the fulfillment of its objects.

Now coming to the last question, whether the Muslim League gained constant strength and importance in all India politics in general and in the Punjab in particular due to the Sikandar-Jinnah Pact, the answer is 'no'. On the contrary, the Muslim League's position in the Punjab started improving since 1943 as it gained in prestige due to the shifting attitude of the Indian National Congress towards its demand and the support of the Communist party and the policy of the British imperialists, who wanted to complicate the communal tangle to serve their colonial interests. If an objective analysis of the contemporary developments is made, the following conclusions can be drawn.[372]

The Muslim League was hopeful that Pakistan would become a reality with the Government's support : the Secretary of State is said to have remarked in about 1940 that India's future house of freedom had room for many mansions. Lord Linlithgow's statement of 8th August, 1940 and Cripps offer of 1942 also conceded the Muslim League's demand half way. Backed by the Government's indirect support in 1942 and with a view to wooing it further. Jinnah strongly condemned the Quit India Movement as an attempt of the Congress to coerce both the Government and the Muslims to submit to establishing a *Hindu Raj.* Treading the same line in its annual session held at Lahore in December, 1943, the All India Muslim League asked the British to divide and quit India. It was meant to counter Gandhi's Quit India Movement.[373]

371. Home Department, File No. 18/5/1944-Political (For more details also see fortnightly reports of the Punjab of the year 1944 and 1945), NAI : New Delhi.

372. Singh, Khushwant, *History of the Sikhs,* Vol. II, 272-73; also see Bajaj, Y.P., *Sir Chhotu Ram and His Works,* unpublished Ph.D. Thesis (Kurukshetra University, 1972), Appendix-XX.

373. Majumdar, R.C., *History of Freedom Movement in India,* Vol. III Calcutta : 1963, 606 and 681.

The Indian National Congress which was responsible for the drastic change in Jinnah's attitude since 1937, now failed to hold out unitedly against his attack while a section of the Congress was half way prepared to meet Jinnah's demand. Gandhi himself wrote on April 1, 1942, in the *Harijan* that of the majority of the Muslims regarded themselves as a separate nation and wanted the partition of India on that basis, they must have the partition. In the following February, C. Rajagopalachari conducted prolonged negotiations with Jinnah, which culminated in Gandhi-Jinnah correspondence that added tremendously to Jinnah's prestige.

It is noteworthy here that negotiations with the League on the basis of Pakistan were conducted at a time when the Secretary of State Lord Ameri, on the demand of the Sikhs and the Unionists, had announced in 1943 in the Parliament that Pakistan would be raised. Similarly, the new Viceroy, Lord Wavell, addressing the joint session of the central Legislature, pointedly remarked that in view of the geographical and economic conditions of India, the two Communities could make arrangements to live together in spite of differing cultures. The holding of negotiations with Jinnah aroused the hostility and suspicion even of the Sikhs and the Hindu leaders including the Unionist leader, Sir Chhotu Ram, and of the *Hindus* of Bengal.[375]

It was this unstable policy of hostility and appeasement of the Congress towards Jinnah, which enabled the Muslim League to form ministries in Bengal, Assam, Sindh and North West Frontier provinces by the close of 1942. This policy had its representations even on the nationalist *Pathans* of the North West Frontier Province. The Pathan delegation of the All India

374. *Ibid.*, 679; Coupland, R., *Constitutional Problem in India,* Vol. II, Oxford : 1945, 298; Menon, V.P., *The Transfer of Power in India,* Bombay : 1957, 163.

375. *Punj Darya* (Lahore), August, 1943, 20; Majumdar, R.C., *History of the Freedom Movement in India,* Calcutta : 1963, Vol. II, 683; Chhotu Ram's letter to Gandhiji disapproving C.R.O. Formula cit. in Ram, T., *Sir Chhotu Ram : Apostle of Hindu-Muslim Unity* (Hindi), Lahore : 1946, 95-105.

Congress Committee, meeting at Allahabad (in 1942) did not vote against Rajaji's resolution on Pakistan by absenting themselves.[376]

In the light of the above, it would be wrong be hold Sikander-Jinnah Pact, which was in force till May 1944 (till the expulsion of Khizr from Muslim League), responsible for increasing the strength of the Muslim League in the Punjab, for that matter in the country. Even if the Pact had not been there, separation and communalism would have grown stronger and most of the Punjab Muslims would have gone over to Jinnah's camp due to the above mentioned factors as well as because of the policy of the British imperialists who were the major cause of communal riots. To cite an example, a member of the British Parliament remarked in 1946 that with the aim of encouraging riots Churchil was sending money to India.[377] Thus, it would be reasonable to conclude that if the Muslim League failed in capturing power in the Punjab, it was mainly due to the non-communal policy and role of the Unionist Party in provincial politics.

However, it would be right to observe here that the Sikander-Jinnah Pact, in spite of the fact that it did not result in making Jinnah strong in the Punjab, did circumscribe the activities of the Muslim Unionists until about May, 1944. Since they constituted a big majority, the Unionist party by itself, even if it so wanted, could not spread out in other provinces, because legislators in those provinces were also the leaders of a considerable section of the Muslims. It is another matter that the communal developments would have been different, but inevitable, if the partition had been avoided. It is to be kept in view that the Unionists, including the Muslims and the non-Muslims who had faith in Unionist ideology, had been doing their to maintain communal harmony in and out side the Punjab, during the period the Sikandar-Jinnah Pact remained in force.

376. Adhikari, G., *Documents of History of the Communist Party of India,* Vol. II, PPH : New Delhi : 1974, 45; Majumdar, R.C., *History of Freedom Movement in India,* Vol. II, Calcutta : 1963, 682.

377. *Punj Darya,* Lahore, November, 1947, 7.

Thus, under the circumstances, the major political factions lost sight of their main task *i.e.*, the upliftment of the rural masses, peasantry in particular. Rather, they were engaged in a neck to neck fight just to acquire political status and recognition in the Punjab politics. The issue engaging political parties was reduced to fighting fascist aggression for winning freedom.[378] Communalism the real bane of national unity could not be absolutely abolished even after discovering a 'scientific definition of Nationality'.[379] The Muslim League was declared to be a party of the Muslim people, and by implication, it was accepted that the Congress represented only the Hindus.[380] Similarly, the other political factions represented one section of the society or the other. Hence, the Communal basis of Indian political parties, so often asserted by imperialist bureaucracy and denied by the Indian Nationalists, was accepted and stamped as 'scientific analysis'.[381]

The left now realised, if national unity was to be achieved without unleashing anti-imperialist mass movement then these two groups must be brought together and the subjective biases between these parties be overcome. Thus, the Congress-League Unity became the key slogan around which the party sought to mobilise the people in the province. The failure of the Gandhi-Jinnah negotiations left the leftists leadership dejected.[382] But, by the very nature of their programme of Congress-League Unity, they had allotted themselves the proud position of being 'non-partisan' and naturally having

378. Adhikari, G., *Pakistan and National Unity* (People's Publishing House, Bombay, August : 1942), 36.

379. Quoted in Joshi, P.C., *Communist Reply to Congress Working Committee,* People's Publishing House, Bombay : 1945.

380. For details see Joshi, P.C., *Congress and the Communists,* People's Publishing House, Bombay, December, 1944, 5.

381. *Ibid.,* 9 and 16 (For details regarding the concept of Nationality see Chandra, Bipan, "Secularisation : Retrospect and Prospect", Secular Democracy, Vol. I, No. 2, Annual, 1973.

382. Joshi, P.C., *They Must Meet Again,* PPH, Bombay : January, 1945, 1-2.

the 'right to make constructive proposals' to both the parties.[383]

The Communists also explained the Unionist-League conflict as a conflict between pre-imperialist landlords and anti-imperialist faction of the Muslim people.[384] They even explained the Sikander-Jinnah Pact as a short-sighted policy on the part of the League. They had realised the fact that the Unionist ministry could be replaced by a people's ministry[385] if the Congress, the League, the Akalis and the Communists joind hands together. It was this understanding of the situation which had led them to join hands with the League and to help its progressive wing to extend its influence in the rural areas. However, the stook of the League was lower than it had been for may months because of in March, 1945, Muslim League ministries were defeated in other provinces and the unity and strength shown by the Unionist Party in the Budget Session.[386] Of course, some progress was made in the urban areas and the League workers resolved to try and carry its message to the villages.[387] However, the fortnightly reports vividly show that the Punjab Muslim League was far from becoming a mass party even in December, 1945 as was claimed by the leftists. It was only able to enroll more members and open more district headquarters but it failed completely to reach out to the rural masses.[388] In an atmosphere of general mass apathy between 1940-45, every communalist group was out to prove itself the only genuine representative of a particular community and true defender of its rights. The conjuncture was such that masses were not choosing their representative instead representatives were choosing the masses.

---

383. *Ibid.,* 2.

384. For details see Sajjad Zaheer, *Light on League-Unionist* Conflict, PPH, Bombay : 1944, 26-27.

385. *Ibid.,* 18 and 33.

386. Home Deptt., File Nos. 18/2/1945-Poll.; 18/3/1945-Poll., NAI : New Delhi.

387. *Ibid.*

388. Home Department, File No. 18/11/1945-Poll (Report on the Political situation for the second half of November), NAI : New Delhi.

Moreover, the leftists, in October 1946, held that the Punjab Muslim League had discredited itself thoroughly. Though its leadership had talked of the common people and better conditions for the tenants, they had done nothing to bring in tenant legislation in the Assembly. Rather, the League leadership remained, in practice, true to the feudal class from which it came.[389] News of struggles against Muslim landlords by the Muslim tenants was pouring in from many districts. In many cases, the landlords themselves office bearers of the local branches. Their tenants' first action was to remove their oppressors from their office.[390] These were the same oppressors who had been eulogised by the Communists for the past three years as the progressive party representing the Muslim people. Ironically, instead of the Communist party, the repository of the most scientific ideology of the age, bringing consciousness to the poor tenants, it was the struggling tenants who suddenly enlightened the party about the truly feudal character of the League. How the tenants fought the British bureaucracy and the landlords class, we have already discussed at length in the third section of the second chapter, as well as the third. However, it will not be out of place to state that from mid 1946 onwards, the struggle of the poor peasants in the province revealed a potential to grow into a major upsurge against landlordism. But the deepening communal tensions not only disrupted the movement but also pre-empted its further developments. To this may be added that after the 1946 election, the formation of Congress-Akali-Unionist coalition ministry instead of soothing the communal tensions, sharply accentuated them. It was also totally against the expectations of the Communists. Particularly for the last four years they had been working for the Congress-League Unity. In brief, the gathering storm of communal frenzy had almost overpowered every political group and factional strife among these groups was getting sharpened. Consequently, the left movement as well as the peasants' movement remained feeble in the province.

389. People's Age, Vol. V, No. 14, October 6, 1946.

390. *Ibid.*

6

Government Policies Towards Agrarian Problems and Agrarian Unrest

The objectives of the Government of Punjab and that of British Indian Policy makers were complex. As the Nationalist movement gathered momentum and the left-wingers began to make their presence felt, the Government had to go beyond purely law and order measures to political manoeuver to keep these forces in check. In this objective the Government was sided by the Unionist Party. As discussed earlier, the Unionist Party was closely connected with the imperialist bureaucracy and big land-holders were by and large loyalists. They distinguished themselves during the war by acting as recruiting sergeant of imperialism. The problem before the Government was how to safeguard the interest of the *Zamindars* and at the same time pacify the suffering peasantry, so that the Punjab might be preserved as the recruiting ground for the imperialist army. If the bureaucracy wanted to follow successfully the policy of stick and carrot, the interests of some exploiting section had to be sacrificed.[1]

Suppression of peasants' activities had to be combined with concessions to the agriculturists, but not at the cost of *Zamindars* who had promised to ensure the support of the moneylenders. Of course, the demands of the tenants-at-will

1. *The National Front,* July 3, 1938. (For details also see the fortnightly reports of the period under review—Home Department, Political, NAI : New Delhi).

who constituted more than 35% of the arable land were neglected totally. It will not be out of place if we take notice of the fact that the Punjab was politically very significant, and had a strong potential in its revolutionary petty bourgeois and peasant elements. Though the left group was not very sound in this province, the bureaucracy was well aware of this potential danger. If the army was the target of the leftists and revolutionary Nationalists in particular and other political groups in general, in turn they were the specific target of the wrath of the imperialist bureaucracy. It was always very careful to suppress and scatter any movement which under their influence tended to take a militant turn.

Keeping the above mentioned points to view, we shall be discussing the policy of the imperialist Government under two separate heads. The first section covers the repressive aspects of its policy and in the second section, the reformist aspect of the Government policy are discussed.

That Punjab was a sensitive province was known to the British bureaucracy. In the beginning of 1920, the Viceroy of India had noticed that the Punjab was in a highly inflammable condition and he informed the then Governor of the Punjab that the Government of India was more anxious about the Punjab than any other region of the country.[2] Perhaps, it was all due to the significance of the province as a frontier region and a base for the recruitment of the Indian Army. Punjab being the 'Sword Arm of India', it was feared that if the Punjab was lost, India would be lost.[3] So it became essential in imperial interests to maintain as absolute control on the province. The tide of nationalism had to be checked. The articulate middle class had to be isolated from the rural masses.[4] Even during

2. *Disorder Inquiry Committee,* Vol. VI, 1920 (Sir Michael O'Dwyer Evidence), 72; Home Department, File No. 164/1/1923-KW-I-Political, NAI : New Delhi.

3. Leigh, M.S., *The Punjab And The War* (Lahore : Government Printing, 1922, 8.

4. Hussain, A., *Fazl-i-Hussain : A Political Biography,* Bombay : 1946, 9.

the agrarian disturbances, in the South-West Punjab, in 1915, some of the rural leaders had posed as the agents of the Crown Prince and the German Kaiser and had proclaimed that the British rule was over.[5] These tendencies had to be checked and the rural peasantry was not to be allowed to join the main stream of the National movement. To substantiate, it would be appropriate to state that during the war, Sir Michael O'Dwyer had the aim of creating class betrayed. His technique was manifest in his own words :

> 'I refer primarily to the rural masses loyal but not subservient, brave but not boastful, enterprising but not visionary, progressive but not pursuing false ideals or mistaking the shadow for the substance'.[6]

It will not be out of place to cite an instance to expose the mind of O'Dwyer in regard with the disturbances in the province. Towards the end of 1919, Pt. Jawaharlal Nehru who was travelling from Amritsar to Delhi in the same compartment in which General Dwyer and his companions were travelling, heard from the General that the latter had the whole town at his mercy and he had often felt like reducing the rebellious city to shambles but he took pity on it and refrained from doing so. This was the state of mind of General Dwyer when the state of emergency was proclaimed and all meetings were

5. *Punjab Administration Report :* 1915-16, Lahore : 1916, 8.
6. *Proceedings of Punjab Legislative Council,* April 7, 1919, Lahore : 1919, 297. (For details regarding the Policy of O'Dwyer, also see Home Political Deposit, March : 1917; Proceeding No. 32, 13; Imperial Legislative Council Debates, September 10, 1918, 299-303; Evidence taken before *Disorder Inquiry Committee,* Vol. VI, 191, 196; *Chelmsford Papers,* Roll No. 22, Letter No. 239, Chelmsford to O'Dwyer, May 12, 1919; Roll No. 23, Letter No. 341 of Roll No. 22, O'Dwyer to Chelmsford, May 12, 1919; Letter No. 386-b, O'Dwyer to Chelmsford, August 21, 1919; (We are here by our own moral superiority, by the force of circumstances and the will of providence. These alone constitute our Character of Government and in doing the best we can for the people are bound by our conscience and not theirs) Vide. O'Dwyer, *India As I Knew It : 1885-1925,* London : 1925, 407.

declared illegal.[7] Soon, several districts were placed under Martial Law and severe punishments were resorted to. Twelve hundred persons were killed and atleast 3600 injured. Mobile columns were sent round the villages to punish the villagers for their participation in the agitation. Hostages were taken from the villages for the purpose of creating impression.[8] Martial Law courts were instituted to inflict heavy punishments on the people. The British entirely forgot the services done by the people of this province during the war in saving the empire.

It will not be out of place if we cite were an instance from the 'Agrarian Disturbances' of 1907 in connection with the policy of the bureaucracy. During the course of these disturbances, the people were not allowed to attend public meetings. In case any meeting was held, after the meeting the people were prevented from going towards European inhabited parts of the city by the police which apprehended damage to the European quarters located there. The crowds shouted slogans like 'Bande Matram' and refused to disperse, the police worked themselves to an unusual degree of frenzy and heat and began to trample people under their horses without making the least discrimination. Many innocent people were belaboured by the police with lathis and the butt ends of their murkets.[9]

Let it be noted that outwardly, a show of love and affection was maintained. To purchase loyalty, the peasants were given false hopes, empty promises and smoky dreams. The rural masses, peasantry in particular, were successfully exploited.[10]

---

7. Nehru, Jawaharlal, *An Autobiography,* Delhi : 1962, 43; Arthur Swinson, *Six Minutes to Sunset,* London : 1964, 45, 64 (For details of atrocities also see *Congress Punjab Committee Report,* Vol. I, 52-60; Vol. II, 10 & 107.

8. *Disorder Enquiry Committee Report,* 211, 227; Singh, Khushwant, *A History of the Sikhs,* Oxford, 1966, 166; For details also see Mohan, H.P., *Imaginary Rebellion,* Lahore : Khosla Bros., 1920, 169.

9. *Amrit Bazar Patrika,* Calcutta, May 8, 1907; Ahluwalia, M.M., *Freedom Struggle in India : 1858-1909,* Delhi : 1965, 348.

10. Home Department, Deposit No. 37, July, 1919, Political, NAI, New Delhi.

Darbars were held, supporters were given lands, titles and honorary posts. Just when the was over, the discontented peasantry were sought to be bribed into submission through remission of land revenue.[11]

The police were mobilised for house searches and for patrolling in villages. This frontal attack proved successful against the weaker leadership. Those who were sitting on the fence returned to become loyal and the people became cautious and circumspect.[12] The risk of this policy proved true, when a leader like Lajpat Rai was struck down by the bureaucracy and the moderates held demonstrations against such an action. The ministry in Great Britain, obviously under pressure, found it difficult in defend this policy. Consequently the policy of frontal attack against the leaders was given up for some time. They were against the nationalists at the political level could be successfully waged with the help of the loyalists. In the first decade of the 20th century, the bureaucracy took care to cultivate such groups and their efforts resulted in the formation of the Unionist Party which dominated the Punjab politics till 1940. Let us summarise the "measures and powers", suggested by Denzil Ibbetson, in 1909, to overpower the sedition in the province. He suggested :[13]

1. The power at notify that in any specific areas no public meeting shall be held...............
2. The power to prohibit any such meeting without assigning reasons............
3. The power to prohibit any specified person from

11. Home Department, B-June-1917, No. 450; *The Tribune,* September 7, 1917, 6; Sir Michael O'Dwyer, *India As I Knew It,* London : 1925, 419.

12. Hewett, J.P. to Lord Minto, August 4, 1907, Minto Correspondence and Government of India, Home Political-4 August, 1907, Deposit, NAI : New Delhi.

13. Lala Lajpat Rai, *Autobiographical Writings,* 1965, Appendix-11, 238-39; Josh Sohan Singh, *Hindustan Ghadr Party,* PPH, Delhi : 1977, 31-32; Josh Bhagwan, *Communist Movement in Punjab,* Delhi : 1979, 20; Leigh, M.S., *The Punjab and The War,* Lahore : 1922, 21.

addressing public meetings without assigning reasons..........

4. Press Laws : The law should empower the executive to suppress any paper, after warning, and should provide against its reappearance under the same management, though under another name.............
5. With the conviction under criminal law, a paper should ipsofacto be suspended from publication.

Let it be noted here that the above noted suggestions of Denzil Ibbetson, which he gave soon after the agrarian disturbances of 1909, became the main features of the British Government policy under review. These principles were repeated time and again at short intervals just to suppress the nationalist' movement. These suggestions and much more, were promptly and more vigorously carried out in practice in the years to come day.

Now, we shall discuss the various methods, the Government employed to pacify the resentment of the soldiers in particular and others in general : *(i)* The Government was fully prepared to consider cases of hardship involving leaders if represented through the proper channel. *(ii)* The Government was not prepared to receive mass representations and Jathas and would take measure to punish participants in such *Jathas.*[14] *(iii)* These measures would include : *(a)* pensioners joining an illegal assembly would be deprived of their pensions; *(b)* any ex-soldier joining forbidden *jathas* would be arrested and prosecuted; *(c)* Remission of land revenue and other civil privileges etc. at that time enjoyed by villagers under suspicion would be forfeited and the inhabitants of these villages would be convicted if they joined the *jathas.*[15]

The authorities had considered it essential to suppress national movements in the villages especially in the districts of Lahore, Amritsar and Sheikhupura whose inhabitants lived comparatively near the educated and politically conscious

14. Home Department, File No. 265/1920-Political, NAI : New Delhi.
15. *Ibid.*

people in cities.[16] Sedition Meeting Act had then been enforced in the districts of Lahore, Sialkot, Ferozpur, Gurdaspur, Hoshiarpur and Ludhiana.[17] The leading newspapers were, moreover, being gagged one after another.[18] The confiscation of the securities of newspapers and the infliction of severe punishments on them, and the prohibition of public meetings at a time like that created strong reactions.[19]

The Punjab Government had, it seems, once against started on a policy of repression, much against the expectation of ever right thinking men in the province. As stated earlier, the Press Act had been freely made use of but the Defence of India Act and the Seditious Meetings Act had also been called to its aid by the bureaucracy.[20] Moreover, the administration of the Punjab was Unsympathetic in its attitude towards the peasants' demands.[21] Not only this, the Government committed all sort of illegalities under Section 144 of the Criminal Procedure Code in order to crush the non-co-operation movement.[22]

On the other hand, the Government issued a statement and promised to help the small agriculturists and other affected

16. *The Zamindar,* Lahore, October 28, 1928 (The early way to check the non-co-operation movement was repression) Vide *The Tribune,* Lahore, November 27, 1920.
17. *The Tribune,* Lahore, December 23, 1920 (What makes this Act of repression all the more regrettable was the fact that it was calculated to do more regrettable was the fact that it was calculated to do more harm already existed among the people.......The effect of injuring the bulk of population, of course, innocent and law abiding, for the same of a few could not but give a fresh cause of complaint and legitimate grievance to those who had none. In fact, while extending the operation of this Act for more period the Punjab Government had done no less injury to itself than to the people). Vide. *The Partap,* June 8, 1921; and December 17, 1920; *Bande Matram,* December 15, 1920; and June 2, 1921; *The Siyasat,* Lahore, December 16, 1920; *The Vakil,* Amritsar, December 18, 1920; Home Department, File No. 922/1922-Political.
18. *Bande Matram,* December 15, 1920; April 22, 1921; *The Pratap,* April 24, 1920; June 6, 1921.
19. *Paisa Akhbar,* Lahore, November 14, 1920; *The Tribune,* Lahore, April 7 and 27, 1921; June 10, 1921.

people, so that they should not be exploited by the various political factions for their political purposes The statement issued by the Government was, however, bold but said nothing with reference to the then economic situation beyond a categorical denial on the question of export.[23] The Communique did not contain a word of sympathy for the suffering people or encouragement in the way of promise to investigate the cases responsible for the high prices and afford relief to those who had been hit by the drought.[24] No effort was made in official departments to study the rates of grain. The Government seemed to possess less information than even the public.[25] The same was the case in matters like famine, rising prices etc. which concerned the peasantry particularly.

The Government was not even prepared to accept the suggestion that it be prepared to fix an average minimum price and to sell the colony lands to deserving persons approved by the Government.[26] Besides the Government confiscated *jagirs* from those who took part in the civil dis-obedience and non-co-operation movement. When it was asked to supply the names of such persons the Government was not prepared to give the names. Whether those persons even committed violence, the reply was negative, but the authorities conveyed that the condition of good conduct and loyalty attached to

20. *The Liberal,* Lahore, December 19, 1920, *The Zamindar,* Lahore, May 3, 1921; *The Punch,* May 4, 1921; *The Vakil,* May 28, 1921; *The Siyasat,* May 29, 1921.

21. Home Department, File No. Pros. April, 1920-21-Deposit-Political; File No. 94-97, April-1920-Political; *The Kesari,* May 6, 1921; *The Pratap,* May 20, 1920; *The Swaraj,* May 29, 1921; *The Gazette,* May 18, 1920.

22. *The Zamindar,* Lahore, March 8, 1921; Home Department, File No. 74-108, 1920-Political, NAI : New Delhi.

23. *The Tribune,* Lahore, August, 27, 1921.

24. *Ibid.*

25. *Ibid., The Siyasat,* Lahore, October 29, 1921.

26. P.L.C.D. Vol. VIII-Part-B, 1925, 325.

these grants was violated.[27] Moreover, to meet the possibility of the adoption of civil disobedience in an intensive form in particular districts or parts of districts in the Punjab, the Government was drawing up a scheme for strengthening of the civil and police staff in the threatened tracts. Order regarding the action to be taken in the event of an incitement to withhold Government dues and taxes were issued from time to time.[28]

At the same time it was decided to throw a wide net and a list of persons was prepared from reports, etc., who were suspected of being in touch with the *Babbars* if not actually active members of the gangs. Simultaneous raids were made in 39 villages on April 22, 1923 and 71 persons were arrested.[29] Where-ever black-turbaned Sikhs were found by policemen, they were attacked. Even shopkeepers of Rajah Sansi, while sitting on their shops, were dragged out and beaten for no other fault than waring black turban.[30] The police did not spare even respectable men like Sardar Sunder Singh Ramgarhia, Sardar Tara Singh, Jaidev Singh, Shiv Dev Singh, Takhat Singh and many more members of the Khalsa Diwan.[31] The press lamented that the Sikhs were being kicked down as if they were mere logs of wood and no human-beings.[32] Many Akalis lost consciousness and then they were lifted up, and hurled like a gunny bag of sand on the road side and in the drain. If any Akali regaining consciousness lifted his head, he was again kicked down.[33] However, it is to be noticed that the spirit of the Akalis did not appear to have been crushed in any way by the beating policemen. On the other hand, their enthusiasm

27. *Ibid.,* 336-37.
28. File No. 71-Sunder Singh Majithia Papers (Private Paper Section), NMML : New Delhi.
29. Home Department, File No. 1/10/1924-Political, NAI : New Delhi.
30. Home Department, File No. 914/II/1922-KW, NAI : New Delhi.
31. Home Department, File No. 914/II/1922-KW, NAI : New Delhi.
32. *Ibid., The Akali,* August 8, 1926; *The Milap,* August 20, 1926.
33. Home Department, File No. 914/II/1922-KW, NAI : New Delhi, *The Tribune,* Lahore, September 6, 1922; *The Nation,* August 24, 1926.

was distinctly on the increase.[34] The Government was hostile towards Akali agitation and Akali *Jathebandi* because the Akalis were not only supporting the demands of the peasants but were also in the forefront of the militant nationalist movement. The Government wanted to crush the Akali movement[35] and therefore, one of the objectives in the Government policy was to break up the *Jathebandi* system and never to allow it to be revived.[36] Besides, those who assisted the Government against Akali agitation and rendered other services had been granted *Jagirs* of the income of Rs. 500/-, Rs. 350/- and Rs. 250/- per month.[37]

Similarly, the Punjab Government had kept a very close watch on the activities of the *Naujawan Bharat Sabha* (hereafter NBS) since its very inception. The militant attitude of the *Sabha* and its fast rising popularity among the public was noticed by imperialist authorities.[38] The declaration of the NBS and allied bodies as unlawful associations, on 3rd May 1930 and the simultaneous application of the Seditious Meetings Act to Peshawar district, finally put an end to this revolutionary association, and all its objectives.[39] Thus the Punjab Government had decided to curb all the militant associations which struggled for liberation of the country.

34. *The Akali,* March, 1926; *Akali-te-Pardesi,* March 4, 1926 (For more details regarding the British policy towards Akalis who were actively supporting the demands and agitations of the peasants, also see *The Pratap,* Amritsar, August 4, 1926; *The Babbar-Sher,* March 5, 1926; July 26, 1926; *The Qaumi-Dard,* Amritsar, March 5, 1926; *The Zamindar,* Lahore, March 5, 21st, 1926; *The People,* Lahore, March 7, 1926; *The Hindustani,* Lahore, March, *The Desh Sewak,* Jullundur, March 11, 29, 1926; *The Muslim Outlook,* Lahore, June 11, 1926; *Akali-Te-Pardesi,* September 6, 1926; *The Bhisham,* Lahore, March 19, 1926; *The Tribune,* Lahore, August 19, 1926.

35. Prime Minister's Office, File No. 595, Basta No. 20, Case No. 485 of 1929, PSA : Patiala.

36. File No. 66-Sunder Singh Majithia Papers, NMML : New Delhi.

37. Sadhu Singh Kakka, Choudhary Ghulam Mohammad, Dewa Singh were some of the loyalists. Vide P.L.C.D., Vol. X-B, 1927, 743.

38. Home Deptt., File No. 13 & KW-Political-1930, NAI : New Delhi.

39. Home Deptt., File No. 464/1930-Political, NAI : New Delhi.

As stated earlier, the printing presses had been so much terrorised by the Punjab police that no press at Lahore was prepared to print the *'Kirti Kisan'*, the only socialist weekly in the province, though its editor Giani Mubarak Singh, a member of the National Executive of the All India Congress Socialist Party had already deposited Rs. 1000/- as security for this paper on the demand of the Punjab Government.[40] Similarly, in 1920, the Government had directed that a sum of Rs. 1000/- deposited by the keeper of the Peoples' Press, Lahore, at which the Akali newspaper was published, be forfeited together with all the copies of the issues of the *Akali* dated 7th, 8th, 9th and 10th October, 1920.[41] With it many other papers were banned. The police also searched out the offices of the Universal Advertising Co., National Press and *'Desh Sewa'* newspaper. The police took with them the ledgers and files of *'Kirti'* magazine.

The office of the *'Kirti'* newspaper was searched out and the work of the Akali newspaper was set at naught. The employers were not permitted to go in or come out. The house of Sohan Singh Josh was also searched and he was arrested.[42] The house of S. Balwant Singh manager of *'Kirti'* magazine was searched. The police carried with it the ledger books, the chits of the customers and many other papers.[43] The house of Dr. Hari Singh of Chakwal was also searched out and the police took many papers concerning the youth movement, labour movement and Revolution in Russia. During the search made at the office of the *Kirti* magazine and the *Akali* newspaper, the library of the Akalis was also searched out and various papers were taken into custody. All the persons,

40. File No. 41, 1936-37-AICC (Private Papers Section) NMML : New Delhi.
41. Home Deptt., File No. 319-20/1920-Political, NAI : New Delhi.
42. Home Department, File No. 18/6/1933-Political, NAI : New Delhi.
43. File No. RP-39-Institution, 1-3 (Private Paper Section), NMML : New Delhi.
44. For details see Home Department, File No. 137/1930-Political, Appendix-I, to notes, 1-10; P.L.C.D.,Vol. XIV, 1929.

arrested in this connection under Rule 121-A had been taken to Meerut and were treated like ordinary prisoners.[44]

If the voice of the people could be silenced, the Lieutenant Governor Sir Fransis O'Dwyer said in October, 1918, that the people would once again be peaceful and loyal. After a lot of search, the regulation 3 of the Act 1818 was invoked to imprison without trial anybody suspected of revolutionary activties.[45] On November 1, 1918, a bill to ban anti Government meetings was introduced and regarding this the Viceroy said, "we can not forget that in Lahore, Englishmen were harassed without any provocation and there were riots in Rawalpindi and many other places, we cannot close our eyes to the fact that the Governor had taken a serious view of the matter." Hence, in the name of prestige and in order to tech a lesson to the people of this province in particular and this country in general for having shown a spirit of revolt, the Government resorted to drastic measures of repression.

After studying the Government policy towards the disturbances in the province, let us now discuss some facts and figures of far as the Government's attitude towards the *Kisan* agitation and the activities of the left group *i.e.*, the Communists in the province, is concerned.

The attempt of the *Kirti Kisan Sabha* workers to influence the various *Zamindara Sabhas* and the unite them into a single body was considered by the Government to be very dangerous.[46] English imperialist, thirsty for the blood of Indians, with the help of *Rajas, Nawabs, Jagirdars* big *Zamindars,* moneylenders and big traders were making every possible effort to suppress the ever-increasing struggle of the labourers and peasants for bread, land and independence.[47]

45. Sedition Committee Report : 1918, 141; The Tribune, Lahore, March 31, 1929; File No. R-III/2/3-Institution (Private Papers Section), NMML : New Delhi.

46. Home Department, File No. 18/7/1931-Political; Williamson, *The India and Communism,* 1935, 276-77.

47. Rasul, M.A., *History of the All India Kisan Sabha,* Calcutta : 1974,

(Contd.)

So far as the repressive measures of the Government were concerned, it was alleged by the leadership of the *Kisan* Party that prohibition of meetings, *Lathi* charges, firing, detention without trial, orders of internment and externment, collective fines on whole villages, humiliating restrictions on the press and other forms of repression had become a normal feature. Even Committee meetings and closed-door meetings were not allowed in many places.[48] The reign of repression was established by the Punjab Government in their attempt to put down legitimate *Kisan* agitation. It also prohibited *Kisans* from entering into their own lands and forced them to pay unjust taxes imposed by the *Zamindars*.[49] A large number of *Kisans* and *Kisan* Comrades were arrested. *Kisan* Conferences were banned. It, promulgated Section 144 of the Criminal procedure Code and confined a large number of *Kisan* within their villages. However, the *Kisan Sabhas* carried on their organisational and propaganda activities undauntedly despite the threat of repression and reprisal on the ground of disseminating class hatred and Sedition.[50]

The Government had decided to curtail the activities of some of the *Sabhas'* most prominent members; one was being prosecuted under Section 124-A, IPC and three had been restricted to their villages under the Punjab Criminal Law

100-04; Home Department, File No. 6/8/1936-Political, NAI : New Delhi (The British Government established by force and fraud in India, has arbitrarily divested the *Kisans* of their natural rights in land and signed these away to *Zamindars* and planters and made alien laws that subjected the peasants to the tyranny of *Zamindars* and *Sowkars.* It is with the aid of these agents and allies that the British Government has held in bondage and ruthlessly exploited the millions in the country for more than a century till they are driven to the last stage of poverty, ill health and misery that is unparallel in the annals of the world History) Vide. Home Department, File No. 7/4/1940-Political, NAI : New Delhi.

48. *Ibid.*
49. *Ibid.*
50. *Ibid.*

(Amendment Act) and forbidden to make speeches.[51] Similarly, about a dozen peasants were reported to have been arrested from various villages in the neighbourhood of Lahore for non-payment of land revenue.[52] In fact, if the call for the non-payment of land revenue was given, the Government would take stern steps and police might be required to realise the land revenue. Another important example of repression that may be cited here is that Comrade Tehl Singh, General Secretary of the District *Kisan* Committee, Lahore had been interned in his village Bhaugali because he was working among the peasants and organising them into *Kisan* Committees and Congress Committees. This was intolerable to the Unionist Government[54] and therefore this internment.

An order under Section 144 was imposed on 19th July, prohibiting any procession in the areas around the Government office. As a result of it, the members of the *bandobast* Committee and allied bodies decided to stage a big demonstration on this issue on July 19, 1938, in the civil lines outside the Canal and Settlement Offices.[55]

Another significant point in this connection worth noting is that the Government made use of the dual tactics of force and elemency. It released 70 persons but arrested almost all the important socialist leaders. Kartar Singh Gill, the Secretary of the P.K.C. was interned in his village for an unlimited period. Prominent leaders of the P.K.C. including *Baba* Inder Singh, Harnam Singh, Sohan Singh Bhakna, Karam Singh Dhut, Gopal

51. Home Department, File No. 18/6/1934-Political, NAI : New Delhi (One of the objects of the Bill (The Criminal Law Amendment Bill) was to check the growth of Communism in this country). Vide. P.L.C.D., Vol. XXVII, 1935, 1938-39.

52. File No. 41/1936-37, AICC (Private Papers Section) NMML : New Delhi.

53. *Ibid.*

54. It is to be noticed that the Unionist Government was fully backed by the British Bureaucracy. In fact, the Unionists were the representatives of the British Imperialism on one hand and spokesmen of the Landlord Class on the other.

55. Home Department, File No. 18/7/1938-Political, NAI : New Delhi.

Singh, Rattan Singh, Dalip Singh, Ram Singh, Jaswant Singh Kairon, Daya Singh and several others were arrested.[56] Almost all the *Jathas* were intercepted by the police and later on arrest of prominent agitators started in several villages.[57] As the war was approaching, the Government decided to take firm action against the volunteers in order to stop further misleading.[58] On June 11, the Government had issued a communique warning that firm action including the use of ordinary Criminal Law and Criminal Law Amendment Act would be taken against the organisers of *Kisan Satyagraha* in Lahore.[59] About 4000 persons were thrown behind bars.[60] Let it be remembered that the repressive policy of the Unionist Government of interning, externing and imprisoning of *Kisan* workers in the Punjab was severely condemned by the All India *Kisan Sabha*.[61]

As we have seen in the 3rd section of Chapter II, the peasants' movement was in full swing and had touched new heights. So the Government also became alert and most repressive towards this movement after 1935. The *Kisan Sabha* in the Punjab was ultimately banned.[62]

During the peasants' agitation in the Nill Bar region, the *Kisan* workers, after being released, became active with a new vigour against the exploitation of the peasants of that *illaqa*. However, the British Bureaucracy was not unware. It detained the *Kisan* leaders of other districts in their respective villages. The company owners too discarded the *Muzaras* who were associated with the *Kisan Sabha*. Only a few *Kisan* leaders such as Comrade Tikya Ram, Wadhawa Ram etc. were left

56. *Kirti Lehr,* Meerut, July 31, 1939.
57. Home Department, File No. 18/6/1939-Political, NAI : New Delhi.
58. Home Department, File Nos. 18/6/1939-Political, 18/7/1939-Political, NAI : New Delhi.
59. *The National Front,* June 11, 1939.
60. *Kirti Lehr,* Meerut, July 9, 1939.
61. *The National Front,* October 9, 1938.
62. *Ibid.,* August 27, 1939; Rasul, M.A., *History of the All India Kisan Sabha,* Calcutta : 1974, 106-108.

who were entrusted with the responsibility of reviving the disorganised, broken and crushed *Kisan* Oganisation and they continued their efforts in this regard even in 1942-45.[63]

Another instance of Government repression worth noting was that on 15th February, 1939, the people attacked a *Kisan* gathering at the village Sajam. The peaceful farmers were beaten so mercilessly that many of them got injured grievously and one peasant named Sati Ram was killed. In connection with his martyrdom, a huge *Kisan* gathering was held at Sajam which was attended by the Congress leaders and also by several *Kisan* workers which establishes repression.[64] Similarly, there were many encounters with the police and several political workers were injured and the Government again started making arrests. With this, the Government declared the following organisations in the Punjab as illegal and consequently their activities were banned :[65]

(a) The Anti-Imperialist League, Punjab, its Branches, Committees and Sub-Committees.

(b) The Punjab *Kisan* League.

(c) The Punjab *Kirti Kisan* Party, Amritsar, its branches, Committees and Sub-Committees.

(d) The Amritsar District *Kisan Sabha.*

(e) The Punjab Provincial NBS, Lahore, its Committees and Sub-Committees.

However, after the ban, individuals active in the above

63. Ram, Wadhawa, 'Some Memorials of Nili Bar-*Banne-Utt-Ado-Adh'*, Master Hari Singh, *'The Peasant Movement in the Punjab Before And After Independence'*, (published in Souvenir issued by the C.P.I. on January 26, 1976.)

64. Home Department, File Nos. 94/2/1940-*(i)*-Political; 7/4/1940-Political, NAI : New Delhi, Nurpuri, Chanan Singh, *The Great Morcha of Lahore and Harsha Chhina'*, published in the *Souvenir* issued by the CPI on January 26, 1976; Rasul, M.A., *History of the All India Kisan Sabha,* Calcutta : 1974, 100-02.

65. Roy, Subodh (ed.), *Communism in India* (unpublished Documents 1925-34, 1972, 198.

organisations sought to group themselves under banner of Punjab *Kisan Qarza* Committee, the first meeting of which was held at Amritsar on March 3, 1935. It held small village meetings at which speakers "combined agrarian agitation with Communist propaganda".

Let us now discuss the Punjab Government policy towards the Communist movement in the Punjab. A brief sketch of this party and its activities in connection with the peasants' agitation has been given in the first section of the 4th Chapter. The Government never tolerated the progress of this left group in the Punjab. Every attempt was made by the police to frustrate attempts to organise meetings in connection with May-Day Celebration in Lahore and Amritsar.[67] Moreover, the *Kirti Kisan* party office was raided on June, 22, 1932 and among other literature, the police seized copies of a cyclostyled *Urdu* pamphlet entitled, "The Programme of the CPI".[68] To put a halt to the ever-increasing influence of Communism, the Unionist Government organised *Zamindara* Conference in various district to convince the peasants that their ministry was a *Zamindara* Government working for their welfare and best interest.[69] Ultimately in July, 1934, the Government declared the CPI an unlawful organisation and banned it. However, the Communists, by forming a strong Central Committee, strengthened their position; They had proved that they were invincible.[70] Now, it had been active as an under-

66. Home Department, File No. 18/II/1935-Political; For further details also see File No. 18/3/1935-Political, NAI : New Delhi; *The Kirti,* December 22, 1935.

67. Home Department, File Nos. 18/5/1933-Political; 18/II/1934-Political, NAI : New Delhi.

68. William, H., *India and Communism*-1935, 270; Home Department, File No. 18/6/32-Political, NAI : New Delhi.

69. Home Department, File No. 18/9/1938-Political, NAI : New Delhi; Gopal, Madan, Sir Chhotu Ram : A Political Biography, Sterling : 1977, 116.

70. Rajeshwara Rao, C., 'The Decade After the Split : The Party Position and Programme, published in a *Souvenir* issued by the CPI on January 26, 1926.

ground organisation. Banning this party and the decision of the bureaucracy to detain its leaders without trial was considered a glagrant violation of elementary civil liberties of citizens and therefore, CPI leadership in particular as well as the other political factions strongly condemned them as such.[71]

It was this accepted policy of the Government to do all that was essential to counter the activities of the Communist International and it was considered to be important that when Moscow-trained Indians were found to be very actively engaged in the work for which they had been carefully trained by the Communist International, drastic action should be taken against them.[72]

In the course of three years from 1933 to 35, eight Moscow trained members of the *Ghadr* Group were intercepted and interrogated by the Punjab police. They were brutally tortured to extort information about the net-work of their party, training in Moscow and instructions which they had brought for their Indian Compatriots.[73] Till 1935, the police authorities were able to establish the identity of some 15 to 20 of the 40 trained Communist who had returned to India and were working at different places. The returned Communists included some of the more active members of the *Ghadr* party such as Teja Singh Swatantar, Gurmukh Singh, Prithvi Singh, Iqbal Singh, Harbans Singh Basi, Chanan Singh and Bhagat Singh Bilga.[74] But soon they were restricted to their respective

71. File No. 16-AICC (Private Papers Section) NMML : New Delhi.

72. Home Deptt., File No. 44/79/355-1935-Political, NAI : New Delhi.

73. William, H., *India and Communism*, 1935, 268-72; Nurpuri Chanan Singh, The Great *Morcha* of Lahore and Harsha Chhina, published in the *Souvenir*, issued by the CPI on January 26, 1976, Personal interview with Sohan Singh Josh on November 20, 1977, Ajoy Bhavan, New Delhi.

74. Home Department, File No. 44/79/355-1935-Political; William, H., *India and Communism*, 1935, 270 (Regulation III of 1818 was issued against Santa Singh, Dasaunda Singh, Gajjan Singh, Karam Singh, Harjap Singh, Gulam Mohammad, Abdul Waris, Teja Singh Swatantar and Wasdev Singh—they were considered Moscow trained Indian Communists).

villages under the Punjab Criminal Law (Amendment Act).

The Punjab Government Premier had already declared in July, 1938, his willing and unconditional help to the empire and refused to tolerate the embarrassment "being caused by the left wing of the Congress under the leadership of Kitchlew and Sardar Sohan Singh Josh".[75] To fulfil the promise, the Punjab Government issued a circular letter in September 1939, directing political workers to refrain from delivering seditious and particularly anti-recruitment, speeches.[76] The state authorities, with all their power, commanded, "that as a matter of policy outsiders should not be allowed to hold meetings in Patiala and the tenants' movement be dealt with a strong hand".[77] The Inspector General of Police, also, could not think beyond asking the Superintendents of Police" to collect information about the ringleaders" and contemplating action against them under the Defence of India Rule.[78] The S.P. Barnala, too contributed to the collective wisdom "so long as political parties continue to enter the state, there is not only the likelihood but surely of the tenants' movement assuming a very dangerous form".[79] Merely the Superintendent of Intelligence seemed to have grasped the significance of the various policy measures tried out in 1939, when the movement had first raised its head, and drawn the right conclusions. His own recommendations were very similar to the line of policy followed with great success in 1939—a policy that had combined conciliation at the level of the village between *Biswedars* and *Muzaras* with a wider policy of isolation and repression of political elements.[80] To facilitate this he recommended that a Board of three Gazetted Officials of the

75. Home Department, File No. 18/9/1939-Political, NAI : New Delhi.
76. *Ibid.*, (For further information also see File No. 18/5/1939-Political; Gopal, S., *Jawahar Lal Nehru : A Biography*, Vol. I, 1975, 210-13).
77. Patiala State Records, Prime Minister's office File No. 770.
78. Margin note by IGP on CID Secret Abstract of Intelligence, dated 17.6.1942, Patiala State Records, P.M. Office File No. 1573.
79. *Ibid.* (CID Secret Abstract of Intelligence, dated 27th Aug., 1942).
80. *Ibid.*, also File No. 1577.

Revenue, Judiciary and Police, one each, he set up and a reasonable strength of the Additional Police force placed at its disposal. He, too, emphasized that the tendency of the said Board should be towards effecting an amicable settlement between *Biswedars* and *Muzaras*; for if a *muzara* was rendered homeless,[81] and would naturally join a hostile agitation. Commenting on the prevailing sate of affairs, he lamented, "District authorities even are not using such tacts as are necessary for patching up the strained relations between the *Biswedars* and *Muzaras* except forcibly effecting *Batai* through police and revenue officials.[82] More cautiously, he criticised the "higher authorities" for not "adopting such measure as may suppress the *Muzara* movement". Finally he pleaded : "It is the crying need of the time that officials, exercising their influence, have the people satisfied in order to maintain law and order" and that "such a line is chalked lead a peaceful life". Needless to add, his appeal remained a cry in the wilderness, and the state authorities continued to stumble along its suicidal path.

In June, 1940, the Punjab Government resolved that the increasing subversive activities of the Communists directed towards disturbing the internal peace of the province and interfering with the efficient prosecution of the war had necessitated the issue of orders under Rule 26 of the Defence of India Rules for the detention of 84 of the more dangerous Communists including five members of the provincial Legislative Assembly. Of these 84 persons, as many as 40 were trained in the Communist's School of Moscow. All had as their common object, the overthrow of the present structure of Government by an armed mass insurrection and the establishment of some form of social rule through a National Democratic Revolution. Their methods had included vigorous

81. This is obviously a reference to those *Muzaras* who had to flee their villages and home to escape the atrocities of the police. Vide. Extract from CID Secret Abstract of Intelligence dated 19.6.1942 under the heading 'Muzara Movement', Patiala State Records, P.M's Office File No. 1573.

82. *Ibid.*

anti-war and anti-recruitment propaganda and attempts to tamper with the loyalty of the Army.[83] In June and July, 1940, over 40 Communists and Socialists from all over the province were arrested under D.I.R. These included Sohan Singh Josh and Master Kabul Singh who were also the members of the Provincial Congress Committee.[84]

It was alleged by Sir Sikander Hyat that the Communists alone were criminals whom the Government wanted to crush. He also described the arrested persons as "fifth columnists" who had no relation with the Congress. Sir Hyat quoted from the Communists' publications and recounted the life sketches of the arrested leaders to prove that they were agents of Russia and were trying to get the Russians to invade India.[85] On 13th December, 1940, three other prominent Communists—Karam Singh Mann, Harkrishan, Singh Surjit and Nawabzada Mahmud Ali—were arrested. In fact, their arrest was a severe blow to the left activities in the Punjab. It is significant to state that the only 'Crime' of the Communists was that they had been working for the freedom of the country even before the Russian Revolution.[86] Mian Iftikharuddin was arrested in the first half of November, 1940. The arrests against anti-recruitment, anti-war propaganda and refusal to pay land revenue, continued. In the later half of December 1940, orders were received from Gandhi to suspend *Satyagrah* in the Punjab.[87] However, before the Civil-Disobedience could be suspended, a number of leading political figures including Pt. Neki Ram Sharma, Mrs, Duni Chand, Master Nand Lal, Mangal Singh, M.L.A., Dev Raj Sethi, M.L.A. and Raghbir Kaur M.L.A. were arrested. Arrests of Political activists continued throughout the year 1941. Till the first half of May, 1941, 1879 Political workers had already been convicted for anti-war and

83. Home Department, File No. 18/6/1940-Political, NAI : New Delhi.

84. *The Communists,* August, 1940.

85. *Ibid.*

86. *Ibid.*

87. Home Department, File No. 18/2/1940-Political, NAI : New Delhi.

political propaganda.[88] 'May Day' was celebrated by the Communists and Socialists. When the Government could not curb the left movement absolutely, it decided to release 8 of the leading communist leaders of the province, on May, 1, 1942, because of a visible increase in the volume of pro-war propaganda.[89] However, the process of arrests continued. In the early months of 1942, 31 leaders were originally arrested and one more was subsequently added. S.A. Dange, Philip Spratt, M.A. Majid, P.C. Joshi, Sohan Singh Josh and Kedar Nath Sehgal figured prominently.[90]

The Punjab Government felt strongly that, if inspite of the long term dangers of the leftists' movement the second choice was to be adopted, it should be made abundantly clear to the CPI and its leadership in all provinces that any attempt to undermine orderly Government or to disturb the efficient administration or peace and tranquility of any province would inevitably necessiate action against them under the law of the land or the Defence of India Rule.[91] With this, the Punjab Government imposed the condition of security and also stopped publication of *Jang-i-Azadi,* a Communist paper.[92] Meanwhile, the Punjab Government made it clear that it was an essential part of its policy that the Communists should be punished like any one else if they violated or broke the law. The authorities believed that the Communists well understood this position and the Government doubted whether warnings would have much effect. Consequently, when some representatives of the Communists Party approached the Government for a number of concessions under the recent Paper Control Order in view of the tone of the *'Peoples' War'* and the objectionable nature of much of the propaganda indulged in by the Communist and other organs of the party, the bureaucracy decided that their request should be refused.

88. Home Department, File No. 18/5/1941-Political, NAI : New Delhi.
89. Home Department, File No. 18/5/1942-Political, NAI : New Delhi.
90. *Ibid.*
91. Home Department, File No. 7/5/1944-Political, NAI : New Delhi.
92. *Ibid.*

The result, it was expected, would probably be to put them in considerable difficulty about paper supply and this might lead to an improvement in the tone of their propaganda.[93]

As stated earlier, during 1945 to 1947, the Punjab *Kisan Sabha* fought many small tenant struggles much as *'Half-Batai'* agitation of Montgomery tenants, the agrarian agitation in Mamdot estates, agitation of Una (Kangra) tenants, agitation of Patiala occupancy tenants and local tenant agitations in Ferozpur district.[94] To meet this fresh challenge, the Unionist Government had established punitive police *Chowkis* (posts) in villages which were considered to be strong holds of nationalism. In the district of Hoshiarpur, these were 60 to 65 such police posts, in Ferozpur 22, and in Ludhiana and Gurdaspur 10 each.[95] Similarly during the course of the Harsha Chhina Canal *Morcha*, blank signed warrants were taken by the police who went in search of *Kisan* leaders. They organised raids in the villages, beat up people and even abused the peasant women. The police also attacked the property of Communist leaders. Often clashes occurred between the *Kisans* and the Police. In all, about one thousand volunteers courted arrest in this struggle.[96]

In the end, let it be admitted that the British bureaucracy from time to time, granted many concessions to the peasantry just to pacify them. For instance, in 1939, it decided to split up some of the colony lands to be auctioned for temporary cultivation, into small plots to suit lessees of slender means. But the *Kisan* Committee could see through the Government plan of diverting the attention of the tenants and tried to

93. *Ibid.*

94. Mehta, Deva Singh, 'Tenant Struggles in Ferozpur District' (unpublished manuscript) in the possession of the author, who was the Secretary of the district *Kisan Sabha* in 1946.

95. *Peoples' War,* Vol. III, No. 42, April 15, 1945.

96. *Peoples' Age,* Vol. V, No. 3, July 21, 1946; Vol. V, No. 6, August 11, 1946; Vol. V, No. 7, August 18, 1946; Vol. V, No. 8, August 25, 1946; (For more details also see Nurpuri, Chanan Singh, *"Memoirs of Famous Struggles", Nawan Zamana* (Panjabi), December 26, 1975); File No. 16-AICC (Private Papers Section), NMML, New Delhi.

dissuade the small tenants from submitting tenders.[97] Another significant point worth noting is that the repressive policy of the Government that followed the agitation in the Punjab gave rise to revolutionary activities in the province.

As pointed out earlier, during the course of the peasants' struggle in the Punjab, the Punjab Government which was following the policy of stick and carrot, now began to realise that it should have pursued a policy of sympathy which constituted the right remedy for unrest and dissatisfaction; and that if it continued to pursue repressive policy, unrest and discontent would go on increasing which would prove more injurious for both the Government and the country. In brief, when the Government failed to suppress the agrarian unrest as well as the agrarian movement through its repressive policy, it decided to follow the policy of carrying out reforms in various fields in order to pacify the resented peasantry in particular and the rural masses in general.

In the next section our aim will be to point out the response of the Government to the peasants' grievances by way the repressive policy described hitherto.

The Government in Punjab was faced with the dilemma as the need to respond to peasants' Socio-economic grievances in a positive way on the one hand, and, on the other hand, the obvious political disadvantage of alienating the upper strata of rural society whose exploitative role gave rise to peasants' grievances. The Governmental policy was a compromise between these two opposite poles, a compromise that took the form of repression of peasant unrest on the one hand and amelianative reformism on the other. Of course, the later policy touched upon somewhat marginal issues, leaving the essential mechanism of exploitation untouched (there we shall discuss only British Punjab since the character of state policy

97. Home Department, File No. 18/2/1939-Political, NAI : New Delhi; Master Hari Singh, The Peasants' Movement in the Punjab Before and After Independence, published in a Souvenir, issued by the CPI, January 26, 1976; Nurpuri, Chanan Singh, The Great Morcha of Lahore & Harsha Chhina, published in the *Souvenir,* issued by CPI, January 26, 1976.

in the East Punjab States has already been described in Chapter III above).

The period before the Unionist Ministry took over, the Government did not initiate much activity in the direction of 'rural reform'. However, the little that was done by way of reform, the references to this have been made in this Chapter frequently, did not satisfy agrieved peasantry, nor could it calm their agitation. With the formation of the Unionist Government in March 1937 there began series of ameliorative rural upliftment measures in the fields of education, cottage industries, health, public welfare etc.

In the area of public works development the Government initiated a road building programme that fundamentally affected the Marketing of agricultural commodities. The road system in Punjab, as the Royal Commission on Agriculture of 1931 had noted, was one of the best among the provinces, then enabling the agriculturists to reach local *mandis* and market towns. This was, of course, an advantage chiefly for the risk peasantry marketing crops on a larger scale.

Quite an important effort in the field of social-welfare, especially for bettering the lot of the rural backward areas, was the improvement in the means of communication like roads and railways. The views of the party were expressed by a number of the members of the Unionist Party who held the opinion that communication led directly towards the prosperity of the province as a whole. The Unionist claimed that roads benefited the *Zamindars* who got better price for their produce, they benefited the purchasers who could get the goods from the market at cheaper rates and they also helped the people who had to go about for every kind of

98. P.L.C.D., Vol. VIII, 7.5.1925, 1088; Vol. XXIII, 13.3.1933, 399, 1018-19 (Maine, Baden Powell and R.K. Mukherjee expressing similar views, noted that in times of scarcity and famines, lack of roads etc. prevented the carrying of Corn from surplus areas to those of scarcity; Vide. Maine, H.S., *Village Communities in the East and West,* London : 1976, 125-26; Mukherjee, R.K., *The Foundation of Indian Economics,* London : 1916, 3-5; Baden and Powell, B.N., *The Origin and Growth of the Village Communities in India,* New York : 1908, 9-10.

business.[98] It may also be noted that the development of link lines was desirable from another angle too *i.e.* for supplying immediate relief to the famine hit areas.

The first step in this direction was taken by the Government when it provided a sum of Rs. 5 lacs for the development of roads in 1925.[99] Quite a significant result of its efforts in this sphere was that the Government in 1926-27 took over on itself the responsibility of the construction of new roads and where-ever necessary the maintenance of the existing ones.[100] Government also approved construction of the Rohtak-Hansi, Bhiwani-Hansi-Hissar and Hansi-Hissar-Fatehabad-Pak-Pattan-Montgomary roads, and took over the responsibility of maintaining Panipat-Gohana-Rohtak and Jhajjar-Rewari roads.[101] Still another equally important step was to impress upon the Government of India the need of laying Rohtak-Gohana-Panipat and Rohtak-Bhiwani Railway tracks and to contact Jhajjar district by a few railway links.[102] As a result, Government of India sanctioned the above mentioned three schemes in 1927.[103]

Let us now turn to the efforts made by the Government in the field of education for the people of the province, especially the agriculturists, who were comparatively far less literate than the urban people.[104] Let it be clear that the

99. P.L.C.D., Vol. VII, 7.5.1925, 1088.

100. *Jat Gazette,* 15.6.1927, 4.

101. *Ibid.*

102. *Ibid.,* 10.8.1927, 4; See Railway Department Year 1927, File No. P-September-688, 20-79—Part-A, P-June, 1928-33-1233—P-1-2-Part-B; Year 1929, P. Dec.-P-681-R-28, 27-Part-B; *Punjab Government Gazette,* Part-I (General), 13.1.1927, 475-76.

103. (Rohtak-Gohana and Panipat Railway link was completed in 1928) Vide. *Jat Gazette,* 15.6.1927, 4; 4.6.1941, 3; P.L.C.D., Vol. VII, 18.11.1927, 3-6; Bargue, A.M. (ed.), *Eminent Sikhs of Today,* Vol. I, Lahore : 1942.

104. P.L.C.D., Vol. X, 24.10.1939, 63; *Punjab Government Report of the Compulsory Education Committee,* 1930, 4; *Punjab Government : Land of Five Rivers,* 2-6; *Proceeding of the Department of Education : Government of India,* Nos. 1-2A, October, 1917.

increasing indebtedness was the result of the policy which had been followed by the Government in the past in neglecting the education of the rural masses. So with a view to spreading education among the backward rural masses, the Government in the Punjab based its efforts on the following principles :

(a) While pointing out the shortage of educational institutions in the rural areas, the leadership of the various political factions impressed upon the Government the need to open more institutions in these areas and further asked that their number should be commensurate with the contribution made by the rural people to the state exchequer;[106]

(b) In professional Colleges, seats should be reserved for the agriculturists, proportionate either to their population or the revenue they paid;[107]

(c) The agriculturists class should be given representation on the management, staff and in the allocation of scholarships in private educational institutions;[108] and

(d) No reduction should be made in educational expenditure by the Government even during financial emergencies.[109]

From the above principles, it is obvious that the various political groups, particularly the Unionists desired the Government to provide maximum facilities for the education of the backward areas. Not only this, they wanted the rural masses to make the best use of the existing educational institutions. Even during the non-co-operation movement, in the teeth of the Congress policy, the Unionist Party urged the

105. P.L.C.D., Vol. XXIV, 26.10.1934, 333.

106. *Jat Gazette,* 24.4.1927, 13; 16.4.1928, 4.

107. *Ibid.*

108. *Ibid.*

109. In 1931, Chhotu Ram Condemned the retrenchment in the Provincial budget for education by Rs. 8 lakhs as against the meagre reduction in the Public Works Department of Rs. 9 lakhs. Vide. P.L.C.D., Vol. XVIII, 7.3.1931, 406.

people not to boycott the Government institutions.[110] Thus we may conclude that the Government followed the policy of the promotion of education not because it wanted to educate the peasants in particular and the others in general but its aim was to win over the support and sympathies of the Unionists who represented the upper section of the agriculturist class. Hence they could succeed in creating a permanent gulf between the upper and the lower classes of the agriculturists. However, their immediate purpose was to appease the agriculturists so that the agrarian unrest and agrarian movement could be pacified and finally averted. Let it be noted that on the instance of the Unionist leadership and others the resolution for the boycott of Government schools was passed.[111] Of course, it was a contradiction of their own policy but they did so just to secure sound footing for themselves in the rural areas, where many other political groups were becoming popular among the peasants as well as the common people.

Shortly after, the ruling party brought forth some important proposals in 1923, with a view to improving the existing state of education in the Punjab. It proposed to set up primary and middle schools in rural areas, high schools in towns and one intermediate college in each district.[112] It also decided to open rural libraries instead of spending a huge amount on the Public Library, Lahore which had already become a costly affair. Hence, about 2 thousand libraries and

110. For more details see *Jat Gazette,* 23.6.1930, 5; 18.8.1920, 3; 8.9.1920, 3; 29.9.1920, 3; 20.10.1920, 9.

111. India in 1921-22, 41.

112. The aim of opening intermediate colleges was to provide equal educational opportunities for the inhabitants of the Urban and Rural areas.......Students from rural areas will pass their inter-examination with greater ease at smaller expense, and shall enter into these colleges where standard for admission had been fixed at intermediate pass. Vide P.L.C.D., Vol. X, 7.3.1925, 141; Vol. XV, 7.3.1930, 330-31; *Jat Gazette,* 15.6.1927, 4 (By 1926, Punjab had the largest number of intermediate colleges in the country) Vide, Hussain, A., *Fazli-Hussain : A Political Biography,* Bombay : 1946, 134.

a number of night schools for adults were opened during 1924-26.[113]

Another significant step taken in this field was that in 1924, a resolution was passed by the various professional and technical institutions, such as Medical College, Lahore, Agricultural College, Lyallpur and Centre Training College, Lahore[114] and laid down that special concessions should be given to the sons of the agriculturists in admission to these colleges.[115] This too happened when the Government issued instructions to these institutions.

During 1924-25, the efforts of the Unionist Ministry resulted in an enormous increase in admission of students from agriculturists families to the Centre Training College, Lahore. To cite the figures, in B.T. class in 1924, 'agriculturist' students formed 20% of the total strength, which rose to 60% in 1925 and 75% in 1926.[116] Still another effort of the then Government for promoting the education of the agriculturists was to urge the Government in 1927 to grant the concession of half fee to agriculturists in two most backward and poorest districts in the South-east Punjab, two in the West Punjab, one in the Central Punjab and one in the North-West Punjab.[117] A little later, Sir Manohar Lal, took up the proposal with a view to examining the possibilities of giving concession in school fees to all the agriculturists not only in the above mentioned districts but all over the province.[118] This objective was finally realised under the Unionist Government after 1937, when self

113. Report of the Education Department cited in P.L.C.D., Vol. XX-A, 17.3.1926, 817-18, 824, 826-28; Hussain, A., *Fazl-i-Hussain : A Political Biography,* Bombay : 1946, 134; *Jat Gazette,* 15.6.1927, 4.

114. *Punjab Administration Report,* 1920-21, 137 (United October, 1920. This school was at Lahore, when it was shifted to Amritsar).

115. P.L.C.D., Vol. VII, 5.8.1924, 106, Trevaskis, H.K., *The Punjab of Today* : 1931, 228 (This institution was set up at Lahore in 1881 to train the teachers for Secondary Schools, afterwards, it gave educational training to the degree teachers).

116. P.L.C.D., Vol. X, 23.11.1927, 1269.

117. *Ibid.*

118. *Ibid.*

fee concession was granted to all the students from agriculturist families. When Sir Manohar Lal (Non-Unionist Minister for Education) was rather indifferent to the cause of education, he was criticised for his educational policy.[119] Even in the Unionist Government, the education policy of Sir Firoz Khan Noon, the Unionist Minister, was attacked on the ground that he had curtailed the grants of the schools run by the local bodies and private management etc.[120]

The over all result of the Punjab Government while pursuing the educational policy discussed so far is notable. For instance, expenditure on education in the province rose from Rs. 6.76 lacs in 1920-21 to Rs. 11.5 lacs in 1925-26 and Rs. 154.19 lacs in 1936-37. In 1944-45, Rs. 201-69 lacs were provided for the development of education.[121] This excludes additional expenditure on the education of Europeans and Anglo-Indians, and on Industrial education. To cite the figures, while there were 156 primary schools in the rural areas in 1923-24, under the primary compulsory Education Scheme, their number rose to 2947 in 1938-39; the numbr of Middle Schools and High Schools rose from 363 and 161 respectively in 1917-18[122] to 3309 and 406 respectively in 1938-39,[123] while in 1923-24 there were only 5 intermediate colleges,[124] in 1938-39, there were as many as 38 degree colleges in the Punjab.[125] In the file of female education, the success was revealing : in 1938-39, 165599

119. P.L.C.D., Vol. X, 23.11.1927, Infra Appendix; XVII, Vol. XV, 20.3.1930, 760.

120. As a result of this curtailment, many local bodies had to close their schools *e.g.* District Boards, Rohtak, on not receiving any grant-in-aid from the Government, had to stop annual increments of its teachers and closed many schools. Vide P.L.C.D., Vol. XXV, 26.6.1934, 45; Vol. XXVI, 1935, 173-74.

121. Punjab Budget with detailed estimates for 1920-21 to 1944-45.

122. *Annual Reports on the Progress of Education in the Punjab* : 1918-19, 20.

123. *Ibid.*, 1938-39, 2-3; P.L.C.D., Vol. XXIII, 27.7.1933, 1071.

124. *Punjab Administration Report,* 1923-24, 106.

125. *Annual Report on the Progress of Education in the Punjab* : 1938-39, 2.

and 12558 were attending primary and high classes.[126] As regards University education for women, their number rose from 161[127] in 1929-30 to 564 in 1938-39.[128]

After setting the educational machinery in order, the Government took another radical step for the social upliftment of the rural masses (Particularly peasantry) by providing sanitation, drinking water, medical and other facilities. It is important to note that in 1924, the Government neglect these essential amenities to the rural areas. The Government was merely spending 10.3% of the funds allocated for the purpose for rural development,[129] and the remaining part was spent in Urban areas. Although it was an uphill task to get this unjustice undone, the Government raised the share of rural areas to 15.7% in 1925-26, 26.4% in 1926-27[130] and 53.2% in 1927-28.[131] It is further notable that such a high allocation for rural health was perhaps never made again till 1933-34.[132]

With these enhanced funds for rural health, the Government made quite a large number of achievement during 1924-26. To cite a few examples, wells, for providing drinking water to the local populations, were sunk at a depth of 300-400 feet at Jahazgarh, Salhawas and Mianwali and some more places.[133] Similarly, schemes casting several lakhs of rupees

126. *Ibid.*, 2-3.

127. *Ibid.*, 1929-30, 2-3.

128. *Ibid.*, 1938-39, 2-3.

129. P.L.C.D. Vol. VI, 13.3.1924, 565.

130. *Ibid.*

131. P.L.A.D., Vol. X, 15.3.1927, 165.

132. It raised expenditure on rural health to an amazing figure of about five times in 1926-27 to that of 1919-20. Vide *Jat-Gazette*, 20.4.1927, 3; P.L.C.D., Vol. VI, 1924, 565; Vol. XXVI, 25.2.1935, 97; For details about Public Welfare Works in the rural areas in various fields, also see P.L.A.D., Vol. I, 13.7.1939, 1440; Punjab Budgets with detailed estimate for 1936-37 to 1944-45; *Punjab Government Gazette* (Extra Ordinary) 2.5.1940, 257; *Mitra's Annual Register*, 1941, 266; Shastri, R.S., *Chaudhari Chhotu Ram : Jivan Charitra* (Hindi), Rohtak, 1965, 628; P.L.C.D., Vol. VIII, 7.2.1925, 1088; Vol. XXIII, 13.3.1933, 359, 1016-19.

133. *Jat Gazette*, 15.6.1927, 4.

were also drafted for Gohana, Rohtak, Pehwa and Thaneswar.[134] During 1937-41, it took another step by inaugurating the scheme of tube-wells; one tube-well was sunk at Mianwali and two in Rohtak district suppling drinking water.[135] Another noticeable accomplishment of the Government during the period 1924-26 was that a large number of dispensaries both for human beings and animals were established. It was claimed by the Government that atleast one dispensary for human beings and another for animals was available to the inhabitants of every village within a radius of 5 miles.[136]

The Unionist leaders were justified in opposing the setting up of the Department of rural construction, because the funds provided for it were meagre. These meagre funds could be utilised in the best interest of the rural areas by distributing them among the beneficent departments like education and public health.

During 1937-44, the Unionist Party's Government considerably expanded its public health activities as vouchsafed by the fact that the budgetary provisions for this purpose, which stood at 10.83 lakh rupees in 1936-37 were speedily raised every year and stood at 36.06 lakh rupees in 1944-45.[137] With a view to protecting the public health, the Government got enacted the Vegetable Colouring Act in 1940.[138]

The Punjab Government made a provision of equal facilities and opportunities for the backward classes, whether rural or urban.[139] The Unionist Party was pledged to get them

134. *Ibid.*

135. P.L.A.D., Vol. I, 13.7.1939, 1440.

136. *Jat Gazette,* 15.6.1927, 4-5.

137. See Punjab Budgets with detailed estimates for 1936-37 to 1944-45.

138. *Punjab Government Gazette* (Extra-Ordinary), 2.5.1940, 257; *Mitra's Indian Annual Register,* Year-1941, 266; Shastri, Y., *Kashtri Jaton Ka Uthanopattan* (Hindi), Haridwar : 1956, 628.

139. P.L.A.D., Vol. XV, 24.1.1941, 270.

Government lands on easy terms of payment. To cite a few instances, after the first Great War, on its persuation the Government conferred about 20,000 *bighas* on the *Kamins* many of whom belonged to backward communities.[140] Again during 1924-26, it improved the lot of the higher category of scheduled castes by giving them proprietory rights of the Crown lands of Arya Nagar, district Multan and saved them from being evicted and also reserved another full *Chak* in Multan (Haveli Project).[141] Similarly during 1940-41, it got distributed among them nearly 3000 acres of crown land in the Punjab and another 1000 acres among the members of the criminal tribes, of whom 75% of the beneficiaries were again the scheduled castes.[142]

The most remarkable measures improving the working condition of the workers and labourers enacted by the members of the Unionist Party was the Trade Employee Act,[143] (which did not affect the agricultural profession). Another important step taken by the Punjab Government was during 1924-26, namely the enactment of the Opium (Punjab

140. *Jat Gazette,* 9.1.1946, 3.

141. *Ibid.*, Shastri, R.S., *Chaudhari Chhotu Ram : Jivan Charitra* (Hindi), Rohtak : 1965, 301-02.

142. P.L.A.D., Vol. XXII, 10.3.1944, 488-89.

143. P.L.A.D., Vol. XXIV, 19.2.1945, 2; *Mitra's Indian Annual Register :* Year 1941, 266; *Indian Year Book :* 1940-41, 527-30; P.L.A.D., Vol. XIII, 30.4.1940, 1237 (For more details about this Act also see *the Tribune* (Chandigarh, 13.7.1969), 4; Dutta, D., *Humayun Kabir—A Political Biography* (Bombay : 1969), 36; P.L.A.D., Vol. X, 24.10.1939, 66, 767-75; Vol. XXIV, 19.2.1945, 5. (Some of the important Provisions of this Act are as follow : Every employee should get 4 paid Holidays in the month; no employee could be compelled to work for more than 11 hours a day and 40 hours a week; no employee could be dismissed without having been given a month's notice before; all employees with one year's continuous service were entitled to 15 days leave with pay; all employees with 15 days continuous service was to get their salaries for the Holidays; in the establishments covered by this Act, Children below the age of 14 could not be employed, etc.).

Amendment) and the Punjab Excise (Amendment) Act.[144] By virtue of these Acts, for both the offences against Opium and Excise Acts, fine was raised from one thousand rupees to two thousand rupees and the term of imprisonment was enhanced from six months to one year.[145] It is a point to note that this was part of the programme of reducing consumption of liquor as a social evil, inspite of the fact that the Government might lose quite a handsome portion of Rs. 1.30 crores, which it was receiving in the shape of Excise duty on liquors.[146] One of the results of these steps was that by 1927, the consumption of liquor was reduced to a great extent; secondly, the number of country liquor shops declined from 1250 in 1901-02 to 741 in 1938-39.[147] Again, the Unionist were prominent in supporting the Punjab Suppression of Immoral Traffic Bill of 1935 presented by a non-Unionist member, Nanak Chand.[148] In 1939, this party too supported the prevention of extravagant Dowries Bill, introduced by a Congressite Munshi Hari Lal,[149] To sum up, a wide range of social welfare measures were introduced or supported by the Punjab Government.

Though the Unionist Party Government faced tough opposition from different quarters, such as, from the non-

144. *Punjab Government Gazette,* Part-II, 12.2.1926, 75; P.L.C.D., Vol. VIII, 5.3.1925, 311-13, 316-17; Vol. VII, 12.11.1924, 355.

145. *Ibid.*

146. Excise Duty was raised from Rs. 4 per gallon in 1908-09 to Rs. 6.56 in 1939. Vide *Punjab Administration Report :* 1908-09, 35; *Excise Administration Report :* 1938-39, 5; *Jat Gazette,* 25.5.1927, 12.

147. Rohtak and 4 other districts in Ambala Division, and other three districts with minimum consumption of liquor were Dera Gazi Khan, Muzaffar Nagar and Jhang. In the whole province consumption fell from 2.14 gallons per 100 persons in 1912 to 1.4 gallons per 100 persons in 1939. Vide. *Punjab Administration Report,* 1912-13, 5; 1938-39, 5; 1941-42, 5.

148. *Punjab Government Gazette* (Extra-Ordinary) ending 31st December, 1935, 77-80; P.L.C.D., Vol XXVI, 21.2.1935 and 22.2.1935, 44 and 80.

149. *Punjab Government Gazette,* Part V, 3.11.1939, 89-90, 92-95; P.L.A.D., Vol. X, 20.10.1939, 146.

agriculturists' Hindu Party[150] (This Party later on, styled itself as National Progressive Party), The Muslim League, the Akali Party (till 1942)[151] and a number of times, from the Congress and the British authorities it continued in the face of all opposition, to advocate and give practical shape to the measures, like due representation to all classes, Communities and areas on Governmental positions and legislatures; the enlargement of franchise, Indianisation of Government services; just distribution of Government funds between the agriculturists and the non-agriculturists.[152]

The financial achievements of the Punjab Government were as follows : An annual saving to the tune of Rs. 1.45 crores in the provincial expenses was made.[153] The rich were made to pay more taxes like the Punjab Tobacco Vend Fee (1934), Entertainment Duty (1937), The Punjab Immovable Property Tax (1941), revised revenues on Urban agricultural lands (1928), and Central Sales Tax (1941).[154]

On the contrary, the Government paid due attention to the problem of land revenue which concerned its main supporters the landlords. In 1928, ceiling of land revenue on rural agricultural land was reduced to 1/4th of the net assets (previously it ranged upto 50%); in any subsequent resettlement it could not be enhanced by more than 25% of the previous settlement, and the land revenue thus revised

150. Singh, Gurcharan, *Ankhi Surma* (Panjabi), 130 (Some Agriculturists and rural Hindus like Baldev Singh and Nanak Chand had also joined this group.)

151. The Akali opposition to the then Government ended in 1942, when Sikander-Baldev-Pact was signed on June 15, 1942 and Baldev Singh replaced Dasaunda Singh on June 26, 1942. Vide Gulati, K.C., *The Tribune,* Lahore, 16.6.1942; *The Akali Patrika,* 16.6.1942; *The Akali Patrika,* 16.6.1942; Mohinder Singh, *Sardani-Azam,* 103-04.

152. *Ibid.*

153. *The Tribune,* Lahore, 5.6.1931, 5; 14.6.1931, 5; 26.6.1931, 5; 2.3.1971, 5; 8.7.1931, 5; 1.8.1931, 5; 4.8.1931, 5; *Jat-Gazette,* 16.9.1931, 1; 9.12.1931, 3.

154. Mitra's *Indian Annual Register,* Year 1939, Vol. II, 187; Year 1941, Vol. I, 267.

could in no case exceed 25% of the net asset (1928).[155] Consequently, the foregoing principle coupled with the sliding scale system (1938) of assessment brought down the land revenue assessment lower than 25% of the net assets and thus the Punjab peasant became the lowest land revenue payer throughout India.[156] *Chahi* rate was rationalised from 1927 onwards.[157] Reduction made in irrigation duty (during 1933-42) placed the peasantry in the enviable position of the lowest water rate payer in the whole country.[158] Appreciable reductions were made in land revenue and irrigation duty.[159] Peasant welfare fund aiming at making special efforts for the progress of agriculture and the rural folk was instituted.[160] Due to the efforts made by the Punjab Government in the field of irrigation, agriculturists became self dependent. Practical shape was given to the *Kharif* Canal extension scheme (1940).[161] *Thal* Project (1924-42), *Haveli* Project (1940) and a canal in Pind Dadan Khan area were completed.[162] New Schemes of tube well irrigation and lift irrigation from Western Jamuna Canal were taken in hand,[163] and many more works were completed. A number of wells and tubewells, for

155. Hussain, A., *Fazli-Hussain : A Political Biography,* Bombay : 1965, 119 and 160.

156. Finance Department Year 1938, File No. 22 (80) F-D, 1948; *The Tribune,* Lahore, 22.11.1938, 2 and 15.

157. *Jat Gazette,* Rohtak, 22.8.1927, 2-4; P.L.C.D., Vol. XXIII, 28.2.1933, 95; Mitra's *Indian Quarterly Register,* Year : 1927, Vol. I, 369.

158. P.L.A.D., Vol. XIX, 10.3.1942, 184; Vol. XXI, 10.7.1943. 357.

159. *Ibid.*

160. *Jat Gazette,* 8.9.1943, 8 (For details also see Deptt. of Education, Health and Lands, Year : 1926, File No. Lands-May-20-21, B; Year : 1941, File No. 17(27) F.D./1944; 22(79) F.D./1948; 20(80) F.D. (1948); *The Tribune,* Lahore, 12.1.1939, 4.

161. P.L.A.D., Vol. XII, 5.3.1940, 132.

162. Mitra's *Indian Annual Register Year :* 1940, Vol. II, 187.

163. P.L.C.D., Vol. XII, 7.3.1925 and 13.3.1925, 140 and 506; Vol. XXVIII, 1936, 59 and 993; P.L.A.D., Vol. I, 22.6.1937 and 2.7.1937, 501 and 947; X, 29.3.1939, 860-61.

providing drinking water to the ruralities were sunk at a depth of 300 to 600 feet.[164]

With the two fold objective of fighting the problem of literature and illiterate unemployment, both rural and urban, and for bringing greater prosperity to the agriculturists, the Government worked hard to install industry in the province, in districts based on agriculture and locally available raw materials, with special attention to the setting up of the cottage and rural industries.[165] As in order to reduce these objectives into reality, the Government assured the various political factions in the House that it would do its best to industrialise the province at a quick pace.[166] Now many Acts were passed with a view to redeeming the Punjab people especially of the rural and backward parts politically, economically and socially.[167]

To substantiate it, let us cite some of the measures of the Punjab Government in this direction. During 1924-25, six new industrial schools were set up at a cost of Rs. 5000 each and it raised their total number in the province 22 with 2000 pupils on their roll.[168] These schools were set up to promote cottage

164. *Jat Gazette,* Rohtak, 15.6.1927, 4; P.L.C.D., Vol. XXVI, 28.2.1935, 173; P.L.A.D., Vol. I, 13.7.1937, 1440; *Jat Gazette,* Rohtak, 22.1.1941, 8.

165. P.L.C.D., Vol. VIII, 8 March, 1925, 140; Vol. XII, March 7, and 13, 140 and 506; Vol. XXVIII, 1936, 59 and 993; P.L.A.D., Vol. I, 22.6.1937 and 2.7.1937, 501 and 947; Hussain, A., *Fazli-Hussain : A Political Biography* (Bombay : 1946) 134; Abbot, A. and Wood, S.H., *Report on Vocational Education in India,* Delhi, Punjab and United Provinces, 1936-37; Delhi : 1937, 110; Darling, M.L., *Wisdom and Waste,* 370; *Report of the Indian Industrial Commission,* Calcutta : 1928, 162; Anstey, V., *The Economic Development of India,* London : 1939, 228.

166. P.L.C.D., Vol. IV, 25.3.1938, 268; Vol. III, 8.3.1938, 577.

167. P.L.C.D., Vol. VII, 25.3.1938, 268; Vol. III, 8.3.1938, 577. Shastri, R.S., *Chaudhari Chhotu Ram : Jivan Charitra* (Hindi), Rohtak : 1965, 146; Bajaj, Y.P., *Sir Chhotu Ram and His Work* (unpublished Ph.D. Thesis), Kurukshetra University : 1972, Appendix-XXV.

168. P.L.C.D., Vol. VIII, 13.3.1925, 515; Punjab Government's Review of the Report of the Industries Department for the year ending 31st December, 1925, in *Punjab Government Gazette,* Part-II, 17.12.1926.

industries in the Punjab in the rural area and also to help remove illiteracy.[169] It was also declared by the Government in the Punjab Legislative Council in the beginning of 1925, that an Engineering College might be started in 1925.[170] For the promotion of industries in 1925, the Government sanctioned, in the Public Sector, the Mandi-Hydro-Electric Scheme by the Punjab Legislature. The Supply to both industrialists and the agriculturists was completed in 1933-34 at a cost of nearly 6.25 crores.[171] It is also to be noticed that the annual budget provision during 1937-44 for the industrial department touched a high mark. For instance, budget provision for this department in 1940-41, was almost 183% of its counterpart in the Budget of 1933-34 which further rose to about 272% in 1944-45, vis-a-vis 1933-34.[172] But, still feeling the funds usually allocated for the industries as insufficient, the Government constituted a special department fund in 1937.[173] To substantiate it, for hosiery development in Ludhiana district during 1937-38, loans amounting to Rs. 1,20,000 were given.[174] The number of hosiery factories rose to 62 in 1939 as against 6 in 1934.[175] To cite another example, budgetary provision earmarked to encourage the industrialists was enhanced by more than 100% in 1940.[176]

169. P.L.C.D., Vol. VIII (V.P. Gray), 6.5.1925, 1067-69.

170. *Ibid.,* 1068-69.

171. In 1925, the Cost of the Mandi Hydro Electric Project was estimated at about 4.6 crores rupees. Vide P.L.C.D., Vol. VIII, 1925, 499; Vol. VIII-B, 8.12.1925, 1945-49, 60; Vol. XVIII, 30.7.1929, 217, 242-43; Vol. XXIII, 27.2.1933, 61, 96-97, 307-27, 347-48, 360; Vol. XXIV, 1.3.1924, 383.

172. *Five Years of Provincial Autonomy in the Punjab : 1938-42,* 21, 27, 47; P.L.A.D., Vol. XVIII, 20.3.1941, 120.

173. *Ibid.,* P.L.A.D., Vol. XIX, 10.3.1942, 185; Vol. IV, 29.3.1938, 263.

174. P.L.C.D., Vol. IV, 25.3.1938, 264-66; Vol. XXVII, 19.11.1935, 996-98; Vol. VIII, 13.3.1925, 514.

175. *Report of the Indian Tarriff Board on the Woollen Textile Industry,* Delhi : 1935, 346.

176. This conclusion has been drawn from the figures cited in P.L.C.D., Vol. VIII, 20.3.1938, 439.

It will not be out of place to state that the Unionist Government discouraged every such foreign article from being displayed as in any way could compete with the Indian Industrial goods.[177] Further to promote *Swadeshi* goods, it issued an order in 1939 to all the departments that indigenous goods should be preferred to foreign goods.[178] Now the provincial Store Purchase Department was set up and was given a free hand in purchasing the requirements of the Government from the local authorities.[179]

Another significant point in this connection worthnothing is that the Punjab Government also undertook survey of the province, in 1938, both district as well as industry-wise.[180] Professor K.T. Shah was invited and requested to prepare a comprehensive plan for the industrial development of the Punjab and his recommendations proved valuable.[181] Institution of Industrial Research Fund, industrial measures at provincial and district levels and designing section at the Mayo School of Art, were a few more significant measures introduced by the Government in the Punjab.[182]

The Government at this stage realised the need and importance of setting up co-operative societies, which could supply raw materials to the village industries and purchase the products manufactured by them. The Punjab Government also set up a marketing organisation for the sale of Cottage Industries' goods with the central depot at Amritsar and its

177. *Punjab Government Gazette*, Part-I, 30.12.1939, 621.

178. P.L.A.D. Vol. X, 2.11.1939, 439.

179. Provincial Store Purchase Department also saved Rs. 1.2 lacs annually in the shape of one percent, commission and other one percent on inspection of stores. Vide, P.L.A.D., Vol. XVII, 17.3.1941, 127.

180. It is also shown as the three years industrial survey of the Punjab. Chhotu Ram headed the Survey Committee, appointed for the purpose Vide. P.L.A.D., Vol. III, 16.3.1938, 846; Vol. XI-A, 2.2.1940, 55; Vol. XVI, 7.3.1941, 253; *India Year Book* : 1940-41, 593.

181. Shah, K.T., *Industrialisation of the Punjab* (Punjab Government; 1941), 205; P.L.A.D., Vol. XVI, 7.3.1941, 253.

182. *Report on the Working of the Industries Department : 1939*, 1 : Also of 1940, 41.

branches at Hoshiarpur and Multan.[183] Now it was also suggested to the Central Government in 1938, that in the interest of the industrial progress of the Punjab, due representation on tarriff Board should be given to the industrialists, growers and consumers.[184] Another step to promote Cottage Industries was to increase the number of co-operative Industrial Societies, of which the most prominent were, the Weavers Societies. They earlier bought yarn from bania at a high rate of interest and sold the manufactured cloth again to him at a cheaper rate.[185] Now they did not depend upon *banias.* They could obtain cash advances from the societies against their finished goods, but without furnishing any security.[186] Besides, small loans were also given to weavers. In 1937-38, to the weavers of Panipat, alone Rs. 65,000 were loaned out.[187]

In the beginning, due to financial stringency, the Government had sought working capital from the capitalists with the result that profits went into their pockets, but in 1941, it set spart a sum of rupees fifty thousand for this purpose, so that the return from it could also be reinvested for their further expension.[188] Again it made efforts to encourage poultry and bee-keeping industries, *e.g.*, one bee-keeping industry was set up at Nagrota (Kangra district) and another in Kulu Valley.[189] Another step was the appointment of a

183. *Report on the Working of the Industries Department :* Punjab : 1936, 29.

184. P.L.C.D., Vol. III, 1.7.1938, 536, 541-42.

185. P.L.A.D., Vol. VIII, 20.3.1939, 439.

186. The number of Weavers' Co-operative Industrial Societies in 1909, stood at 205 (It was 57 in 1921) Vide. *Annual Report on The Working of Co-operative Societies* : 1920-21, 31; also of 1939, 38-39.

187. P.L.A.D., Vol. IV, 25.3.1938, 264; Vol. XVII, 17.3.1941, 128.

188. *Ibid.*, (For more details also see the *Annual Report on the Co-operative Societies,* in the Punjab : 1930, 48; also of 1938, 7; also of 1939, 42.

189. In 1938-39, Advanced Training in Dairying, bee-keeping, poultary farming, and fruit preservation was being imparted in te Punjab Agricultural and Research Institute, Lyallpur. Vide, *Annual Report on the Working of the Education Department,* Punjab : 1938-39, 74; 1935-36, 62; P.L.A.D., Vol. VIII, 20.3.1939, 861.

Central agency for the revival of the pottery industry, for which a sum of Rs. 60,000 was provided.[190]

Considerable progress was recorded in the field of industrial education for women. While the number of institutions, where a good number of women trainees were receiving industrial education, stood at about 200 and 1400 in 1920 and 1937 respectively, it rose to about 2015 in 1939.[191] Funds were also increased. To quote the figures, it was Rs. 6000 in 1920, but in 1940, it stood as high as Rs. 79,000.[192] Another important measure of the Government was that it provided Rs. 30,000 in 1941 for giving loans to those educated unemployment who desired to set up industries but did not have the resources.[193] Another significant point is to be noticed that a sum of Rs. 10,000 was set aside,[194] in the annual budget, in 1938-39,[195] so that trainees to foreign countries could be sent to acquire knowledge in the modern industrial technology. Hence, the growth of industries strengthened the hands of the working class as well as the rural people who depended on agriculture.

Moreover, the British Government in the Punjab came to depend, by this time, on the exploited ruralites and thus started giving them maximum concessions like remission and reduction in land revenue and *abiana,* funds for expanding irrigational facilities and developing rural social welfare,

---

190. P.L.A.D. Vol. VIII, 16.3.1939, 210.

191. *Punjab Government Gazette* (Extra-Ordinary) 20.12.1938, 626; *Punjab Administration Report*: 1925-26, 24-30; P.L.A.D., Vol. XII, 11.3.1940.

192. P.L.A.D. Vol. XII, 11.3.1940, 330-31.

193. P.L.A.D. Vol. XVIII, 17.3.1941, 123; Vol. XIII, 25.3.1938, 263; *The Tribune,* Lahore, December 15, 1937, 3; Vol. XII, 11.3.1940, 328.

194. Abbot and Wood also had suggested that even those who were already engaged in imparting vocational education on were in alike professions, should visit abroad in order to understand the practice of the Craftmen there. Vide. P.P.R.A. Vol. III, 16.3.1938, 209; Vol. VI, 21.11.1938, 486; Abbot, A. and Wood, S.M., *Report on Vocational Education in India* (Delhi, Punjab and United Provinces), 1936-37, Delhi: 1939, 4.

195. *The Indian Labour Year Book : 1946,* 10.

industrialization etc.[196] The Government's objective apparently was the uplift of the down trodden and backward section of society.[197] In brief, there grew a gulf between the British Government and the money-lending classes in the Punjab, as the former had passed many Acts which were against the interests of the latter. It will not be out of place if we cite here some of the measures adopted by the Government in this connection.

It took first step by opening a large number of land mortgage banks both in private and co-operative sectors and co-operative societies helping to release agriculturists' lands mortgaged with the moneylenders and also to issue the loans on easy terms.[198] Another important step taken by the Government in 1930, was the Regulation of Accounts Act (Punjab Act I of 1930), where under moneylenders were to maintain their accounts in the prescribed form and furnish half yearly or yearly ligible debt statements to their debtors regularly.[199] Penalty for failure in maintaining proper accounts

196. *Inqlab*, Lahore, 11.1.1945; *Zamindar*, Lahore, 11.1.1945; *Milap*, Lahore, 10.1.1945, 4; *The Tribune*, Lahore, 10.1.1945, 3; also of 11.1.1945, 3; *Jat Gazette*, Rohtak, 3.9.1941, 1 (For details also see : P.L.A.D. Vol. XV, 24.1.1941, 270; *Pioneer*, Allahabad, 12.1.1945; *The Tribune*, Lahore, 12.1.1945, 3; *Milap*, Lahore, 12.1.1945, 3; *Daily Herald*, London, 11.1.1945; Ram, T., op. cit., 73, 79-82, 84-85, 88; *Jat Gazette*, Rohtak, 10.12.1941, 2.

197. For details see Ram, T., *Sir Chhotu Ram : Apostle of Hindu-Muslim Unity*, Lahore : 1946, 84, 87, 90; P.L.A.D. Vol. XXIV, 19.2.1945, 6; *Shbhez*, Lahore, 10.1.1945; *Ajit*, Lahore, 10.1.1945; *Punjab Government Gazette* (Extra-Ordinary) 10.1.1945; *Veer Bharat*, Lahore, 10.1.1945, *Jat Gazette*, Rhotak, 17.2.1941, 2.

198. *Punjab Administration Report : 1920-21*, 68; also of 1924-25 137; *Annual Report on the Working of Co-operative Societies :* 1924, 15; of 1925, 13; of 1926, 16-17; of 195, 60; of 1939, 19; also see for the year 1918, 1923 and 1938; *Jat Gazette*, Rohtak, 25.5.1927, 7; 15.6.1927, 4; P.L.C.D., Vol. XXI, 7.5.1925 1085-88; *Punjab Government Gazette* (Supplement), 11.2.1927, 25-26.

199. In fact, it was enacted by the Punjab Legislative Council in 1926, but was vetoed by the Governor. Vide. *Punjab Government Gazette*, 1931, Part-I, 657; 29.11.829, 51-52; Hussain, A., *Fazli-Hussain : A Political Biography*, Bombay : 1946, 147.

was the loss of interest wholly or in part, and also of the cost of suits.[200]

Another achievement of the Government was the revival of the *Panchayat* Board to arbiterate disputes among the àgriculturists and thus it saved them from indebtedness,[201] put significant results of its efforts appeared when the Punjab Relief of Indebtedness Act VII of 1924 of 1934 and the Punjab Debtors Protection Act II of 1936, were passed, of which the latter was the supplementary to the former. Both the Acts materialised the Unionists' long desire which they had incorporated in their Punjab Moneylenders Bill of 1924 that was passed by the Punjab Legislative Council in 1926, but was turned down by the Governor.[202]

Another important measure of the Punjab Government for releasing the peasants' land was the enactment of the Resolution of Mortgaged Land Act, 1938 (Punjab Act IV of 1938).[203] This Act restored without any payment about 42 lacs acres belonging to nearly 3,64,780 small landholders, which was mortgaged prior to 8th June, 1901,[204] with the moneylenders for approximately Rs. 4,13,00,000. The underlying progressive principle of the Act was that any mortgager who had benefited from the mortgaged lands twice or more than the principal advanced, was not entitled to any

200. Punjab Act I of 1930, Section 4 (b).

201. *Jat Gazette,* Rohtak, 15.6.1927, 4.

202. Hussain, A., *Fazli-Hussain : A Political Biography,* Bombay : 1946, 160; Ram, T., *Sir Chhotu Ram : Apostle of Hindu-Muslim Unity,* Lahore : 1946, 7; P.L.C.D., Vol. VII-B, 14.12.1925, 1735-97 (For more details also see *Jat-Gazette,* Rohtak, 20.4.1927, 5; 8.1.1927, 6.

203. *Punjab Government Gazette* (Extra Ordinary) 6.9.1938, 115-17.

204. This Act was to be effective in the case of mortgages made before 8 June, 1901, the date on which the Punjab Alienation of Land Act, 1900, Came into force, this alienation of Land Act, became effective from 12.4.1939 Vide. *Punjab Government Gazette* (Extra-Ordinary) 5.12.1939, 113; Punjab Respitution of Mortgaged lands (Amendment) Act 1942; *Punjab Government Gazette* (Extra-Ordinary) 6.4.1943, 49.

205. P.L.A.D., Vol. XII, 5.3.1940, 134-35.

further compensation. The land so mortgaged, by any one of any one stood restored to the original owner without any payment.[205] During the same period, its efforts resulted in the enactment of another beneficial measure, namely the Punjab Registration of Moneylenders Act (Act III of 1938).[206] When during 1936-37, the spirit of the above legislations, especially of the Punjab Debtors Protection Act aiming to uproot the evils linked with indebtedness, was violated, the Punjab Government issued the following three notifications in 1939 protecting the debtors.

The first notification exempted from attachment the whole of the fodder crop and 1/3rd of all other crops but no less than 20 maunds grains;[207] under the second notification issued under Section 68 of the Criminal Procedure Code, agricultural land belonging to un-notified agriculturists was protected against sale in execution of decrees,[208] and through the third notification issued under Section 61 of the Criminal Procedure Code Carts, Milk, Cattle, animal sheds, manure, fodder spurs etc. of the agriculturists were protected against attachment or sale in execution of decrees.[209]

The work of the Punjab Government in the field of irrigation was indeed important. In the very first Chapter we have seen at length the defects in the entire system of irrigation which were to the long standing anomalles in the Northern India Canal and drainage Act (1873). With a view to removing these defects by occured since 1873, the ruling party through a resolution made the following suggestions :

---

206. *Ibid.*, also Page 140; Vol. IX, Finance Department Year 1938, File No. 22 (78)-F(D-1938); *Punjab Government Gazette* (Extra-Ordinary), 2.9.1938, 111-14, also Part I, 9.6.1939.

207. P.L.A.D., Vol. VIII, 20.3.1939, 443.

208. *Ibid.*, 1146.

209. The Punjab Government also gave liberal loans for land development *e.g.*, in 1937-38 and 1938-39, it gave liberal loans for 1,79,429 rupees and 2,82,568 rupees for this purpose respectively vis-a-vis Rs. 1,33,243 given for this purpose in 1936-37, Vide. *Ibid;* Saini, B.S., *The Social and* Economic History of the Punjab : 1901-39 (including Haryana and Himachal Pardesh), Delhi : 1975, 420.

I. The clause relating to forced labour *(Begar)* to work on the Canal, should be abrogated;[210]

II. A Committee of the representatives of the agriculturists should be formed to advise the irrigation department about the closures of the canals, so that the loss to the crops on this account should be minimised;

III. Agriculturists should be allowed to appeal in *Aabi-Zai* cases to the district judges for fair play;

IV. Water rates should be charged at 40% to 50% of the existing rates;

V. Those fields for which *Kharaba* be claimed must be inspected by the Canal Officers within a specified period from the date of submitting the applications;[211] and

VI. If the produce was less than six annas in the rupees, no water rate should be charged.

Several political groups strongly opposed *Chahi* rates; as the cost of sinking the wells was to be entirely borne by the cultivators themselves, the Government had no right to change it. This demand, however, was also opposed by many such as Gokal Chand Narang, Raja Narinder Nath and many others.[212] When the cultivators of Rohtak demanded the abolition of *Chahi* rates, the Unionist Party included this demand in its manifesto.[213] Consequently, the Punjab Government in 1933 abolished *Chahi* rate in the Rohtak region.[214]

---

210. In fact, it was not difficult to do so because the forced labourers were paid better wages than those prevailing in that area at the time of exploiting them. Vide. P.L.C.D., Vol. XXII, 24.11.1932, 677.

211. P.L.C.D., Vol. XXIII, 27.3.1936, 626, 656-57.

212. Gokal Chand Narang, Raja Narinder Nath and Others opposed the resolution of the Cultivators of Rohtak, demanding the abolition of *Chahi* Rates. Vide P.L.C.D., Vol. X, 7.3.1927, 17.3.1927, 135-39, 529-37, 1445; *Jat Gazette,* 25.5.1927, 3.

213. *Jat Gazette,* 10.8.1927, 4; 27.5.1931, 2.

214. P.L.C.D., Vol. XXIII, 28.2.1933, 95; *Jat Gazzette,* Rohtak, 27.5.1931, 4.

Bringing down of *abiana* was another significant contribution of the Governmnet in the Punjab. It was alleged by several political leaders that the rates of the agricultural commodities had declined steeply during 1929-33 in comparison to those of 1924, when the water-rates were last fixed in the Punjab.[215] But on the other hand, the cost of production stood as high in 1933 as it was in 1924.[216] As a result of the constant pressure of the various political parties, the Punjab Government appointed the *abiana* Committee in 1933, to review the abiana rates,[217] which recommended that the irrigation duty should be permanently reduced atleast by Rs. 80 lacs to Rs. 1 crores.[218] As a result of this recommendation, the local Government reduced the abiana in a permanent way in 1933 by Rs. 37 lacs.[219] It is to be noted that the Punjab was the first province where the water rate *(abiana)* was reduced. By 1942, the Punjab peasant paid the second lowest abiana rate in the whole country.[220]

Due importance was attached to the irrigation work in the province. The Government of the Punjab gave an assurance to the various political groups that in case the experts declared the site suitable for the Bhakra Dam project, money should be no problem.[221] It will not be out of place to state that in the

215. *Jat Gazette,* 27.5.1931, 2; P.L.C.D., Vol. XXIV, 5.3.1934, 515; Vol. XXII, 21.3.1933, 645; Bajaj, Y.P., *Sir Chhotu Ram* and His Work (unpublished Ph.D. Thesis) Kurukshetra University, 1972 (See Chapter of Agricultural Work).

216. P.L.C.D., Vol. XXIV, 5.3.1934, 95.

217. P.L.C.D., Vol. XXIII, 21.3.1933, 643, 655, 662-63.

218. *Report of the Abiana Committee* (Appointed by the Punjab Government, 1933 (Lahore : 1934), 47; Ram, T., *Sir Chhotu Ram : Apostle of Hindu-Muslim Unity,* Lahore, 1946, 12.

219. P.L.A.D., Vol. XXI, 16.3.1943, 357; Vol. XIX, 10.3.1943, 84; Vol. VI, 1.12.1938, 846; Ram, T., *Sir Chhotu Ram : Apostle of Hindu-Muslim Unity,* Lahore : 1946, 11-12.

220. P.L.A.D., Vol. XIX, 10.3.1942, 184; Vol. XXI, 26.3.1943, 357.

221. Ram, T., *Sir Chhotu Ram : Apostle of Hindu-Muslim Unity,* Lahore : 1946, 7; *Jat Gazette,* Rohtak, 7.12.1927, 3; P.L.C.D., Vol. XII, 27.2.1929, 522-24.

irrigational work, even the peasants put pressure on the Government for the execution of the Bhakra Dam Scheme. When three ministers, Sunder Singh Majithia, Fazl-i-Hussain and Feroz visited Rohtak during 1925-27, the agriculturists of the area through memoranda urged upon them to start this Project immediately.[222] Finally an American expert was invited to the Punjab to look into the suitability of the proposed site for the Bhakra Dam.[223] A detailed report in connection with this project was submitted in January, 1928, that was passed on for the Government of India's approval.[224] Of course, this Project could not materialise before the country's liberation but the Punjab Government gave practical shape to some other irrigational project with a view to providing immediate relief to the South East Punjab.

Kharif Extension canals Scheme costing Rs. 60 lacs was undertaken in 1940.[225] One non-perennial canal irrigating the Hissar district was commissioned in June 1941, and some more non-perennial canals were in progress.[226] The total capital out lay on such canals in the province was allowed to touch Rs. 1.25 crores,[227] by March 1942, as against the original allocation of Rs. 60 lacs in 1940, as mentioned above. Similarly, *Thal* Project was completed in 1942 which extended irrigational facilities to 1.5 million acres of land.[228] Thus, it added to the

222. *Jat Gazette,* Rohtak, 25.11.1925, 7; 1.12.1926, 4; 7.12.1926, 3; 10.8.1927, 3.

223. The American expert landed at Bombay on November 11, 1927. Two officials of the Government of India and one of the Irrigation Department assisted him in the study of the site of Bhakra Dam, Vide. *Jat Gazette,* Rohtak, 29.4.1927, 5; 7.12.1927, 3.

224. P.L.C.D., Vol. XII, 3.12.1928, 274.

225. This scheme was calculated to provide non-perennial irrigation (during Kharif only) to 3.5. lacs acres. Vide P.L.A.D., Vol. XII, 5.3.1942, 132.

226. P.L.A.D., Vol. XIX, 5.3.1942, 132.

227. Shastri, Y., *Kashtri Jation Ka Uthanopattan* (Hindi), Hardwar : 1956, 628.

228. P.L.A.D., Vol. XIX, 13.3.1942, 185 and 255; Shastri, T., *Kashtri Jation Ka Uthanopattan* (Hindi) Hardwar : 1956, 628.

people of that area and add to the revenues of the Government through irrigation duty and by sale at a better price of the Crown waste lands situated in the *Thal* areas.[229]

Another noteworthy irrigational scheme better known as the Haveli Project was competed in 1939, by the sincere efforts of the Unionists' ministry. This project costed Rs. 3.66 crores[230] and proposed to provide perennial and non-perennial irrigation to 7 lacs and 8.5 lacs respectively.[251] Another scheme costing about 2.5 crores was prepared to raise the water level of the wells in Doabs,[232] (the area lying in between the rivers Sutlej and Beas), in 1942, a small canal was dug in Pindi Dadu Khan areas.[233] Again with a view to exploring irrigational possibilities in the western parts of the province and especially in the *barani* districts of Rawalpindi, a sub-division was created in 1943 which was converted into a division with three sub-divisions in 1944.[234]

229. P.L.A.D., Vol. X, 15.3.1927, 455-57, 459-61.

230. *(i)* Originally planned in 1916, the Secretary of State for India sanctioned this project in April, 1937, while the actual work on the project commenced in October, 1937; It was commissioned on April 2, 1939; it diverted the waters of the Jhelum and Chaneb rivers into the river Ravi near Sink and by constructing a barrage near Trimmu. It was during 1939-40, that the Karam, Ganesh and Tabri Canals of the Muzafargarh canal system; Sidhnai canal and the Chenab Innudation Canals were amalgamated with the Haveli project, (It was completed within a small period of 18 months), *(ii)* Originally its estimated cost stood at Rs. 636 lacs in 1926-27. Vide *(Punjab Administrative Reports of the Canals for 1938-39,* 40, 45; 1939-40, 52;)); P.L.C.D., Vol. XII, 6.3.1940, 132; Vol. XV, 31.1.1941, 602.

231. During 1939-40, total area irrigated by the Haveli Canals stood at 7238 lac acres but inspite of that the project earned a net profit of 0.98% in its total investment Vide *Administration Reports of the Canals for 1939-40,* 52; 1938-39, 40; P.L.C.D., Vol. XXVI, 28.2.1935, 175; Vol. XII, 4.3.1940, 132.

232. It is notable that in the beginning when the tube-wells were introduced in the province, nothing was changed both for the successful and unsuccessful barinys. Vide : P.L.A.D. Vol. 31.1.1941, 602; P.L.C.D. Vol. XIII, 6.2.1933, 219.

233. P.L.A.D., Vol. XIX, 10.3.1942, 185.

234. P.L.A.D., Vol. XXII, 7.3.1944, 404-05.

Hence, it may be concluded that the efforts made in the field of irrigation were comprehensive aiming at a prosperity of both the poor agriculturists of unirrigated areas and of the province as a whole, while for releasing the former the Punjab Government tried and also succeeded to some extent in bringing water to the thirsty barran lands and getting the irrigation duty reduced. In its aim the Government succeeded as is borne out by the figures *e.g.* canal irrigated area had increased from about 8.8 million[235] acres in 1923 to 16.5 million[236] acres in 1938-39. Similarly the area under the cotton cultivation rose from about 1.95 million[237] acres in 1920-21 to 3.13 million acres[238] in 1938-39. Attesting the same point Mr. Darling and the National Planning Committee observed that the M. Darling and the National Planning Committee observed that the irrigational improvements during the period resulted in a great stimulus to the trade and industry in the province.[239]

Coming to the question of agriculture, the Government passed the Punjab Act V of 1938, restraining the alienation of the land of an agriculturist debtor to a moneylender of his own tribe.[240] But inspite of it, peasant proprietors dominated in the political organisation of the agriculturists. To cite an example, in 1935 the ruling party had 7 out of the 8 members representing the Ambala Division in Punjab Assembly from among the peasant proprietors and out of its 11 Sikh members, 8 belonged to the self-cultivators class.[241] Besides, it is also worth mentioning that landlords adopted a very sympathetic

235. *Board of Economic Enquiry,* Publication No. 52, 47.

236. *Ibid.,* Supplementary 3 to Publication No. 52, 1.

237. *Statistical Abstracts of British India : 1911-12 to 1920-21,* 346-51.

238. Report on the Operations of the Agriculture Department, ending 30th June, 1939, 72.

239. Darling, M.L., *Wisdom and Waste,* London : 1936, 15; *Report of the National Planning Committee : River Training : 1947,* 32.

240. *Punjab Government Gazette* (Extra-Ordinary), 16.6.1938, 80; Singh, Bakhtawar, *The Social and Economic History of the Punjab,* Delhi : 1975, 246; Barrier, N.G., *Social and Economic History Review,* 161.

241. P.L.C.D., Vol. XXVIII, 12.11.1935, 1091.

attitude towards the tenants and self cultivators *e.g.*, Janal Khan, on of the big landlords, strongly supported the scrapping of the Jansi Batai (sharing of Crops) system.[242] While supporting the resolution proposing the application of income tax principle to the assessment of land revenue, Muhammad Hyat Qureshi admitted, "It is the result of his (peasant proprietor) strenuous labour that we, the big landlords are living the life of ease and confort.[243] Still further, these big landlords pleaded the exemption of the small peasant proprietor from the payment of local rates and took upon themselves the responsibility to pay the whole amount.[244]

The Punjab Government's efforts in the field of Land Reforms began in 1926, when the Punjab (Amendment) Bill was passed by the Punjab Legislature Council.[245] The Bill asked the Government to fix the Land Revenue at not more than 1/3rd of the net assets instead of the then existing rate of 1/2 of net assets.[246] However, the Governor immorally vetoes it, because he had political differences with the ruling faction.[247] But without being discouraged the Unionists intensified their efforts and further raised their demand by asking that maximum land revenue should be assessed at 1/4th of the net assets with the proviso that in no subsequent resettlement it should be enhanced by more than 25% of the preceding

242. *Ibid*.

243. P.L.C.D., Vol. X, 22.2.1928, 79.

244. P.L.A.D., Vol. XII, 4.3.1940, 50-51.

245. Hussain, Azim, *Fazli-Hussain : A Political Biography,* Lahore : 1946, 160.

246. The Notable feature of the Bill was that in every subsequent year reassessment land revenue was not to be enhanced by more than 1/3rd excepting areas, either Urban or where irrigation would develop fast, Vide. Department of Education, Health and Lands, Year : 1926, File No. Land-Feb.-3-B, NAI : New Delhi.

247. Only fast of the Unionist Party was that while scrupulously defending the democratic rights of the people, it had elected Abdul Qadir as the President of the Punjab Legislature Council against Governor's expressed desire that its out going official President should be elected Unanimously. Vide : Hussain, A., *Fazli-Hussain : A Political Biography,* Lahore : 1946, 160.

assessment.[248] The Government ultimately gave way by legislating the Punjab Land Revenue Act, 1928, conceding the preceding demands.[249] By the implementation of this Act in resettlements, wherever these became due, land revenue was considerably slashed. For instance, in 1930, it was out down by Rs. 2.23 lakhs, Rs. 1.04 lacs, Rs. 2.28 lacs, Rs. 0.86 lacs, Rs. 0.36 lacs, Rs. 1.38 lacs and Rs. 1.83 lacs in the settlement circles of Shahpur, Gujranwala, Sheikhupura, Attock, Mianwali, Gujrat and Jhang respectively.[250]

During the period between 1928-33, with a view to benefitting the owner cultivators, the ruling party went on urging the Government that the land revenue should be determined on the basis of self-cultivators' net assets instead of rent receiving landlords' and that it should properly account for the cost of cultivation including the amount due to cattle depreciation connected herewith.[251] Though the Government did not accept this proposal, it introduced the sliding scale of assessment of land revenue on experimental basis in Montgomery and Lyallpur districts in 1930.[252] But this wholesome feature came to be applied on a large scale only since 1937,[253] the year, the Unionist party made a mark. However, the only existence of the foregoing land reforms, though solutary, did not result in much benefits to the agriculturists until 1937, whereafter these were enforced anxiously by then Government. Significant results of this combination of salubrities was that in the resettlement made

248. P.L.C.D., Vol. XI, 8.5.1928, 1009, 11, 47; P.L.A.D., Vol. XIII, .3.1940, 49; Vol. 27.1.1941, 313.

249. Punjab Land Revenue Act 1928, Section 48-B; Hussain, A., *Fazli-Hussain : A Political Biography,* Lahore : 1946, 149; The Tribune, Lahore, 6.2.1933, 7; P.L.C.D., Vol. XXVI, 6.2.1935, 818.

250. *The Tribune,* Lahore, 27.4.1930, 3.

251. *Ibid.,* 6.9.1933, 7; P.L.C.D., Vol. XI, 8.5.1928, 913-21, 926.

252. Report of the Land Revenue Committee appointed by the Punjab Government in 1937, 47 (Punjab Government in 1938).

253. P.L.A.D., Vol. VIII, 30.3.1939, 962; Ram, T., *Sir Chhotu Ram : Apostle of Hindu Muslim Unity,* Lahore : 1946, 12.

during 1937-44, land revenue was assessed much below 25 percent of the net assets,[254] and thus the Punjab cultivators became the lowest land rate payer in the country.[255]

The Punjab, Government, since 1937, did not need to adopt underhand means for affording relief to the agriculturists because they were satisfied with the success of the sliding scale of land revenue system. The Government also thought that the illiterate cultivators would be able to maintain their accounts if more reformed system was followed.[256] Apart from the slashing of land revenue, the ruling faction impressed upon the Government especially during the economic depression to give very liberal remission in land revenue.[257] What it stressed upon was the abolition of Acreage rates which was charged by the Government to recover, in 7 years, Rs. 60 lacs which amount the Government had incurred on digging water courses, construction of culverts and preliminary survey and demarcations. This effort resulted in an assurance by the Government that acreage rates would either be remitted or abolished.[258] At this time, the Government suspended the realisation of *malikana* for three harvests and further assured to reconsider the issue at any opportune time.[259] At the same

254. The illustrate the point in resettlement made during 1937-44, in the assessment circles of Gurgoan and Jhelum districts and the tehsils of Lahore, Chunian, Kasur, Amritsar, Taran-Taran and Ajnala rate of land revenue (in terms of net assets) was reduced specially from 40-45% (Gurgoan, Jhelum and Lahore) 30.5%, 22%, 25.5.% to about 23.2% (Gurgaon, Jhelum and Lahore) 15%, 16%, 15.3%, 14% and 14.1%, Vide P.L.A.D., Vol. XXI, 12.3.1943, 214-15, Vol. XIV, 6.2.1940, 856.

255. P.L.A.D., Vol. XV, 27.1.1941, 962; Vol. XIX, 10.3.1942, 184.

256. P.L.A.D., Vol. XII, 4.3.1940, 47; Vol. XIX, 13.3.1942, 327-28.

257. *Ibid.*

258. P.L.C.D., XXVIII, 10.3.1936, 320, 515, 521, 547.

259. (The Unionists had criticised the excessive *malikana* rate, that was realised as a part of rent from the grantees in colonies. It should be also noted that land revenue was not leviable on Crown-lands). Vide. P.L.C.D., Vol. XXIII, 5.3.1934, 515; Vol. XXVIII, 10.3.1936, 314; Vol. XXIV, year 1934, 312 and 322.

time, one section in the party opposed the Government's policy selling crown land through auction, whereby only capitalists could purchase that.[260] They demanded its distribution among the agriculturists of famine-stricken areas.[261]

The Government also made efforts to introduce many modern technique for increasing the agricultural yields.[262] Consolidation of lands was the first step taken by the Government in 1924-25.[263] For this purpose, the number of co-operative Societies (engaged in this work) was increased from 133 in 1924 to 237 in 1926, which made a mark since 1937 *i.e.*, their number stood at 1477 in 1939.[264] Area consolidated in Punjab increased steadily, improving the prospect of large scale farmers. From 5376 acres consolidation in 1923, it rose to 21258, over 100,000 and 1,57,211 acres respectively in 1926, 1938 and 1939,[265] and thus, by the close of 1939, more than a

260. *Jat Gazette,* Rohtak, 22.11.1930, 3.
261. *Ibid.*
262. Need for improving agriculture had also been emphasised by the Indian Industrial Commission with a view to ensuring the supply of food to the growing population; bettering agriculturists lot as well as the enhance the progress of industries, Vide, Report of the Indian Industrial Commission 1916-18 (Calcutta : 1918), 88.
263. The Unionist leadership attached so much importance to this need for enhancing agricultural interests because very few holdings were economic. Darling also pointed out that the fragmentation of yields had been carried so far as to prevent all attempts at cultivation. Vide. Darling, M.L., *Punjab Peasant in Prosperity and Debt,* London : 1925, 29-30, 84, 133-34 and 264.
264. The Annual Reports on the working of Co-operative Societies in the Punjab for the years ending 31st July, 1923 to 31st July, 1927, also year ending 31st July, 1940; *Jat Gazette,* Rohtak, 15.6.1927, 41.
265. The Achievements of these societies is further brightened when it is studied bearing in mind their work was stealthily opposed by the Patwaris, because, thus, practice of legal gratification were greatly slashed. Vide. *Ibid;* Ullah, A., Co-operative Movement in the Punjab, London : 1937, 257-58; P.L.A.D., Vol. VIII, 16.3.1939, 210; Vol. III, 8.3.1938, 570.

million acres had been consolidated.[266] The policy as well as the contribution of the Government is further revealed by the fact that while co-operative societies were doing this difficult task in as many as 22 districts of the Punjab, the Revenue Department was carrying it on in much less area *i.e.* the remaining seven districts of the province namely, Gurgaon, Rohtak, Sialkot, Gujrat, Jhelum, Mianwali and Muzaffargarh.[267] The Government also ended a long standing injustice to the small holders, when the reclamation of waste lands was pressed by the Unionists. While under the old policy, big landlords managed to get much above the quota of additional canal water allowed for the purpose, under the new policy introduced by the Government, reclamation work commenced from the head of a tributary with the lands affected greatest by Ahur (Barrenness), whether these belonged to small agriculturists or big landlords and gradually reached the tail.[268]

For further betterment of agriculturists, stress was laid on protecting the producers against the frauds being jointly perpetrated by the commission agents, weightmen, sackmen and brokers etc.[269] For selling their produce, agriculturists actually got nine and half *annas* of every rupee paid by the

266. In order to expedite it, the Unionist Party got enacted the Punjab Consolidation of Holdings Act 1936 (Further amended in 1945) introducing compulsion in this regard, if it was objected by any owner of land. Vide. P.L.A.D., Vol. VIII, 16.3.1939, 210; Bakhtawar Singh, *The Social and Economic History of the Punjab : 1901-39*, Delhi : 1975, 204; *Punjab Government Gazette* (Extra-ordinary), 33.

267. To expedite the consolidation work through the Revenue Department, Consolidation Officers assisted by *Canungos* and Patwaris were appointed in each district. The result was that the consolidated acres increased from 13472 in 1937 to 27,149, 51,666, 72,841, in 1938, 1939 and 1940 respectively. Vide. Annual Report on the operations of the Department of Land Revenue Records for the year ending 30th September, 1935 to 30th September, 1940.

268. P.L.A.D., Vol. XXI, 16.3.1943, 355.

269. *Punjab Provincial Banking Enquiry Committee Report*, 1929-30. Vol. I, 219-20, 52-53; P.L.A.D., Vol. XVII, 594; Vol. VI (Sohan Singh Josh) 14.11.1938, 555.

consumer and the remaining amount was fraudulently snatched away by the above mentioned usurpers. To eradicate these evils, a modest beginning was made in 1924, by increasing the number of co-operative Commission ships for the sale of agriculture produce,[270] and the following year the Government introduced the Punjab Agricultural Produce Marketing Bill, but it was vetoed by the Governor.[271] However, the ruling party succeeded in getting enacted the Punjab Agricultural Produce Marketing Act in 1939.[272]

Thus, it may be concluded that the contribution of the Punjab Government to farms and fields covered almost all their aspects. The policy that it had adopted to accomplish its aim to pacify the agriculturists was significant, while using its authority to bring about the changes, it laid distinct emphasis on using the media of the social and democratic institutions like arbitration and conciliation Boards, Marketing Committees and Co-operative Societies of various kinds which endeavoured to give a training to the agriculturists for self improvement by involving them in their activities which let to nonetheless satisfactory results.[273]

From the above discussion though it seems that the Punjab Government had achieved a lot, in reality, it has failed

270. *Report of the Committee on Co-operation in India : 1915,* para 9 (Simla : 1915); *Punjab Administration Report for 1919-20,* 69; *Report on the Working of Co-operative Societies in the Punjab* for the year ending 31st July, 1929, 31; also for the year ending August, 1939 to July 1944.

271. *Jat Gazette,* Rohtak, 13.6.1927, 4; P.L.C.D., Vol. XXVII, 25.10.1935, 245.

272. *Punjab Government Gazette* (Extra-ordinary) 11.5.1939, 105-111 *Jat Gazette,* Rohtak, 4.6.1941, 3; P.L.A.D. Vol. VII, 19.1.1939, 384, 466-67, 594-903; Vol. XV, 28.11.1941, 71; Vol. V, 7.7.1938, 783-814; Vol. VI, 14.11.1938, 231-308, 321-23 and 555.

273. While the number of Cattle breeding societies rose from 20 in 1923 to 150 in 1930 and 352 in 1939. There were 62 *Cho* (Water logged lands) Reclamation, 183 Better Farming and 61 Fruit Plantation Societies in 1939; all doing much useful work. Vide, *Annual Reports on the Working of Co-operative* Societies in the Punjab : 1923, 32; also of 1932, 32 and also of 1939, 24.

miserably in having a hold in the rural areas among the peasants. The reason was obivious, it could not come to their expectations. During the period under review, internal differences within the ruling party precipitated and became public, and its leaders were repeatedly disobeyed by the members. As a result, its strength progressively dwindled in the Punjab Legislature for about a decade (1926-35). In the election of 1929, its strength was further reduced to 37, whereas that of Hindu Sabhites who had formed themselves as National progressive Party rose to 20 from 9 in 1926.

Secondly, the ruling party failed to solve the communal and political tangle. After 1938-39, its leadership had realised the incompatibility of their dual position because on all important issues like the Second World War. The future constitution of the country, the Communal problem et., the fuling faction and the Muslim League differed widely. Contrary to the latter's attitude, the former extended support to the Government right from the outset and concluded Sikander-Baldev Pact, on June 15, 1942, although the Akalis were the staunch opponents of the Muslim League's demand of Pakistan. Hence, at this stage, the various political factions were involved themselves in the then political activities in the province in order to acquire strength and establish their position in the rural areas. However, they forgot their main task of helping and improving the conditions of the agriculturists. It is also to be noticed that the British Government in general and the Punjab Governor in particular followed the policy, initiated by the ruling party in the province because the latter had been supporting the former since the day it captured power. Moreover, it suited the British imperialists, as they could continue ruling till they enjoyed the support and favour of the ruling faction.

From the above discussion though it appears that the Punjab Government had achieved a lot, in reality, it had failed miserably in having a hold in the rural areas, especially among the peasants, Because it could not come to the expectations of the small landholders. Reforms made by the Punjab

Government and the measures it had undertaken to improve the lot of the poor peasantry were politically motivated and this aspect we have already discussed in the Second Section of Chapter. This can also be proved if we take into account the number of seats it could win in the Punjab Legislative Assembly in the election of 1946. The ruling faction got only 20 seats and out of this number 13 were Muslims. On the other hand, the League won 75, the Congress 51, the *Panthic* Sikhs 23, and the Miscellaneous 4, out of the total of 175, while 2 seats were vacant. In brief, the ruling party as well as the British bureaucracy failed to satisfy the agriculturists because they paid little attention to the problems and sufferings of the peasants, rather they were more attached to the issue of their position and stability in the Province. But this made them unpopular and finally both collapsed.

7

Summing Up

Now we try to prepare the balance sheet of the achievement as well as the weak points of the peasants' movement during the period under review. One of the most favourite myths about Punjab was that it was predominantly a province of peasant proprietors. But this nation had hardly any basis in reality. Punjab was as much a land of *Zamindars,* rich peasants, middle and small proprietors, occupancy tenants, tenants-at-will, agricultural labourers and agricultural servants. And, the pattern of land ownership was highly differentiated. In 1925, 58.3% owners owned less than 5 acres of land, had average holding of 2.6 acres, and cultivated 12% of the total land, 26.2% of the owners with holdings between 5 to 15 acres owned 26.6% of the land. Besides, 33% of the owners with holding of over 50 acres owned 25.7% of the land, while 7.5% of the owner with holdings of 20 to 50 acres owned 27.2% of the land. A similar enquiry was conducted by the Board of Economic Enquiry, Punjab in 1939. This enquiry also showed that the size of holdings in case of small landlords had further decreased while the holdings of big owners had increased.

Tenants formed a significant section of the rural society and played an important role during the peasants' struggle in the Punjab. In 1932, the tenants-at-will held 48.2% of the area while occupancy tenants held 7.3% of it. In 1935, the tenants constituted 31.8% of the rural working population. The discrepancy between the two figures is explained by the fact that many small owners rented out their small pieces of land and themselves worked as tenants at bigger holdings. However, their number was going up very rapidly. The rate of their increase was 58.7% between 1921 and 1931, while population as a whole went up only by 13.5%. The agricultural labourers lived in extreme poverty. They had hardly any credit to enable them to borrow, for they were a poor risk. They were the first to appear at the famine relief work in case of natural calamities.

As mentioned earlier, an important section consisted of rich peasants of upper stratum of the peasantry. The benefits of commercialization, irrigation and rise in prices were concerned the *Zamindars* through the *batai* system and by the upper stratum of the peasantry who had surpluses to sell whereas the rise in costs went against the tenants. Rich formers and *Zamindars* were also the beneficiaries of the Punjab Farmers' debt legislation which enabled them to branch out and expand into rural moneylending in a big way; thus adding to surplus drawn through usury to lend rent on profit of cultivation. On the contrary, the benefits of co-operative credit were also monopolised by the rural rich. The same stratum was also acquiring greater control over land transforming many of the small owners to the status of tenants-at-will.

The nature of the peasants' unrest and struggle would be affected, or its objectives determinants provided by the varying nature of contradictions or alignments between various agrarian classes and strata, between agrarian classes and urban social groups, and between the urban and the rural people of the province and the colonial state. The principal contradiction of Indian society (including Punjab) within which frame work all other contradictions operated, was between the Indian people and colonialism which blocked their social progress and under-developed their economy. Any political and social movement would have to keep in view the *Zamindars* peasant proprietors and tenants-at-will, who often paid half of the *abian* and land revenue. We have to remember that in the central Punjab there were a large number of tenants who were the proprietors as well; the distinction between these categories is observed more clearly in the Western and Eastern-Southern regions of the province. The rich upper stratum of the santry was able to exploit the mutual differences between sections of the poor peasantry, tenants etc. and thus establish a controlling influence in the rural polity.

Since the very beginning of the period under review, the principal objectives of the British policy in this province were, first to insulate this province from the anti-British sentiments, and, second, to preserve the social and economic structures the failure of which might have led to an atmosphere engendering disloyalty. Moreover, the Government's desire to protect the British armed forces and the recruiting base of the British Indian Army conditioned the Government's approach and strategy in the Punjab. In British strategy and thinking the central place was occupied by the small peasants. The imperialists thought that as long as the small peasants reposed their faith in British rule, agrarian unrest, militant nationalism and the leftist ideologies could find no place in the Punjab. At the same time, the Government was not ready to forgo revenue from the small peasants event during the calamitous depression years when as a result of the steep decline in the agricultural products, the burden of Government taxes was increased manifold. The average remission of land revenue during the five years from 1929-30 to 1933-34 amounted to only 6%. Other peasants' demands would stem from the internal contradiction within rural society, *e.g.* conflicts between the tenants-at-will and the *Zamindars* and the agricultural labour and the peasant proprietors and landlords. These conflict were complicated by the operation of rural credit.

The enormous size of the debt burden of the peasantry can be seen from the fact that it was in 1921 more than 19 times the amount of the land revenue. As early in 1920, 80% of the peasant proprietors were in debt. And, it was estimated in 1920's that atlest 80% of the cultivators sold about 80% of their produce in the village to the shopkeeper-cum-money-landers. This borrowing, when it reached high levels and brought threats of sale of land in execution of decrees sought by money-lenders, became a serious political problem. The Punjab Land Alienation Act which tackled this problem at the turn of the century merely sought to protect from the sale of the land of members belonging to agriculturist tribes and did nothing at all to provide for the essential credit requirements of those that needed to borrow for survival.

During 1920's various changes in the rural society shattered the old static society, transforming it gradually from a community pattern into an individualistic one. The census reports of the period of our study show (see Chapter I) the clow pace of urbanization. For the prosperity of the people of the province and to tackle the issue of unemployment both in urban and rural acres, and to improve the lot of the agriculturists, there was a strong as well as urgent need, especially of agriculture based industrialization as well as the development of cottage industries in this province. Capital was extremely unorganised in the rural areas and as a matter of fact not much of it was available. Another noteworthy feature of the older socio-economic system was the communal pattern which became increasingly apparent in the second half of the 19th century. It had its roots in the social and political structure of the British Punjab. Here was a society composed of three different but some times overlapping, segments—Hindus, Sikhs and Muslims, each with its customs, boundaries and traditional elites. Casteism also prevented the evolution of a strong consciousness and it was probably the greatest political handicap under which the Indian laboured. The high-ups in the social scale were unmindful of the well being of low castes, and objected to their admission to educational institutions. This laid the foundation of communal tensions and the socio-economic effects of communal strife cannot be easily ignored.

We have seen that right from the beginning of the period of our study *i.e.* 1920, a wave of militant nationalism spread throughout the Punjab and to some extent the peasants were awakened in some parts of the province. The militant spirit strengthened the mass movement to fight the imperialist exploitation and oppression. In this, way, the peasants' problems and their demands and aspirations gave birth to the militant struggle of the people which they fought against the British bureaucracy and the highhandedness of the

Zamindar class and the moneylenders in the beginning of this movement but after 1930 this movement declined for sometime. However, it gave birth to an economic, political and social revolution in the shape of peasant's struggle. The feelings of nationalism and national solidarity, and the anti-landlordism and anti-imperialist feeling roused the people particularly in the rural areas. The leftist group also gained strength. The extremists within the peasants organisation continued their attacks on the weaknesses of the Congress policies as also on the politics of the Unionists. During 1920-30, they aimed at co-operating with the Congress and creating an awakening in the Punjab. The declaration of the various parties of forming a front with the Congress, the boycott of the Simon Commission and the emphasis on total independence did not bring immediate success. At this stage the leadership of the youth organisation, which in the province was a part of the peasants' organisation, wanted to give a new shape to the policies of the Congress to make it a party of the masses through propaganda, speeches, messages appeals and by sending leaflets to labourers, farmers and prominent leaders of the province as well as the country.

The Punjab *Kisan* Organisation in particular and other radical parties in general brought to the force the demands of the common man and also provided a wider outlook to the Congress programme through their hold criticism, continuous propaganda and powerful agitation. They tried to pressurize the Congress to enlarge its objective and to include the social and economic demands of the farmers in its programme. Their several campaigns and struggle against imperialism and landlordism created a sizeable group within the congress having sympathies with them. Although the leadership of the PKC tried to give a socialistic orientation to the Congress programme, they continued in general, to look upon the Congress as a bourgeois party. The real object of the PKC's efforts was to enlist Congress support in their fight against imperialism and landlordism as well as against the moneylender.

Above all the radical left groups created a tradition of left ideology which left its mark on Punjab. The Peasants groups *i.e.*, the PKC and NBS held parallel sessions in Karachi, which gave further strength to their demand for total freedom. In a specific resolution, they preached a mass militant struggle to strengthen the peasants' and workers' organisations. Another noteworthy achievement of the left was that the Punjab Scialist Party was organised in 1933. The Punjab continued to be a fountain head of revolutionary thought for other provinces which had united under the banner of Hindustan Socialist Republic Party. Since 1920, Lahore always remained a centre of revolutionary activities. It attracted revolutionaries from the whole of the Punjab and others states as well. While on the one hand, radical elements, particularly the leftists and the Congress socialists, started organising peasants in the form of *Kisan Sabhas,* conservatism found expression through the leadership of the landlord class which had a close association with the imperialist government. As a result, strong resistance was encountered by the Congress Socialists as well as the Communists in their efforts to provide a leadership to the poor peasants. Moreover, the moneylenders and men belonging to the business community were the pillars of the social base of the Congress and their influence did not allow the congress to take a lead in the agrarian movement.

The Akali agitation which at first remained purely religious in its nature, organised the *Zamindars* and the middle class Sikh peasants in the national struggle. The most significant and lasting contribution of the Akalis was that their struggle brought about political awakening among the rural masses, particularly the Sikh peasantry. In brief, it gave rise to militant nationalist element and prepared the ground for the formation of the Punjab *Kirti Kisan* organisation. In the final analysis, the contribution of the *Babbar* Akali agitation was that by intensifying revolutionary activities in the Punjab, it quickened the pace of the Indian National movement. Their martyrdom strengthened the determination of the Indian revolutionaries to eject the foreign government out of the country. Another important point worth mentioning is that only the Sikh peasants participated in the movement during 1928-45. The participation of the Muslim and Hindu peasants was negligible. The upper strata of the peasantry and the landlords made the peasants rally round them with the slogan that the rate of the *abiana* and land revenue should be reduced. But no attention was paid by the then Government to other grievances of poor peasants, such as reduction in rent, abolition of debt, forced labour *thickriphera* etc. The other group of the landlords (Unionist Party), loyal to the British Government, attacked those sections of the moneylenders who were considered to be the non-agriculturists. They, supporting the peasants' demands for abolition of debt, could win them over. The strategy they prepared was to reduce revenue and *abiana* only through pressure on and compromise with the British administration.

Under the prevailing conditions, only a leftist political party taking up the demands of the peasants and tenants, might have started a militant struggle against the high-handedness, exploitation and atrocities of the moneylenders, the *Zamindars* and the British imperialists. All the efforts to form such an organisation during the period under review as an alternative proved to be futile. During this period, the leftist failed to attract the peasants, not only because of the repressive measures of the British but also because of the policies of the CPI and its contradictions and split into two factions. Their factional hostilities continued even at the time when the united front had been formed with the opposition groups in the Punjab provincial Congress. It was merely during the period of the United Front that the leftist assembled under the banner of the CSP and the PKC was formed, and it remained a target of criticism of the Unionists. Even before they could establish themselves among the peasants and tenants, the Unionist Party snatched away this initiative from them, when they introduced some agrarian bills against the moneylenders. The neutrality observed by the Congress towards these bills also enabled the Unionist Party to curb their opponents. The policy of carrot and stick was adopted simultaneously in order to satisfy the agriculturists and check the rising agrarian movement in this part of the country.

The British bureaucracy in 1923 had helped the Unionist Party to gain strength. It tried that the peasants should rally round the unionists who had constituted the constitutionalist *Zamindara* league. The league in its manifesto included some of the demands of the peasants and held out an assurance that their party would help the peasants financially and thus relieve them of the debts to the moneylenders, but in reality they paid to attention to the demands and problems of small peasants, agricultural labourers and tenants because their real strength depended on the support of the top crest of the rural society and the tacit support of the British Government. The Unionists Government called itself the government of the agriculturists whereas they represented only the rural upper strata. The purpose of such a posture was to divert peasant discontent from militant lines of action. In the beginning of 1930 itself, the local agriculturists' organisations started coming into existence; the pace of such a development depended on many things such as the deterioration of the economic condition, the differential impact of the depression on different strata of peasantry, and the attitude and programme of the organised parties. In the beginning, a large number of peasants used to assemble in the meetings of the *Zamindara* League, after 1930, when the organisation failed to move the Government, the thinking of the peasants also went on changing. Now they started leaning towards organisations more responsive to their grievances, like the *Zamindara Sabha* (close to the Akali Party), and the *Kisan Sabha* (led by the *Kirtis,* the Congress Socialists and the Communists). It was this latter group which exposed ruthlessly the dreadful reality of imperialisms, exposed the stooges and the allied forces of imperialism, *Rajwarashahi, Jagirdari* and Capitalism. The first task of the NBS was to organise labourers and the peasants by means of newspapers and setting up libraries of socialist literature in certain villages. As we have seen, during the powerful movement of the peasants between 1937-40, the strongest opposition was manifested by the peasants of Nilibar when 25,000 of them launched agitation against exploitation and repression. The *Zamindars* were asked to concede some of their demands and the Government was also forced to intervene. Even after 1940, agrarian unrest in the Nilibar region continued and it was the PKC which took up the organizational and propaganda work in that area.

Now a question arises, why the peasants and the tenants of the north-west Punjab, failed to respond in the same way as the Nilibar peasantry. It has been shown that the influence of the leaders in the north-west Punjab was very limited and the leaders of the PKC toured this region only in 1940 for the first time. Of course, they tried their best to organise the peasants of this region but they failed to make a mass base, one reason being that most of the leaders belonged to the central Punjab. Moreover, there was no such leadership in this area which could act as a link between the rural masses and the provincial leadership. Apart from the defects of organisation another factor was that during the entire period under review, not only in the Congress but in all the other political parties, there were serious differences of opinions. Internal factionalism existed in all the political parties which weakened the movement itself (Chapter V). Under the circumstances, the major political parties after 1937 lost sight of the task of upliftment of rural masses in general and the peasantry in particular.

As the nationalist movement gathered momentum and the leftists began to make their presence felt, the Government had to go beyond purely law and order measures to political measures to keep these forces in check. The problem for the Government was how to safeguard the interests of the *Zamindars* and at the same time pacify the suffering peasantry, so that the Punjab may be preserved as the recruiting ground for the imperialist army. Suppression of the peasants activities had to be combined with concessions to the agriculturists, but not at the cost of *Zamindars* who had promised to secure the support of the moneylenders. As we know, the Punjab was politically very significant and a strong potential in tis revolutionary petty bourgoeis and peasant elements. Though the left group was not very strong in the province, the bureaucracy was well aware of this political danger. It became essential in the British interest to maintain an absolute control on the province. The tide of nationalism had to be checked. The articulate middle class had to be isolated from the rural masses. In the first decade of the 20th century, bureaucracy took care to cultivate loyalist groups and their efforts resulted in the formation of the Unionist party which dominated the Punjab politics till 1940 and this we have discussed at length in Chapter V.

The Punjab Government also kept a very close watch on the activities of the *Naujawan Bharat Sabha*, the Communists, the Congress Socialists, etc. and at the same time, undertook 'reforms' in various fields in order to pacify the peasantry in particular and the masses in general. But the little that was done by the way of reforms (the reference of this have been made in detail in Chapter VI) did not satisfy the aggrieved peasantry, nor could it calm their agitation. These measures were evidently politically motivated.

In the British Punjab the agrarian movement remained confined mainly to the districts of the central Punjab. It remained every weak and almost negligible in the western Punjab. The same can be said about the south-eastern Punjab (the modern Haryana). It was limited mainly to the Sikh peasants, the contribution of the Hindu and Muslim peasants being very little. In other words, the movement confined itself to the small Sikh *Jat* peasant proprietors of the Central Punjab. Perhaps, this movement could reach the *Jat* Sikhs of the central Punjab due to their traditional hostility to the British imperialism and the existence of the militant religious reform movements. The movements of 1938-40, in the Nilibar, Montgomery, Multan, Lahore, and Harsha-Chhinna alone can be called the effective peasants movements in which their demands were taken up and the attention of the masses was drawn to their problems. The leadership of the agrarian struggle opposed the illegal increase in rent, *begar* and eviction. It also demanded that the rent be reduced and the share-croppers be relieved. However, these movements could not continue for long. Secondly, their spread remained limited specially and large areas remained unaffected. Moreover, the target of these movements were not only the Indian *Zamindars*, Hindu moneylenders but also the British bureaucracy and the foreign companies which had acquired land on lease particularly in the Nilibar region. Above all the leadership of the agrarian struggle did not pay attention to the demands mostly concerned the tenants-at-will, share-croppers and the agricultural labourers, such as better service conditions and higher wages. One possible explanation could be that the leadership was working with a view to organising all the sections of the peasantry as a part and parcel of the anti-imperialist struggle. That was why the leadership neither encouraged nor accentuated the class conflict in rural areas. Under the prevailing circumstances this was perhaps a justified strategic approach. As a result of the policy adopted by the leadership of the peasants' movement, the peasants of the middle and the rich classes came to acquire a hegemony over this movement. We have also seen that its leadership did not take up the issue of the indebtedness with vigour and enthusiasm. It is a fact that during 1935-42, *morchas, dewans*, conferences and demonstrations were held in which emphasis were laid on this problem, but not to the extent warranted by the indebted peasants' misery.

The social base of the agrarian movement, reflected in its demands and programme, were limited in the following directions. Firstly, the small land proprietors could not enlist the support of their neighbours who were comparatively well off. Secondly tenants-at-will and the farm labourers were out of the sphere of this movements. The social composition of the peasants' movement and its leadership left the scope of the demands it look in hand limited. The rich peasants who were, in the colonial context actual or potential landlords as well as actual or potential employers of labour, were hardly likely to favour the taking up of demands of tenants, whare-croppers and agricultural labourers. To some extent casteism was also responsible for limited participation in the agrarian movement. In the Central Punjab, the agricultural labourers belong to the lower castes. They were, therefore, generally disinclined to join up with the Jat peasants. On the other hand, the common caste and social position of the peasantry of the middle class as well as the rich class not only organised them but also helped them to establish their authority over the small land proprietors. Another important reason why the social base of this movements remained limited was that its radical leadership failed to understand and appreciate the differentiation and the varied character of the peasantry. Once the peasantry was seen and viewed in an undifferentiated manner it was easy for the leadership to identify the interests, demands and aspirations of the prosperous peasant proprietors with those of an undifferentiated category, "the peasantry".

Here it is also necessary to assess the form of this struggle. The form it came to acquire in the British Punjab was mainly on the lines of the Indian National Congress and agitational. It includes holding of meetings, peasants' conferences, rallies and processions, marching of *Jathas* and ultimately courting arrest by the peasants. The strategic perspective, guilding the forms of struggle, at no stage was that of making an agrarian revolution, peacefully, or otherwise, that is, of bringing about changes in agrarian structure through direct peasant action. This perspective were more in the nature of putting pressure on the Government through varying degrees of mass mobilization in order to persuade or pressurize it to accept the peasants' demands, wholly or in part.

The demands of the peasants' movement did not question the basic fundamentals and legitimacy of the agrarian structure. Their main objective was the abolition of the illegal and undesirable exactions. They opposed the unrepresentative, unjust and imperialistic administration. All the radical demands of the peasants' movement like the abolition of land revenue, small uneconomic holdings, etc. were limited to speeches and resolutions and were never made the basic of active movement. It is true that there had come a wide spread awakening among the peasantry but the position of the rich and middle class peasants was neither fundamentally challenged nor weakened.

So far as the question of the connection between the

peasants' struggle and the Indian National Congress is concerned we can perhaps say that the links were not strong. The Congress in the Punjab drew strength from the support of the traders and other urban sections and could not draw the peasants and the tenants into the strong anti-British struggle. At the same time, another significant dimension was the fact that the peasants' struggle succeeded in creating an atmosphere for opposing the political authority simultaneously with the struggle on economic grievances, for the peasants' movement in the Punjab was a struggle against the loyalists, 'the feudal rulers' and the *Zamindars*'.

As we have seen in the second section of Chapter V, the feeling of communalism played a part in weakening the peasants' struggle particularly in the region of Western and South-Eastern areas of the Punjab. The Muslim *Zamindars* and the British Government clearly exploited the fact that is the Western Punjab landlords and tenants were Muslims whereas the moneylenders were Hindus. Their objective was to change the peasant politics and to rally the peasants behind the landlords on the basis of religious communalism against the moneylenders. The Hindu moneylenders were also not averse to promoting their interests through Hindu Communalism. Communalism was so pervasive that even the peasdants of the central Punjab who were guided by the leftists could not keep aloof from the communal elements. Under these conditions of communalism and casteism in the Punjab, the struggle against *Zamindars*, moneylenders and the British imperialism remained weak. Another significant reason for the failure of this movement was the strength of the Unionist party, duly supported by the British bureaucracy, in the Western Punjab and South-eastern Punjab and that of Muslim communalism in the Western Punjab. The British Government and the landlords succeeded in maintaining these two areas as their power bases with the active support of landlords, the rich peasantry and emerging agriculturists moneylenders and the general body of peasantry.

Let us now turn to the *Muzaras*' movement in the East

Punjab States. We should recall that since the beginning of the period under review, the *Muzaras* had come a long way in their struggle against the repression of the states, the exploitation by the *Zamindars* and also against the help and protection given by the British to the rulers of the States. However, it is yet to be seen whether or not they succeeded in their objective. As far as *Muzaras* were concerned, the reply would be probably 'Yes' because they only wanted the land, lost by their forefathers to be restored to them. Even the communists in practice envisaged nothing beyond, though their theoretical vision encompassed the setting up of socialistic society. To them socialism in simple terms meant that a tenant should own a piece of land for cultivation. For the leftists of the Punjab it had already been an article of faith, with their roots in the self-cultivating peasant proprietors of central Punjab. Moreover, the *Muzaras* seemed to be fairly substantial tenants. The fact that before the settlement they owned the land they now cultivated as occupancy tenants or were occupancy tenants on land now held as tenants-at-will is a pointer in the same direction. Their capacity to resist oppression for a long time is no evidence of their being sound economically; rather they had been forced by their hardships and miseries to continue the struggle against exploitation and oppressive policies of the State's authorities. They desired to be the owners of the land as they generally believed that as a matter of right they were either the owners or at least the occupancy tenants. Consequently, their perspective was that of a land owning peasants.

Similarly weaknesses were visible in the understanding of the nature of the British rule. It was thought that the British Punjab was better-placed as it had representative institutions and enjoyed the civil liberties. Many *Muzara* movement leaders believed that in the British Punjab the burden of land revenue and other taxes was not much and the agriculturists received remunerative prices for their produce. The comparison between the Phulkian States and the neighbouring territory is understandable but it tended to go much further. Several speakers in the Conferences and the posters stressed their demand that they wanted nothing more than what their counterparts in the British territory were already enjoying (See Chapter III). The limited nature of the civil liberties, the heavy land revenue against which the peasants in the British Punjab had been agitating, and the unrepresentative nature of the councils and the assemblies, in fact, the whole nationalist critique of the British rule was not sufficiently clearly conveyed to the peasants of the Punjab States. Nor was the connection between the continued resistance of the British rule and the survival of the princely rule disclosed. Hence, the British were looked upon as the supreme power and the princes as their subordinates. The deputations to the political agents made an attempt to get the British to put pressure of the rulers of these states. Yet the realisation that it was the British support which in the last resort enabled the princes to maintain their autocratic rule was lacking or was inadequately expressed. It was a serious weakness, without removing which no real unity could be achieved between the people of the British Punjab and the people of the Punjab states.

Again, no emphasis was given by leaders in the Punjab states to the connection betwεen the maintenance of the *Biswedari* system and the existence of the British rule. The princes were urged in the capacity of rulers, to interference and protect them from the high-handedness of the officials as well as that of the *Biswedars*. This further strengthened their claim that they were the real fountain-heads of justice to the different sections of the society. Thinking that the serious agrarian struggle posed a great danger to their existence, the rulers of the states put their entire force at the back fo the *Biswedars*.

The *Muzara* movement which was led by the leftists in the Punjab states certainly lacked strength, particularly against the Akalis and these forces which helped the rich agriculturists against the small and poor peasantry. They merely criticised the Akalis led by Master Tara Singh for being more inclined towards compromise and collaboration with the reactionary conservative and even anti-national forces and they claimed to be more honest than the Akalis. But this emphasis on the individual dishonesty, hypocrisy and such other matter diverted the attention from the deep roots of communalism which was the whole notion of the existence of separate interests of different communities. It was thus not surprising that the leftists by 1945 had started supporting the demand of a separate Muslim Pakistan. Similarly, a section of the leftists expressed their sympathy for a separate Sikh homeland. It limited their appeal only to the Sikh peasants, although it intensified the immediate potency of the appeal. But in the Punjab states this communal appeal could not be used to any advantage because of the hold of the Akalis on the masses. However from 1940, Master Tara Singh began to openly help the British and the Maharaja of Patiala. Master Tara Singh was able to rally the Sikh peasants in large numbers round him; those swayed by religion sentiments still considered the Akalis as the militant fighters against the atrocities and exploitation. However by 1942 if the Sikh peasantry had to choose between the Akalis on the one hand and the Praja Mandalists and the leftists on the other, they opted for the latter.

Only the Biswedars could remain untarnished from influence of communal forces. They did not feel insecure because of the presence of their representatives in the administration and because of the active state help extended to protect their interest in the beginning of the tenants' struggle. Even then, they had to learn much from their counterparts in the British Punjab who were leading the Unionist Party, which used not only the communal and caste identities (the Muslim *Zamindars* hailed from the west Punjab while the *Jat Zamindars* from the East) but also with the help of the British rulers developed a new identity around the presumed opposition between rural as against urban interests such as moneylenders, traders, etc. Thus, the *Biswedars* succeeded in dividing the rural society into two sections and forming a separate rural block in which the *Zamindars,* the peasants and the tenants could be included. This was an obstacle in the way of the rising peasants' struggle in the British Punjab. The *Biswedars* failed to develop such a strategy. At the most, they could form an association, pressurize the rulers and threaten to organize an armed force of their own. They also started trying to win the sympathy of the right wing leaders. One remarkable feature of the politics of the states during 1925 to 42, was that the leftists were non-sectarian. After 1930, they joined hands with the militant Akalis, secular *Praja Mandalists* and the Congress. In course of time, particularly since 1942, the left leadership was compelled to make some compromise with communal elements and thus lost their secular non-sectarian image.

We must accept the truth, the *Muzaras'* struggle with its militant approach, sacrifices and success remained a limited economic struggle of the Punjab peasants. In fact, it could not go beyond the *Biswedari* system; nor could it reach even the interior of the Punjab, states. Further, it did not develop strong links with the peasants' struggle in the neighbouring British Punjab. Hence, this struggle could gain neither the opportunity nor the help for political and ideological advancement for the future. In brief the political activities in the East Punjab states remained far away from framing long term objectives and programme. No compaign of "No Tax" was 1 launched in the non-*Biswedari* region (where the Government demands of land revenue and *abiana* rate were never opposed by any of the leaders), nor was there a call for "No *Batai*" which would have associated with them the whole peasantry. The Punjab *Kisan* Committee which on behalf of the communist party guided the peasants movements in the British territory and the East Punjab States, failed to get help from outside the states, on the lines of the *morchas* like the *Kisan Morcha* of Lahore of 1938-39 or like the *Jathas* sympathising with the peasants' movement in the British territories.

In fact, there is not even a single conference on record where the peasants expressed their support to the tenants. The peasants in their individual capacity did help the *Muzaras*. They also addressed their conferences and made efforts to get their grievances redressed when they tried to bring about a compromise between them and the states' authorities but no particular solidarity was achieved. In this way, the impact of this movement did not go beyond the leftist peasants and the *Praja Mandalists*. The Congress leaders of the national level generally failed to appreciate the significance of this movement publicly. So far as the leaders of the movement itself were concerned, it was usual for them to mention the name of some leaders of national status in order to gain popularity at the provincial and local level. The people outside the states were never properly informed of the significance of the movement.

Now, we come to the concluding part of the balance sheet of the agrarian movement and the tenants' struggle in the East Punjab States respectively. Of course, by the end of 1945, the peasants' struggle in the Punjab and the tenants' struggle in the East Punjab States had almost lost their impetus and appeal. Inspite of the radical and progressive outlook of the militant nationalist leadership in the Punjab, the pace of the growth of the mass movement in this province gradually slackened in the 1940's. The repeated acts of terrorism on moneylenders, landlords and the British revenue officers clearly showed that the peasants' leaders had lost their hold over the peasantry and could not appreciate the limitation of personal terrorism in bringing about revolution. It is significant that during 1938-39, the "No Tax" campaign did not spread in the Punjab and Bengal as it did in the U.P.

Nevertheless, it will be mistake to under rate these movement. They brought about a rapport between the anti-*Zamindar* and anti-imperialist forces and it strengthened the growing awareness among the various sections of the society, that they should fight a united and organised battle. At the same time, these movements as well as the agrarian unrest in British Punjab and East Punjab States succeeded in creating an awareness among the peasants, workers and youngmen and in impetus to launch a meaningful struggle against imperalism and landlordism. Moreover, the activities of the leftists and the Congress socialists groups derived strength from the prevailing agrarian unrest and they succeeded in encouraging anti-imperialist elements and traditions and also in creating an atmosphere for opposing the political authority of the British bureaucracy on the one hand and the Princes of the states on the other. Further, so far as the peasants' struggle in the British Punjab is concerned, it was a struggle against the allies of the British, the feudal rulers and *Zamindars,* and consequently gave birth to the feelings of national solidarity alongwith anti-landlordism. It is not these movements always cooperated with the Indian National Congress and created an awakening in this region of the country. In short, the peasants' struggle in the province was to oppose such policies as could hinder India's achievement of freedom and to promote the programmes and policies which could help achieve this end.

Above all, the peasants' organisations, particularly those led by left nationalist leaders, provided a wider outlook to the Congress programme through their bold criticism, continuous propaganda and powerful agitation. It was this movement, in fact, which gave birth to the leftist ideology in the Punjab and at the same time created a leftist wing in the congress having sympathies with these movements. The left programme was a step ahead of the Congress programme and the leadership of the PKC tried to give a socialistic orientation to the Congress programmes. Its real object was to make the Congress a more militant organisation and to enlist its ideological support in their fight against landlordism, moneylenders and imperialism as well. In brief, the Punjab Socialists Party organised in 1933, was also a gift of the militant nationalist and socialistic ideas of the PKC's leadership and the NBS. Finally, the experience of the peasants' struggle in the Punjab from 1920 to 1945 revealed the potentialities of rural upsurge against landlordism, exploitation and imperialism.

Bibliography

Abbreviation

NAI : National Archieves of India

PSA : Punjab State Archieves

ACHI : Archieves of Contemporary History of India

PCSL : Punjab Central Secretriate Library

DDL : Dwarka Dass Library

Primary Sources : Unpublished

Proceedings of the Department of Education, Health and Lands : 1923-25, GOI, NAI, New Delhi.

Proceedings of the Department of Revenue and Agriculture : 1900-10, GOI, NAI, New Delhi.

Proceedings of the Department of Industries and Labour : 1924-36, GOI, NAI, New Delhi.

Proceedings of the Finance Department : 1915-30 and 1934-35, GOI, NAI, New Delhi.

Proceedings of the Home Department : 1920-40, GOI, NAI, New Delhi.

Proceedings of the Home Department (Political) : 1919-45, GOI, NAI, New Delhi.

Meerut Conspiracy Case (1929-32) selected files :—(NAI, New Delhi) :

(a) Files on the Workers' and Peasants' Parties;

(b) Gurumukhi Exhibit;

(c) Urdu Exhibit;

(d) Punjab and U.P. Speeches;

(e) Statements of the Punjab Communists (especially of

R.S. Nimbkar and others) involved in the Case : Abdul Majid, Sohan Singh Josh and Kedar Nath Sehgal;

(f) Meerut Conspiracy Case Judgment delivered by R.L. Yorke—Additional Session Judge in the Meerut Conspiracy Case, Vol. I.

Amritsar Conspiracy Case : 1919—Proceedings, Exhibits and Judgement, (One Roll, in Microfilm), NMML, New Delhi.

Delhi Court Papers : Assembly Bomb Case, Trial No. 9 of 1929, Vols. I & VI (in original), Private Paper Section, NAI : New Delhi.

Assembly Case Session Judgement dated 7th October, 1930, Phase III A/9/3 (in original), NAI : New Delhi.

Punjab States' Agency Records (Political) : 1925--35, PSA : Patiala.

Punjab States' Agency Records (General) : 1920-36, PSA : Patiala.

Patiala State Records : Prime Minister's Office Files : PSA, Patiala 6157, G-2155, 541, 547, 548, 549, 552, 553, 556, 563, 564, 566, 567, 569, 578, 608, 609, 613, 623, 624, 630, 639, 642, 644, 654, 655, 667, 669, 670, 672, 675, 689, 690, 692, 697, 700, 702, 703, 710, 713, 715, 724, 727, 729, 730, 733, 734, 737, 742, 744, 745, 746, 747, 750, 756, 770, 772, 774, 1534, 1546, 1547, 1550, 1553, 1554, 1555, 1559, 1561, 1563, 1573, 1574, 1575, 1650, 1657, 2077, 5804, 2226/100, 238/SPC, Case No. 565/C of 1943-44, 565/C, CB, 1-2 of 1944-45, CB, 1-2 of 1945-46, T-1 of 1945, etc.

Chamber of Princes' Records, File-CAS/L-9 (Subversive movements from across the border) Press Clippings pertaining to the States and the Political Movements, PSA, Patiala.

Proceedings of the Punjab States Council Meetings held at Lahore on 17th & 18th March, 1940 and at Simla on 30th & 31st March, 1943, PSA, Patiala.

Nabha State Records : Confidential Meetings Files—82-B, 49-C, 62-C, 337, PSA, Patiala.

Faridkot State Records : Political Movement Files—23, 37, 82, 226, 243, 264, 265, 291, 336, 369, PSA, Patiala.

Kalsia State Records : Files—(Confidential)—1, 2, 132, 164, PSA, Patiala.

Kapurthala State Records : Files—A5-1, M/3-14, M/3-14, M/3-39, PSA : Patiala.

Reports on the operations for the Relief of distress caused by floods in the districts of Rohtak, Gurgoan, Karnal and Ambala during September, 1933, File No. B/14468, PSA : Patiala.

Assessment of the Pakpattan Tehsil of the Montgomery districts, 1922, File No. R/1689, PSA : Patiala.

Assessment of the Gujranwala Tehsil, Gujranwala District, 1912, File No. R/1548, PSA : Patiala.

Assessment Report of the Kharian Tehsil of Gujarat District, 1913, File No. R/1591, PSA : Patiala.

Annual Administration Reports of Patiala, Nabha, Kapurthala, Faridkot and Kalsia States for the period 1911-39, PSA : Patiala.

Annual Report of the Canals in the Punjab : 1919-20, PSA : Patiala.

Primary Sources : Printed

Following Selected Publication of the Board of Economic Enquiry, Punjab, PCSL, Chandigarh :

(a) *The Size and Distribution of Agricultural Holdings in the Punjab,* 1928, No. 4.

(b) *The Size and Distribution of Cultivators Holdings in the Punjab,* 1928;

(c) *The Size and Distribution of Proprietory Holdings in the Punjab,* 1939;

(d) *Punjab Farm Accounts : 1930-33.*

(e) *Soldiers' Savings,* No. 68, 1939.

(f) *Note on the sale of Gold and ornaments in 120 Punjab Villages,* from October, 1933 to December, 1933, published in 1936, etc.

Punjab Legislative Council Debates, Proceedings : 1920-45, Vols. VI-XXIX, NAI, New Delhi.

Punjab Legislative Assembly Debates, Proceedings : 1937-40, Vols. I-XX, NAI, New Delhi.

Punjab Budgets with detailed estimate : 1920-21, NAI, New Delhi.

Report of the Abiana Committee appointed by the Punjab Government, Lahore : 1934, PSA : Patiala.

Report of the Joint Select Committee on Indian Constitutional Reforms : 1933-34, Vol. I, Part II (London : 1934), NAI : New Delhi.

Report of the Land Revenue Committee, appointed by the Punjab Government in 1937-38.

Report of the Punjab Provincial Banking Industry Committee : 1929-30, Vol. I, Calcutta : 1930.

Report of the Retrenchment Committee appointed by the Punjab Government in 1931, Lahore : 1931.

Report of the Punjab Sources of Revenue Committee, 1931, Lahore : 1931.

Abridged Report of the Royal Commission or Agriculture, Calcutta : 1928.

Royal Commission on Agriculture—Appendix to Report, Bombay : 1931.

Nehru Committee (All Parties Conference) Report : 1928. Allahabad : 1938 (Third Edition).

Reserve Bank of India Preliminary Report on Agricultural Credit, Bombay : 1936.

Review of the work of the Irrigation Department, Statistical and Statement : 1938-39.

Statistical Abstracts of British India : 1920-21 to 1938-39, London : 1932 and Delhi : 1941.

Dufferin Enquiry into the Economic Conditions of the Lower Classes of Agricultural Population, December : 1888.

Abhyankar, G.R. and Trivedi Manishanke, S., *Report of the States Peoples' Conference,* Bombay Session : 1928.

Land Revenue Administration in the Punjab : 1919-20.

Annual Reports of the Canals in the Punjab : 1919-20.

Annual Reports of the Public Works Department, Punjab 1931-32; 1938-39.

Annual Reports on the Operation of the Department of Land Records, Punjab : 1936-40.

Annual Punjab Administration Reports : 1919-21, 1922-23 to 1925-26, 1938-39.

Annual Reports on the Working of the Punjab Alienation of Land Act (1900), 1902-03 and 1906-07.

Confidential Papers of Home Secretary and Governor General of India : 1920-45.

Board of Enquiry, Punjab Publication No. 52, Agricultural Statistics of the Punjab : 1920-21 to 1939-40, Lahore : 1940.

Agricultural Statistics of the British Punjab : 1938-39, Supplementary 3-10, Publication No. 52, Lahore : 1940.

Bulletin of the Joint Development Board Punjab : 1930.

Annual Administration Reports of the East Punjab States and Khalsa States : 1919-37.

Director Information Bureau, Punjab—*A Review of the Administration of the Punjab* from April 1, 1937 to September, 1938.

India in 1921-22 (Calcutta : 1922).

India in 1925-26 (Calcutta : 1926).

India in 1927-28 (Calcutta : 1928).

Memorandum prepared by the Punjab Government for the use of the Indian Statutory Commission, Vol. I, 1928.

Punjab Government Gazettees : 1916-40.

Punjab Revenue Act, 1928.

Punjab Act of 1930.

Punjab Act VII of 1934.

Punjab Act II of 1936.

Punjab Act III of 1938.

Punjab Act IV of 1938.

Punjab Act X of 1938.

Indian State Committee Report, London : Printed and published by His Majesty's Stationery Office : 1929.

Indian States, Calcutta, Central Publication Branch : 1928.

Indian States Today, New Delhi Publication Bureau Government of India : 1948.

India in 1917-35, Vols, I & XI, Government of India, Calcutta : 1936.

Collected letters of Bhagat Singh and his Comrades (Punjabee) edited by Amarjeet Chandan, Balraj Sahani, Yadgar Library Publication, Amritsar : 1974.

Report on the Native Newspapers (Punjab) : 1920-40 (A few issues missing), NAI : New Delhi.

News-Papers and Journals

The Kirti (Punjabee), Kirti Lehr (Punjabee) : February 1926 to November, 1939 (The copies of *Kirti* and *Kirti Lehr* are available in Bhai Mohan Singh Vaid Section : Library Punjabi University Patiala; Desh Bhagat Yadgar Hall Library, Jullundur; NMML, Teen Murti, New Delhi (Microfilm Section) and NAI, Library-Proscribed Literature Section, New Delhi).

Hind Samachar : 1920-45, D.D.L. Chandigarh; Desh Bhagat Yadgar Hall Library, Jullundur.

The Milap, Lahore : 1932-35, NAI : New Delhi.

The Tribune, Lahore : 1920-45 (Microfilm) NMML, Teen Murti, New Delhi; and Department of Historical Studies, Punjabi University, Patiala.

Jat Gazette (*Urdu* weekly), Rohtak : 1916-40, Dr. Y.P. Bajaj, Reader in History, Punjabi University, Patiala—Personal Collection.

Daily Nawan Zamana (Punjabee) selected issues.

Sada Yug (Weekly) *(Punjabee),* selected issues, Office Library Punjab Council of the CPI, Sector-21, Chandigarh.

The People (weekly issued from Lahore) : 1926-29—edited by Lala Lajpat Rai till his death in 1928, DDL, Lala Lajpat Rai Bhawan, Sector-15, Chandigarh.

National Front (weekly Newspaper of the CPI), Vol. I, Nos. 1 to 5 (February 13, 1938, to February 5, 1939); Vol. II, Nos. 1 to 33 (February 12, 1939 to December 17, 1939), ACHI, J.N.U., New Delhi.

The Communist : The Official organ of the CPI section of the CI—some selected issues of the years 1935 to 1938, Vol. I of each year and years 1939-41, Vol. II of each year and also Vol. III of 1941, ACHI, JNU, New Delhi.

International Press Correspondence : Organ of the Communist International : 1922-38, CHI, JNU, New Delhi.

Communist International (Journal of the CI) Selected issues : May 1919 to April, 1928, ACHI, JNU, New Delhi.

The Congress Socialist : Organ of the All India Congress-Socialist Party : Vol. I, No. 182, 1934; Vol. I, Nos. 7, 8, 10 to 12, 1935, ACHI, JNU, New Delhi.

The Punjab Past and Present (Various issues), issued by the Historical Research Department : Punjabi University, Patiala.

The Pioneer (Allahabad), 1929.

The Punjabee (Lahore), 1907.

Indian Review, Vol. VIII, 1907.

Journal of Asian Studies, Vol. XVIII, February, 1968.

Journal of Indian History, Vol. I *(ii)*, August, 1972; Vol. I, December, 1973; Vol. XXXVII *(i)* April, 1959.

The Quarterly Review of Historical Studies, Vol. XVI, No. 2; Vol. XVIII, No. 2.

Adhudaya (Allahabad), 1929-31.

Bombay Chronicle (Bombay), 1919.

Civil and Military Gazette (Lahore) 1919-1923.

The Indian Annual Register (Calcutta) : 1919-47, Edited by Mitra, H.N.

Census Report and Gazetters :

Kaul, H.K. Census of India-1911 (Lahore : 1912) Pt. II.

Middleton, L. Census of India-1921 (Lahore : 1923) Vol. XI-Part-I.

Martin, J.J. Census of India-1921 (Calcutta : 1923) Vol. I,Part-II.

Khan, A.H. Census of India-1931 (Lahore : 1933) Vol. XVIII.

Census of India-1941 (Lahore : 1943).

A Macfarquhar Punjab District Gazetter : Amritsar District (Chandigarh : n.d.)

Punjab District Gazetter : Amritsar District (Lahore : 1913) Vol. XXV.

Imperial Gazetter of India : Indian Empire, Vol. IV, Administrative (Oxford : 1907).

Private Papers

Prathvi Singh Azad Papers, NMML, Teen Murti, New Delhi.
Dr. Chaman Lal Papers, NMML, Teen Murti, New Delhi.
Sir Sunder Singh Majithia Papers, NMML, Teen Murti, New Delhi.

AISPC—Papers, NMML, Teen Murti, New Delhi.

AICC—Papers, NMML, Teen Murti, New Delhi.

Transcripts of Interviews : Private Papers Section, NMML, Teen Murti, New Delhi.

Dr. Sunder Lal

Sri Ram Sharma

Bhim Sen Sachar

Gokal Chand Narang

Sri Gurdial Malik

Bhai Jodh Singh

Ajit Prasad Jain

Zaheer Shri Sajjad

Indulal Yajnik

Shri Shaukat Usmani

In Microfilms—Private Papers :

Papers of Lord Willingdon, MSS, EUR, D.256, Roll, I to XIII, NAI, New Delhi.

Papers of Joseph Austin Chambarlain, Secretary of State for India, Roll, I to XVI, NMML, New Delhi.

Linlithgow Papers, MSS, F 125/86-Correspondence with the Governor of the Punjab and his secretary Vol. I-II, June-August, 1938, NAI : New Delhi. Selections from the despatches addressed to the Government of India from the Secretary of State from India : 1932.

Indian News-Papers : 28.12.1935 to 26.12.1936 (In Microfilm), NAI, New Delhi.

Montagu Papers : Private Papers of E.S. Montagu, Secretary of State for India : 1917-22, EUR E 523, Rolls, I-XIV, NAI, New Delhi (India Office Library Records, London).

Zetland Papers : Private Papers of Second Morquis of Zetland, Secretary of State for India : 1935-40, MSS, EUR, 0.609, Vol. 23, 24, 25A, NAI, New Delhi.

Erskine Papers : 1934-40 MSS, EUR, E. 286, Roll, I-XI, (India Office Library, London), NAI, New Delhi.

London : India Office Library Records, A.P. Home Collections : *Paper of A.P. Hume,* Indian Civil Services : 1927-47, NAI : New Delhi.

Birkehead Papers (Frederick Edwin Smith, 1st Earl), MSS, EUR, D. 703, Rolls, I to VII, NAI : New Delhi.

Chelmsford Papers (Frederic Johan, Napier, Thesiger, 1st Viscount), MSS, EUR, E. 264, Rolls, I-XXVIII, NAI, New Delhi.

Halifax Papers (Edward Frederick Lindleywood, 1st Ear), MSS, EUR, C. 152, Roll, I-XIX, NAI : New Delhi.

Morley Papers (John, 1st Viscount), MSS, EUR, D. 573, Rolls, I-XIII, NAI : New Delhi.

Reading Papers (Rufus Daniellsaacs, 1st Marquas) MSS, EUR, 238, Rolls, X-XII, NAI : New Delhi.

Harikrishan Papers, No. 238 (in original), Private Papers Section, NAI : New Delhi.

Unpublished Ph.D. Thesis :

Bajaj, Y.P., Sir Chhotu Ram and His Works (Kurukshtra University, Kurukshtra : 1972).

Lakhanpal, N.K., The Governors of the Punjab : 1901-39-A Constitutional Studies (Punjab University, Chandigarh : 1962).

Mohan, Kamlesh, Militant Nationalism in the Punjab (Guru Nanak Dev University, Amritsar : 1980).

Raja Ram, Impact of the First World War on the Punjab (Punjab University, Chandigarh : 1972).

Puri, H.K., *The Ghadr Party* : A Study in Militant Nationalism (Guru Nanak Dev University, Amritsar : 1975).

Barrier, N.G., Punjab Politics and the Disturbances of 1907 (Duke University : 1966—in Microfilm).

Secondary Sources

Abbot, A. and Wood S.M. : *Report on Vocational Education in India* (Delhi, Punjab and Uttar Pradesh), (Delhi : 1937).

Abdul Latif : *Industrial Punjab*—Calcutta : 1911. *An Economic Survey of Bhambu Sandila,* a village in the Muzzafargarh district of the Punjab (Lahore : 1936), edited.

Agricultural and Trade Statistics (British) Punjab—1939-40 (Lahore : 1941) edited.

Abdur Rauf : *West Pakistan Rural Education and Development* (Central Press : 1970)

Abhednand Swamy : *India and Her People* : (Calcutta : 1963)

Adarkar, B.N. : *The History of India Tariff—1924-39* (Lahore : 1940).

Adarkar, B.P. : Indian Monetary Policy (Allahabad : 1939) Principles and Problems of Federal Finance (London : 1941).

Aderson, G. : *British Adminsitration in India* (London : 1923).

Aderson, J.D. : *Peoples of India* (Cambridge : 1913).

Adhikari, G. : *'The First Indian Communist Conference' Marxist Miscellany* (PPH, New Delhi : 1974)

Pakistan and National Unity : The Communist Solution (Bombay : 1944).

Documents of History of the Communist Party of India, Vol. I & II (PPH, New Delhi : 1972 & 1974 respectively).

Ahluwalia, M.L. : *Kukas : The Freedom Fighters of the Punjab* (Bombay : 1965).

Ahmad, Muzzaffar : *The Communist Party of India and Its Formation Abroad* (Calcutta : 1962).

Myself and the Communist Party of India : 1920-29 (Calcutta : 1970).

Communist Challenge Imperialism from Dock (Calcutta : 1967).

Ahmad Zahir : *Dust and Dawn in Village India* (London : 1965).

: *Communist Challenge Imperialism from Dock* (Calcutta : 1967).

Ahmad, Z.A. : *The Agrarian Problems in India* (Lahore : 1936).

Ahmad Dhari : *Economic Possibilities of Kapurthala* (Punjab : 1921).

Present Situation with Special Reference to Punjab Disturbances (Dehradun : 1919).

Alston, W.P. : *Education of India* (London : 1910).

Allen, G.C. : *The Economic Development of India*, 3rd edition, (London : 1939).

Aderson, G. : *British Administration in India* (London : 1923).

Aderson, J.D. : *Customery Law of Muzzafargarh District* (Lahore : 1925).

People of India (Cambridge : 1913).

Anstey, V. : *The Economic Development of India* (London : 1939).

Antonova, K., : *A History of India* (Moscow : 1978).

Bongoral Levin, G. :

Kotovsky, G. :

Arther Swinson : *Six Minutes to Sunset* (London : 1964).

Ashok, Shamsher Singh : *Punjab Dian Lehran* (Punjabee) (Dhuri-published by Narain Singh, n.d.)

Atta Ullah : *Co-operation Movement in the Punjab* (London : 1937).

Aulakh, Jagjit Singh : *Ikk Jiwan Ikk Itihas* (Panjabi) n.d.

Avtar Singh : *Din Dehare Rattan* (Panjabi) n.d.

Baba, Karam Singh (ed.) : *Abhinandan Granth*—86th Birth Commemoration Vol. Baba Kharak Singh Abhinandan Committee, New Delhi.

Babbar, Sunder Singh : *Babbar Akali Lahar* (Amritsar : 1961).

Baden Powell, B.H. : *The Origin and Growth of Village Communities in India* (New York : 1908).

Bagchi, A.K. : *Private Investment in India : 1900-39* (London : 1972).

Bajwa, Fauja Singh : *Kuka Movement* (Delhi : 1965); *Who is Who : Punjab Freedom Fighters* (ed.,) (Patiala : 1975).

A Brief Account of the Freedom Movement in the Punjab (ed.,) (Patiala : 1975).

Bal, S.S. : *A Brief History of Modern Punjab* (Ludhiana : 1977).

Bala Shastri Hardas : *Armed Struggle for Freedom : Ninety Years of Independence : 1857 to Subhash Bose* (trans) Apte, S.S. (Poona : 1958).

Balabushevich, V.V. and Dyakov, A.M. : *Contemporary History of India* (PPH, New Delhi : 1964).

Bamford, P.C. : *Histories of the Non-Co-operation and Khilafat Movements* (Delhi : Government of India : 1923, reprinted in Delhi : 1974—Confidential CID handbook).

Banerjee, G.L. : *Dynamics of Revolutionary Movement in India : Housekeeping of Revolution in Russia and India* (Calcutta : 1970).

Banga Indus : *Agrarian System of the Sikhs,* late Eighteenth & Early Nineteenth Century (Delhi : 1978).

Bargue, A.M. (ed.) : *Eminent Sikhs of Today,* Vol. I (Lahore : 1942)

Barrier, N.G. : *The Punjab Alienation of Land Bill of 1900* (Monograph : Duke University, 1966).

Punjab Politics and Disturbances of 1907 (Microfilm, NMML, New Delhi).

Batalvi, A.M. : *Iqbal Ke Akhari Do Saal* (Panjabi) n.d.

Beasant, Annie : *How India Wrougth for Freedom* (Madras : 1915); *India Bond or Free : A World Problem* (Putnami : 1926).

Beoli, B.P.L. : *Monstrous Rule in Faidkot* (Delhi : n.d.).

Bhandari, Som Nath (ed.) : *Eminent Hindus of Punjab* (Lahore : 1943).

Bhatnagar, N.L. : *Transport in India and Abroad* (Meerut : 1951).

Bingley, A.H. : *The Sikh—Handbook for the Indian Army* (Calcutta : 1918; reprinted-Patiala : 1970).

History of the Caste and Culture of Jats and Gujars (Delhi : 1978).

Blunt, Sir Edward : *Caste System in Northern India* (Madras : 1931) *Social Service in India* (Madras : 1931). *An Introduction to Some Social and Economic Problems of the Indian People* (London : 1938).

Blyn, G. : *Agricultural Trends in India : 1891-1947*(Philodelphia : 1966).

Boris, Ponomorgov : *Some Problems of the Revolutionary Movement* (Prague : 1975).

Bose, Nemi Sadloan : *The Indian National Movement—An outline* (Calcutta : 1965).

Bose, A.C. : *Indian Revolutionaries : Abroad, 1905-1922* (Patna : 1971).

Bose, Subhash Chandra : *Indian Struggle 1920-42* (Bombay : 1964).

Brailsford, M.N. : *Ain-i-Hindustan* (Urdu) n.d.

Brecher Michal : *Nehru : A Political Biography* (London : 1958).

Brij Narain : *The Agricultural Workers and the Punjab Land Revenue Committee* (Lahore : 1939).

India in Crisis (Allahabad : 1934).

India Before and Since the Crisis, Vol. I and II (Allahabad : 1939)

Indian Socialism (Allahabad : 1937).

Economic Structure of Free India (Lahore : 1946).

Brij Narain : Board of Economic Enquiry Punjab : Eighty Years of Punjab Food Prices, 1841-1920 (Lahore : 1920).

Charkha Marxism : Indian Socialism (Lahore : 1941).

Rational View of Life : Punjab Socialist Party (Lahore : n.d.)

Indian Economic Problems : Essays on Indian Economic Problems (Lahore : 1922).

Marxism is Dead (Lahore)

Broyne, P.L. : *Better Village* (Oxford : 1937).

Rural Reconstruction : A Note (Lahore : 1934)

Brown, Emily C. : *Hardayal : Hindu Revolutionary and Rationalists* (Delhi : 1976).

Buck, C.H. : *Faiths, Fairs and Festivals of India* (New Delhi : 1917).

Butler, Sir Harcowt : *Indian Resistance* (London : 1951)

Cab, G.D.H. : *Communism and Social Democracy : 1914-31* Part I (London : 1931).

Calvert, H. : *The Wealth and Welfare of the Punjab* (Lahore : 1936).

: *Size and Distribution of Agricultural Holdings in the Punjab* (Lahore : 1928).

: *The Law and Principles of Co-operation in India* (Lahore : 1921).

Carr, B.H. : *The Bolshevik Revolution :*

1917-23, Vol. III (London : 1966).

: *Twenty Years Crisis : 1919-39* (London : 1954).

: *Socialism in Our Country,* Vol. I (London : 1966)

Carver, J.N. : *Principles of Rural Economics* (Baston : 1911)

Caveeshar, Sardar Singh : *Sikh Politics* (Delhi : 1950)

: *Non-Violent Non-Cooperation* (Lahore : 1934)

Chadha, T.R. : *A Study of the Communist Movement in the Punjab* (Gaziabad : 1954).

Chandra, Bipan : *"Ideological Evolution of the North India, Terrorists"* in *Socialism in India,* edited by Nanda B.R. (Delhi : 1972).

: *The Rise and Growth of Economic Nationalism in India* (PPH, Delhi : 1977).

: "Peasantry and National Integration in Contemporary India" *Social Scientists,* Vol. V, No. 2, September, 1976.

: *Economic Principles of Indian National Leadership : 1880-1905* (PPH, 1966).

Chatterjee, J.C. : *In Search of Freedom* (Calcutta : 1967).

Chatterjee, M.P. : *Indian Revolutionaries in Conferences* (Calcutta : 1980).

Chaudhary, Sukhbir : *Peasants' and Workers' Movement in India :* 1905-29 (PPH, Delhi : 1971).

: *Growth of Nationalism in India : 1919-29,* Vol. II (Delhi : 1973).

Chhabra, G.S. : *Social and Economic History of the Punjab : 1849-1901* (Jullundur : 1962).

Chirol Valentine : *Indian : The Modern World* (London : 1926).

: *India : Old and New* (London : 1921).

: *India Unrest : A Reprint,* revised and enlarged from *'The Times'* with an introduction by Sir Alfred Lyall (London : 1910).

Chitra, V.R. & Jekhumall Vishwanathan : *Cottage Industries of India* (Madras : 1948)

Chopra, P.N. : *Role of Indian Muslims in the Struggle for Freedom* (Delhi : 1979).

Chudgar, P.L. : *Indian Princes under British Protection* (London : 1929).

Clarke John : *The Sikhs* (Oxford : 1946).

Claudin, Fernando : *The Communist Movement From Comintern to Cominform* (London : 1975).

Cohen, S.P. : *Indian Army : Its Contribution to the Development of a Nation* (Berkeley : 1971).

Cole, D.G.H. : *Communist International Between 5th and 6th International* (London : Communist Party of Great Britain : 1928).

Cotten, H.J.S. : *New India* (London : 1904).

Coupland, R. : *Constitutional Problem in India*, Vol. II, (Oxford : 1945).

: *India : A Restatement* (London : 1945).

Craddock, Reginald : *The Dilemma in India* (London : 1929).

Crooke, W. : *Natives of Northern India* (London : 1907).

: *Religion and Folklore of Northern India* (London : 1926).

Damodran, K. : "Memoirs of An Indian Communist", *New Left Review,* London No. 93, September-October : 1975.

Dange, S.A. : *Gandhi Vs. Lenin* (Bombay : 1921).

Daniel Argav : *The Moderates and the Extremists in Indian National Movement : 1883-1920* (Bombay : 1967).

Darling, M.L. : *The Punjab Peasant in Prosperity and Debt* (London : 1925).

: *Rusticus and Loquitur or The Old Light and the New in the Punjab Village* (London : 1930)

: *Wisdom and Waste in the Punjab village* (London : 1934).

: *At Freedom Door's* (London : 1949).

Das Gupta, M. : *Dshbandhu Chitranjan Das* (Delhi : 1940)

Dass, R.K. : *The Labour Movement in India* (New York : 1923)

Dass, Tarak Nath : *Sovereign Rights of the Indian Princes* (Madras : 1924).

Davey Bargain : *The Economic Development of India : A Marxist Analysis* (London : 1975).

Dayanand, Swami : *Hand Book of the Arya Samaj.*

Degras Jane : *Communist International 1919-1943, Documents,* Vols. I, II, & III (London : 1971).

Deol, G.S. : *The Role of the Ghadr Party in the National Movement* (Jullundur : 1969).

: Sardar Bhagat Singh (Patiala : 1978).

Desai, A.R. : *Social Background of Indian Nationalism* (Bombay : 1948).

Desai, Meera : *Women in Modern India* (Bombay : 1957).

Desai, R.C. : *Standard of Living in India and Pakistan 1931-32 to 1940-41* (Bombay : 1953).

Desai, T.B. : *Economic History of India under the British* (Bombay : 1968).

Dewan Raj Kumar : *Modern Kapurthala and its Makers* (Kapurthala Government Publication : n.d.)

Dewan Jermani Dass : *Maharaja :* Lives and Loves and Intrigues of Indian Princes (Bombay : 1969).

Dewett, K.K. : Indian Economics (Delhi : 1948).

Dorothy Norman : *Nehru : The First Sixty Years,* Vol. I (Bombay : 1961).

: *History of the Indian National Congress : 1935-37*, Vol. II (Bombay : 1947).

Douie, J.M. : *Punjab Settlement Mannual* (Lahore : 1930)

Drummond, J.C. : *Punchayats in India* (London : 1937).

Dubois, J.D. : *Hindu Manners Customs and Ceremonies* (Oxford : 1906).

Dukhi Munsha Ram : *Jiwan Bhai Sahib Mohan Singh Vaid* (Panjabi) (Amritsar : n.d.)

Duie James : *The Punjab, N.W.P.P. and Kashmir* (First published in 1931, Reprinted Delhi : 1974).

Dunber, Sir George : *India and the Passing of Empire* (London : 1951)

Duni Chand : *The Ulster of India : An Analysis of the Punjab Problems* (Lahore : 1936).

Dutta, D. : *Humayun Kabir : A Political Biography* (Bombay : 1969).

Dutt, R.C. : *The Economic History of India in Victorian Age : 1837-1900* (Delhi : 1960).

Dutt, R. Palme : *India Today* (PPH, Bombay : 1947).

Dutt, V.N. : *Jallianwala Bagh* (Punjabi Univ. Patiala : 1972)

Ewart, J.M. : *Terrorism in India : 1917-36* (Simla, Government of India : 1937, reprinted Delhi : 1974).

Fagan, Sir Patrick : *Possibilities of Agricultural Development in the Punjab* (Lahore : 1923).

Farquhar, J.N. : *Crown of Hinduism* (London : 1913).

Fuller, Bompfylde : *The Empire of India* (London : 1913).

Ganda Singh : *History of Gurdawara Shaheed Ganj* (Amritsar : 1935) : *Some Confidential Papers of the Akali Movement* (Amritsar, S.G.P.C. : 1930—edited).

Gallegher, John and Seal Anil (ed.) : *Locality, Province and Nation : Essays on Indian Politics : 1870-1940* (London : 1940).

Gandhi, M.K. : *Young India : 1919-22 & 1924-26* (Madras : 1927)

: *Hindu-Muslim Tension* (Ahmedabad : 1927).

: *Correspondence with Mr. Gandhi from August : 1942 to April, 1944* (Delhi : 1944).

: *The Indian States' Problems* (Ahmedabad : 1941). *Quit India* (Bombay : 1942).

: *His Life, Writings and Speeches* (Madras : 1918)

: *Collected Works of Mahatma Gandhi*, Vols. XVI; XLI, XLII (Ahamedabad : 1965, 1970 & 1971 respectively).

Gangulee Nagendra Nath : *The Indian Peasant and His Environment* (London : 1935).

Gankovsky, Yu V. : *The People of Pakistan : An Ethnic History* (PPH, Lahore : 1968).

Gautam Chattaopadhayya : *Communism and Bengal's Freedom Movement : 1917-19,* Vol. I.

Ghosh, Ajoy Kumar : *Articles and Speeches* (Mascow : Publishing House for Oriental Literature : 1962)

Ghosh, Shanker : *Political Ideas and Movement in India* (Calcutta : 1975).

: *The Western Impact on Indian Politics 1885-1919* (Calcutta : 1967).

Ghoshal, U.N. : *Bhagat Singh and His Comrades* (Bombay : 1945).

: *The Agrarian System in Ancient India* (Calcutta : 1973).

Ghurye, G.S. : Caste and Race in India (Bombay : 1932).

: Caste, Class and Occupation (Bombay : 1961).

: *Indian Customs* (Bombay : 1951).

Giani, Gurmukh Singh : *Biography of Master Mota Singh* (Panjabi) n.d.

: *Prescribed Literature,* NAI, New Delhi.

Giani, Kehar Singh : *Praja Malerkotla Di Dard Kahani* (Panjabi) n.d., published by Jagir Singh Joga, Amritsar : n.d.

Giani Nahar Singh : *History of Freedom Movement in India* (Amritsar : 1950).

Giani Partap Singh : *Akali Lehr Da Itihas* (Panjabi) (Singh Bros., Amritsar : 1951).

Gibbs, H.A.R. : *Mohammedanism* (n.d.)

Gidwani, B.S. : *History of Transport in India* (Delhi : 1954).

Glading Perey : *India Under British Terror* (London : 1931).

Gopal, Sarvepalli : *British Policy in India : 1885-1905* (Cambridge : 1965).

: *The Viceroyality of Lord Irwin* (Oxford : 1957).

: *Jawaharlal Nehru : A Biography,* Vol. I, (London : 1975).

Gopal, Thakur : *Bhagat Singh : The Man and His Ideas* (The Manifesto).

: *Bhagat Singh* (Hindi) (Delhi : 1963).

Government of India (Compiled by) : *Terrorism in India* (1917-37) (Delhi, n.d.)

Gulab Singh : *Under the Shadow of Gallows* (Delhi : 1964).

Gulati, K.C. : *The Akalis : Past and Present* (Delhi : 1974).

Gupta, Parthasarthi : *Imperialism and the British Labour Movement : 1914-64* (Macmillin : 1974).

Gurbux Singh : *Manzil Dis Pai (Panjabi)* (Ludhiana : 1969).

Gurcharan Singh : *Ankhi Surma (Panjabi)* (Hoshiarpur : 1950).

: *Babar Akali Lehr (Panjabi)* (Hoshiarpur : 1950).

Gurdev Singh : Nationalism and Nationality—India : Role of the Ghadr Party with National Movement (A Thesis for Ph.D. Punjab University, Chandigarh : 1965).

Gurdit Singh : *The Voyage of Kamaghata Maru* (Calcutta, n.d.)

Gwyer Maurice and Appodrai (ed.) : *Speeches of Documents in India Constitution : 1921-47* in 2 Vols (London : 1957).

Hadson, J.C. : *India Census Ethnography : 1901-31* (Lahore : 1931)

Haithcox, John Patric : *Communism and Nationalism in India : M.N. Roy and Comintern Policy : 1920-39* (Bombay : 1971).

Handa, R.L. : *History of Freedom Struggle in Princely States* (Delhi, n.d.)

Harbans Singh : *The Heritage of the Sikhs* (Bombay : 1964)

Harbans Singh and Jagjit Singh : *Singh Sabha Lehr in Punjab : 1849-1960* (Ludiana : 1962).

Hardyal, H. : *Hindu Revolutionary and Nationalist* (Delhi : 1976)

Hardy, G.S. : *Report on The Import Tariff on Cotton Piece Goods and on External Competition in the Cotton Piece Goods Trade* (Calcutta : 1929).

Harris, D.G. : *Irrigation in India* (Lahore : 1923).

Hasan Mushirul : *Nationalism and Communal Politics in India : 1916-18* (Delhi : 1979).

Heath, Lionel : *Review of the Conditions of Head-Weaving in the Punjab* 1930 (Lahore : 1931).

Herger, Gerald, A. : *Politics of Integration Community : Party and Integration in Punjab* (University of Chicago, thesis : 1971 in Microfilm-unpublished, NMML, New Delhi).

Hough, E.M. : *Co-operative Movement in India* (London : 1939)

Housewirth, E. : *Purdah* (Lahore : 1932).

Howard, A. & Howard, G.L.C. : *Indian Crisis : The Background* (London : 1943)

Hussian, Azim : *Fazl-i-Hussain : A Political Biography* (Bombay : 1946).

India : *The Civil Dis-obedience Movement, 1930-34* (Compiled in the Intelligence Bureau : Home Department, New Delhi, Government of India : 1934).

: *Study Village India.*

Isemonger, F.C. & Slattery, J. : *An Account of the Ghadr Conspiracy* (Lahore : Government of India : 1916).

Iyer, C.S. Ranga : *India in the Crucible* (London : 1928).

Jagjit Singh : *Ghadr Party Lehr* (Amritsar : 1955).

Jain, M.K. : *Freedom Movement in India during 1909-19* (Punjab University, Solan : 1954).

Jather, G.B. & Beri, S.C. : *Indian Economics*, 1939, Vol. II (Oxford : 1948).

Jayantanuja Bandyopadhyaya : *Indian Nationalism Versus International Communism* (Calcutta : 1966).

Jayaswal, K.P. : *History of India* (Lahore : 1933).

John, S. Hoyland. : *India Crisis : The Background* (London : 1943).

James, Kenneth, W. : *Arya Dharma Hindu Consciousness in the 19th Century.*

Josh, Bhagwan Singh : *Communist Movement in Punjab : 1926-47* (Delhi : 1980).

Josh, Sohan Singh : *Hindustan Gadar Party* (PPH, New Delhi : 1977).

: *Immortal Heroes : Lives of Communist Leaders* (Communist Party Publication : 1975).

: *Baba Sohan Singh Bhakna* (PPH, New Delhi : 1966).

: *My Meetings with Bhagat Singh and on other Early Indian Revolutionaries* (Communist Party of Indian Publication : 1977).

: *Akali Morchian Da Itihas* (Panjabi) (Delhi : 1972).

Joshi, P.C. : CPI : Its Policy And Work in the War of Liberation (Communist Party Publication, September, 1942).

: *Congress and the Communists* (PPH, Bombay : 1944).

: *Communist Reply to Congress Working Committee* (PPH, Bombay : 1945).

: *They Must Meet Again* (PPH, Bombay : 1945).

Joshi, Shashi : *Ideological Origins of the Communist Movement in India, 1920-45* (J.N.U. New Delhi—Unpublished).

Joshi, Vijay Chandra (ed.) : *Writings and Speeches of Late Lala* Lajpat Rai (Univ. Publisher, Jullundur : 1966).

Kanji Dwarkadas : *India Fight For Fredom (1915-37)* : An Eye Witness Story (Bombay : 1966).

Kapur, S.N. : *Scope of Industrial Development in the Punjab* (n.d.)

Kartar Singh : The Panjabi Folk-lore, *The Tribune,* November 10, 1957.

Karkaria, R. : *India : Forty Years of Progress and Reforms* (London : 1896).

Karunakaram, K.P. : *Religious and Political Awakening in India* (Meerut : 1965).

Karr, J.C. : *Political Trouble in India : 1907-17, Confidential Report* (Calcutta : 1973).

Karasan Khanun K.S. : *Inside India* (London : 1937).

Kay, Sir Cecil : *Communism in India : Unpublished Documents from NAI, 1919-24* ed., by Subodh Roy (Calcutta : 1971).

Kenneth Jones : *Communism in the Punjab.*

Keith, A.B. : *Speeches and Documents on the British Dominions 1918-31* (Oxford : 1932).

Kermit, E. Makanzie : *Comintern and World Revolution : 1928-43)* (New York : 1964).

Karr, James Compell : *Political Trouble in India : 1907-17* (Calcutta, *Government of India : 1917,* reprinted Delhi : 1973).

Khambett, K.J. : *Wealth and Taxable Capacity of India* (Bombay : 1924).

Khan, Aga : *Indian in Transition : A Study in Political Evolution* (Bombay : 1918).

Khan, A. : *Founder of Pakistan (Through Trial to Triumph)* (Cambridge : 1942).

Khan Bahadur, Kazi Azizuddin Ahmad : *Situation in India*, Year 1930 (Allahabad : 1930).

Khan, F.K. : *The Making of Pakistan* (Lahore : 1944).

Khan Ghulam : *Tari-i-Trade Union* (Lahore : 1922).

Khan, Ikramullah : *Technique of Agricultural Propaganda* (Lahore : 1910).

Khosla, R.P. : *India and the War*, Part I & II (Lahore : 1924).

Khushwant Singh : *A History of the Sikhs,* Vols. I & II (Oxford : 1966).

Khushwant Singh & Satindra Singh : *The Sikhs of Today* (London : 1953); *Ghadr* : 1915 (Delhi : 1966).

Khazan Singh : *A Correspondence on Indian Freedom Movement : 1930-34* (Cyclostyled Copy, JNU, New Delhi).

Kirpal Singh : *The Partition of the Punjab* (Punjabi University, Patiala : 1972).

Korson, J. Henery (ed.) : *Contemporary Problems of Pakistan* (E.J. Brill London : 1971).

Krishna Hathi Singh : *With No Regrets* (Bombay : 1943).

Lajpat Rai : *England Debt to India* (Delhi : 1967).

: *The Problem of National Education in India* (Calcutta : 1920).

: *The Agony of the Punjab* (Madras : 1920).

: *Young India : An Interpretation and the History of the National Movement from within* (Lahore : 1927).

: *The Political Future of India* (New York : 1919).

: *Autobiographical Writings* edited by Joshi, V.C. (University Publication, Delhi : 1965).

: *Unhappy India* (Calcutta : 1928).

: *A Historical Narration of Britain's Fiscal Policy in India* (New York 1920).

Lalwani, K.C. : *Essays on Economic Planning* (Calcutta : 1957).

Language Department, Patiala : *Punjab Castes* (Patiala : 1970).

Latif, A. : *The Industrial Punjab : A Survey of Facts, Conditions and Possibilities* (Calcutta : 1911).

Latif, S.M. : *History of the Punjab* (Lahore : 1916).

Leigh, M.S. : *The Punjab and the War* (Lahore : 1922).

Lothian, A.C. : *Kingdom of Yesterday* (London : 1951).

Lovett, Sir Verney : *History of the Indian National Movement* (London : 1920)

Lenin, V. : *Alliance of the Working Class and Peasantry* (Mascow : 1971).

: *Report on an Inquiry into the Silk Industry,* Vol. I (1917).

Levy Reuben : *The Social Structure of Islam : 1957,* 2nd Ed., CUP (The former Title (Sociology of Islam).

Maclagan, E. : *Report of the Committee on Co-operation in India* (Lahore : 1915).

Mahmud Ahmad : *Ahmadiya or The True Islam* (n.d.).

Main H.S. : *Village Community in the East and West,* 3rd Edition (London : 1966).

Majumdar, R.C. : *History of Freedom Movement in India,* Vols. II & III (Calcutta : 1963).

: *British Paramountcy And Indian Bennaisance* (Bombay : 1965).

Madan Gopal : *Punjab Tenancy Act* (n.d.).

Makhsuspuri, Sunder Singh : *Babbar Akali Lehr,* 2nd edition (Panjabi) (Amritsar : 1970).

Malhotra, S.L. : *Gandhi : An Experiment with Communal Politics—A Study of Gandhi's Role in Punjab Politics : 1922-1931* (Chandigarh : 1958).

: *Agricultural Problems of India,* (Allahabad : 1953).

Mamoria, C.B. : *Labour Problems and Social Welfare in India* (Allahabad : 1958).

Manmathnath, Gupta : *Reminiscences of A Revolutionary : History of the Indian Revolutionary Movement* (Bombay : 1972).

Mathur, Y.B. : *British Administration of Punjab* (Delhi : n.d.)

: *Hindu Home Life* (: 1890).

Marshall Alfred : *Principles of Economics* (New York : 1949).

: *Industry & Trade* (London : 1932).

Marshall, Windmiller : *Communism in India* (California : 1939).

Masani, M.R. : *The Communist Party of India : A Story History* (London : 1954).

Masan, Philip : *Matter of Honour : An Account of the Indian Army, Its Officers and Men* (London : 1976).

Mathew Arther : *Education of India* (Lahore : 1926).

Mayo, K. : *Mother India* (London : 1927).

Mazumdar, Anvika Charn : *Indian National Evolution : A Brief Survey of The Origin & Progress of the Indian National Congress* (Madras : 1915).

Mehta, H.R. : *History of the Growth of Development of Western Education in the Punjab : 1846-84* (Lahore : 1929).

: *Failure of Provincial Autonomy in India* (Lahore : 1944).

Menon, V.P. : *The Transfer of Power in India* (Bombay : 1957).

Misra, B.B. : *Indian Middle Classes : Their Growth in Modern Times* (London : 1961).

: *Administrative History of India : 1834-1947 : General Administration* (Oxford : 1970)

: *Bureaucracy in India : An Historical Analysis Development upto 1947*(Delhi : 1977).

: *Indian Political Parties : An Historical Behaviour upto 1947* (Bombay : 1976).

Misra, B.R. : *Indian Provincial Finance : 1919-39* (Bombay : 1942).

Mittal, S.C. : *Freedom Movement in the Punjab : 1905-29* (Delhi : 1977).

Mohan, H.P. : *Imagination Rebellion* (Lahore : 1920).

Mohinder Singh : *The Akali Movement* (Macmillion, Delhi : 1979).

: *The Faith and Progress of the Brahmo Samaj* (1882).

Morland, W.H. : *India At The Death of Akbar* (London : 1920)

Moor, R.J. : *The Crisis of Indian Units : 1917-40* (Delhi : 1974).

Morrison, Th. : *Economic Transition in India* (London : 1911).

Mosley Leonard : *The Last Days of the British Raj* (London : 1961).

Mukherjee, A.K. : *Economic Problems of Modern India* (London : 1939), Vol. I.

Mukherjee, Hiran : *Remembering Marx* (New Delhi Communist Party Publication : 1967).

Mukherjee, H.C. : *Congress and the Masses* (Calcutta : 1945).

Mukherjee, H.N. : *Indian Struggle for Freedom.*

Mukherjee, R.C. : *Land Problems of India* (London : 1933).

: *The Foundation of Indian Economics* (London : 1916).

Mukherjee, H. and Mukherjee, Uma : *Bande Matram and Indian National Congress*

: Bipin Chandra Pal and India's Struggle for Swaraj (Calcutta : 1958).

: *Growth of Nationalism in India* (1857-1905) (Calcutta : 1957)

: *India's Fight for Freedom : The Swadeshi Movements : 1905-1906* (Calcutta : 1958).

: *Origin of the National Educational Movement : 1905-10* (Calcutta : 1957).

: Agrarian Relief in Four Countries (Allahabad : 1937).

: Rural India, Peasants Poverty, It causes and Cure (Allahabad : n.d.).

: *Rural Reconstruction* (Allahabad : 1946).

Mukhtiar Singh : *Kisan* (Urdu) n.d.

: *Cottage and Small Scale Industries* (Allahabad : 1947).

Mundy Alfred : *Indian Unrest : 1919-20* (Dehradun : 1921).

: *Present Situation with Special Reference to Punjab Disturbances* (Dehradun : 1919).

: *Revolution or Evolution* (Lahore : 1922).

Mundy G.S. : *Report on the External Competition in Cottage and Small Scale Industries* (London : 1947).

: *Piece Goods* (London : 1929).

Nahar Singh : *Development in Sikh Politics : 1900-11* (Delhi : 1965).

: Gooroo Ram Singh and the Kuka Sikhs : Rebels against the British Power in India : Documents, 1863-71 (Delhi : 1965).

Nanavati, Manilal, B & Anjaris, J.J. : Indian Rural Problems (Bombay, 1945, 1947 (2nd & 3rd Ed.), 1951 : 4th Edition.

Nammodripad, E.M.S. : *Economics and Politics of India's Socialist Pattern* (Delhi : 1966).

Narahari Kaviraj : *Peasant Uprising in Bengal* (PPH : Delhi : 1972)

Naroji Dada Bhai : *Poverty and British Rule in India,* (Delhi : 1969).

Natrajan, S.A. : *A History of the Press in India* (Bombay : n.d.)

Narang, G.C. : *Brief History of Patiala State* (Patiala : 1911)

: *Brief History of Malerkotla State : 1914-18* (Lahore : 1920).

: *Real Hinduism* (Lahore : n.d.).

Navinson, H.W. : *New Spirit in India* (London : 1908).

Nayar, Baldev Raj : *Minority Politics in the Punjab* (Princeton New Jersy : 1961).

Nehru, Jawaharlal : *An Autobiography* (London : 1963).

: *The Discovery of India* (New York : 1946).

: *Soviet Russia : Some Random Sketch and Impressions* (Bombay : 1929).

: *India's Freedom* (London : 1962).

Nicholas, M.N. (ed.) : *India Transfer of Power* (1942-47).

Niemeyer, Sir, Otto : *Indian Financial Enquiry Report* (Delhi : 1936).

Niranjan Singh : *Akali Lehr Dian Kuj Yaadan* (Panjabi) (Singh Bros., Amritsar).

: *Master Tara Singh* (Panjabi) (Singh Bros., Amritsar).

Nurullah, Syed & Naik, G.P. : *Students' History of Education in India :* 1800-1944 (Bombay : 1945).

O. Dwayer Michael : *India As I Knew It : 1885-1925* (London : 1925).

Overstreet, Gene, D. & Windmillar, Marshall : *Communism in India* (Bombay : 1960).

Padmasha : *Indian National Congress and The Muslim : 1928-47* (Delhi : 1980).

Panandikar, S.G. : *Some Aspects of Economic*

Consequences of The War for India (Bombay : 1921).

Panchhi, Pritam Singh : *Ghadr Ki Gunj Aur Kamaghata Maru Ka Romanch* (Delhi : 1961).

Patel, A.D. : *India Agricultural Economics* (Bombay : 1937).

Patel, S.J. : *Agricultural Labourers in Modern India and Pakistan* (Bombay : 1952).

Pathak, G.S. : *Some Reflections on the Civil Revolution in India* (Delhi : 1972).

Peare Arro, S. : *Cottage Industry of India* (Delhi : 1930).

Prasad, Amba : *The Indian Revolt of 1942* (Delhi : 1958).

Prasad, Beni : *Hindu Muslim Question* (Lahore : 1943)

Petric, D. : *Communalism in India : 1924-27* (Compiled in the Intelligence Bureau, Home Department : Government of India, Calcutta : 1927).

Prasad, Bisheshwar : *Security of Punjab during the British Period* (Patiala : 1968).

Plunkett, M. : *Co-operation* (Oxford : 1925).

Punjab Government : *Land of the Five Rivers* (Patiala : 1970-Reprint).

Puri, Sahib Chand : *Ahalkari Sazshan* (Phulkian Samachar Publication, Patiala, n.d.)

Rai, Satya M., : *"Revolutionary Terrerist Movement in the Punjab".*

: *Teaching Politics,* Vol. II, Nos. III & IV (Delhi : 1976).

Raja Ram, : *The Jallianwala Bagh Massacre* (Punjab University, Chandigarh : 1969).

Ram, T. : *Sir Chhotu Ram : Apostle of Hindu-Muslim Unity* (Lahore : 1946).

: The Law of Crimes (:1945).

Ramesh Dutt : *The Economic History of India,* Vol. II (Delhi : 1970).

Randhawa, M.S. : *Kangra* (Panjabi) n.d.

: *Haryana De Lok Geet* (Panjabi) n.d.

Randhir Singh : *Ghadr Heroes : Forgotton Story of the Punjab Revolutionaries* (PPH : Bombay : 1945) of 1914.

Ranga Iyer, C.S. : *India : Peace and War* (London : 1930).

Ranga, N.G. : *Right for Freedom* (Delhi : 1968).

: Revolutionary Peasants (Delhi : 1949).

Rapson, E.J. (ed.) : *Ancient India :* From the Earliest Times to the First Century A.D. (Cambridge : 1922).

Ravinder Kumar (ed.) : *Essays on Gandhian Politics* (London : 1971)

Rasul, M.A. : *History of the All India Kisan Sabha* (Calcutta : 1974).

Raychaudhari, Tapan (ed.) : *Contribution to Indian Economic History,* Vol. I & II

(Calcutta : 1960 & 1963 respectively).

Ray Jhankhande : *Bhartiya Kranti Kari Andolan : Ekk Vishleshan* in Hindi (PPH, Delhi : 1974).

Read Margret : *The Land and Life of India* (London : 1934).

Read, Sir Stanley & Cadell, P.R. : *India : The New Phase* (London : 1928).

Rees, J.D. : *Real India* (London : 1908).

Reginold Craddock : *Dilemma in India* (London : 1929).

Roberts Sir William & Kartar Singh : *Text Book of Punjab Agriculture* (Lahore : 1947).

Row, M.R. : *Truth About Japanese Competition* (n.d.)

Rowlinson, H.G. & Garrether H.L.O. (ed.) : *The Great Men of India* (London : 1939).

Rothermund Dietmar : *The Phase of Indian Nationalism and other Essays* (Bombay : 1970).

: *Government, Landlord and Peasant in India.*

: *Agrarian Relations under British Rule : 1865-1935* (Wiesbaden : 1978).

Roy, M.N. : *India in Transition* (Geneva : 1952).

: *The Future of Indian* Politics (London : 1926).

: *Memoirs* (Bombay : 1964).

Roy, M.N. & Evelyn : *One Year of Non-co-operation* (Calcutta : 1923).

Roy Santinoy : *Role of Indian Muslims in the Freedom Movement* (PPH, Delhi : 1970).

Roy, Subodh (ed.) : *Communism in India : 1925-34*—Unpublished Documents (Calcutta : 1972).

Rushbrook William : *Three Fold Problem* (London).

Russell, J. : *Report on the Work of the Imperial Council of Agricultural Research* (London : 1937).

Sahni, Ruchi Ram : *Struggle for Reforms in Sikh Shrines* (SGPC, Amritsar : 1964).

Saini, B.S. : *Social and Economic History of the* Punjab : 1901-39 (Ess Ess Publishers, Delhi : 1975).

Sainsara Gurcharan Singh : *Oh, Vee Din San (Panjabi)* (Ludhiana 1965).

Sandhu Virendra : *Yugdrashta Bhagat Singh Aur Unke Mrityunjava Purkhe* (Hindi) (Varanasi : 1920, reprinted Delhi : 1968).

: *Sardar Bhagat Singh Pattar Aur Dastavez* (Hindi) (Delhi : 1977).

Sanyal Sachin : *Bandi Jiwan* (Hindi) (Delhi : 1963).

Sapra, B.G. : *Economics of Agricultural Progress* (Lahore : 1926).

Sarkar, B.N. : *The History of Indian Tariff Board : 1924-39* (Delhi : 1940).

Sardesai, S.G. : *India and the Russian Revolution* (New Delhi : 1967).

Sarkar, J.N. : *Economics of British India* (Calcutta : 1947).

: *India Through The Ages* (Calcutta : 1944).

Satyarthi, D. : *Rajput Songs of War* (Modern Review : January, 1939).

Sayeed, K.B. : *Pakistan : The Formative Phase, 1857-1948* (London : 1968).

Sen, N.D. (ed.) : *Punjab's Eminent Hindus* (Lahore : 1943).

Sen, S.R. : *Growth and Instability in India Agriculture* (Calcutta : 1971).

Sethi, R.R. & Mehta, J.L. : *A History of Punjab University,* Chandigarh.

Shadi Lal : *Commentaries on the Punjab Alienation of Land Act* (Lahore : 1933).

Shah, K.J. : *Ancient Foundation of Economics in India* (Bombay : 1954).

Shah, K.T. : *Industrialization of the Punjab* (Punjab Government, Lahore : 1941).

: *Wealth and Taxable Capacity of India* (Bombay : 1924).

: *Russian Experiment, 1917-1927* (Bombay : 1927).

: Congress Select Committee on the Financial Obligations between Great Britain and India Vol. II-Annexture to Report (Ahmedabad : AICC-1930).

: *Federal Finance in India* (Bombay : 1929).

: *How India Pays For The War* (Bombay : 1943).

: *India's Place in Post War Reconstruction* (Bombay : 1943).

: *Economic Background* (London : 1944).

: *Trade, Tariff and Transport in India* (Bombay : 1923).

Sharma, Jagdish : *Indian Struggle for Freedom : Selected Documents and Sources* (Delhi : 1965).

Sharma, J.S. : *India Struggle for Freedom,* Vols. II & III (Delhi : 1965).

Shastri, S.R. : *Punjab in Ferment* (S. Chand & Co., Delhi : 1971).

: *Haryana Ka Itihas* (Rohtak : 1966).

Shastri, R.S. : *Chaudhari Chhotu Ram : Jivan Charitra* (Hindi) (Rohtak : 1965).

Shastri, Y. : *Kashtri Jation Ka Uttanopattan* (Hindi) (Hardwar : 1956).

Singh, M.A. : *A Students History of Educational Thought,* Vol. II, n.d.

Sir Denzil Ibbetson : *A Glossary of the Tribes and Castes of the Punjab and NWFP,* Vols. I & II (Language Department, Punjab, Patiala : 1970).

: *Punjab Castes* (Patiala : 1970).

Sir, K. Fitz : *Twilight of the Maharaja* (London : 1956).

Sita Ram Singh : *Nationalism and Social Reforms in India : 1885-1920* (Delhi : 1968).

Sitaramaya Pattabhai : *History of the Indian National Congress,* Vols. I & II (Bombay : 1947).

Sinha Sardhar : *Indian Independence in Prospectives* (Bombay : 1964).

Sehata Dharam Singh (ed.) : *Dudhike De Ghadri Baba* (Panjabi) (Dudhike Lajpat Rai study Forum : 1972).

Sohan Lal : *Development of Irrigation in the Punjab* (Lahore : 1926).

Spare, B.G. : *Economics of Agricultural Progress* (Lahore : 1929).

Spratt Philip : *Blowing up India : Reminiscences and Reflections of a farmer Communist Emissary* (Calcutta : 1955).

Srinivasraghavan, T.A. : *A Modern Economic History of England and India,* Vol. II (1955).

Stricland, C.J. : *Studies in European Co-operation* (Lahore : 1922-23)

Sunder Lal : *Bharat Mein Angrezi Raj* (Publication Division, Delhi : 1960).

Surinder Nath : *History of the Congress Movement* from 1919-35 (A thesis, Punjab University Solan : 1954).

Strickland, R.B. : *Indian Co-operative Studies* (London : 1920).

Suri, V.S. : *Punjab Ke Lok Geeton Mein Azadi Ki Goonj* (Jullundur : Daily Partap : 1956).

Syed, K.B. : *The Pakistan : The Formation Phase.*

Syed Mohammad Hussain : *Terikh-i-Patiala* (Amritsar : 1877).

Syed Wasti : *Lord Minot And The Indian Nationalists Movement : 1905-10* (Oxford : 1964).

Talib Gurbachan Singh : *Sardar Sewa Singh Thikariwala* (Patiala : 1971).

Tandon, P.D. & Others : *History of Hindu-Mulsim Problem in India*

Tara Chand : *History of the Freedom Movement in India*, Vol. III (Publication Division, Delhi : 1972).

Tara Singh : *Meri Yaad (Panjabi)* (Amritsar : 1945).

Teja Singh : *The Gurdwara Reform Movement and Sikh Awakening* (Jullundur : 1943).

Tndulkar, D.G. : *Mahatma* 'Life of Mohan Das Karamchand Gandhi', Vol. I (Bombay : 1951-54).

Thomas, P. : *Christians and Christianity in India and Pakistan* (1954).

Thakur Gopal : *Bhagat Singh : The Men and His Ideas* (Delhi : 1965).

Thornburn, S.S. : *Report on Peasant Indebtedness And Land Alienation to Moneylenders* (Lahore : 1896).

: *The Punjab in Peace and War* (Language) Department, Patiala : 1970.

Thompson, Edward : *A Letter from India* (London : 1932).

Thompson, W.P. : *Punjab Irrigation* (Lahore : 1925).

Tirlok Singh : *Bhagat Singh (Panjabi)* (Amritsar : 1963).

Trevaskis, H.K. : *The Punjab of Today : Economic Survey of The Punjab in Recent Years : 1890-1925* (Lahore : 1931).

: *Land of the Five Rivers* : On Economic History of the Punjab from the Earliest time to the year of grace-1890 (London : 1928).

: *Indian Babel* (London : 1935).

Trotsky Leon : *Against Individual Terrorism* (New York : 1974).

Ujjagar Singh : *Amar Shaheed Sewa Singh Thikariwals* (Panjabi) (Patiala : 1970)

Usmani Shaukat : *Autobiography* (Manuscript), Ajoy Bhavan CPI Office, New Delhi.

: *Sojourn in the Soviet Union* (New Delhi : 1977).

: *Peshawar to Mascow : Leaves from an Indian Mahajir Diary* (Delhi : 1927).

Van-den Dungen, P.H.M. : *The Punjab Tradition : Influence And Authority in the Ninteenth Century in India* (London : 1972).

Yatyne, Clande M.D. : *Indian In Persuit* (London : 1923).

Visvesvarya, M. : *Reconstructing India* (Bombay : 1944).

: *Planned Economy for India* (Bangalore : 1936).

: *Reconstruction in Post-war India* : A Plan of Development all round (Bombay : 1944).

: *Rural Reconstruction in India* (Bangalore : 1935) : *Unemployment in India* (Bangalore : 1932)

: *Our Economic Problems* (Bombay : 1948).

Wadia, P.A. & Merchant, K.T. : *Our Economic Problems* (Bombay : 1948).

Wadia, P.A. & Joshi G.N. : *Wealth of India* (Lahore : 1925).

Walia Ramesh : *Praja Mandal Movement in East Punjab States* (Punjabi University, Patiala).

Wallace, Paul : *Poltical Party System of Punjab State, India : A Study of Factionalism* (University of California, Berkeley Thesis : 1966-Microfilm, NMML, New Delhi.).

Waltaz, H.A. : *The Ahmadia Movement* (Delhi : 1918).

Wasti, Syed Razi : *Lord Minto and the Indian Nationalist Movement, 1905 to 1910* (Oxford : 1964).

Weld, W.B. : *India's Demand For Transport* (New York : 1920).

Williamson, H. : *India And Communism : 1935* (Compiled in the Intelligence Bureau, Home Department Government of India, Calcutta : 1936).

Wolff, H.W. : *Co-operation in India* (London : 1929).

Wood, S.M. : *Report on Vocational Education in India.*

Yash Pal : *Sinhavalokan* (Hindi) Vols. I & II & III (Lucknow : 1951, 1952 and 1955 respectively).

Yusuf Ali, A. : *A Cultural History of India* (London : 1940).

: *Making of India* (London : 1925)

: India Science Congress : Glimpse of the Punjab; a Souvenir of the 14th Meeting of the Indian Science Congress held at Lahore in January, 1927, edited by C.H. Reed (Lahore : 1927).

: *Medieval India :* Social and Economic Conditions (Lahore : 1932).

Yusuf Ali : *Life And Labour of the People of India* (London : 1907).

Zaheer Sajjad : *Light on League : Unionist Conflict* (PPH, Bombay : 1944).

Index

D

E

F